Hush My Mouth

Ken Farrington

HUSH MY MOUTH

The Thoughts, Beliefs, Observations,
Triumphs and Disasters of a Jobbing Actor

First published in 2018 by Fantom Films
fantomfilms.co.uk

Copyright © Ken Farrington 2018

Ken Farrington has asserted his moral right to be identified
as the author of this work in accordance with the
Copyright, Designs and Patents Act 1988.

A catalogue record for this book is available from the British Library.

Hardback edition ISBN: 978-1-78196-302-9

Typeset by Phil Reynolds Media Services, Leamington Spa
Printed and bound by CPI Group (UK) Ltd, Croydon, CR0 4YY

Photographs not specifically credited are from the author's personal collection.

In memory of
Michael Croft, OBE (1922-1986)

Contents

1

1950 to 1955 • Alleyn's School • Michael Croft • John Stride • Julian Glover

I USED TO HAVE a theory, some fifty years ago, that the basic motive behind the desire to be an actor was not a very attractive one. If you strip the whole thing down to its roots you are, in essence, of the belief that when you stand up on stage and recite lines that you have learnt by rote, it is worth other people paying to come and see and hear! Since I had thought out this theory, as I imagined, pretty much by myself, I felt a bit proud of its originality and didn't question it too much. Of course, in this day and age no thought is entirely original and now that I come to rethink the premise, I'm not so sure that it is entirely true. At some stage during the process of deciding whether or not to take up acting as a career it is an aspect that must be faced and there has to be a degree of arrogance if the final decision is 'yes'. I am no longer sure that it is as great an influence in the decision making as my teenage theory suggested, but nevertheless that arrogance has been a significant factor in the make-up and in the success of many an actor!

On the other hand, there are many great and wonderful actors who have managed to exude humility and have shunned attention: Sir Alec Guinness, Sir Paul Scofield, Dame Judi Dench, to name the most obvious. Perhaps it is that the initial arrogance is dissipated when faced with the wonder and brilliance of writers the like of Shakespeare, Shaw, Wilde, Miller et al. Perhaps that humility comes with familiarity with the theatre and the wonder of its history. Or perhaps the stark reality of the bump and grind of the professional theatre with its cruel injustice forces one to a state of humble acceptance that it is not always the best that rise to the top.

Analysing my own decision to become an actor, at the age of 18 or 19, there was no family connection or even interest in the theatre. I can't even remember being taken to a pantomime! I did however take myself to the music hall at the Camberwell Palace, in South East London, creeping into the gallery at a tender age, something like 12 or 13, tipped forward in 'the gods' at a perilous angle to train the binoculars, rented from the back of the seat in front, on the nudes that stood frozen in tableaux, forbidden by the Lord Chamberlain to move a muscle! I think the height of my theatrical experience and sexual arousal was watching Jane with her dog 'Fritz' (from the *Daily Mirror* comic strip) undressing to take a bath, silhouetted in black behind white screens, with the odd flash of colour as an undergarment was carelessly and seductively tossed over the top of the screen.

The seats in 'the gods' were on such a rake that I must have been in danger of tipping forward onto the stage!

Shakespeare and Chekhov I hadn't yet discovered. I went alone and told no one of how I was squandering my hard-earned pocket money. I did the usual paper round and saved my fare money to school by walking the four and a half miles there and back. I am of course forgetting the school matinees at the Old Vic, which almost escaped my memory because they were more like an extension of the lunch break when we were all trooped off to the South Bank to join with other gangs of noisy schoolkids, some of them girls, which was quite a novelty and incitement since I attended a boys-only school. We were let loose for two hours in the dark; and, to many of us, the object was to see what damage could be wreaked on the drama of the situation on stage with a witty, and sometimes not so witty, interjection, designed to impress one's peers and of course the girls!

It wasn't until some six years later when I was in my late teens that I saw my first proper drama, in a proper theatre with a proper audience and a proper attitude. Michael Croft, who was then my English teacher at Alleyn's School, took me to see *Dial M for Murder* in the West End with Bernard Lee playing the lead. He also took me backstage to meet his old schoolboy chum Russell Enoch, who had been appearing in the play, and Richard Wattis, a very recognisable face from films and TV, who was sharing a dressing room with Russ. (Russell Enoch later changed his name to William Russell and became quite a star as Ian Chesterton, sidekick to the first 'Doctor Who' and whom, some years later, I was to parody in a light-entertainment sketch with the not wildly funny comic Joe Baker for ITV.) Chatting and drinking with them in their dressing room was a heady experience for the son of a builder and decorator from Peckham, and I think it sowed the seeds of desire to join what seemed to me a most glamorous profession indeed.

Michael Croft had been in the Navy during the war, and had, on demobilisation, gained an ex-service place at Keble College Oxford where he developed his love of English literature, theatre, and poetry. On leaving university, and after a brief involvement in the professional theatre where he was rumoured to have understudied Kenneth More in *And No Birds Sing*, he took up a post as English teacher at Alleyn's School. Alleyn's was at that time a direct-grant school and there were few, if any, fee-paying pupils. The pupillage was made up of bright young boys who had somehow managed to excel in the 11-plus examination. In some cases, on looking at the pupil, one would have to question the means employed to pass the exam! They were a pretty mixed bunch, with the sons of the well-to-do and the professional classes mingling with the sons of coal merchants and manual labourers.

The school had a very good reputation for music, and although it had been founded by Edward Alleyn, a Shakespearean actor and contemporary, it had no special accent on drama, other than the usual annual school play, which was more than a little eclipsed by the Gilbert and Sullivan productions. Prior to the arrival of Michael Croft at Alleyn's in 1948/49, only a handful of its alumni had taken to the theatre. Leslie Howard (known at school as Leslie Stainer) went on to carve out an illustrious career playing such parts as Ashley in *Gone With the Wind* and the lead in *The Scarlet Pimpernel*; and also there was Frank Thornton from *Are You Being Served?* and the actor/manager/playwright Ray Cooney who left school early to 'tread the boards,' much to the disgust of his parents and tutors. However, in the last forty years the school has gained a considerable reputation for its drama and has seen some thirty of its ex-pupils, including Sam West, Julian Glover, John Stride, Simon Ward and Jude Law, to pick out the most recently successful, take up acting as a career.

It was at Alleyn's that Croft spawned the idea of what is now the National Youth Theatre, and I count myself lucky to have come under his influence at the very start and to have been in at the birth. There is little doubt that Croft changed the lives of many young people; indeed, with the continuation and growth of the National Youth Theatre his influence is still in evidence, long after his death. However, I have always felt that Croft was responsible for a great sea change in my life, and that I owe him a debt I will never be able to repay.

Sidney 'Soapy' Hudson, the then headmaster of Alleyn's, fought long and hard to maintain the traditions of an English public school; but, bearing in mind the complete cross-section of social strata, it is not surprising that he found it an uphill task. The sons of the professional classes were the ones that usually ended up with the power, wearing the silver badge for house prefect or the gold for school prefect. However, there was a considerable groundswell of resistance from the working-class lads from the back streets of Peckham, Brixton, Nunhead and the like. This resistance took various forms and was frequently castigated from the stage in the Great Hall at early-morning prayers and dismissed as the 'lunatic fringe' by a somewhat harassed Soapy. Punishment took the form mainly of detention on a Saturday afternoon as, rather strangely, unlike any other school in the area, we had Saturday-morning lessons. Caning wasn't used to any great extent, but it was quite an occasion when it did happen. I overstepped the bounds once, taking the piss out of Colonel Snowdon during an English lesson, and was taken down to the master's changing room where, witnessed by another master, I was made to bend over the end of a table and dear old Colonel Snowdon (who was so called more because of his appearance – white hair and a military moustache – than his rank and who must have been near retirement age) took a run at my backside along the duckboards. It wasn't too bad really; I don't think his heart was in it. Either that or he was on his last legs!

In the main, however, I seemed to spend my Saturday afternoons in detention. In fact, I never bothered to check, but just stayed on at school every Saturday afternoon. One Saturday, I went to the detention room to find I wasn't on the list and was about to leave and take an unexpected half-day off. Unfortunately Mr Cox, the maths teacher, who had a fine line in acerbic sarcasm, happened to be taking the detention and said, 'Sit down Farrington, you can do an hour anyway, I'm sure you deserve it.'

It was he too who brought about my final slide to the lower depths of the 'lunatic fringe'. I had just moved up to the fifth form, and on the first day of term I cheerily greeted him as he entered my new class as form master. He turned on his heels, muttering 'I'm not having this!' and returned a few minutes later with the news that I had been transferred to Form Vd. This was the 'remove' form, full of pupils who were not wanted in the sixth form, but who were either quite useful to the school, or were on the point of being thrown out. They were the hard mob of the school rebel element, and I was pretty scared as I entered the class on that fateful day.

It was around about this time too that I had been in big trouble for pausing by the main gate, as I left school on the last day of term, to take off my school tie and my cap and light up a fag. The headmaster, from his study window, observed this rather foolish act of bravado; and when I returned in the afternoon for the detention that I had momentarily forgotten, I was summoned to his office, the detention was trebled and there was talk of asking me to leave the school. So in a way I had earned my place with the hard core of the 'lunatic fringe', although I don't think I was anything other than misguided and unfocused rather than downright wicked. I didn't really have an agenda for my disobedience; I wasn't fighting against anything. I think I was simply trying to be funny or to show off and it just came out all wrong sometimes!

However, it was at this point that I came more directly under the influence of Michael Croft, as he entered my life as my English teacher. He was himself fairly new to the school, having only been there for a term or two, but his reputation had already been established by one or two incidents. First, he had confiscated a dirty 'girlie' magazine from one of the hard mob, and instead of taking disciplinary action, as was expected, after reading it, handed it back! Second, he had shown himself to be a more than difficult adversary on the soccer field, but not because of his ball skills. He had appeared on the right wing, I think it was, in the end-of-term masters-versus-boys match, looking most frightening with his shock of reddish crinkly hair and his shirt tails flying. He was probably the dirtiest player they had ever encountered, although coming from 'up north' I think he was having trouble adapting from the game he used to play for the Heaton Moore Rugby Club. He could only have been about thirty at the time, although to us boys that was already old, and was a terrifying picture of uncontrolled energy. He also proved to be quite useful at cricket, which was a game he loved and had more knowledge of.

By such means, he acquired the reputation of being 'one of the boys', gradually gaining the trust of the unruly element that saw him as allied with them against the establishment. Although in some quarters the dirty-magazine trick was seen as something of a ruse, they liked his interest in sport and his laid-back method of teaching. He didn't push the lessons at them: he just talked and they could take it in or not, as they pleased. Alan Bennett's *The History Boys* comes to mind.

The first step in my conversion came I suppose with football. Like most boys, I enjoyed kicking a ball around, but had not managed to stand out as having any particular talent. On being demobbed from the Army after the war, my father had concentrated on teaching me to box. A two-edged sword really: it did teach me to be able to look after myself, but it also developed an aggressive side to my nature, which I didn't really need as I had inherited it from him in the first place! However, when I graduated from junior to senior school at the ripe old age of 13, I was small for my age and was more or less forced to box for the house in one of the lower weights – because, as they said, there was no one else of my size that would know how to put the gloves on! Unfortunately, I was drawn, for my first bout, against 'Chinky' Grant, a tough 19-year-old who was of Chinese origin and therefore much smaller than average for his age group, and who hadn't been known ever to lose a fight at his weight. It proved to be one hell of a battle, with blood and sweat flying everywhere. I didn't win; the first three rounds were declared a draw, and we were invited to fight a deciding round, but as Chinky and I were absolutely out on our feet, we both declined and he was given the decision. Nevertheless I had gained a reputation as a bit of a battler, at 13 being able to give a 19-year-old a run for his money, and apart from aligning me with the undesirable 'lunatic fringe' even more, this probably gave Croft the inspiration to put me in the school under-14 football team. There I blossomed as something of a ball winner, with some of the same wild enthusiasm that Croft had shown (and probably the same level of ball skills).

Apart from giving me something to aim at, playing for the school also meant that I had to stay out of detention as most of the interschool matches took place on a Saturday afternoon. This didn't happen overnight, but I developed a method of bartering with the masters and usually managed to arrange to do an hour on the allotment after school instead. I began to develop as something of a sportsman and branched out into athletics and swimming. My conversion had begun – but not yet academically!

Croft hadn't been long at Alleyn's before he took over the directing of the school's annual Shakespearean production, the first of which was to be *Julius Caesar*. How it came about I'm not quite sure, but there must have been some considerable infighting in the masters' common room. Croft's apparent championing of some of the less accepted pupils certainly didn't gain him approval from the headmaster and it became clear that the staff were becoming divided between those that were on Croft's side and those against. One of his first tasks, after casting the main parts, was to enlist as many of the dropouts as he could to make up the crowd scenes, which were to prove one of the major high-lights of the production. With this regard he approached the under-16 football team and asked us to enlist *en masse*. The initial response was a resounding 'no' from the majority, who did not want to be 'poofy actors', but when the word got around that there was to be free ale at the end of the action we all swallowed our objections and signed up! One of our lot – the right half, Johnny Stride – even got a couple of lines as Pindarus.

Julius Caesar was to be staged in modern dress and in the open air. This in itself was highly innovative for an annual school play, but Mike also brought with him a wonderful ability to inspire verse speaking of a level not previously heard in school productions, and to direct crowd scenes that pulsated with energy and excitement and yet were decidedly disciplined. It didn't come easily. I remember hour upon hour of rehearsal, listening to speech after speech being repeated time after time so that in the end I knew everybody's part. I can't say that, at this juncture, I enjoyed it much. It was like dripping water, and I couldn't understand why they were having such difficulty; Croft would repeat each line the way he wanted it said and, quite frankly, I could rarely see the difference. Rehearsals went on and on until late into the night, and there were many objections from parents and teachers as the school seemed to be taken over by the magnitude of the production. Bert Spring, the junior school head, was heard to complain that it was the first time the school play had been directed from 'The Dog' – the Greyhound pub in Dulwich Village where Croft seemed to spend much of his time between rehearsals.

Croft had frequently to fight against the authorities and was consequently often short tempered and tired, not to mention hung over. We too were not accustomed to this sort of concentrated and prolonged effort and were often fractious and difficult to control. However, we were not all novices; Croft was lucky enough to discover Julian Glover, who was soon bitten by the acting bug and became established as the school's leading actor. He gave us his Mark

Antony, and somehow John 'Navvy' Stride, so called because of his big hands, had, as I have previously mentioned, managed to get himself a few lines as Pindarus. Also in the cast were a couple of the school's intellectuals, already used to treading the school boards; Michael Barnes, who ended up as a professor at Queen's University and the director of the Belfast Festival, and David Keene whom I later came across as Bishop of Southall when I was playing Nottingham.

Somewhat to the dismay of the headmaster, we made the papers before the play even opened! Allegedly, a passer-by in Townley Road saw what they thought to be a master in mortarboard and gown being attacked by rebellious pupils, and called the police. They had of course witnessed the dress rehearsal of the lynching of Cinna the poet by the rioting Romans. I say allegedly because I don't recall the police arriving at rehearsal and I'm not at all convinced that the story wasn't cooked up by Croft – the first spin-doctor! This suspicion is inspired by the fact that a few years later when visiting Manchester with the Youth Theatre's *Henry IV Part 2* and confronted with poor advance booking and a lack of publicity, Croft organised a parade in full costume to the city centre where we performed excerpts from the play in Piccadilly Gardens, accompanied, inexplicably, by our own skiffle group. We were eventually asked to 'move on' by the police. The next day Croft managed to get front-page coverage in the *Manchester Evening News* with the story that the prostitutes of Piccadilly had complained to the police that we were interfering with their trade and had us shifted!

However, the Alleyn's production was early days and we were as yet unaware of the lengths that Croft would go to. Despite the early publicity, however, I don't think any of us were prepared for the reception on that first night. The crowd scenes and the battles were momentous. No professional company, at that time, could have afforded to put so many bodies on stage, and being in the open air allowed us to exceed even the wildest dreams of any entrepreneur. We performed on the football pitch in front of the pavilion, and as night fell the audience were stunned as the blanks fired, the thunder flashes exploded, and the lunatic fringe took over the world! *Julius Caesar* was an unprecedented success and we played to full and enthusiastic crowds. The audience was composed not only of proud mums, dads and girlfriends, but attracted some of the West End critics who were very fulsome in their praise and were to become, in the main, great supporters of Croft. It was a heady time: none of us had experienced this sort of team success in the past and at last many a school rebel was given a shove in a different direction. Croft had taken the energy and vigour of the uncommitted and made it not only acceptable but also applauded – and laudable.

I think it true to say that, although the speaking parts were highly praised and were thought to be superior in verse speaking and maturity of characterisation to those of any previous school production, it was the crowd and fight scenes that ended up as the star of the show. The sheer scale and magnitude afforded by being in the open air was jettisoned the next year for the intimacy and the limitations of the school stage in the Great Hall. Croft decided to try his hand at *Hamlet*. He had seen what he wanted – John Stride had caught his eye – but he was unable to ignore Julian Glover who had, by this time, established himself as the school's leading actor, and he and 'Navvy' were front-runners for the title role. There followed endless rounds of readings and auditions with Julian and Johnny in competition. When Mike told Julian that they had decided to split the part and let them have three performances each, Julian declined the offer and told them to give the part to Johnny. Exactly how he declined is up for conjecture, but he did get to play Laertes so it couldn't have been too acrimonious!

Because of the success of *Julius Caesar* and Mike's previous connections with the professional theatre we were beginning to attract attention, not just locally, but from the national press; and *Hamlet* was an even greater artistic success with Johnny winning universal acclaim for his verse speaking and mature performance. Pretty well all of the West End critics came. W. A. Darlington of the *Telegraph* wrote of Navvy, two years later when he came to see *Antony and Cleopatra*:

> I saw him do well as Hamlet two years ago, when he was 15, but he has made great strides since then. No experienced critic dares to praise an amateur actor too highly for fear of sending him on the stage; but in the first act I seriously debated with myself whether I ought not to say that Mr Stride must turn professional.

I had not at that time been bitten by the acting bug, but I had acquired a taste for the 'amber nectar' at the last night parties and volunteered to serve again as a courtier-come-soldier. My main task was to carry Hamlet's dead body at shoulder height, together with three others of course, at the end of the play. After the nerves of the first night we amused ourselves by trying to get the corpse to squirm, interfering with his body in unspeakable ways, as we solemnly slow-marched off stage with the body held aloft!

Laertes was to be Julian's last role at the school as he was to leave and go to RADA – the first of many. His departure came possibly a little sooner than we all expected. At the end of that term when Soapy was giving out prizes, at assembly in the Great Hall, he called Julian to come and receive the Collins prize for shooting. As Julian was half way up the centre aisle Soapy noticed that he was sporting a pale green shirt instead of the regulation white, or grey. Drawing everybody's attention to the fact that Julian was improperly dressed, he told him to return to his seat; at which point Julian turned on his heels and marched right out of school, only to return some forty years later to give out prizes from that same stage in that same school as an invited celebrity, having carved out a fine career for himself as a classical actor with the RSC, in the West End theatre and in films.

I think because of exams I was not involved in the next production, *Macbeth*. By now commitment to the annual school play was total and rehearsals went on late into the night, and nearer production time into the early hours of the morning. This really seemed to trouble Soapy, who was still more than a little wary of Croft and perhaps jealous of his acknowledged success, so it was given out that anybody sitting exams was not allowed to be in the annual production. This was despite the fact that figures were to prove that boys involved in the productions did better than those not involved. In my own case, when I took my 'O' levels in a class where nobody else got more than two, I got nine, and was immediately looked upon as sixth-form material! This, I can assure you, was as great a surprise to myself as it was to everybody else. In those days, instead of waiting for the results to come in the post, you could go to the school on a predetermined day and the results would be pinned up on the noticeboard, under the arches. I wandered around in a trance, returning to the board every five minutes to check and see if they'd rectified the error! I can't say that I was aware of any real effort upon my part, except for the last-minute swotting; I think it was simply that Croft had instilled in me not only a desire to learn, but also the discipline and concentration necessary to study and achieve.

My rise to the sixth form was cathartic and the floodgates of achievement were opened. I became House Prefect, House Captain, and then School Prefect. I got First Eleven colours for football, half-colours for athletics and swimming, and quarter-colours for cross-country. I became drum major of the school military band, which was at the time one of the best in the country, playing at the Queen Mother's garden party in the Mall and the Bishop of London's garden party at Lambeth Palace; although, if I am honest, I was probably given the rank of drum major to prevent me from playing the trumpet. Much to the annoyance of family and neighbours I tried desperately to master the trumpet. I would have loved to be a musician; but while I had rhythm, I had no aptitude! I spent all of my waking hours at the school, involved in some activity or other. Quite a sea change from being on the verge of expulsion; and all due to one man's interest and inspiration. There were of course others who had a hand in my conversion. There was 'Loopy' Young, my housemaster, who apparently, I was to learn later, made me House Captain against the headmaster's wishes and then fought for me to be a School Prefect. There were also the French teachers, Miss Wiggs and 'Rolly' Barker.

When I was aged 14 my mother had arranged, through the school, a French exchange. I can remember going to Victoria station with her to pick out my exchange partner Bernard Labbé (now a celebrated heart surgeon in Paris) from the milling crowd of foreign students. I can equally well remember the excitement of getting on the Golden Arrow for the return leg when I visited them for the first time: the first time I had ever left these shores. The end result was that I, at that age, took a greater interest in French than any other subject, apart from woodwork and art; helped no doubt by the fact that Miss Wiggs was something of a brilliant teacher, with her fascinating readings about Provence as she perched on a desk at the front of the class. I learned later that she had been involved with the French Resistance during World War Two and had been awarded the *Légion d'Honneur*. In later years, when I was in my forties it must have been, I went to visit her in a home in Eastbourne, only to find that she had gone a bit 'gaga'; she hadn't a clue who I was and persisted in the belief that I was French, embarrassingly speaking to me in that language at the top of her voice. I found the whole thing very depressing and didn't go again.

It would appear that I had a good ear for accents and when, in my first year in the sixth form, 'Rolly' Barker took on the direction of Molière's *Le Médecin Malgré Lui* ('The Doctor in Spite of Himself'), I was given the lead part of Sganarelle: my first speaking part ever, and in French! Until then, I had been overlooked by Croft when it came to dishing out the speaking parts; and there was one of my best friends, 'Navvy' Stride, walking away with the plaudits. There was too my other best friend 'Froggie' French, who had played Macduff to Johnny's Macbeth. We were all in the under-16 football team together and for the next few years were an inseparable trio, as we rose up through the teams to reach the First Eleven.

The Molière production had nothing of the kudos of the annual Shakespeare; and lovely though he was, a real 'gentle man', Rolly had nothing of the pizzazz of Michael Croft. So it was natural that I should go to Croft and ask for his assistance in helping me with the big speeches, and Rolly was such a nice guy that he took no umbrage. I think I must too have had something of a desire to be taken on the Croft bandwagon, like my friends.

The French play was a success, or so it seemed; how could you tell? It played to full houses but there was no press like the Croft productions, only the school magazine, which commented on 'the masterly performance of Sganarelle whose acting and pronunciation were almost professional – for several days afterwards I was trying in vain to convince a French colleague that Sganarelle wasn't an expatriate'.

But then it would say that, wouldn't it?

It did succeed, however, in getting me on the speaking-part list when Croft came to cast the next production. *Antony and Cleopatra* contains some of

Shakespeare's greatest poetry and was a decidedly ambitious choice, particularly since it shifts its scene from Egypt to Rome and back again with such alarming speed, and on that tiny stage in the Great Hall! Then of course there is the unassailable monument where Antony dies in Cleopatra's arms. Cleopatra too was quite a problem; although the part was originally written for a boy actor, the convention of boys playing female parts had long since been forgotten and Cleopatra had become the domain of such great actresses as Peggy Ashcroft, Margaret Leighton, Edith Evans and Liz Taylor.

Since tasting life as a walk-on in two of Croft's previous productions, I was quite chuffed when he asked me to read for the play. The only foregone conclusion was that Johnny was to play Antony. He had by now left school and had followed Julian to RADA; somehow, Croft had managed to persuade the authorities to bend the rules and let him come back as a visiting student. However, all of the other parts were up for grabs and the now ritualistic round after round of readings started. It was a very thorough process (more thorough than I have experienced since, in the professional theatre) and went on for some weeks. We would have sessions with Croft directing us and giving us every inflection, line by line. I found myself in apparent competition with Richard Hampton as we were given the same speeches to work on and frequently found ourselves together after school waiting to be auditioned. I can't remember how it happened, but Richard says he remembers the distraught look on my face as I came out of the room having just learnt that we were in competition for the role of Cleopatra! Sufficeth to say I didn't fancy playing 'a girl' and I lost my appetite for acting. Which is not to say that Dickey wouldn't have come out on top anyway, but it didn't fit in with my image of myself. I was much more interested in playing Enobarbus; however, David Weston had already somehow got that, and I was as distraught as Julian must have been when he didn't get Hamlet. I must admit I felt like crying. I had to swallow my pride and be satisfied with Scarus, a tiny part in comparison. It was the first of many disappointments to come in this cruel profession where injustice not only survives, but also thrives.

By now the Croft bandwagon was on a roll and his productions were attracting the attention not only of the top national critics but also luminaries of the professional theatre. W. A. Darlington writing in the *Telegraph* gave both Johnny and Dickey a rave notice. Johnny having left to pursue a career in the theatre, Croft had found his next lead actor in Richard Hampton. He had also attracted, apart from David Weston and myself, Colin Farrell (who now goes under the stage name of Col Farrell) who had played the Soothsayer and Paul Hill who had played Iras. I have always thought that Paul was one of the few boys who were adversely affected by coming under the influence of Croft and the

Youth Theatre movement. Paul had all of the attributes of a Shakespearean juvenile lead, with a great voice and a wonderful sense of verse; but he was small and slight, with the physical attributes of a character actor. Although Paul didn't become a professional actor, like the rest of us, he was to become Croft's right-hand man in the development of the National Youth Theatre and directed many a professional production. Unfortunately, he also became Croft's drinking partner; and few, if any, could stand the pace and live a balanced life thereafter!

There was at the school, at that time, a drama society called 'The Bear Pit'. It was a society run by and for the boys with the boys taking on the direction and running of all aspects of production. It too was benefiting from this great zest for theatre, and Paul, Colin Farrell and myself appeared in a production of *She Stoops to Conquer*, like visiting guest stars, you might say.

Because of the attention attracted by the annual production, and Croft's previous connections with the professional theatre, we were getting such stars of the theatre as Paul Daneman and Sir Donald Wolfit coming to the school to judge the reading prize, which itself took on greater significance as the standard rose with all of the schoolboy actors vying for the kudos of winning the verse-speaking prize. The year that Paul Daneman was the judge, it was won by Dicky Hampton and I came second, with my reading from *Under Milk Wood*. Since there was no second prize, Paul Daneman went out and bought a book token to be presented to me as runner-up! I still have it stuck away somewhere in my scrapbook of memories.

I think it must have been this strength in depth that prompted Mike to select *Henry V* as his next venture. Dickey Hampton played Henry, Paul Hill the Chorus, David Weston played Pistol, Colin Farrell played Orleans and Doll Tearsheet was played by Brian Eatwell who became a top designer in the film industry and spent most of his time in Hollywood before his untimely death in the year 2003.

During the war, I had been evacuated to Wales, returning to London with a strong Welsh accent which I had long lost but which proved useful as I played Fluellen. At last, a decent part in a Croft production! Unfortunately, it brought the Welsh accent back, good and strong; which was all very well for the play, but since I was by then a prefect and occasionally had to read the lesson at morning assembly, it earnt me a summons to Soapy's study and a lecture on taking the piss out of the Bible (not his exact words of course!).

The leek scene, in which I beat Dave Weston (as Pistol) about the head with the largest leek to be found daily at Covent Garden vegetable market, was one of the comic highlights of the play. At one early performance, however, Dave took it upon himself to indicate that Pistol had been scavenging the battlefield and came onstage sporting bits and pieces of armour that he'd 'purloined' from the slaughtered French. I didn't take much notice until I started to beat him and he began knocking his knees together. The clamour and clatter of the leg armour brought a tumultuous reaction from the audience, making it impossible to continue. As it subsided, I tried to continue with the dialogue – at which point Dave's knees started again and the audience went up again! This happened several times and in the end I had to get really serious with the beating to get him to stop. Needless to say, we kept it in.

I had at last left the ranks of the spear carriers and walk-ons and joined 'the chosen few'. There was a first-night ritual of us staying up boozing after the performance and carousing until dawn when we would all get into Mike's car and go to Fleet Street to pick up the first edition of the papers and consume them over breakfast in a nearby café. Sadly, on this occasion *Henry V* was doomed as there was a press strike; not only was the nation deprived of the knowledge of our success, but I was deprived of my initiation into the ritual, and had to wait another year. We were pretty depressed that our triumph had missed the papers, but some of the more dedicated critics still came and they sent Mike their 'crits' which were published in the school magazine. I did rather well in these reviews and they tipped the balance in my decision not to go to university but to follow Julian and Johnny to RADA.

It seemed, at the time, an easy decision, but it is one that I have learnt to regret. I had just taken my 'A' levels in English Literature and French and had my fill of reading and studying. Mike had managed to get me a provisional place in his old college, Keble College, Oxford, on condition that I got Latin, which would have meant that I had to stay on at school and I couldn't wait to get out and onto the stage. I had become addicted to the feeling of elation, of success, the buzz of making people laugh and the adrenaline rush of the curtain rising. The thought of ploughing through another term studying a subject that I had given up for woodwork in the third form had little appeal.

Meanwhile I had to contend with my father who had no desire to see his son throw away the benefits of a good education. In retrospect, I can see that he was a frustrated man. He by no means lacked intelligence, but had not had the opportunities that were available to me. He had, too, spent four years of the war in India and Burma, leaving me to bond with my mother in my early years; when he returned, I think he must have felt left out and was jealous of my relationship with her, because she had learnt to rely on me as the 'little man of the family'.

I made myself an inner promise that if I got a scholarship to go to RADA I would go. If I wasn't good enough to get a scholarship, then I wasn't good enough to get where I would want in the professional theatre. Mike coached me long and hard and, when it looked like I was ready for the daunting audition for entry to RADA, the subject was then broached to my parents.

So it was that a few weeks later Croft was taken by my mother and father to the local Conservative Club for a drink and a chat about my future and my father agreed to let me go on the stage, *if* I could get a scholarship to RADA. In a way, unbeknownst to him, my place was already assured. Sir Kenneth Barnes, the then Principal of RADA, came to see *Henry V* and told Mike that if I didn't get a scholarship he would pay for my tuition himself; a wonderful offer, which in the end I did not have to call upon.

I don't remember much about the auditions, held in the 'Little Theatre' in the basement of the RADA building in Malet Street; I was in such a fever pitch of excitement. I did Hotspur's 'My liege I did deny no prisoners...' as my free choice and Hamlet's 'What a piece of work is a man...' as a set text. Having got through the first round I was recalled a week or so later to go through the whole ordeal again. Then came the weeks of anxious waiting for the post to inform me that I had got the George V Bursary! This in turn I did not have to call upon as I had the necessary 'O' and 'A' level qualifications for a Major County Award, and RADA asked me to apply for this as it would then release the bursary to be given to someone else.

In my last term at Alleyn's I had won a travelling scholarship in French and Spanish, which consisted of three months in Boulogne at a branch of the University of Lille studying French literature and a month in Spain with a Spanish family. I think I was about a month into my studies in Boulogne when I received the news that I would have to return to England to undergo further auditions for the Major County Award. I was summoned to Morley College, to audition before a panel of adjudicators. It was a little like a village hall stage and was all a bit surreal; I remember an almost 'out of body experience' as I watched a number 68 bus pass the window, looking out over their heads and performing my Hotspur.

I was invited to sit down and face them across the table and discuss my future, and then I was asked to improvise! I had no experience of improvisation; I could only do, parrot fashion, what Croft had taught me. Luckily, I don't think they had much idea of what it was about either. Joan Littlewood was in her early days, and although there was a lot of talk about, and interest in, improvisation, it was still in its infancy. In the event I attempted to take on the dogmatic and bigoted personality of my own father and improvise his objections to my decision to take up acting as a career.

It worked, so in a funny way my father helped me to get my Major County Award; and I started at RADA in September 1955, at the age of 19 following in the footsteps of Johnny Stride and Julian Glover.

2

1955 to 1956 • RADA • Diana Rigg • Birth of the National Youth Theatre • Richard Hampton • David Weston • Colin Farrell • Paul Hill

I HAVE A FREQUENTLY recurring dream of returning to RADA as a mature student. It is extremely vivid and convincing and I am always very happy and successful there. In my dream, I return as a reasonably established actor who is desperate to take every step within his power to improve. I suspect that the underlying explanation for these dreams is a desire to go back and start again. I confess that I am not content with the way my career developed – I have, in the main, not done the sort of work that I set out to do – but I don't feel I can lay that dissatisfaction at the door of the Royal Academy of Dramatic Art.

My first term there was straight from school, and I fear I looked upon it as little different from an extension of the sixth form. I was, too, more than a little overjoyed and overwhelmed at being in the daily company of girls! There were twenty-two of us in the class; twelve of them were women, and some of the lads weren't interested in girls. That is not to say that I did not work hard. I was still very new to acting and felt I had a lot of catching up to do, so I threw myself wholeheartedly into the classes. I had a desperate desire to be 'the best'; a thirst to play the leading part – to be the hero! My concept of what it meant to be an actor was still based on narcissism and the film-star image. I wanted to be James Dean; I wanted to be noticed, admired, and lusted after. I didn't mind what it took.

Technical classes included mime with Mary Philips, and movement with Amy Boalth and later with Rosalind Iden who, strangely, always wore a hat in class, even whilst performing complicated exercises, and was married to Sir Donald Wolfit, the last of the great actor-managers. Dancing was with Miss Fletcher, fencing with Mr Froechlin and phonetics with Miss Brown, the registrar, who, together with Sergeant who manned the Gower Street entrance, seemed to control all that went on at RADA.

Most of these subjects were new to me, but I generally settled in quite well and enjoyed them all. I did, however have some difficulty in coming to terms with the dancing, which tended to be a little on the balletic side and not at all my cup of tea. Prancing around on tiptoe in black tights I found a little embarrassing and consequently sent the whole thing up. I am ashamed to say that I managed to reduce Miss Fletcher to tears on one occasion when we were practising period bows. We took two paces forward and with a flourish bowed forward over the extended right leg. On this unfortunate occasion, I found my face inches away from the black-tight-clad rear end of Gordon Wright and could not resist the temptation to bite his arse; whereupon he screamed and jumped into the air, and a very tearful Miss Fletcher took me to see John Fernald who was now the Principal (Sir Kenneth Barnes having by this time retired). Fernald gave me a lecture; Miss Fletcher explained her emotional reaction by saying that she felt I had great promise as a dancer if only I would take it seriously. I found this quite flattering and was suitably chastened. The last time I saw Gordon Wright, he was a policeman on the beat in Manchester.

No doubt because of my boxing prowess I was also one of the best in the class at fencing; and when Bertolt Brecht visited RADA with some members of his company in 1956, I was chosen by Froechlin to perform a demonstration with Marril Glendenning as my opponent. I didn't quite know how to handle fighting a girl; my exhibitionist streak deserted me and I lost miserably.

My favourite class, of course, was acting with, in the first term, Richard Ainley, the son of Henry Ainley, the great actor-manager of the early 1900s. He was himself a very powerful actor, but had been crippled during the war when a bomb blew up behind him and left him paralysed on the right-hand side. His power, however, was not diminished and he was an inspirational figure, tall and imposing; his handicap seemed to increase his impressiveness. He was also extremely kind; I recall that, on one occasion, I met him at the main entrance and he pressed a fiver into my hand and told me to take my girlfriend for a drink. Since, at the time, I had no regular, I drank most of it myself! In the second term acting was with Judith Gick, but I didn't have such good parts with her and was forced to stage-manage, a task that I am ashamed to say I considered a waste of my talent.

In the third term of my first year Winifred Oughton directed us in *The Good Companions*, and I was lucky enough to land the leading role of Jess Oakroyd. This was to be my first attempt at a north-country accent; it was becoming obvious that I had quite a good ear for accents and dialects.

Shakespeare was a separate subject, taken by another 'old stager' Nell Carter, and was of course another of my favourites. I was surprised at how lacking in experience some of the students were with regard to Shakespeare and I revelled a bit in my superiority. That was until my third term, when Richard Carey took over the Shakespeare. Hearing that we were to do excerpts from *Henry V*, I asked to be considered for the part of Henry, but felt my nose put very much out of joint when my request was dismissed with Carey telling me I was not tall enough! The part was given to Clinton Greyn and I was extremely resentful.

This was not to be the last time that Clinton 'pipped me at the post' for a part; it happened again some few years later in the film *Robbery*. I bore no grudge against Clinton, although I was jealous of his height and classical good looks; but

I did take very much against Richard Carey who was not unlike an older version of Clinton, tall and strikingly handsome with a mop of wavy hair that he seemed to be continually stroking and patting. During rehearsals, he would quite frequently stand gazing out of the window and seemed to be paying little attention. After a term of virtual warfare, again, I was surprised to get a glowing end-of-term report. He must have thought I was someone else!

What has happened to those twenty or so young hopefuls of the class of '56? Robert Kaliban, my great rival, returned to America where I later heard he was thriving in the voice-over market. David Sumner with his smouldering good looks went on to appear from time to time with the RSC and for a while was artistic director at Crewe Repertory Theatre. Shivendra Sinha I last came across in India in 1984 when I toured with *Educating Rita*; he appeared to be living in a disused theatre and suffering from gout. Valerie Pitts became a TV presenter for a while but I have not heard of her for some years now. David Forder ran a rep theatre for a while and then took up an official post at Equity. Mary Duddy, who spurned my advances and inspired some of my more doggerel verse, I have seen from time to time. Martin Hocke, my old drinking partner, wrote novels in Tuscany but passed away some years ago.

The rest seem to have sunk without trace, except for the most successful careerwise – Diana Rigg. She was in my first-year class at RADA, and I can remember her in J. B. Priestley's *The Good Companions*, in which she played the lead role; although she was very good, she did not particularly stand out in that first year and did not seem wildly ambitious. There were many very pushy females around the Gower Street building, but Diana was not in any way one of them: she was very laid back and seemed to be treating RADA more as a finishing school than a springboard to a great career. I remember her as being very tall and distinguished, which I found a little daunting so I kept my distance – tall women made me feel very conscious of my lack of height. She is now of course a Dame of the theatre, which is even more daunting! So from that first class of twenty-two, only three or four managed any sort of sustained career in the theatre.

I took several holiday jobs during my time at RADA; in one break, I worked as a porter at University College Hospital in Gower Street. Since I was required to wear a white coat, I was frequently mistaken for a doctor, but in the main I spent most of the time sitting in a little room with the other porters and waiting to be called to push a wheelchair, move a bed or run an errand. On my first day, I was called to go to one of the wards and help to take a body down to the morgue. I had never before encountered death and I found the whole experience very traumatic, especially when the other two porters involved in the exercise were old hands and chatted irreverently as they lifted the body off the bed and onto a trolley, with such remarks as, 'Cor blimey, 'e's a big bugger, this one – don't drop 'im, 'e'll make a 'ell of a mess!' He was of course in a shroud but it was obvious that he was a tall and corpulent man. I went very silent and looked at his chart hanging on the end of his bed to see who he was. His name was Frederick Valk; it meant nothing to me, but it registered. That evening I started as a dresser at the Piccadilly Theatre, where Peter Ustinov was appearing in his own play, *Romanoff and Juliet*. I was dressing John Phillips and after explaining my duties to me he added, 'I should advise you to keep a low profile at the moment – nerves are a little bit raw; one of our cast died today.' When he told me it was Frederick Valk, I couldn't believe the coincidence of it!

During that first year, I did not feel that RADA was stretching me sufficiently; I was extremely ambitious and hungry for more theatrical experience. So I looked for extramural adventures. My first venture was with the Attic Players in Dulwich Village, who specialised in Greek drama. This was my first experience of 'am drams' and it has to be admitted that it was not the normal run of amateur theatrical companies. It was run by Eleanor Phethean who had been a professional actress and her husband David Phethean, who was still an actor and who directed the plays. Again, I was following in the footsteps of Johnny Stride whom I had seen performing with them earlier, when I was still at school, together with Michael Croft himself who played some Greek or other who had been banished to an island because his feet were rotten and smelt terrible!

In December of that year I was recalled to Alleyn's school, just as Johnny had been, to play Rumour the Chorus for the next production of *Henry IV Part 2*. At the last minute, due to illness, I also took over the role of Westmoreland. By now, I had become very aware of my lack of height and went to great lengths to make sure I was allocated footwear that would allow me to pad up the heel and increase my height. I was always very aware of what I looked like and went to desperate lengths to ensure that I looked good. I wasn't alone in this, however; I think we were all very self-aware. A lasting memory for me is when Paul Hill, who was playing Prince John and had taken to padding out his tights because his legs were so thin, missed his step making a dignified entrance down a flight of stairs and bounced to the bottom on his heels, thus shaking his makeshift newspaper padding to the bottom of his tights leaving him looking rather lumpy around the ankles! This vision stayed with me throughout the scene and I'm not sure that anybody heard a word I said, or indeed if I was able to utter at all! It was a strong cast with Richard Hampton playing Hal, Dave Weston as Falstaff and Colin Farrell as Justice Shallow. As Pistol, Dave Fournel, the then AAA junior long-jump champion, cleared the width of the Great Hall stage with no run-up to speak of and landed on a table in the Boar's Head Tavern!

This was to be Croft's last production at Alleyn's; and I was able to take part, with the permission of RADA, because it was during term time and Croft was able to tailor rehearsals to my availability. In any case, I was not heavily involved; they were not large parts. However, when *Henry IV Part 2* was invited to play at the Southwark Shakespeare Festival, I was presented with a different problem. The Festival was held at Toynbee Hall and I had taken a daytime job bottling beer at Barclay's Brewery, just across the road on the south side of Lambeth Bridge. We were paid by the day and there was a strange mixture of casual labour. One rascal, by repute a member of a gang at the Elephant and Castle, was constantly goading me because he thought I was posh. I reacted to his goading by offering to punch his head in, and after a bit of a scuffle we became great pals! He even brought his Elephant and Castle gangmates to *Henry IV Part 2*, giving them strict instructions to behave themselves. To my amazement this rather strange bunch of reprobates were completely enthralled and professed to have thoroughly enjoyed the experience. My standing went up considerably at the Brewery!

Another extramural experience that I managed to fit into my first year was with an amateur drama company called the Goodrich Players. It was run by Miss Winifred Vigay, whose octogenarian father was the epitome of the old 'actor laddie', and although he was so ancient he could hardly see or walk, he was a powerful presence and very astute with his comments. Winifred herself was an extremely theatrical character, taught speech and drama at the City of London Institute, and seemed to belong, like her father, to another age.

My first Goodrich production was of no real consequence, but the second was an evening of scenes from Shakespeare and I was able to fulfil my inner secret desire to be a romantic lead actor by playing Hamlet in the 'Get thee to a nunnery' scene and the bedroom scene with Gertrude. In the second half of the evening, I played Romeo! On the same bill, Gary Raymond, the first Cliff in *Look Back in Anger* and who had just recently left RADA, was to play scenes from *Othello*, but he was offered a real professional job (I think it might have been the blockbuster film *El Cid*) and was replaced at the last moment.

We did one performance in the school hall at Honour Oak Girls' School and Martin Holmes wrote a critique in which he described my movement as 'crouching in the hams'. By now, you see, I had advanced from padding newspaper into my boots to give me more height and had invested in a proper pair of elevators from Anello & Davide, shoemakers to the profession. These consisted of three-inch cork wedges and had the effect of throwing my weight forward, rather like wearing high heels I should imagine. I was not put off by such perspicacious criticism, however, and continued to totter my way through many a part for many a year, such was my vanity!

In the final term of my first year at RADA, I was very flattered to be offered the part of Private Gross in an independent student production of *Captain Carvello*, which was to be performed in a village hall near Beaconsfield. It was a small cast with Michael Ashton, Dudley Sutton and my mate Martin Hocke in the cast, directed by another classmate, David Sumner. We weren't paid much, as I recall, but we were provided with accommodation and fodder in the village.

So, my first year at RADA had been to say the least eventful. Apart from the RADA productions (which at this point were not public performances), I had managed to cram in a return to Alleyn's and performances at the Southwark Festival, a Greek drama, two productions with the Goodrich Players and a student production, my first paid job. That is if you don't count the two evenings' entertainment that I had organised at the British Legion. My father and mother, both keen members of the Legion, had got them to invite me to provide the entertainment for one of their musical evenings. I enlisted the help of Kal (Robert Kaliban) and Peggy Chichester, two Americans who seemed very capable of standing up and performing with gusto, and Nicholas Smith, who was in another class in my year at RADA and, although very odd-looking, with ears that stood out like a taxi with the doors open, was musically extremely gifted on the piano and guitar. (He later became quite well known as Mr Rumbold in *Are You Being Served?*) We sang songs and did a sort of barbershop quartet; I did a mime of a Phil Harris record, an idea that I pinched from something I had seen at Alleyn's, and we ended with community singing. The British Legion members, who were more accustomed to music-hall comedians and the odd solo singer, were at first a bit stunned, but it would appear that we were a great success and we were surprised to be paid and invited back again. The second visit, however, was a complete and utter disaster. Lulled into a feeling of confidence after our previous success we did little in the way of preparation or rehearsal, feeling that it was all so easy. I think I set things off by starting the first song in the wrong key and things went rapidly downhill thereafter. They didn't actually boo, but they did decline to pay us and the others refused to talk to me for some weeks! I came to the conclusion that I would not pursue a song-and-dance career.

I wasn't long depressed, however; the opportunity had arisen for my first real professional engagement. Michael Hastings, who was a buddy of mine at Alleyn's and a constant companion on the athletics track, had written a play that was to be directed by Robert Peake at the New Lindsey Theatre. As I remember, the play was entitled *Don't Destroy Me* and I was invited to play the part of George, who was based on the character of James Dean. I still harboured the fancy (along with the majority of young actors at that time) that I bore an uncanny resemblance to James Dean, and I was devastated when John Fernald refused me permission to take two weeks off to play the part. I had not yet got used to the concept of not always getting what I wanted.

There were tentative attempts at a steady relationship, but nothing serious until I met Joan. (I will withhold her surname for reasons that will become clear.) In my term but in a different class, she was very attractive and worked in the holidays as an air hostess for KLM; I was completely bowled over. A regular romance at last, although since Joan still lived at home just off the Fulham Broadway she was kept under surveillance by her rather strict mother; and as I was still living in Peckham, well south of the river, it meant rather sore feet and very late nights, or rather early mornings. Usually by the time I had taken her home and managed to tear myself away from the long-drawn-out farewells, the last bus had long gone. The first attempt to cover the distance was disastrous as I was deliberately sent the wrong way when I asked directions from a taxi driver and spent much of the night walking towards Chiswick, with the taxi driving past from time to time to see if I'd given up! Eventually, however, I mastered the route and spent the journey home working on my parts as I walked through the streets, changing to humming to myself, so as not to appear insane, if anybody should chance to surprise me, which was rare at that time of the morning. It kept me pretty fit, saved money, and became a favoured method of line learning for me. I still find that I learn lines much easier on the move.

Once again following in the footsteps of Johnny Stride I decided to fit in my two years' National Service sandwiched between my two years at RADA. I wasn't happy about it – I wanted to get on with my acting career – but it was compulsory and I thought it better to get it out of the way, so I signed up to go in after the revival of Michael Croft's production of *Henry V*, which was to launch the start of what is now the National Youth Theatre of Great Britain.

After the phenomenal success of his productions at Alleyn's, Croft had begun to consider where he could go from there. The overall opinion was that his productions were challenging the professionals because of their vigour and fresh-ness; he was quite brilliant in the way that he could inspire and orchestrate crowd and battle scenes, and he insisted on a standard of verse speaking that was unique in a school production. He was, too, wonderful at spotting talent in young people and developing that talent. Every line was painstakingly repeated and repeated in rehearsal until he was satisfied. I had not experienced anything like it at RADA and I have to admit that I had missed this fanatic attention to detail. When he invited me to play the part of Fluellen again I did not hesitate.

Croft was not only a brilliant teacher; he was also a genius at publicity and raising finance. At the outset he was prepared to finance his production of *Henry V* with the income from his book *Spare the Rod* (which was later made into a film with Max Bygraves playing the lead), but having enlisted the support of many leading members of the acting profession he set about launching an appeal for funding. Sir Ralph Richardson agreed to be President, with Glen Byam Shaw (director of the RSC), Sir Michael Redgrave and Michael Benthall (director of the Old Vic) as Vice Presidents. Dame Sybil Thorndike, Sir Lewis Casson, Anthony Quayle, Terrence Rattigan, John Fernald, Beatrix Lehmann, Sandy Wilson, Peter Hall, Alan Badel and Reggie Smith of the BBC all gave moral support as patrons. With this formidable list of supporters Croft set out the aims of the Youth Theatre:

> To encourage young people towards a better understanding and appreciation of the best of native drama.
>
> To bring together the most talented and lively young actors in the country to take part in holiday productions and set a standard of performance that will be of benefit to school and youth club productions in general.
>
> To show the educational value of drama in terms of team effort and self-discipline.
>
> Above all to give to young people a chance to show what they can do working together as a team for a common aim.

Sir Ralph Richardson wrote:

> As President of the Youth Theatre, I wish Michael Croft and all his players the greatest good fortune in their courageous and worthwhile venture.
>
> I feel that the Youth Theatre deserves the greatest support by young and old alike, for, by encouraging young people to act in great plays, it not only increases their understanding of our playwrights but it will also create a greater enthusiasm for good drama amongst young people throughout the country.

Glen Byam Shaw wrote:

> The general plan of the Youth Theatre seems to me admirable. I feel that what you are going to do will be of such value that I am honoured that you should ask me to be a member of the general committee.

Mr W. A. Darlington of the *Telegraph* wrote:

> Having had three memorable experiences of Mr Michael Croft's special talent for inspiring schoolboys to act, I am delighted to hear that he is to employ it on a scale bigger than was possible for him as a master at Alleyn's School. I welcome the foundation of a Youth Theatre and wish it all good fortune.
>
> What seems to me particularly praiseworthy is Mr Croft's sensible approach to his venture, especially his refusal to make it a nursery for the professional stage.

The *Daily Telegraph*, no doubt urged on by W. A. Darlington, took up the gauntlet and sponsored the first production, thus taking the pressure off Croft financially and providing a guarantee of valuable news coverage. Sir Alec Guinness and Peter Ustinov joined the list of Vice Presidents and Flora Robson, Margaret Leighton, Kenneth More and Richard Burton joined the list of Patrons, together with a number of prominent politicians.

Despite the fact that the cast was to be virtually the same as the Alleyn's School production, with Richard Hampton, David Weston and me all playing our old parts, we had three weeks' full-time rehearsal. Simon Ward was brought in from Alleyn's to play Katherine and Barry Boys, from our rival school Dulwich College, was recruited to play the Dauphin. There were, too, changes in some of the minor parts, and some additions to the list of soldiers, attendants and so on, amongst them my brother Brian. Derek Jacobi's name appears in the programme as one of the crowd artists, but he assures me that he has no recollection of it; he did, however, turn up in the next production.

The first night on Monday September 10th 1956 was everything that the first night of a success should be. Sir Ralph Richardson and Richard Burton were both in the audience and came onto the stage to make speeches of congratulation at the curtain call. The first-night celebrations were followed by the all-night vigil and the trip to Covent Garden, which was then still a vegetable market, for breakfast followed by the journey down Fleet Street to pick up the early morning editions. As we drove back to Dulwich in Mike's car we took it in turns to read out the 'crits', elated and excited by our success. The whole week was a sell-out with many well-known politicians and actors in the audience each night. The last night was a celebration in true Croft manner – the Youth Theatre was on its way.

Five days later Richard Hampton and I boarded a train at Paddington, bound for Oswestry in Shropshire (where strangely enough Croft was born), to start our two years' National Service.

3

1956 to 1959 • National Service • RADA •
Mike Williams • National Youth Theatre • Derek Jacobi •
Hywel Bennett • Michael York

RICHARD HAMPTON AND I weren't together for long; Dickey, as a very accomplished flautist who was also a member of the National Youth Orchestra, was to continue his music in the Royal Artillery Band and I was to attempt a National Service Commission. At Oswestry station we were bawled at by a red-faced corporal and divided into two bunches, 'six eight to the left six nine to the right'. We parted and found ourselves herded into sheep pens to await transport to the camp. I could see Dickey in his pen some few yards away on the other side of the corporal. I stuck my head through the rails and 'baaa'd' at him. This seemed to upset the corporal considerably and he descended upon me in the most threatening manner, demanding to know my name and 'what sort of f---ing comedian' did I think I was!

This was the start of a painful relationship, as I was soon to find that the red-faced, apoplectic Corporal Berry was to be in charge of my section and from that moment he decided to use me as his whipping boy. Fortunately, as I had reached the rank of drum major in the school Combined Cadet Force, the drill and the 'bullshitting' weren't new to me, a fact that seemed to rile the corporal more. He found it quite inspirational that I was going to be an actor and took great delight in overseeing my haircut. I had come into the army with a very full and healthy head of long hair: the 'long-haired actor' personified. One of his first tasks was to gleefully inform me that I could keep anything that was under my beret; he then watched the camp barber shave my head up to and beyond the top of the ears, but leaving a tumultuous mop on the top. Not unlike the modern fashion; but I felt I looked ridiculous, and as soon as I got back to the barrack room I sat on the floor whilst one of my new-found mates cut the remainder down to a quarter of an inch all over with a pair of nail scissors. Later, when he learnt that I was considered officer material because of my schooling and might be going before the War Office Selection Board, Corporal Berry nearly burst a blood vessel!

The six weeks' basic training was painful. In adversity, however, the troop all bonded together and we had many a laugh. I took most of the flak from Corporal Berry, but I didn't mind it too much; it made me more popular with my mates, as I coped by getting quite a few good laughs out of it, which of course increased his fury. He would call upon me using the foulest epithet that his limited intellect could muster; I would frequently ignore him and, when confronted, would say that I had thought he was talking to himself. He once called me and, as I turned, he threw his drinking mug at me and yelled, 'Hey, F---kface, wash that!' I let the mug fall to the floor and shatter, calmly and innocently asking, 'Wash what?'

His special punishment was to make me spend my evenings shovelling coke from the main pile and wheelbarrowing it to our hut, for hours on end. He would invariably set me to work and then go out for the evening, and I found that as long as I was still there looking suitably knackered when he returned it satisfied his sadistic and bullying nature. Dickey would call for me in the evening and I would down my shovel, toddle off with him to the NAAFI or the cinema (where we would sit with our knees up under our chins in the front row, the cheapest seats, with the children of the NCOs who lived on the camp), and return in time to be found exhaustedly hanging over my shovel. Joan came up one weekend and I managed to grab a few moments of sanity with her in the local town – though she was somewhat taken aback when she saw my haircut!

Towards the end of my basic training I was accepted by the War Office Selection Board as an officer cadet. However, the Christmas Revue was coming up at the Oswestry camp, and when Lt Gordon Clyde learnt that they had a RADA student in their midst I was approached and invited to join the company. The first problem was that I was expected to go to Mons, in Aldershot, to begin my officer cadet training, and it was suggested that they should inform Mons that I had broken my arm and would not be able to start until after Christmas! This suited me fine, but the question then arose as to what I should do in the meantime. Most of the cast were officers and their wives and rehearsals were only possible in the evenings. I had no desire to spend my days continuing my basic training! I managed to negotiate that I should be put in charge of the camp theatre, working during the day, painting the sets and fixing the lights. I was now pretty much my own boss, taking great delight in staying in bed when the RSM did his early-morning inspections and revelling in the protection afforded me by my relationship with the officers who were organising the revue. I also took on an added importance when Jon Pertwee visited the camp to entertain the troops and I, as resident theatre technician, had to get the stage ready for him.

The Christmas Revue, called *Spludge* ('Greek for *egdulps*'), was a series of sketches and musical moments which, as all amateur productions are, was a great success. Gordon Clyde was a gifted light entertainer (later writing comedy and appearing with Dick Emery in his TV series); and I also recall that Richard Francis, who joined us late from OUDS, wrote a version of 'Teddy Bears' Picnic' called 'Teddy Boys' Picnic'. Richard eventually went on to be Head of Light Entertainment at the BBC. He too was going to Mons in Aldershot to be trained as an army officer, so we set off after the Christmas Revue together.

At Mons I had a relatively light time of it compared with the brutality of the basic training at Aldershot. I played football for the Army Crusaders, a team of officers, which meant that I spent much of my time away from camp, travelling the country playing soccer. I even returned to my old school, Alleyn's, to play against the First Eleven; I scored the winning goal, which is memorable since I didn't score many! Possibly because of my value to the officers as a soccer player, on April 17th I learnt that I had passed my officer's training and was to be assigned to 39 Heavy Regiment RA. Ironically, though, they were to be posted to Cyprus in October, so I was lost to the team anyway: a pretty fair example of the wonders of military planning!

After the 'pass out parade' I was to be granted a week's leave, which, as luck would have it, allowed me to join Mike and the Youth Theatre to play in the second production at Toynbee Hall. Since it was to be a revival of the production of *Henry IV Part 2* that we had previously done at Alleyn's, it was not too serious that I would miss some rehearsal time, but I relinquished the part of Rumour to Paul Hill and I took over the part of Poins, Prince Hal's sidekick. Richard was unable to get leave from the army, so the young Derek Jacobi played Hal. I also doubled with my original role of Westmoreland, and on one occasion when Dave Fournel was long-jumping in the AAA junior championships, which he won, I played Pistol as well.

I am ashamed to say that there was a certain arrogant complacency setting into the company. Not as far as Croft was concerned, I hasten to add; but, perhaps in order to accentuate their superiority over the 'new boys', some of the old lags started to mess about onstage with 'in' jokes that from time to time got out of hand. One of the most destructive was perhaps the slipping in to the Shakespearean dialogue of certain unlikely words, the most outrageous being 'dustbin'. It was indeed shameful, and I blush to confess that I too was part of this childish gag. The Lord Chief Justice was referred to as 'my Lord Chief Dustbin', and Falstaff exhorted the Hostess to 'empty the dustbin'; stupid little violations of the text, to show how dangerously we could live life. When Mike heard about it he hit the roof and we were all given a dressing down and a lecture on professional attitude.

I have to say that Derek Jacobi was not involved in this childish gag, but was in no way sanctimonious or aloof, taking on the mantle as Dickey's successor with great dignity; no mean task. We were a pretty close-knit group, and Dickey had been the leading member of our company for a long time. There was no way that Derek could have been completely comfortable – indeed I understand that he has often said that he felt a bit of an outsider – but all things considered he did a magnificent job, and his performance was superb, very impressive. When the production was taken to Manchester in the summer of that year, Derek and

Dickey were both unavailable and the part of Hal was played by Peter Papaloizou on this occasion.

Immediately after the production at Toynbee Hall I joined my new regiment, who were stationed at Perham Down on Salisbury Plain. In my new officer's cap and with one pip on my shoulder, I took the train to Salisbury where I was met by my appointed batman, who seemed to sport the most enormous chip on his shoulder and an extreme dislike of commissioned officers, especially me. He threw my kit bag unceremoniously into the back of the Land Rover with a fag hanging from his mouth and grumbling constantly about 'f---ing officers'. The driver, meanwhile, seemed to harbour some sort of death wish and set off at the most alarming speed, cornering madly on two wheels and breaking every rule in the Highway Code. I remained silent all the way to the camp, partly out of fear for my life and partly because I didn't know how to deal with this sort of flagrant insubordination. In reality I felt more in tune with their working-class attitude towards authority than I did with my new privileged position.

On arrival I was informed that the large country mansion that served as the officer's quarters was temporarily full to the brim and I would have to make do with a tent on the lawns for the first night or two. My bolshie batman reluctantly helped me unload my bags by more or less throwing them at me, and I settled in to my tent. By now it was late afternoon and the subalterns of the regiment were assembled on the mansion's terrace enjoying their end-of-the-day gin and tonic. My batman grumbled his way around the tent muttering angry abuse at the apparently high-spirited junior officers, well out of earshot of them, but inviting me to join him in his contempt for them and their sort. I didn't know what to do; if I remember, in the main I agreed with him, as he reluctantly helped me dress in 'patrols' for the evening meal. I had been told to dress for dinner, so I was getting to wear my newly bought evening dress.

I must have been extremely gullible, because I didn't even suspect foul play when I was the only one in evening dress at the long table that night, nor did I recognise the driver or my batman as they joined the officers that they had been reviling; but when my batman turned up with a mug of tea at my tent the next morning and, on ascertaining that I took two sugars, proceeded to stir in two teaspoons of salt, and I could see that I was still being watched from the terrace by a horde of junior officers who were obviously finding something extremely hilarious, I began to feel that I was being set up. But it was not until later when I had my first interview with the adjutant, who asked me why I had opted to sleep in a tent on the lawn when there were plenty of rooms available in the main building, that the penny finally dropped and I realised I had been the victim of an elaborate initiation process.

Having settled in to the regiment, still stationed on Salisbury Plain prior to going to Cyprus, I applied for leave. With a heartbreaking letter from Croft begging me to approach my commanding officer and subtly dropping the name of Sir Ralph Richardson (I later learnt that Croft had got Sir Ralph to write a letter to the War Office!), I managed to get leave to travel north to Manchester with *Henry IV Part 2*: the Youth Theatre's first touring production. The performance at the university theatre, the Arthur Worthington Hall, was to be my first visit to Manchester, but by no means my last. From that time, Manchester was to play a large part in my life.

In one respect, the visit was a failure. The bookings were terrible and, as I have already mentioned, to arouse interest in the production Croft organised a procession, in costume, through the streets of Manchester. We performed excerpts from the play in Piccadilly Gardens, and then set up our makeshift skiffle group in Lewis's arcade where we were later moved on by the police. As a newly commissioned army officer, I was not exactly over the moon about making such an exhibition of myself and didn't enter the exercise with much enthusiasm. Apart from feeling a bit above the whole thing, I have always believed that actors should not appear in costume or make-up in public, except on stage, and have always detested the practice among amateurs of appearing in the bar after their performance with heavy make-up still in evidence, more often than not clumsily applied. Nevertheless, I found myself playing the 'tea chest' bass in the skiffle group as Croft felt that my previous rank of drum major qualified me as a musical authority! The embarrassing procession succeeded in attracting a lot of press attention and the bookings definitely improved; but although we were well received on stage, we still did not play to full houses.

In another respect, though, the production was a success. The flame had been kindled; the seeds for the northern branch of the Youth Theatre had been sown, and many new friendships had been forged. Robert Powell and Anthony Sher were reputedly among the recruited students who helped out, showing people to their seats in the Arthur Worthington Hall and so on.

With the departure of the regiment from Southampton on HMS *Dilwarra* on September 26th, my acting came to a sudden halt. Joan came to wave goodbye from the quayside and it was agreed between us that should our relationship endure the twelve months' separation, we would get engaged on my return! In Cyprus, we were considered to be on active service, keeping the peace between the Greeks and the Turks and searching for Colonel Grivas, the leader of EOKA, the terrorist organisation that was fighting for union with Greece. As an artillery regiment, we had given up our heavy guns and were, to all intents and purposes, infantry. I was in charge of a troop of thirty-six men together with a couple of sergeants, and we spent the year almost entirely under canvas patrolling an area that changed from time to time as we were moved about the island. My life consisted of patrols through the countryside and visits to the nearby villages building up a relationship with the locals and looking for signs of terrorism, and setting up roadblocks from time to time, searching for arms. We were also there to keep the peace between the Greeks and the Turks, who were constantly at loggerheads and frequently rioting and setting about each other.

I found it a lonely existence as I was mostly on my own. As an officer I was not able to fraternise with the men; the closest relationship I had was with my troop sergeant, Sgt Wilding. Rather than spend every night alone in my little tent, I would frequently organise some night patrol or swan around the area in my Land Rover; I was learning to drive and took every opportunity I could to get behind the wheel. I would give my driver the night off, Wilding and I would set off together around the villages under our command and I would take the opportunity for some driving practice.

The roads were often very poor and the number of accidents had risen so dramatically that the army issued a directive that, since a traffic accident was to be made an immediate and mandatory charge, officers were not to drive army vehicles in order to avoid the embarrassing situation of having to take them to court martial. Consequently, when I hit an army truck on a side road off the road to Episkopi one night, I was in trouble, big time. I hadn't even passed my test! There was not a great deal of damage; the wing mirror of the truck had hit my windscreen and shattered it as we had passed each other at some speed crossing a humpback bridge.

The damage to the other vehicle was very slight; a smashed and distorted wing mirror. After ascertaining that the driver had a mate in the Motor Transport Office who would be able to get him a new mirror and cover for him, I sent him on his way and turned to Sgt Wilding for inspiration. He was a Scouser who, prior to joining the army, had been a prison warder in Liverpool, so he was not without a devious turn of mind. We immediately got on the wireless and informed control that we had run into an ambush and been fired at; the windscreen had been shattered and we had driven off the road and given chase. A few days later, we read in the *Daily Telegraph*: 'Last week a security forces Land Rover was ambushed just outside Episkopi – there were no casualties.'

In many ways I regret my attitude during that year in Cyprus. It was a wonderful location to be banished to, but I resented the fact that it had been forced upon me. I wanted to get on with my career as an actor, I didn't want to be a soldier; and, although I made the best of it, I didn't enjoy the year in the sun as much as I would do now. I had one wonderful posting when I was at Zygi, for once not in a tent but in a hut on the sandy beach where I was just able to run out into the Med for a dip before breakfast. This was my happiest month; but in the main I was counting the days to my freedom.

A few weeks before my demob, however, I courted disaster when, after a night of celebrating my upcoming freedom in the regimental mess at Akrotiri, I awoke the next morning with something of a hangover, and when I came to get dressed I realised that I had left my peaked cap in the mess. When I went to look for it, I was informed by the mess waiter that the commanding officer had given it to his second in command to destroy. Now I will allow that it was not in the best of condition; it had taken on a very distinctive shape and, having blown from my head from time to time when driving in the open Land Rover, it had more than lost its new look. Nevertheless, I was very fond of that hat and it had somehow become something of a talisman for me. From a distance the hat was recognisable before I was.

The officer's cap is not army issue, but has to be paid for by the officer himself. However, I wasn't going to buy a new one just for the few weeks I had left. At the same time, I didn't fancy serving out my final days in a beret; I was finding that nobody saluted me, and sensed that one or two were taking advantage of the situation to put me back in my place! So, feeling that I had grounds for an objection, I went to my battery commander to register a complaint. He just laughed and said it was a lousy hat and should have been burnt months ago.

Not to be daunted I called on the adjutant and asked to borrow the Queen's Regulations, the rulebook for army behaviour. He told me that I should first take the matter to my battery commander, but I explained that I had done that and he had just laughed. He then said I should complain to the CO, but I pointed out that I was unlikely to get a sympathetic hearing since he had given the order. In that case, he informed me, I should go to Area Command; if I got no joy there I could complain to the War Office, and if that proved unsatisfactory I had the right as an officer and a gentleman to complain directly to the Queen! I said, 'I do hope it doesn't go that far,' requested an interview with the CO and left.

On the morning of my appointment, sporting my beret and feeling less than sure of myself, I stood before the CO and explained that my hat had been taken from the officers' mess and destroyed, at which point the CO said, ominously quietly, 'I gave the order for your hat to be burnt; it was a disgrace.' I swallowed hard and tentatively said, 'I'm sorry, sir, but I don't believe anybody has the right to dispose of my own personal equipment without reference to myself.' There was a long pause and the CO said, 'Go to my tent; on the bed you will find a hat. I believe it is the right size. It isn't new, but it's in a damned sight better condition than yours was!'

That evening in the mess, I was prevailed upon by the other subalterns to give him back his hat, but I was flushed with success and wasn't going to let go of my trophy. When the CO came into the mess later that evening I boldly approached him and asked if I could buy him a drink. He had famously never accepted a drink from anybody, but he looked at me without a glimmer of humour and said, 'With you, Farrington, I'll have a lager, thank you.'

So I came out of the army with the CO's hat; but even then I managed to mess things up by over-celebrating the night before freedom, ending up on the beach with the squadron leader's daughter and, in the early morning, watching the plane that was to take me to Episkopi for my flight home pass overhead. Perhaps my late development in relationships with the opposite sex had made me more vulnerable to temptation than most. I was not alone in this, however, because when I returned to England on September 15th 1958 after a year away, I was to discover that Joan was three months pregnant!

I wasn't given this news as soon as I arrived home and picked up again with Joan, but I was aware that something had changed, something was wrong; she no longer seemed to be the woman that I had built up in my mind over the year away. It could be that the poor love was aware of her condition and terrified, unable to give herself fully to the relationship; or it could be that my dalliance on that last night in Cyprus had destroyed something in our relationship within myself. I had not told Joan about it, but I think it may have affected my attitude. Whatever it was, by the time she dropped her bombshell twelve days after my return, I had come to the conclusion that I was no longer in love with her; so, in a way, there was an element of relief when she told me of her condition – a way out!

I did not feel it honourable to leave her in times of such trouble; I felt obliged to help, if only to salve my own conscience. Abortion was illegal at that time, but Joan had decided that that was the course of action she wished to pursue. So first of all, having got the name of the guilty party I went to see him at his place of work, which strangely enough turned out to be a forces' club where he was washing dishes. He was a student and hadn't much money, and I think he was somewhat overawed by my rank because he didn't put up much of a fight. I felt insulted that she had chosen to be unfaithful to me with such a wimp!

Nevertheless, I told him to empty his Post Office savings account to pay for the abortion, and I then went and tracked down a backstreet abortionist. The abortion cost £10; the student had had £15 in his account. I rather cruelly gave Joan the extra fiver for her trouble. As so frequently happened in these matters, it all went wrong and Joan was taken into Chelsea Hospital. I visited her daily until it was all over and then, after having tea with her family on October 12th, I left her; but that was not to be the end of it.

I should have returned to RADA on leaving the army in September, but Joan's situation, coupled with the fact that I was somewhat disorientated by re-entering civilian life, led me to ask for a postponement. I was not sure if I still wanted to act. The role of second lieutenant had been a difficult one for me; coming from a working-class background, despite my almost public-school education, I found it difficult to sustain the necessary distance between my men and me. In the officers' mess one was encouraged to believe that, as an officer, you were superior and the men had to be treated correspondingly. I was not overly impressed with some of my fellow officers who, it seemed to me, had to rely upon this sort of brainwashing in order to maintain control. It was probably arrogant of me, but I attempted to lead by example, by being better at anything I asked my men to do than they were. It took me quite a time to come down to earth again.

To reacclimatise, I decided to get a job in the theatre to see if I still had the appetite for it. However, in order to get a job backstage I had to be a member of NATKE (National Association of Theatre and Kinematic Employees), and in order to become a member I had to have a job in the theatre: Catch-22. I cracked the code by taking a job as a cleaner at the Duchess Theatre in Covent Garden, for which I did not have to be a union member, but as a worker in the theatre I was able to claim membership. Thus, two weeks after leading a troop of thirty-six men on active service in the Mediterranean, I was to be seen cleaning the brass on the foyer doors in Drury Lane!

After a few days, I got my ticket and took a job as a stagehand at the Old Vic, working as a 'showman' (that is, just for performances). For a while I did both jobs; two weeks later, I was promoted to 'dayman' at the Old Vic and gave up my cleaning job at the Duchess.

I was very happy at the Old Vic. There were about ten of us daymen in all, and a lot of our time was spent in the staff room below the stage playing cards. On one unbelievable occasion the fireman (of all people), who for some reason always stood up to deal, had just lit his pipe and carelessly tossed his match over his shoulder as he stood. The chair had a canvas seat and by the time he came to sit down again his chair was burning nicely. Nobody said a word but kept a straight face, watching his every move in amazement until he sat down when they all, simultaneously, collapsed with laughter.

At some point during the day we would be summoned; when this happened we would all move off in a group across the road to the scene dock, looking rather like the packs of stray dogs I had frequently seen roaming around Cyprus. I christened us 'the stage hounds'.

The first production that I worked on was *Julius Caesar* with Michael Hordern as Cassius and John Phillips as Brutus: he showed no sign of remembering that I had been his dresser for *Romanoff and Juliet*, and I didn't have the balls to remind him. Ronald Lewis played Antony. I can't claim to have been a model stagehand; between cues we would be playing cards down below in the staff room, and I am ashamed to say that I was frequently 'carpeted' for missing going up to move a chair or take a prop.

My greatest blunder was during a production of Ibsen's *Ghosts* with Michael Hordern as Pastor Manders, Dame Flora Robson as Mrs Alving and to start with Ronald Lewis as the young Oswald. However, he had some sort of mental breakdown shortly after opening night and just disappeared, leaving a note pinned to his dressing-room door to say that he would not be back! I was on 'tabs' for this production, which meant that I had to pull in the curtain at the intervals. However, this was not as simple as it sounds. Some of the furniture was downstage, below the 'tab line', and since the fire curtain had to be brought down at each interval, it was necessary to move the furniture upstage before bringing in the tabs or the fire curtain. This all took place in a blackout, so everything had to be done on timing as nobody could see properly. The sequence was that at the end of the scene the lights would go to blackout; three stagehands dressed in black would come on in the dark, move the furniture upstage behind the curtain line and wait whilst the tabs were brought in, and at that point the fire curtain could be brought in to satisfy the regulation. I would take my cue from the prompt corner, who could just about see when the furniture was safe: first the red light to stand by and then the green light to go.

On the first night, no less, I was stationed at the pulley ropes and, on getting the red light, dutifully gripped the rope up high and prepared to pull. The stage went to blackout, the actors exited and the three stagehands came on, moved the furniture upstage and waited. The green light flashed and I pulled with all my might; the first pull is the hefty one to get the weights away and then it was a simple matter of stopping the momentum at the end. I heaved: nothing happened. I pulled again – nothing happened. By this time, the curtain was expected to be in, and the lights went up to reveal the three stagehands, in their black robes with hoods over their heads, looking rather like monks. The most experienced of the three for some reason dropped onto his hands and knees and crawled offstage into the wings; the second panicked and dashed as he thought offstage only to end up in the channel where the iron fire curtain was due to descend and had to sheepishly return to the stage and find the correct exit. The third, my mate David Miles, simply stood still facing the audience grinning, until I eventually discovered my error: I had forgotten to take the brake off the tabs! The title *Ghosts* took on a different meaning that night; and to cap it all the director of that particular production was John Fernald, the Principal of RADA!

David Miles and I were frequently in trouble together. He was a student at St Martin's Art School in Charing Cross Road; and since we were rarely seen apart, both invariably wore jeans and a sweater (the uniform of the student in those days) and both sported beards, we were known as the 'terrible twins'. Not only did we work together, we socialised together too. In order to maximise our chances with the ladies at the various parties, we worked out a scheme. If we felt that the party was to be a casual scruffy-artist-type 'do', we would go smart, or at least in blazer and flannels which was as smart as we could afford at that time. If it looked likely to be a formal affair, we would go in our jeans. It proved quite successful. There were many parties at that time and we were both pretty heavy partygoers, possibly as a reaction to the restricted life that I had led in the army.

It would be cruel to say that Joan was stalking me; stalking was not a term we used at the time. Nevertheless, she seemed to be at most of the parties I went to. I had no wish to hurt her; I was still very fond of her, and from time to time we got on quite well together. It is probably unfortunate that she turned up, on one occasion, at a Youth Theatre party where she spent most of her time chatting with Shirley Cameron, an actress who was married to David Palastanga. David had been at Alleyn's when Croft first arrived as a teacher, but he was there too soon to take advantage of Croft's revolution of the drama. He was an extremely tall, good-looking, athletic young man who was a fine fast bowler for the First Eleven cricket team, but on accidentally setting fire to the colours room where he frequently took himself off for a smoke, he was 'asked to leave'. After a few high-profile modelling jobs he graduated into acting, his most prestigious appearance being in Tennessee Williams' *Suddenly Last Summer* in the West End. Shirley was very much in love with him and was devastated when he later left her for Hildegarde Neff. However, at this time, they were very happy together and when Joan asked if they were going to have children, Shirley replied, 'I've got David; why should I want a carbon copy?' A remark for which I was going to pay!

In January 1959, having decided that I did still want to be an actor, I returned to RADA for my last year, but I did not at that time give up my job at the Old Vic: I simply went back to being a showman, working only in the evenings, together with David who was then back at St Martin's Art School. I had a new set of classmates. In the final year at RADA, our productions moved into the larger Vanbrugh Theatre and there were public performances. I was not at all happy with my parts for the first term back and, as soon as I had the opportunity, I sought an interview with John Fernald and expressed my disappointment. He was delightful and assured me that he had better things in mind for my next two terms, which were of course more important, so I contented myself with getting on with the parts I had been allocated.

In those first-term casts one of the leading players was Conrad Monk, who seemed to be very well thought of by the establishment, and who seemed to me to be extremely ambitious. He was not without talent, and I am very surprised that he did not seem to last long in the profession, although not at all surprised that he became a millionaire, having started a firm called 'Knobs & Knockers' and sold it for Monopoly money! On sunny summer days we would all get as much exposure on the flat roof of Gower Street as we could, often rehearsing on the roof, and Conrad sold a suntan lotion that he had concocted himself; guaranteed to tan instantly. Since it was a mixture of Nivea cream and iodine, which stained the skin, it was very successful (if a little on the yellow side) and it sold quite well. I believe he even sold some to Ellen Pollock, who directed us the next term in *Saturday Night* and who worshipped the sun to such an extent that she looked as if her skin had been to the tannery!

A new and exciting member of the staff was Peter Barkworth, who taught technique. As a working actor, he had more credibility than most; but not only that, he was a brilliant technician and a brilliant teacher. We all strove for his approbation and I got on with him very well. Because I had little to do with regard to my parts in the productions, I joined the French acting class taken by Pamela Stirling and we did *L'Épreuve* by Marivaux. I played Lucidor, the romantic lead, which pleased me no end: I still nurtured the idea that I was a reincarnation of James Dean, but now I was also Gérard Philipe!

Rehearsal times for the French plays were limited; there was the odd time set aside during the working day, but in general it was expected that the students would get together themselves and organise extra rehearsals. Since I was still working in the evenings at the Old Vic, we would meet up early in the morning and grab an hour or so before classes started. François Landry, another former pupil at Alleyn's (though one who had strangely slipped through Michael Croft's net), was also in the cast having just arrived at RADA, and we got on well; his brother Michael had been in the school production of *Le Médecin Malgré Lui* in which I played Sganarelle. I have always found that there was a style of humour at Alleyn's that even in later years created a bond that made it easier to communicate and get on.

It wasn't all roses, however, because unfortunately Tom Kempinski, who later became a playwright of some distinction but was then playing my valet Frontin, seemed to have great trouble getting out of bed in the morning and never turned up for the early-morning sessions. Since he was heavily involved with Caroline Mortimer at that time, I suppose it was understandable; but as production day was drawing nigh, I was in no mood to understand. We all put pressure on him to pull himself together and when eventually, after some weeks, he did arrive, but late, he marched into the theatre waving his umbrella and announcing his arrival in a loud voice and interrupting the scene that we were rehearsing. I leapt from the stage, ran up the aisle and pinned him to the back wall of the auditorium by the throat; I had to be dragged off. To accompany my aggressive nature I have always had a big thing about punctuality!

I had been asked by Mike Croft to play Claudius in the Youth Theatre's next production, *Hamlet*, to be rehearsed and performed primarily at Dartington Hall in Devon in the Easter break. However, shortly before the end of that first term I received the 'bombshell': Joan was pregnant again, and this time it was me! She had been turning up from time to time at parties that I went to, and even at my home; at some point I had obviously taken advantage of her, having had too much to drink. As Shakespeare puts it: 'It puts a man on and it takes a man off,' but in this case I hadn't had enough to 'take me off'! Obviously the question of an abortion arose, but was quite understandably dismissed after her previous experience. There was also the matter of her wanting 'a carbon copy of me', that particular seed having been sown by Shirley Cameron, which was flattering but… I was in one hell of a state and when the time came to join Mike in Devon, I rather cowardly scuttled off and left my old schoolmate 'Froggie' French to deliver the 'glad tidings' to my parents.

My father had a bit of a soft spot for Froggie, as they both had strong cockney accents that they refused to tone down or improve, and I felt he could divert the flak that was imminent. He did a great job, to such an extent that my father was convinced the baby wasn't mine and wanted to contest the paternity! I didn't know what to do. I certainly wasn't going to follow my father's plan; I was sure it was mine and I knew she was going to have it. We hadn't yet arrived at the 'swinging' part of the sixties, and unmarried mothers were very much frowned upon; but, although I was still very fond of Joan, I didn't love her enough to feel that we could make a go at marriage. In any case, I had selfishly started to dislike her because of the stupidity of her putting me in this position.

At Dartington Hall, I threw myself into rehearsals in an attempt to alleviate some of the stress. The Youth Theatre was still all male, with boys playing the female parts. Mike, who was aware of 'the Joan situation', gave me the young Hywel Bennett, who was playing Ophelia, to take aside and teach him how to speak Shakespeare. Richard Hampton, who had now left the army and was at Oxford, soon to be made president of the OUDS, was to play Hamlet; Simon Ward had graduated from the female roles to play Rosencrantz. Although there were many old mates, the Youth Theatre was also beginning to cast its net wider and many more schools were involved, with youngsters coming from all over the country. Michael York, then known as Michael Johnson, played Horatio; Neil

Stacey, Polonius; John Nightingale, Fortinbras; Michael Cadman, Marcellus; and John Shrapnel, Laertes. All were later to pursue careers in the theatre with varying degrees of success.

The production of *Hamlet* was very well received, and was destined for greater things. We took it to the Sarah Bernhardt Theatre in Paris for the '*Théâtre des Nations*' for two days at the end of May, the whole company flying from Heathrow and put up in a variety of dodgy hostels. This was to be the first of many overseas tours taken by the Youth Theatre and almost, but not quite, my last.

There were still a few days remaining of the Easter holiday before I returned to RADA. Whilst working at the Old Vic, I had struck up a relationship with Norma, a truly delightful young girl from the wardrobe department. She was from another age; she dressed, thought, and behaved like someone from the Victorian era. She was petite, fragile and beautiful in her many petticoats and tight bodice; she had an air of unassailability about her and, apart from the challenging aspect of the relationship, there was too a feeling that it was safer and less liable to get me into the sort of trouble that I was currently finding myself in. She had recently moved from the Old Vic wardrobe to the RSC at Stratford and had invited me down for a few days before I was due back at RADA.

I slept on a sofa in the little cottage that she rented, up an alley opposite the stage door. That season they were performing amongst other things *Othello* with Paul Robeson in the title role and Sam Wanamaker as Iago; Albert Finney (who had been in the year above me at RADA) was playing Claudio. Brian Croft, who had been at Alleyn's and with the Youth Theatre from the beginning as stage manager, was with the company as were my old classmates Diana Rigg and Ted de Souza, and also Julian Glover.

I fell in love with the place; I spent my time reading and discovering Stratford during the daytime whilst I waited for Norma to finish work. Sometimes we would meet up at lunchtime and take a punt out onto the river, and in the evening she got me tickets for the plays in the theatre. The whole thing seemed to me idyllic and ever since that time I have always longed to be a part of that scene. On the last night before I was due to return to RADA, Norma threw a bottle party in her little cottage and after the show the company of *Othello* arrived in dribs and drabs with their bottle contributions. It wasn't until Paul Robeson came up to congratulate me that I discovered that, when the guests were arriving and asking what the party was in aid of, she in her quaint Victorian manner was saying, 'It's in honour of Ken!'

Back at RADA for my penultimate term, I found that my visit to Fernald had been well worthwhile: I had my best parts yet. Ellen Pollock, who had been one of G. B. Shaw's favourite actresses and with whom I got on very well, was to direct

Saturday Night by Jacinto Benavente. It was to be the first production of the play in England and, with a mammoth cast of forty-odd, was to incorporate most of the intake: all of the classes joined together. In order to spread out the parts fairly there were to be two separate casts; Michael Williams was to play the lead in one cast, myself in the other. Mike and I were to become great friends and although we both had a policy of not attending the other's rehearsals except when we had to, strangely we ended up giving such similar performances of the same part that many of the cast said that, listening over the dressing-room tannoy, they found it impossible to tell which of us was on!

Mike became my 'new best friend' at RADA and we frequently socialised together. He had a wonderful 'party piece' of a little north-country man seeing a bargain-price suit in a shop window and being conned by the salesman into thinking he could wear the ill-fitting attire by altering his physique. I never failed to find it hilarious and would engineer situations at parties to persuade him to perform. When I married and left home, Mike turned up at my parents' in 88 Lyndhurst Way and moved into my empty room!

My next part was my most difficult and most prestigious yet at RADA. I was to play Trigorin in John Fernald's production of Chekhov's *The Seagull*. Fernald was regarded as an authority on Chekhov and as the best director of his work in England. Michael Williams was to play Konstantin and Anne Bell, Nina; Freda Keet, who later returned to South Africa, played Arkadina. As per usual, there were two casts with one enjoying the first night in the Vanbrugh, the other the last night. I was in the second group and therefore found myself in the audience on opening night. I was devastated when my rival Trigorin got laughs in the wooing scene! I immediately got hold of Freda Keet and set about discussing with her how we could avoid the laughs; I was certain that they were the wrong sort of laughs and in the wrong place. Fernald, however, was not at all worried and told me there were meant to be laughs, but I remained unconvinced; in the end we got laughs that I still found unacceptable. He must have agreed with me to an extent because when the production was later to play Cambridge, he chose me to play Trigorin.

Working with my first real professional director was a revelation. I'm not sure that he enjoyed the same delight, however, as the Joan situation was coming to a head. Joan's mother appeared outside the RADA building in Gower Street one lunchtime and threatened to take the story of my infamous behaviour to the newspapers! Although I wasn't at all sure they would be in any way interested in small fry like me, I felt that I had to warn Fernald. He was wonderful; he didn't exactly pat me on the back and tell me what a great chap I was, but he arranged for me to see his solicitor, and it was later agreed with Joan that I should pay her

£200, which sounds a pittance now but in 1959 seemed a fortune. I was released from all responsibility and was not to attempt to contact Joan or the child. I was being let off lightly, and a real weight was lifted from my mind when Mike Croft lent me the money until I had started to earn and was able to pay him back.

To arrive at this agreement took a number of weeks and during that time, in the summer holidays, we took *The Seagull* to Cambridge Arts Theatre for one week. Although we were being paid, it was little more than expenses, but still a fortune for us. Mike Williams and I decided to share digs and set out to look for the cheapest we could find on the theatre digs list. We struck gold: in a terraced cottage a short walk from the theatre, a little old lady living alone on her pension offered us bed and breakfast for thirty-five shillings for the week.

At breakfast the next morning, we soon found why it was so cheap. I was up first and discovered, too late, that the milk was off; I had already poured it on my cornflakes. Mike stumbled out, bleary eyed, a few minutes later and I watched him swamp his dish of cornflakes before I pointed it out to him. He sat and surveyed his dish for a few moments before saying, 'I can't eat that.' I said, 'You can't say anything; you'll upset her, and what can you expect for thirty-five bob a week?' But Mike wasn't having that; he called the old lady and pointed out that the milk was off. She took his dish and the jug of milk into the kitchen and came back a few moments later with a jug of fresh milk and the dish of now soggy cornflakes, having poured off the sour milk!

Cambridge was a happy experience: the weather was good, and we spent many a day on the river Cam, jousting on the punts, frequently having had too much sun and being in no real frame of mind for the show. I learnt there that this was foolhardy, and I had to pace my day to build up my concentration towards the performance in the evening. We often appeared on stage with faces burnt red by the sun, and soon discovered that make-up was ineffectual in covering it up when it melted after the first few minutes and the redness shone through again.

At the end of that term, the Youth Theatre's *Hamlet* was to be revived and played for a week at the Queen's Theatre in Shaftesbury Avenue, followed by a week at the Arts Theatre in Cambridge and a week at the Lyric Hammersmith. I remember sitting on the stairs backstage during the dress rehearsal at the Queen's Theatre when Sir John Gielgud came down the stairs and excused himself to pass! I had just seen him in *The Ages of Man*, his readings of Shakespeare pieces, and I was completely gobsmacked. He said something like, 'Working hard?' in that wonderful mellifluous voice of his that could make words sound like musical notes, and I think I just squeaked a smile in response.

In my last term at RADA I had a smallish part in *The Signature*, a play by Roger Holland about Mary Queen of Scots and Elizabeth, directed by my old adversary Richard Carey. The cast included Edward Fox and Derek Fowlds. There were still many of that year that I did not know particularly well. My only previous encounter with Edward Fox was passing him on the stairs whilst he was in the act of smashing a chair. On making enquiries, I was told that he was playing Hamlet and finding the rehearsals very frustrating. Also in that year were David Burke and John Thaw, but I did not work with them. My next production was Dryden's *Love for Love*, a Restoration comedy in which I played Tattle the fop; my performance owed much to Alec McCowan, whom I had seen night after night playing a Restoration fop when I was working at the Old Vic.

Apart from being a wonderful experience, I learnt a lot at RADA; more in my second year than in the first, mainly because I was older and had grown up some-what in the army. The make-up of the classes was so similar that I find it difficult sometimes to remember which student was in which year. There was always the ruthlessly ambitious young lady, the technically aware and clever young man, the outstandingly good-looking, and the rather odd. However, bearing in mind that RADA was at that time the top drama school and, together with Central School of Speech and Drama, more or less had first choice of possible students, what is amazing is how few of them have managed to stay in the theatre and carve out a living on the stage. This is an observation not on the effectiveness of the instruct-ion, but more on the difficulty of the profession. It is probably a truism that you cannot teach someone how to act. In later years I had considerable experience of teaching with the Manchester Youth Theatre, and found that those with talent could and those with no talent couldn't. What you can do, however, is channel that talent and give it taste.

If I had to crystallise my learning at RADA I would say that there I learnt that the great writers have more to say and of more value than my vain attempt to attract attention to myself. Of course, I learnt a lot in terms of technique, but then if I had just gone into rep I would probably have picked up quite a bit of that just through experience, although possibly not voice production. At RADA, I worked on great plays with experienced exponents and with fellow students who were the pick of their era. Although still ambitious, I think I may have picked up a little humility.

I was also awarded the Emile Littler prize of twenty-five guineas, which is awarded apparently to a student thought to have outstanding aptitude for the professional theatre. In truth, I think Fernald may have awarded it to me as he was aware of my financial situation after the Joan affair!

4

1960 to 1961 • **First year in the theatre** •
The Splendid Spur • *Hamlet* in Holland •
An Age of Kings • **The birth of** *Coronation Street*

I LEFT RADA ON December 19th 1959. Peter Sellers gave out the prizes and the diplomas in the Vanbrugh Theatre, and I was hoping to get the chance to chat with him and verify a family rumour that he was a distant cousin of mine by marriage. I had an old aunt on my mother's side who frequently told the story of how Peter Sellers, as a young lad, often helped himself to the fruit at the family-run greengrocers and got his ears clipped. It seemed unlikely, but she was very insistent and I would have loved to check it out. In the event, however, I was just part of a continual procession of students picking up diplomas and prizes – a shake of the hand and off. Since I am no longer in touch with any of the surviving members of that side of the family (the only ones that I knew have 'passed on'), I have missed my chance, but would like to keep the slight hope alive anyway!

I was extremely lucky. I left RADA with a year's work already lined up and an agent waiting to take me on. The BBC television producer Hal Burton had seen *Henry V* at Alleyn's and had been very complimentary about my performance in a letter he had written to Michael Croft which had been published in the school magazine. I think, because he was aware that this letter had been quite influential in my decision to take up acting, he felt a little responsible and offered me a small part in his next production for BBC TV, which of course had only one channel at that time. I was to play the boyfriend of Elizabeth Shepherd in *Where the Party Ended*, starring Michael Gwynn and minuscule Welshman Dudley Jones. The play was about an unexploded bomb in an underground tunnel; I had only a few lines but it was my first real professional role and I was very excited. I had also been invited by David Scase to join his company at the Library Theatre, Manchester, in the New Year. I had auditioned for David, who had seen me in a production at the Vanbrugh Theatre, in my last term and I had accepted the offer. However, when I was offered a six-week serial, playing the lead in *The Splendid Spur* for the BBC Children's TV, David handsomely released me from my promise and I agreed to join the company later – as it turned out, over a year later.

The Splendid Spur, based on the 1889 novel by Sir Arthur Quiller-Couch, is a swashbuckling, romantic tale of Cavaliers and Roundheads, featuring plenty of sword fighting and horse riding, with Patrick Troughton playing the villainous Captain Settle and me playing the romantic bewigged Cavalier juvenile lead. At my interview for the role the producer David Goddard asked me if I could ride a horse. When I honestly admitted that I had never tried, apart from an old cart-horse on a farm, he told me straight away that I had got the job! I was a little bewildered and he explained that he had just finished a similar series that had involved much horse riding and had been told by a young actor that he could ride, but out on location they discovered that he had been more than optimistic and they lost a day's filming while they arranged a stunt rider for him. I had got the part simply because I had confessed my limitations: a strange start.

I did, however, ask that I should be allowed to ride if I could get myself taught in time. As it happened, Simon Ward's father Len (who had a very successful garage business and had become a great supporter of the Youth Theatre) owned two horses which they kept in the paddock at their house in Addiscombe, and I was invited to use them whenever I wanted. After an introductory lesson at a riding school at Hyde Park Corner, I set off daily with a packet of sandwiches to Addiscombe where I spent most of the day on horseback in the surrounding countryside. By the time we came to film the riding sequences I was quite good, although I rode more like a cowboy than an accomplished horseman; but they refused to let me do more than sit on the horse and walk, arguing that if I was injured the filming would stop and the series would have to be withdrawn. To add insult to injury my stand-in rider was a girl.

Apart from the exterior riding sequences and some action scenes filmed in the studios at Ealing, the rest of each episode was transmitted from the Lime Grove studios – live! I coped quite well with the fighting except on one occasion when I had been rehearsing an uppercut so that it missed by a mile but, filmed over my shoulder, would look as if it made contact. When it came to the take, my boxing instinct took over: I stepped in to deliver the blow and floored the stuntman with a beauty! The stuntman/fight arranger was Ray Austin who, half way through the series, had to take over the role of Black Dick when Michael Balfour was rushed to hospital with a perforated ulcer. He simply donned Mike's costume, with a little padding and help from the make-up department, and lurched his way through the part keeping his face as far as possible out of shot. It looked as if Mike had suddenly become very camera-shy!

Although I was now a professional, when the Youth Theatre was invited to take *Hamlet* to Holland for a one-week tour I couldn't resist it and went back unpaid to join all my old mates for what I thought was to be the last time. We played in about five different venues around Holland and were amazed at the standard of the theatres and their facilities. They all seemed so modern, clean and well equipped.

There were still a great number of my old Alleyn's schoolmates in the company and we had many hilarious moments, on and off stage. Brian Eatwell, who later moved to LA and became a very successful production designer, was playing a courtier in the opening scene, and had worked out a subplot to keep his interest going through the repetition, night after night. He was very small, but very good-looking, one might even say pretty; and had decided to play the scene, even though he had no dialogue, as if he were having an affair with Claudius. Every time I looked his way, he would lower his eyes, flutter his lashes and go very coy. I found the only way to get through the scene without 'corpsing' was not to look his way. However, a few days into the tour, in the middle of my long speech in that scene, I heard a strange noise behind me and, on turning to see what was happening, I saw Brian wrapped in a large cloak walking slowly across the stage in a pair of noisy wooden clogs, looking seductively over his shoulder at me.

There was too the scene when Horatio, played by Michael York (who was then Michael Johnson), receives a letter from Hamlet telling of his amazing escape from death on his voyage to England. In Croft's production, the two sailors who have delivered the letter withdraw upstage while Horatio reads it to the audience and then asks the sailors to take him to Hamlet. After the first night the two sailors were joined by a couple of others, who were at a loose end at the time, and the next night there were a few more; eventually, it developed into some sort of crowd scene, with, amongst them, Brian Eatwell dressed as a nun! Once again, matters got out of hand and Mike had to step in with a hefty lecture.

This was my last full-time involvement with the Youth Theatre. Their next production was a revival of the modern-dress *Julius Caesar* at the Queen's Theatre and I would drop in from time to time to join in the jive scene, which more or less started the play. This was the first production that brought in girls to play the female parts and I must admit that I was very much against the idea. Not because of any misogynistic leanings, but on two counts. First, I believed that it was part of the Youth Theatre's attraction that they were doing Shakespeare as he had originally written it, for boy actors. Second, I felt that the inclusion of women would only disrupt the camaraderie that was, for me, a great part of the wonder of the Youth Theatre. In retrospect, I see that it would not have been possible to continue without bringing girls in; it was the next logical step, and has introduced many a fine actress to the profession, not least Helen Mirren, Paula Wilcox, Diana Quick, Nicola McAuliffe and Kate Buffery.

On returning from Holland I started work straight away on *An Age of Kings*. This was a BBC TV serialisation of Shakespeare's history plays, from *Richard II*, through the three *Henrys* and on to *Richard III*. The series was produced by Peter Dews who, apart from overall control, directed the actors with Michael Hayes as co-director concerning himself more with the photography; a new concept. I had missed the first episode, due to my involvement with the Youth Theatre, but joined the cast for part two of *Richard II*. There was a permanent company of about twenty-plus actors, and we were joined from time to time by visiting leading classical actors to play some of the main parts. My first involvement was minimal: I played a courtier and soldier and was thrilled when David William, who was playing Richard, paused in front of me when delivering his 'Down, down I come like glistering Phaethon…' speech.

My other main involvement was in the murder of Richard in Flint Castle. The king was kept in a dungeon, which was accessed by a flight of steps about twenty feet high. There were twelve murderers who entered silently and took up threatening positions, one on each step, up to the full height. On a given verbal cue, we were to jump in sequence starting from the top so that we arrived to surround the king at, as near as possible, the same dramatic moment, and with a loud and frightening thump. On the top step was Anthony Valentine (who later made his name playing Raffles) who would turn up at rehearsals sprucely dressed ready for a night out with his make-up girlfriend and take the highest jump without flinching. One step down was Derek Ware, who had been a compatriot of mine at RADA, but had now graduated to stuntman and fight arranger. Derek took the whole thing a lot more seriously and, during rehearsals for the murder scene, would change into tracksuit and plimsolls, limber up and get into the right mood for his death-defying leap. When it came to transmission, which was live, we all jumped on cue except Derek who ran down the whole flight of steps to take up his position for the murder. There was the dramatic thump as we all landed, followed by the pitter-patter of Derek coming down the steps!

My first speaking role of the series was in the first part of *Henry IV Part 1* when I played Gadshill. Although it wasn't done intentionally, I somehow got hold of a rather outlandish battered hat with a large feather that tended to draw the eye to my performance whenever I was on screen. 'If you want to get ahead, get a hat!' I also attracted the attention of Lady Hotspur, played by Patricia Heneghan who was later to become my wife! Percy Hotspur was played by Sean Connery and the wooing scene, with 'Paddy' and him together, attracted quite a bit of attention. Peter Dews, who had a very quick wit, called it the 'I trouble you to keep a civil tongue in my head' scene. Hal was played by Robert Hardy, Falstaff by the wonderful Frank Pettingell, Henry IV by Tom Fleming and Angela Baddeley played Mistress Quickly.

The two parts of *Henry IV* were further split into two, thus making four episodes. As a minor member of the company I was expected to play a variety of parts from priest to lord, peasant to soldier, and I took a great deal of pleasure in attempting to disguise myself from one part to another. I had grown a beard, which I reshaped for each part, and the make-up department joined in with wigs.

In those days, television followed much more the format of the theatre when it came to production. We would rehearse each episode for two weeks in a drill hall at Shepherd's Bush and then go into the studios at Riverside for two days when the cameras were rehearsed into the scenes. There would be four cameras that were moved around the floor photographing the action and four boom operators on moveable sound platforms with microphones on long poles like fishing rods, with the control room switching from one to the other during the performance. The whole thing was transmitted live, so there was no room for anything but the greatest accuracy. We did of course have the luxury of the occasional filmed insert, but since there was an obvious difference in quality of picture between the studio and the filmed inserts these were kept to a bare minimum. If anything went wrong, we just had to carry on. The floor manager had a cut-out key that would cut the sound if needed and I suppose there was always the facility of switching off the cameras, but it never happened; we just went on. When I was later married to Paddy, she told me a story of once being in a TV play set on a Tube train when one of the actors died and the rest carried on and kept the scene going, improvising dialogue even! Sometimes nowadays it's impossible to tell if some of them are alive or dead.

When the action changed from one scene to another, two of the cameras would peel off and set up for the next scene; the other two would continue until the end of the scene in progress, and when it was over they would scoot across the studio and join the new scene. One of the major difficulties was making sure that the cables linking each camera to the control room didn't get tangled as the action progressed. Another was making sure that the microphone didn't appear in shot at the top of the screen. It was a long and tedious process working the whole thing out in the studios, and the end of the two days followed by the transmission was very like a first night, but without the feedback from the audience. Like the Blitz, it drew us all together as a company. The post-production drink-up in the local is something that is sadly lost with the modern method of recording everything in short clips; it is now possible, indeed common, to not meet your fellow actors unless they are actually in the scene with you!

Things did occasionally go wrong, however, and poor old Derek Ware seemed to be at the centre of most of them. In the battle scenes of *Henry IV Part 1*, Derek, as fight arranger and resident stuntman, was engaged in hand-to-hand combat on a bridge and at the culmination of the fight was to be thrown off the bridge onto a pile of mattresses out of shot on the floor below. During the long and tedious camera rehearsal, whilst the cameras were elsewhere, Derek was quietly practising his fight sequence on the bridge, miming his opponent and grunting dramatically to himself with the effort. On seeing this strange 'bridge dance' I called some of the others to come and look; whereupon Derek, on seeing that he had a little audience, put more than necessary effort into the fight and, on throwing himself off the bridge, missed the mattresses – and also missed the show as he had to be taken to hospital with concussion and bruised ribs.

It was during the weeks of the *Henry IV* episodes that my philandering took another turn. I was walking from Shepherd's Bush Tube station with Michael Graham Cox and met Patricia Heneghan coming from rehearsals. We stopped and exchanged pleasantries; I can't remember what was said as it was of no particular import, but as we continued on our way to the rehearsal room having said goodbye to her, Mike said something like, 'You're well in there.' At the time I was surprised and didn't really know what he was talking about; I hadn't even considered the possibility. For one thing, she was one of the guest stars and in a very much more elevated position than I was. For another, she was an established and much admired actress who had played many a lead in TV plays. When Sydney Newman was head of drama at ABC TV, he started to gather together a company of actors who were to be put under long-term contract and would form the nucleus of a regular drama company. Patricia Heneghan, Mary Peach and Neil McCallum were the first and more were to follow, but alas Sydney Newman went to BBC TV and the plans and contracts were dropped!

I didn't consider I was in the same bracket and therefore did not entertain ideas above my station. However, when I received a telephone call from Patricia one evening to hear her ask if I could come across to St John's Wood, I dropped everything and took the Tube. I was pretty well bowled over: she was a star, she had her own flat, she knew lots of famous people, and there was no mother looking over our shoulder all the time. Her mother was Doris Yorke who had been a concert artist and had appeared in many films playing the Peggy Mount sort of parts; and then, when her husband, Wing Commander Heneghan, retired from the forces, they ran the Grand Theatre Croydon together. On top of all this, I found Patricia sensuous and attractive. I didn't go home for a few nights; I was in love. I severed all other relationships, and entered into this new partnership with fervour and with pride – 'Look who I've got on my arm!'

It was while we were doing the *Henry IV*s that I learnt that the part of Fluellen in *Henry V* had not yet been cast. There were many genuine Welshmen in the running and although I didn't hold out much hope, I did let Peter Dews know that I was hungry for the part. Dudley Jones, who had been in my first 'tele', was the front-runner and was a very good friend of Peter's. Dudley was unusually small and apparently, on seeing a cat flap on Dudley's kitchen door, Peter christened it 'Dudley's Door'! There was some question as to whether Dudley would be available and various other possibilities were rumoured, none of them being me. One day, however, when Peter was taking Paddy (as Patricia Heneghan was mostly called) and myself in his little VW Beetle to Oxford to see the OUDS production of *Tamburlaine*, he just quietly dropped the bombshell that he had decided to let me play Fluellen! I nearly went through the roof of the car with delight; I couldn't believe my luck. Because of my previous success with the part, I was convinced that I was going to stun the entertainment world with my outstanding performance; I had at last left the ranks of the walk-ons and bit parts and joined the big boys.

Robert Hardy, who was playing Henry, had previously also played Fluellen and was very kind and helpful to me, giving me the odd tip. It all went well until one day when I was rehearsing the leek scene with George A. Cooper, who was playing Pistol. I had been beating George about the head with a padded cudgel, and when we had finished the scene he descended threateningly upon me, took the cudgel from my hand and brought it down heavily on my head. Angry and very red in the face, he shouted, 'That hurts, doesn't it?' I was very frightened but managed to say, 'No, not really,' which rather took the wind out of his sails. He calmed down and said, 'Well, you've got hair; just remember I'm bald.' George was a delightful and amusing man with no illusions of grandeur and I was very distressed that my amateur enthusiasm had once again made me go over the top. A lesson well learnt again.

This aside, *Henry V* was a wonderful experience; but with Judi Dench playing Kate, William Squire playing Chorus, my old school acquaintance Julian Glover as Westmoreland and Tony Valentine playing the Herald, not to mention Robert Hardy as Henry, I did not, as I had expected, walk away with the plaudits. I was completely ignored and learnt another valuable lesson. There is a wide gulf between being successful on the amateur stage and holding your own on stage with good professional actors.

It was in *Henry V* that matters came to a head with Derek Ware, the accident-prone stuntman. In the siege of Harfleur Derek was due to mount a scaling ladder and ascend to the top, at which point the ladder was to be pushed away from the wall and Derek was to be thrown back onto some bales of hay; but when it came to the crunch, perhaps remembering his previous accident, he chickened out and only went up halfway, a few rungs. The somewhat bemused actor waiting at the top of the ladder to send him hurtling backwards did a perceptible shrug and pushed the ladder anyway; Derek limply fell to the floor, screaming madly. Thus, the siege of Harfleur was almost unsuccessful; Henry nearly lost the battle!

Derek was not in the least an unpopular character; in fact we were all very fond of him. As an accident-prone stuntman he was the source of much amusement, and he also told tales against himself. When once he had no theatre work he was employed by a private detective to tail a wayward husband in a divorce case. Derek told of how he kitted himself out with a white raincoat and trilby hat pulled down over his dark glasses and stationed himself beneath a lamp post outside the house of his prey, unobtrusively reading a newspaper, just like in all those 'B' pictures. When the suspect came out, Derek folded up the newspaper, slipped it under his arm, and set off on foot in pursuit. His prey took him down several back streets before eventually turning down an alley. Derek paused and carefully put his head around the corner to check that it was safe to follow and immediately met the clenched fist of his prey, with his nose!

It was after the transmission of *Henry V*, when we were all in the pub swapping Derek Ware stories and having a good laugh, that Peter Dews said, 'I'm going to have to sack him.' We all went very quiet and felt riddled with guilt. The next day we all went *en masse* to Peter and asked him to reconsider. Derek stayed.

After Fluellen, I returned to the ranks and played a variety of smaller parts in *Henry VI* in which Eileen Atkins, who was married at that time to Julian Glover, played Joan of Arc. Frank Windsor was the Earl of Warwick, and Terry Scully King Henry VI. In the first episode I played a serving man and in one scene I had to be involved in a street fight, my main adversary being Terry Wale, who was of similar stature to me: that is, lacking in inches. At the end of the scuffle we had a few lines of dialogue, aggressively nose to nose. At the dress rehearsal, I noticed that Terry had put in elevators, and although he didn't tower over me, my nose was considerably lower than his. During the live transmission, when it came to the fight, I dived for his feet and in the ensuing struggle took his boots off. It gave the fight an added impact; it became not just a pointless push and shove affair.

I hasten to add that this was done in a spirit of good fun and was not given or taken maliciously; we were indeed 'a band of brothers' – although I had, for some reason, taken against an actor called Jeremy Bisley. I have often found that I have taken violent dislikes; it seems almost chemical. Within the theatre, the first was Barry Boys and now, poor old Jeremy Bisley; others were to follow. Our antipathy was mutual and well known. At one point it almost reached fisticuffs, and it looked as if I was about to attack him in the green room during the coffee break! Peter Dews took me aside and said that if I did hit him he would have no choice but to sack me, reluctantly.

I controlled myself and continued through the *Henry VIs* with performances of first the Duke of Buckingham and then the Earl of Northumberland, who only had one speech of a few lines, which I attempted to do in the dialect of the region, taking out records from the BBC library and practising for hours on end. When it came to the crunch, however, I delivered the speech in the Northumbrian dialect and brought the rehearsal to a standstill as they all looked at me in quizzical amazement, not having understood a word I said. I had always thought that I had a good ear, but that was one I had to give up on. Nowadays of course actors are very rarely called upon to play anything but their own dialect, which is a shame: I used to enjoy the challenge.

In the last episode of *Henry VI*, I played Earl Rivers, brother to Queen Elizabeth, played by Jane Wenham who was married, for a while, to Albert Finney. Rivers survived Henry only to be hung on the orders of Richard III, played magnificently by Paul Daneman. In mid-November of 1960, *An Age of Kings* came to an end having won the Golden Rose of Montreux.

While working as a stagehand at the Old Vic I had made the acquaintance of Elizabeth Robinson, who worked in accounts; she had made the decision to set up as an agent, and as I was about to leave RADA she had asked me if she could represent me. Since I already had a year's work lined up, I was reluctant to lose the ten per cent, but I agreed to allow her to handle the contracts for me and signed up with her on condition that she did not charge me commission on the work that I had already got. I was extremely lucky and it was unbelievable to have had such a start. Towards the end of my time in *An Age of Kings*, she arranged for me to have an interview with Josie Scott who was casting for a new 13-part series to be called *Florizel Street*.

Florizel Street was to be a twice-weekly serial set in the back streets of Salford, and transmitted from the Granada studios in Manchester. However, my first interview with Josie was in her office in London, where she asked me to read through a scene for her. She explained that it was to be set in Salford and asked if I could do a Manchester accent. Jess Oakroyd, the character in *The Good Companions* that I had played at RADA, had been Yorkshire, not Lancashire, and I had previously only spent two weeks in Manchester with the Youth Theatre; but, remembering that Albert Finney came from Salford, I opted to try it with him in mind. Some year or so later Eddie Judd came into the *Coronation Street* studios looking for Albert Finney as he had been convinced that he had heard him over the tannoy in his dressing room!

We read the scene together and Josie then explained to me that they were very keen to get genuine north country actors; she was going to recommend that I should be invited up for a screen test, but told me not to mention that I was not from the north.

A few days later, I found myself in Manchester for the day, rehearsing in the morning and performing in front of the cameras in the afternoon, for the test. The part I was reading for was that of Dennis Tanner, and my test scene was a violent row with Elsie Tanner, who was played, in the test, by Pat Phoenix. I think she had already been cast and knew she would be playing the part. Violet Carson, whom I already knew since she had played the Duchess of York in *Richard III* in *An Age of Kings*, was also there screen testing for the part of Ena Sharples.

We rehearsed in the morning and, during the break for lunch, I met up with David Scase from the Library Theatre. We went for a drink and a sandwich at the New Theatre Inn, to talk over my delayed employment at the Library Theatre. The pub (which is alas, no more) was behind the Royal Opera House in Quay Street, and was frequented by all of the actors in Manchester. Although I had only one pint of beer, it served to relax me when it came to the test. When I let rip in the scene I must have overdone the anger because I didn't get the part: they said I was somewhat too strong. It went instead to Philip Lowrie, and I returned to London. Some fifty years later I read in Harry Kershaw's memoirs that it had gone to a choice between me and Philip, and there had been quite a lot of discussion before I was placed second. I had no idea of the magnitude of that test and wonder how different things would have been if I'd won!

In early December, the series started with two transmissions a week under the new title of *Coronation Street*, and was such an instant success that they decided to continue the series for a further six months. I was approached and asked to play the part of Billy Walker, son of Jack and Annie Walker, the landlords of the Rovers Return, the street local that was to become the most famous pub in the world. My first appearance was in Episode 13, written by Harry Kershaw, and my part was described as a smiling cheerful youth. It was especially written for me, and the smiling bit was based on the fact that at the camera test, when I was so completely at ease after my lunchtime beverage, they had kept the cameras running and picked up the way I was smiling and relaxed before and after the scene. The other happy coincidence was that, as Billy Walker, I was returning to the pub after National Service and still had an army uniform. Perhaps that's how I got the part; I had my own costume!

I didn't start in *Coronation Street* until February and in the January of 1961 I was able to slip in another job. I was approached by John McGrath, a writer and director, who explained that he was trying to set up a film of *The Loneliness of the Long Distance Runner* by Alan Sillitoe. In order to raise some interest and money, he wanted to film an excerpt for the BBC TV programme *Bookstand*. In the event of him getting the finance, he wanted me to play the part. Cross-country running had been one of my fortes at school: I had quarter-colours for cross country, I had won the Rover Scouts' cross country in two successive years and had been a member of the South London Harriers, who boasted Gordon Pirie as their star runner, so I felt well qualified and we set off for a day's filming in the woods.

I had a wonderful day running across fields and through woods, skipping up paths and hurdling tree trunks, but when it came to the close-up shots it proved to be too difficult on the rough terrain and we moved onto the road, where the camera was set up on the roof of the Land Rover and I ran behind. Since the camera was focused in closely on my face, the background of the tarmac would not register. This too proved unsuccessful, however, as the distance from lens to subject was crucial and it was impossible for me to keep an accurate distance from the vehicle. Since it was just a head-and-shoulders shot, I suggested that I should be tied to the rear of the Land Rover so that all I had to do was keep the rope taut. We set off at a predetermined slowish pace and the camera started to roll. Being not as fit as I thought I was, coupled with the fact that I had been running on soft ground and was now on hard tarmac, it wasn't long before my jarred leg muscles seized up and I was in agony, yelling to them to stop. The driver couldn't hear over the noise of the engine and the cameraman thought I was acting dramatically as I was pulled yelling and screaming for what seemed an interminable distance.

The ordeal over, I was relieved to collapse in the back of the car and we set off back to London. Halfway home it was decided to stop for tea, but when it came to getting out of the car, I found it impossible to move; I couldn't even straighten up, let alone stand! I was carried into the restaurant by the crew, frozen in a sitting position, and carried out afterwards in a like manner. It took me some few days of hot baths and horse oils to fully recover.

The show went out and I waited for the call. I had agreed to do six months in *Coronation Street*, but knew that the film would take some months to set up and that they wanted me so much that they could accommodate this. A few weeks later I received a distressing phone call from John McGrath to say that a full feature film of *The Loneliness of the Long Distance Runner* was going to be made but that he had been ousted by John Schlesinger, who was going to direct. He was extremely upset and told me that he had asked them to at least see me for the lead role; there was nothing else he could do.

A few weeks later, I was summoned to meet Schlesinger at the Hilton Hotel. On my way up to town for the interview, I called in at the Old Vic to see 'Navvy' Stride, who was now starring in the company there. We were having tea in the café opposite, no longer there but a favourite with the company then, known as 'The Greasy Spoon'. Tom Courtenay, whom I had known slightly at RADA, came into the café and during the conversation I happened to mention that I was on my way to see Schlesinger with reference to a film, at which point Tom informed me that he had signed a contract that morning to play the lead in *The Loneliness of the Long Distance Runner*!

I went on my way to the interview, sat in the plush hotel room, and went through the sham interview with a sinking feeling in the pit of my stomach. In retrospect, perhaps I should have said something to Schlesinger, but I was (a) overawed and (b) feeling very dispirited and lacking in confidence. All of the disappointments I had had so far were as nothing compared to this; this was to be the first lesson in just how cruel and unfair the acting profession could be.

In February 1961, I started my first spell in *Coronation Street*. The Walker family consisted of Annie, my mother, played by Doris Speed; Jack, my father, played by Arthur Leslie; and my sister Joan, played by June Barry. In that first episode, I had just been demobbed from the army and arrived home with a kitbag over my shoulder to discover that there was a gas leak in the street and we were all to spend the night in the Mission Hall, run by Ena Sharples. The cast was nowhere near as large as it is today. There was the Barlow family, and the Tanners; there were the three old ladies in the 'snug', Minnie, Martha and Ena; there was Albert Tatlock, and Harry Hewitt, and the barmaid Concepta Riley. Then there was the corner shop run by Florrie Lindley, later to be joined by her assistant played by a very young Patricia Routledge, with her regular customers the 'barm cake girls', plus the slightly upmarket Esther Hayes, played by Daphne Oxenford. I met them all in the Mission Hall in that first episode and was to spend, on and off, the next twenty-five years in their company. Over that time I have seen many changes. Characters have come and gone, writers have come and gone, directors have come and gone, and the wonderful family feel that we had in those early days has just gone – or at least it had when I was last there.

We transmitted twice a week in black and white. We rehearsed two episodes from Monday to Wednesday in the rehearsal room above the studios in Quay Street, Manchester, with the sets taped out on the floor and substitute furniture. On the Wednesday afternoon we would have the technical run-through, when the camera operators and the sound boys were brought in to watch and work out with the director how they were going to record it. Then on Thursday we would go into the studio where the sets had been erected and furnished, and we would rehearse for the next day and a half with cameras and sound. On the Friday evening the first episode would go out live, and the second episode would be recorded immediately afterwards for transmission on Wednesday evening. Each episode was done in its entirety, with a break for the advertising. I can still hear the floor managers call 'Stand by studio!' and then the countdown from ten to one and action.

It was just as exciting and adrenaline-racing as a first night, and had the same effect: that of bonding us as a team, going through the trauma together. Towards the end of my first six months, I had a scene where I was working in the garage under a car and my boss came to say goodbye as I was returning to London. As I rose to face him I looked into his eyes and saw that he had frozen: he wasn't going to say a word. He didn't have a very large part and I suspect was not what you would call an experienced or accomplished actor. It was a live show and there was no stopping so I improvised the farewell with a mute and terrified actor just staring bewildered into my face! I confess that I really enjoyed the feeling of having 'saved the day' and was quite exhilarated afterwards, although I also felt sorry for the actor; I never saw him again.

In those days, Granada was a much smaller concern, with just two studios. The Bernstein brothers, who owned Granada, were frequently to be seen in and around the place. There was a canteen but no bar; and the local pub, the New Theatre Inn, was the centre of most of the socialising, with writers, producers, technicians and actors all mixed in together. There was a wonderful family feel about the whole thing. Of course, the whole concept of 'soap stars' was unheard of; there hadn't been anything like it before.

As the series gathered momentum over those first six months, the popularity, which started mainly in the north, was spreading south and in fact all over the country. At first, the public appearances were organised by the press office and we would all go together. They weren't very grand affairs: working men's clubs and the like. I remember arriving late at one such function with June Barry, who was playing my sister Joan; we entered the club to find that the introductions had been done and the *Coronation Street* cast were all sitting at a table at the other end of the hall. We had to weave our way between the tables of applauding working men and their families as we were announced from the stage; and, on arriving at the cast table, Pat Phoenix hissed to me, 'Kiss your mother.' I was a little taken aback at first and thought I had misheard her, but she repeated, 'Kiss your mother!' It was then that I realised that I was expected to play the part both on and off screen, and I started to have serious misgivings. I wasn't prepared to assume a northern accent and answer to the name of Billy wherever I went.

It was the first of a number of little 'spats' that I had with Pat Phoenix, who seemed to be taking on the role of 'head girl'. After I had been in the series for about three months, I made the mistake of asking how to pronounce a certain line. I even remember the line: it was, 'Look what you've done to my hair.' I wasn't sure whether 'look' should be pronounced more like 'luke' or not. I happened to ask Pat, who seemed surprised to learn that I was not from 'up north'. From that time onwards she started to give me little tips on accent, and this developed into tips on acting; and since I wasn't over-impressed with her performance, which I found a little obvious and self-indulgent, I once told her so and thus started a feud that was to last a number of years.

At that time, her boyfriend was Bill, a taxi driver who had become quite a friend of mine. He was such a regular visitor that he was almost like one of the cast and I frequently drank with him in the New Theatre Inn as he waited for Pat. Pat, upset with my attitude, sent Bill to sort me out and thus ended another friendship; we didn't fight, but we had quite a row.

In later years I came to like Pat: she had a wonderful generous nature; but in those early days when she was working hard to don the mantle of 'star' of the street, she aggravated me intensely with her thirst for attention. She was hungry for the limelight – and, I have to give it to her, she succeeded. Perhaps I just resented her success. As the series progressed the invitations came in for individual stars to open fêtes or shops, give out prizes and make all manner of personal appearances, and Pat was very much at the top of the list. The days when we all went out as a cast were over. There were no stars as such, but it was becoming obvious that Ena Sharples, Elsie Tanner and Annie Walker were rising to the top of the pile. Tony Warren had created three gigantic characters and *Coronation Street* was off on its matriarchal roller-coaster ride.

Tony, who had written the first episodes, was now joined by a team of writers amongst whom were John Finch, Harry Driver, Vince Powell, Harry Kershaw and a young Jack Rosenthal. I think it true to say that 'the Street' owed much of its success to the wonderful innovative scripts and its novel style. Tony Warren was still writing a number of scripts and was frequently in and around the company: it was still very much his baby. I would often share a dressing room with Philip Lowrie, who played Elsie Tanner's wayward son, Dennis: the part I had originally tested for. My nose was regularly put very much out of joint when he and Tony, who had struck up a real friendship, would sit in the dressing room that I shared and discuss script ideas for the character of Dennis. I remember them getting quite excited as they discussed the possibility of Dennis taking a bath in the tin bathtub on the mat in front of the fire. It was a smashing idea as many families were still without bathrooms, but I just felt out of it and very frustrated that my character was not getting the same degree of attention.

Many of my most enjoyable scenes were with the 'barm cake' girls, Sheila and Doreen, played delightfully by Eileen Mayers and Angela Crow, who didn't stay as long in the series as they deserved to. Realising that I was not going to become the star of this particular set-up, at the end of my six months I decided not to renew my contract. It was not an easy decision and I remember discussing it with Arthur Lowe who had joined the cast as Leonard Swindley, running the little haberdashery shop, with Eileen Derbyshire playing his adoring assistant Miss Nugent. They were a wonderful double act, with a beautiful gentle humour. We were sharing a dressing room at the time and in the long discussions over what I should do, he advised me to get out. 'You don't want to get stuck in a series at your age,' he said. Since he went on to 'get stuck' in a spin-off with his character of Leonard Swindley and then to 'get stuck' in *Dad's Army* for many years, I can only assume that he had grown tired of the conversation and wanted to draw the discussion to a close, or that he wanted to see the back of me anyway!

Apart from the genuine feeling that I did not want to play the same character day in and day out – this was not what I had become an actor for – I was also planning to get married. My relationship with Paddy had developed quite considerably and when I was in London I spent a lot of my time at her flat in St John's Wood, which just so happened to be around the corner from where John Stride was now living, married to Virginia. We would frequently meet up for a drink and visit each other. Johnny was still at the Old Vic and was about to do Romeo with Judi Dench as Juliet and directed by Franco Zeffirelli. At a party in his flat he introduced me to Zeffirelli, who after a few minutes of conversation turned to Johnny and said, with his attractive Italian accent, 'This boy would make a good Mercutio;' to which Johnny replied, much to my surprise, 'Over my dead body.' At the time, I took it as a compliment, and indeed it is impossible to know just how serious either of the remarks were, but I have often wondered how different a path my career would have taken if Franco had been serious and if Johnny had been more enthusiastically in favour!

Paddy had joined me in the Street for ten weeks as a librarian who was having an affair with Ken Barlow, played by Bill Roache. Although her contract was for ten weeks, they had only used her for about three or four episodes and we had taken a little flat together in Didsbury. Up until that point I had been staying with Irene Rostron, a leading light in the amateur theatre whom I had met via the National Youth Theatre when we had come up with *Henry IV Part 2*. She was a widow and had two very spoilt and overindulged cats that were allowed to do pretty much as they liked. Breakfast time was particularly distressing to me as they climbed over the table and interfered with milk, cereal and whatever took their fancy. I couldn't wait for her to go to work in the morning so I could impose my own discipline on her precious cats!

Margot Bryant, who played Minnie Caldwell, had taken a shine to me (having taken against Bill Roache because of the way he held his knife and fork); and when Paddy and I rented the flat in Didsbury, Margot took a flat in the same large old Victorian house. After finishing *An Age of Kings* and as soon as I was able to pay off my debt to Mike Croft, I had bought a little Austin 7 Ruby for £25; I suspect that some of my attraction as far as Margot was concerned was the fact that I had a car, and it soon became obvious that I was expected to act as her chauffeur. I ended up parking around the corner and creeping in the back door!

As Minnie Caldwell, one of the trio of old biddies that became famous as 'the snug ladies', Margot was a sweet little old lady who loved cats, was bullied by Ena and wouldn't say boo to a goose. In reality, she was a cantankerous snob who swore like a trooper and was continually griping about people, although she was indeed fond of cats and would tell endless stories in which she endowed them with the power of speech and personality. She certainly liked cats more than she did people, and eventually paid the price; when she went 'gaga' and ended her days in Cheadle Royal, a mental hospital just outside Manchester, she was a lonely and unvisited lady. In the early days, a great number of the cast still lived in the south and would take the train down after the show on a Friday night, returning from Euston on the Monday morning. Apart from often making the porters blush with her ill-tempered and foul-mouthed outbursts, Margot had a wonderful way of ensuring that she had a carriage to herself. At that time the carriages were divided into individual compartments, each holding about eight passengers. On boarding the train at Euston, Margot would sit at the window and, if she saw anybody coming towards her compartment looking as if they were going to join her, she would leer at them with a maniacal glint in her eye and invite them in with a beckoning finger; they soon changed direction and she travelled in solitude on a crowded train.

In spite of her confrontational manner, I found Margot to be frequently amusing; but she was not popular with the cast, and I too eventually went off her some years later when she engineered the termination of Harry Markham's contract. Harry had been brought into the Street as Handel Gartside, an OAP to team up with little Minnie. He was a delightful and amusing old man who was thrilled to get the job as her companion so late in his career, but Margot didn't take to him and 'had a word' with the producer; his contract was not renewed.

The demands of the script would vary from week to week and frequently I would not have much to do. In consequence, I would find myself with money in my pocket and time on my hands. I joined forces, as it were, with Peter Adamson, who was playing Len Fairclough, a customer in the Rovers Return. The Rovers' drinking area was originally divided into the two bars: the 'snug' where the three old ladies were frequently found, sometimes with little old Albert Tatlock, and the slightly larger public bar. Peter did not have much of a part at first; he was more or less an extra, playing darts, with the odd line to say; and I have often felt that it was because I suggested to Harry Kershaw, whom I got on very well with, that Peter deserved better, that his part was written up and he was to become one of the main characters for many years. At that time, however, Peter had little to do and we would frequently meet up after rehearsals and set off together to 'paint the town'. It wasn't long before I upgraded my little Austin Ruby for a more upmarket Wolseley and it became our little 'party wagon' as we lurched from pub to club, usually ending up at the Cabaret Club, where we were welcome regulars. There was no breathalyser at that time, but of course one could still be arrested for drunken driving. Having been well schooled by Michael Croft in the art of 'drinking deep', I was well able to hold my drink but frequently had to close one eye as I drove home in the early hours of the morning because I was seeing double. Peter was my constant companion in these late-night forays and, in later years, I was distressed to find that it had turned into a major problem for him.

My life in Manchester then was pretty lively, but when Paddy was written in to *Coronation Street* it became a little more sober and normal. We decided to get married; when my first six-month stretch in the Street ended, I took instruction in the Catholic faith and we were married on August 4th 1961, by her cousin Father Peter Cooney, in the Catholic Church in Fulham Road. The traditional stag night took the form of a pub crawl, starting south of the river with Froggie French, my mate from Alleyn's, Peter Adamson and Howard Romp who had married my younger sister; when the pubs closed in the south, we picked up Johnny Stride after his performance at the Old Vic and hurried across Westminster Bridge to grab the extra half-hour drinking time north of the Thames. We were all a little fragile, as was customary, on the big day!

The reception was at the Knights of Saint Colombo Club in Ladbroke Grove and was attended by Violet Carson, Margot Bryant and Peter Adamson from the company of *Coronation Street*. The best man was Froggie French, and Johnny Stride was the chief usher. Mike Williams also came to the wedding, although I didn't see much of him after we left RADA; he went to Stratford and started a long association with the RSC that I was very envious of.

We rented a flat on the top floor of 11 Bolton Gardens, which was owned by Paddy's elder sister Maureen who was a costume designer with the BBC. She had in fact worked on *An Age of Kings* but was about to leave the country and lecture on costume design in, first of all Canada, and then ended up at Boston University. It was a beautiful flat at the top of a five-storey building; and our marriage, my career and my life nearly ended there when we moved in and, having hired a van, I moved the furniture from the flat in St John's Wood and up the many flights of stairs, on my own. Paddy stood at the top of the stairs in tears, begging me to stop, as I struggled up with furniture on my head and down again to the van, sweating and exhausted, unwilling to let up until it was finished. Thus started my married life and, shortly after, my first real professional theatre engagement when I was at last able to honour my promise to David Scase who had released me a year earlier to do the 'tele'. I joined the Library Theatre, Manchester.

5

1961 to 1962 • Library Theatre, Manchester •
David Scase • *Nil Carborundum* • Nicol Williamson •
The West End • Sir Donald Wolfit • *Billy Liar*

IT IS REMARKABLE THAT the Library Theatre, Manchester, was so successful. Set in the basement of the Library in St Peter's Square, it was a very depressing place to work with no natural daylight, except from the small windows at ceiling height in the rehearsal room, where all you could see was the occasional passing pair of shoes through permanently grubby glass, and where one had the continual feeling that the air was second hand, passed down from above. It is no great wonder that resistance to colds and flu was very low and once one person went down with the sniffles, it was fairly certain that the rest would follow. It says a great deal for the Artistic Director, therefore, that such a high standard was achieved and it was much respected within the profession. What mattered was what happened on stage, and it enjoyed a reputation for excellence that was well deserved and owed much to the inspirational leadership of David Scase.

David was one of the most approachable directors I have ever known, and tremendous fun to work with and for. It didn't feel like work; he made it seem like a bunch of mates who had got together to enjoy themselves. That is not to say that the atmosphere was anything but extremely professional: it was just very unpretentious.

The company spirit was not without its downside, however, because I found a certain amount of resentment towards my presence. This was understandable really, because this was my first professional engagement in theatre proper and I was not starting as an assistant stage manager as so many had to do: I was coming straight in and getting the plum parts, in a company that had been together for a considerable time; some of them had been there for more than two years. My three-play contract over six months started with Brendan Behan's *The Hostage* in which I played Leslie, the British soldier held hostage by the IRA; followed by Claudio in *Much Ado About Nothing* (I had been asked to play Benedick but I uncharacteristically did not feel myself ready, or perhaps I just wanted to play the more romantic role). Finally there was *Pinocchio*, the Christmas production of the Brian Way and Warren Jenkins version, in which I played the name part.

John Normington, a very clever and accomplished actor, was probably the one most put out by my arrival, as I was told that he was hoping to play Leslie and Pinocchio. To be fair, I never felt any antipathy from him, but he had been with the company for some years and I sensed the resentment of those who felt he had been hard done by. This feeling of being alone in a somewhat hostile atmosphere mirrored that of my character in *The Hostage*; and, to be perfectly honest, in retrospect I am not sure where the truth behind my discomfort lay. Was it resentment of my lucky start, or was it an onstage feeling that was carried off stage? I have never had much sympathy for the concept of living the part off stage and have always tried to draw a line between my work and my home life, or my offstage life. However, I have often found that the character I happen to be playing influences my offstage character. This has never ever been deliberate; the only explanation I can think of is that during the rehearsal period, when one is trying to get under the skin of a character, certain aspects of my own personality come to the surface, just as others are submerged, as one tries to search for motivation. That is not to say that when playing a murderer one has to become murderous, but it does mean that one has to explore the possible emotional journey that leads to the committing of the act.

For the second play David Weston, my old school pal, joined the company and we rented a flat together in the Whalley Range area of Manchester. It was a large run-down Victorian house, divided up into 'bedsits', very cheap and very draughty. We had one large bedroom with two beds in opposite corners, an inadequate gas fire that worked off a meter which we were reluctant to feed, and a wardrobe with a door permanently open because the latch didn't work and the floor sloped so alarmingly that the door just swung open! The only other bit of major furniture was a rather lumpy sofa in the middle of the room. It was winter, cold, wet and miserable, but since we were playing *Much Ado* in the evening and rehearsing *Pinocchio* in the daytime it didn't much matter to us: we were too busy. At weekends, after the Saturday night performance, we would get into my car and set off for London, driving back up on Monday morning to go straight to rehearsals for the afternoon.

This friendship with David was soon to be put under a severe test. In the Christmas show Dave played the circus ringmaster but, towards the end of the run, Clive Graham, who was playing the policeman, had to go into hospital for an operation on his haemorrhoids, and Dave was to take over his part for the last few performances. On the afternoon of Dave's takeover we rehearsed him into the scenes and came to the point where Pinocchio comes running on from one side of the stage as the policeman comes running on from the other, and the two collide in the middle, much to the amusement of the children in the audience. Dave explained that he had his best trousers on and didn't want to sit on the floor for the rehearsal, so I talked him through it. I was to run on at high speed with my head down, not looking where I was going; Dave as Mr Policeman was to come running on from the opposite wing and, on seeing me, was to stop, put his hands on my shoulders and take the force of my impact on his padded stomach and just sit back onto the floor.

During the performance, Dave was doing very well and getting the between-scene plaudits from his fellow actors in the wings. When it came to the collision scene, with shades of his improvisation as Pistol years before, Dave decided that the collision would be funnier if Mr Policeman was also not looking where he was going. Dave was a big boy, and as I hit his stomach at top speed and him at top speed too, my back concertinaed and I fell to the floor choking for breath and in great pain. Much concerned, Mr Policeman got up and bent over and, under cover of the great laugh that he had succeeded in getting from the audience, asked if I was all right. Pinocchio's reply was unprintable and I would hope unintelligible to the little children. I staggered to my feet, went into the wings and was sick.

The show went on and during the interval Dave came to my dressing room to humbly apologise and show concern, but I was in no mood to talk to him or even to let him in. He was full of contrition and enlisted the help of other members of the company to try and get them to convey his remorse to me, but I was still in agony and in no mood to kiss and make up. After rejecting a number of emissaries I became the bastard and Dave became the poor misunderstood victim!

I still have trouble with my back, and I still have Dave as a very special friend. From that moment I was a regular visitor to the hospital to visit Clive and help his speedy recovery with a regular supply of bottles of Guinness concealed in a voluminous raincoat.

Colin Welland, who later wrote *Chariots of Fire* and starred in *Kes*, was also in the company, playing amongst other parts 'Rio Rita', an out-and-out effete 'poofter' in *The Hostage*: very strange casting, but oddly effective, and very funny. We did have one little 'spat' when, at the end of the play, Leslie, my character, is reading aloud the newspaper report which announces that his captors are about to assassinate him. It was quite a dramatic moment as his initial delight at seeing his name in print changes to disbelief as he comes to the bit that says they are planning to end his life. I found that I was getting an unusual, sniggering reaction and, on turning round, I discovered that Colin was reading the article over my shoulder and mouthing, camply and slightly ahead of me, the contents. I tried many ways of hiding the article, moving so that he couldn't see it, but it didn't seem to work and in the end gave up and just handed the article to him.

I have always had a problem with 'upstaging', as it is called, and reacted rather badly. I think I am a little over-sensitive to it; there is a strong argument for leaving it to the director to sort out – it is after all their job – but they never seem to see it as soon as I do, and often they don't mind, or don't think it important. Perhaps I should have read the signs and tried my hand at directing earlier in my career.

These sorts of spats are quite common in the theatre and although they can often sour the team spirit, it did not cause a rift between Colin and myself. In fact at one point, since I was the only one of the company to own a car, he asked me to help him move flat; when I turned up in the car, late one night after the show, I discovered that I was helping him and his young wife to do a 'moonlight flit'! Colin had been a teacher and didn't have much, mainly bedding, to move and I felt rather sorry for the pair. Other members of that talented company were Jennie Goossens, who played Beatrice in *Much Ado*, and Helen Fraser, who was very good at comedy, far from her later role in *Bad Girls*. She deserved better.

On leaving the Library Theatre in February I went almost immediately back to the BBC TV in Noël Coward's *This Happy Breed*, directed by Hal Burton, my first ever professional employer. It was a very starry cast with Richard Johnson, Brenda Bruce, Fay Compton, Dinsdale Landen, Avril Elgar, and Adrienne Corri who had a reputation for being somewhat of a firebrand and difficult to work with, but in the event was great fun. I didn't have a very big part but it was good company to be seen in; and I was glad to have a little spare time as we learnt that Paddy was pregnant and we decided to move out of the flat we were renting from her sister in Bolton Gardens and find a house of our own. Julian Glover took over the lease of Maureen's flat; and we bought a terraced house in Canonbie Road, Forest Hill, on top of the hill and very much the area in which I had grown up.

Apart from needing more room because we were expecting a baby, I was keen to get my foot on the property ladder; I resented paying rent and seeing nothing in return. In order to help pay the mortgage, which now seems a pittance, we took in a lodger, Tony Whelan, who had been in the Library Theatre company. As a Roman Catholic Tony had a built-in empathy with Paddy, and he had also proved a very good friend to me, and very supportive when I found it difficult at the Library. There was much to do finding, decorating and moving into a new house, so I was quite pleased not to be put too much under pressure at work; although in another respect I was frustrated at not getting more showy parts – I preferred playing the lead!

I was further frustrated in this respect when I was booked by the Royal Shakespeare Company to play in Henry Livings' *Nil Carborundum* at the Arts Theatre, just off Leicester Square in London. Once again, I didn't have a very big part, but it was a large cast and the only ones with more than a few scenes were Nicol Williamson, James Booth and Terry Palmer who were playing the leading roles. The minor roles were, however, littered with names that have since become well known: Edward Fox, Graham Crowden, Arthur Mullard and Timothy West amongst them. The play was set in an army barracks and I was playing the commando corporal. I had also been asked to 'cover' (which is a euphemism for 'understudy') James Booth, who had a reputation for being somewhat volatile and unreliable. The play was directed by a young Anthony Page, who was very much 'flavour of the month'.

Since I was one of the few in the cast with recent army experience, I was frequently consulted when it came to drill procedures et cetera and I effectively ended up directing the commando scenes. I must say I enjoyed the extra respons- ibility, until it came to the technical rehearsal and the first night. The main commando scene, which I had taken over as 'my baby', depended on a complete and utter blackout, smack on cue at the end of the scene, but in the technical and in the dress rehearsal this had not happened. I approached Anthony Page and he said, 'Leave it to me, I'll sort it out.' At that all-important first performance it was even worse than before: there was no blackout, we were all left embarrassingly on stage in full light, and when I approached Tony in the pub afterwards he was very dismissive and in fact downright rude.

It may have been just bad timing, but I was very hurt and felt as if I had been taken advantage of. So when I was telephoned at home one weekend and asked if I would go on for Nicol Williamson, who had been taken ill, my first reaction was to point out that I had been asked to cover James Booth, not Nicol, and how much would they pay me? Their response was to point out that everybody in the company was on the same wage and that they were not prepared to pay anything. I then declined their offer and rang off. A few moments later, the phone rang and I was offered five pounds; I accepted.

This all happened on the Sunday, so I set about learning the part. They had said that I wasn't expected to know it and could carry the script, but I was quite a quick study and managed to get the first act more or less 'under my belt' before the rehearsal that was called for the Monday afternoon to give me a chance to go through my paces prior to the evening show. Most of my scenes were with James Booth who was, to say the least, rather an odd character. He first complained about being called in for extra rehearsals, and then in the evening performance spent his time trying to get me to put the book down, so that he could grab it and leave me stranded.

This sounds like a particularly vicious thing to do, but I got on very well with James and I knew that he quite liked me; it was just his humour and his idea of fun. In the event I found that, far from upsetting me, it helped to relax me and took my mind off the tension of the situation. An announcement had been made before curtain up informing the audience that I would be taking over and carrying the book, and they were given the chance to get their money back. I don't think anybody did; they rarely do when they have made the journey, parked the car and settled into their seats. Taking over in this way is always a 'no lose' situation; the audience's sympathy is almost guaranteed. I got a very good reception and was looking forward to getting the second act under my belt for the next performance on the Tuesday, but Nicol made a rapid recovery and was back in top form!

I did, however, find it amazing that he never once spoke to me. We had rehearsed the play in the Duke of York's Theatre in St Martin's Lane, and I used to get there an hour before rehearsals were due to start. It is something I have always attempted to do, not solely in order not to be late, but to make sure that I have time to settle after the journey and prepare myself to be in the mood to work. Most times, I found myself going through my part alone on the stage in an empty theatre; but on this production, Nicol occasionally came in early too, and he never even acknowledged my presence. There were the two of us on stage in opposite wings in a large and completely empty theatre, and not a word of greeting or otherwise was uttered between us. When I took over his role for that one performance he didn't even come and say, 'Sorry for dropping you in it, mate. How did it go?'

I did hear that once in an interview he professed to not liking actors; which, since they come from all backgrounds with all shades of opinions, beliefs and personalities, is a particularly stupid statement. It would probably be more accurate to say that actors did not like him. That is not to say that his work is not admired – he was, in my mind, a particularly unique and brilliant actor – but he was unbelievably selfish and would think nothing of destroying another actor's performance to improve his own.

I was therefore delighted beyond measure when, at the end of one performance, the curtain came down after we had taken our first bow and Terry Palmer smacked Nicol on the nose. The curtain went up and they both turned to the audience and took another bow; the curtain came down and Nicol hit Terry, but a bit like a girl – he scratched his face. After the next bow the curtain stayed down and the skirmish was stopped. Since Terry was only small and Nicol quite tall, the event was not without its comic element. As I understood it, Nicol had been selfishly indulging in his own performance at Terry's expense, and Terry was not a man to mess with. He was a smashing little Welsh actor with lots of vitality and integrity, but completely uncompromising. He said what he felt and felt what he said. The last I heard of him he was directing, which I imagine he would be good at, but very choosy and wouldn't do rubbish. *Nil Carborundum*, or don't let the bastards grind you down, was a good title.

Next came the first of many returns to *Coronation Street*. This time it was just for four weeks – eight episodes – and I returned with a glamorous blonde on my arm, much to the consternation of Annie Walker, my mother, who set about busting up the relationship. It was a little under a year since I had left, and not much had changed. It had, however, now lost much of that documentary feel, and had really taken off with the public as a serialised drama, especially in the North; it was still very real, with a unique touch of humour. Ena Sharples and her little cabal in the Rovers Return snug bar had particularly caught the public imagination; they were unique and extremely amusing as they sat in judgement over their milk stout. Violet Carson as the leader was vinegary and aggressive, and looked very formidable and frightening with her trademark hairnet and her overcoat buttoned tightly across her chest to give the appearance of a metal breastplate. She was constantly at loggerheads with Elsie Tanner, and dominated the other two of the triumvirate. Minnie Caldwell played the Stanley to Ena's Oliver Hardy, with her simple and slightly dim-witted approach to life. The third member was Martha Longhurst, played by Lynne Carol, shuttled backwards and forwards between the two.

They were inseparable in the series, but in reality had very little to do with each other. Violet lived in the Blackpool area and shot off every day as soon as she could to miss the crowded train. Margot made her weekend trip to Hove where she had a flat, and Lynne was fairly local. Before becoming a national icon in her hairnet, Vi had been well known (if not visually) as Wilfred Pickles' pianist in his radio show *Have a Go* with his catchphrase 'Give 'em the money, Barney'. Violet was therefore no stranger to being well known; but she found it difficult, in later years, to support the busloads of sightseers that paused at her house as the Blackpool guides announced who lived there and the tourists peered over her garden hedge. She was becoming as vinegary as her character; but I got on very well with her, partly because she had been in *An Age of Kings* and was rather proud of that credit as it gave her CV a certain look of class. She made the effort to travel south for my wedding, and also took the trouble to knit my firstborn a little woollen jacket.

The friendship was put to the test from time to time as I was constantly taking up rehearsal time with requests to do the scene again or questioning the action, and she would be champing at the bit to get the train to Blackpool. There was too the occasion when, in the studio for a final run-through, the three ladies were poised in the snug with two of the cameras in position, waiting for the preceding scene to finish and the floor manager to give the hand signal to start. As I passed on my way from the studio, I jokingly gave the hand signal, expecting them to be aware that it was me and to ignore it. Unfortunately, like good professionals, they were not looking directly at the floor manager in order not to be caught 'cue-waiting', and just caught my signal in their peripheral vision, immediately setting off at a great lick into the scene. The other scene not having finished, the two were running concurrently, each one getting louder as they bravely tried to save the day and continue despite opposition. Violet was not amused, but her anger was short-lived!

The fact that I got on with Vi did not please Doris Speed who played Annie, my mother. She and Vi didn't get on too well, although nothing was said: they just kept out of each other's way. Doris had turned professional late in her life: in fact at the age of 60, having been a secretary for Guinness for many years in order to keep her parents, who were music-hall artistes and consequently often out of work. As a child Doris was taken around the touring theatres, never stopping long enough to go to school, and eventually ended up teaching herself to read and write. She loved books and her first job was in a library at the age of 13.

Her acting started, she told me, at a local amateur company where they would all share a dressing room backstage with a blanket hung up to separate the men from the women. She was spotted by a radio director and invited to read excerpts from books, and eventually to act in radio plays, which she did with time off allowed by Guinness. (The famous brewing firm remained loyal to her to the end, and throughout her life she received a Christmas gift from the management.) So used to radio was she that when she was invited to Birmingham for a small part in a TV play, she was unaware of the fact that it was to be screened and couldn't understand why they kept asking her what she would be wearing for the part. It was only after she reached the age of retirement that she took the plunge, turned full-time pro and landed the part of Annie Walker, which she was to play for the next twenty-five years.

By this time her father had died; but she continued looking after her mother for many years, hiring a nurse to care for her during working hours and dashing home by bus to Chorlton-cum-Hardy to relieve the nurse at the end of the day. Consequently, until her mother died she had no social life to speak of. We always got on well at work and she would call me over to her little corner of the rehearsal room to chat to her while she applied her make-up in the morning. This was her ordinary daytime make-up; she would travel in on the bus, unmade-up, arrive early for work and after lighting up a cigarette would set about applying her face with the fag hanging from her lips. In those days she spoke little of herself as she applied her make-up and chatted away, punctuated by the occasional spit into her mascara; it was just general gossip, which she loved. I didn't learn the facts about her early life until she had retired from the Street and I used to visit her in her retirement home. Although there was much of Annie Walker in Doris, Annie lacked the humour and readiness to laugh at herself that for me characterised my surrogate mother, Doris. She did, however, take her work very seriously. She had to: it was all she had!

Arthur Leslie, who played my father Jack, I think found Doris a little tiresome and, in the same way that his character stoically said nothing but suffered in eloquent silence, Arthur just kept his mouth shut and got on with the job. He was a lovely, gentle and elegant man with wonderful warmth. He had been a 'rep' actor for many years and enjoyed the financial security that the Street afforded him in his later years; it was just tragic that he was to die in 1970 and only had ten years of that comfort and acclaim. He was one of the rocks upon which the success of the Street was built; but it was the ladies that grabbed the limelight, headed by Violet, Doris, and Pat Phoenix as Elsie Tanner, the lovable tart. They were all three now national icons, and the star system had shaken these to the top of the pile, all of them women; the men really were shoved in the back seat.

There was too the Hewitt family, who had been in the cast from the beginning and were still there. Bus driver Harry Hewitt was played by Ivan Beavis, whom I believe had been a local amateur actor who had also struck lucky. Harry was a single parent with a daughter from his first marriage, and was later to marry Concepta Riley (often referred to as Contracepta), the Irish barmaid at the Rovers played by Doreen Keogh. She helped him to bring up his troublesome daughter Lucille, played by Jennifer Moss who couldn't have been much more than 14 at that time. Jennifer herself was to find that growing up as she did in the public eye was to provide her with great personal problems and she was ill equipped to cope. She stayed with the Street until 1974 when she was sacked, having developed a drink and drug problem. I remember, in one of my frequent returns to the Street, going to a party at her flat and experiencing my first 'joint', which she had expertly rolled for me at double or treble strength, and being a little sick!

Another who later disintegrated but at this point was still a mate and on the up was Peter Adamson, playing Len Fairclough, who had been written up as a drinking pal for Harry Hewitt and was much more ensconced as a regular. As a bachelor figure he was of much greater interest to the writers, getting some really good storylines, and was now emerging as the 'main man'. Since for much of my year out I had been just up the road at the Library Theatre, I didn't feel as if I had been away at all! It was like joining up with old mates. Bill Roache of course was still there and so was Alan Rothwell who played his brother, David Barlow. There were newcomers too: Graham Haberfield as Jerry Booth, Len's sidekick, and Ken Cope as Jed Stone, the Scouser scallywag lodger of Minnie Caldwell. Anne Reid playing Valerie Tatlock was still there but was now teamed with (and eventually became Mrs) Ken Barlow. Anne always struck me as being much more seriously talented than the usual run of soap actresses, an assessment that has subsequently been borne out by not only her performance in *Dinnerladies* but also a number of other wonderful performances in serious drama.

On my return trips to London I had frequently given a lift to Gordon Black, who had been involved in casting at Granada but had recently left to work for the agents Fraser and Dunlop in Regent Street. At Gordon's invitation, I joined their impressive list of clients. They were indeed a very classy set-up and I would often call in to find some well-known faces waiting to be seen. On one occasion I was flattered to be consulted by Barry Took and Marty Feldman who asked my opinion of a storyline they were discussing. I had hoped that, by being with the 'big boys', I would get my nose into bigger and better productions; but it didn't quite work out like that. Despite the big talk, I found I was small fry for Peter Dunlop and Jimmy Fraser, and when Gordon left the agency I was somewhat lost at the bottom of the list. Once again, Hal Burton came up with an offer and I played a small part in the BBC *Sunday-Night Play*, 'Undercover Cat', with Roland Culver playing the lead. I was cast as 'Animal Clinic Man'; unlikely casting, but I enjoyed the trust that Hal had in my ability to play character parts. This happens very little these days when casting against type is virtually unheard of.

Although I had already played in the West End with the Youth Theatre's production of *Hamlet* at the Queen's in Shaftesbury Avenue, to me it didn't really count as part of my career as a professional actor; so when I was offered a small part in *Fit to Print*, a new play set in a newspaper office by Alastair Dunnett, the then editor of *The Scotsman*, I jumped at the chance. An added attraction was the fact that the lead part was played by Sir Donald Wolfit, who was coming to the end of his most illustrious career, and was the last of the dying breed of actor-managers. (The character of 'Sir' in the film *The Dresser* was based upon him.) He was reputed to have been the definitive Lear; he certainly had the most mellifluous of voices, and was a heavyweight in every sense of the word. He was, however, a megalomaniac and, as many of them are, very insecure. My wife Paddy had worked with him years before, when she was little more than a child actor, and he had grandly offered her the job of cleaning and carrying, from one theatre to the next, his brass doorplate with his name and title engraved on it. It was delivered to her in the form of an honour and it was her job to make sure that it was cleaned and fixed to the door of his dressing room at each venue.

Wolfit was renowned for his touring company, taking Shakespeare to the provinces; when he got his knighthood in 1957, it was wickedly proposed that Olivier got his for being a 'tour de force' while Wolfit was 'forced to tour'! He was also reputed to have surrounded himself with mediocre talent in order to enhance his own magnificence; a questionable practice since it is well accepted these days that if one is surrounded by excellence, one's own performance is enhanced rather than overshadowed. In this instance, however, it was not in his gift to cast the play and he had quite a strong cast with Ewan Roberts, Basil

Henson, Charmian Eyre, Frances White and Valerie Bell in the main parts, and they were all capable of standing their ground. Indeed Basil and Sir Donald did not get on at all and they were at daggers drawn from the beginning.

It seemed to be part of his megalomania that he required you to like him or dislike him; he just couldn't stand to be simply ignored. I had of course come across Sir Donald before: first at Alleyn's School when he came to judge the reading prize, and later when his wife Rosalind Iden had been movement teacher at RADA; I had visited them in their house at Hurstbourne Tarrant when I found myself in that area after being commissioned in the Royal Artillery. Since I had only a small part in the play, I kept myself very much to myself and out of the cast conflict. This seemed to set a challenge to Sir Donald who kept inviting me into his dressing room for a glass of port, something that was supposed to be very good for the voice. (Indeed, I have often had trouble with my voice and have frequently been advised to try gargling with port. I have never been sure whether one was supposed to swallow it afterwards or not; afraid of being told that I should spit it out, I have never asked!) I didn't feel that I could knock on his dressing-room door and say, 'Good evening, Sir Donald, I've come for my glass of port,' and also I did not want to get drawn into the dispute between him and Basil Henson, and so I never went.

I don't know why he seemed to take such a shine to me, apart from the fact that I think he wanted me to like him. It was not all roses with him, however, because although I didn't have a large part it was quite showy. I was playing a young cub reporter. In one scene, I had quite a nice laugh line that seemed to annoy Sir Donald and he set about trying to kill the laugh. Just before I delivered the punchline that fired the laugh, he started to laugh himself and killed it; so the next night I paused for his laugh before completing the line, which won the laugh again; so he shifted his laugh, and so it went on until it became a little onstage duel. It was never spoken of or discussed and it became a nice little technical exercise for me.

Sir Donald was no slouch when it came to stage technique; he knew all the tricks. I noticed early on how he encouraged an entrance round by clicking the fingers of his upstage hand as he made his first entrance; since this sounded like distant clapping, it inspired the audience to applaud. We opened in Nottingham, and despite this being Sir Donald's birthplace we did not play to full houses. Nevertheless, Sir Donald insisted on making a curtain speech at the end of the performance, often very dramatic and emotional, castigating the audience for not being more numerous; this, I think, was the basis of the upset between him and Basil Henson. The management was Peter Saunders who was best known as the impresario behind the long-running production, *The Mousetrap*. I had nothing much to do with him except when he sent me for a shorthand lesson with his secretary to make my miming seem more realistic! I felt it was a waste of time, and that Peter Saunders wanted to feel that he had had some input and just picked on that as something to say. In the end it mattered little as the play didn't run for very long: one week in Nottingham and six weeks in the Duke of York's Theatre in St Martin's Lane.

I loved the West End; I really felt part of the theatre world. The Salisbury was the actors' pub where one could drink and meet up with the likes of Peter O'Toole, Ronnie Fraser, Peter Bowles, J. G. Devlin and Eddie Judd every night before the show. There was also the Buckstone, behind the Haymarket, which was a basement club exclusively for actors after curtain-down and closing time which was heaving every night with the stars of the West End; and there was too Gerry's in Shaftesbury Avenue which catered likewise for the late-evening drinking of the West End elite. Although the atmosphere at the Buckstone did from time to time get a bit tense and dramatic with all of those big egos around, it was a warm, friendly and inviting place to relax after seeing, or being in, a show. I felt I had been accepted into a rather large and special family. Something else that seems to have vanished with progress!

Although we had hardly settled into our new home and Paddy was now fairly large with child, I could not turn down the offer to take over the role of Billy in *Billy Liar*, which was now touring the country. Written by Keith Waterhouse and Willis Hall, the part had been instrumental in launching the career of Albert Finney. He had been followed by Tom Courtenay, who started the post-London tour and was then replaced by Trevor Bannister, who had been the understudy in the West End. Oscar Lewenstein was looking to extend the tour for a further ten weeks; and after rehearsing in the new cast members, with Paul Stone directing, we opened in Hull at the end of September 1962. Not surprisingly, since it is such a good play, it was a great success. Frank Pettitt played the garrulous father; Eileen Dale, the long-suffering mother; Nan Marriott-Watson, the grumbling granny; and Annabel Barton, Sheila Eves and Gillian Eddison the three girlfriends. Ralph Broome was Billy's bewildered friend.

Billy Liar has some unforgettable moments, the greatest being the mime scene where Billy, alone on stage, plays with a cane from the garden and transforms it to a fishing rod, a crutch, a rifle et cetera, ending up with the playing of the 'Last Post' in memory of his grandma, who has just died. The first two acts are just about as funny as you will get on stage and the third is just about as sad as you can get with the futility of the situation.

We got fantastic reviews wherever we went and I came out of them very well. I did, however, learn some pretty important lessons. First: never drink before a performance! In Hull, we were invited by the Mayor to join him for lunch after a tour around the Town Hall. The wine flowed freely and, flushed with success after the opening night, I'm afraid I was a little greedy! That night I thought I had given the best performance yet, full of energy and uninhibited invention, but that was not the consensus of the rest of the cast and after a talking-to from Ray Kelly, the company manager, I resolved never to drink before a performance again. I later adapted this resolve, or rather interpreted it, as I took to having the odd bottle of beer during a performance, if I felt that the part warranted sustenance!

I was also taken down a peg or two in Golders Green, where we played the Hippodrome. We were by now a fairly close-knit company, as often happens on tour after weeks of being alone together in the provinces, and used to meeting up after the show in the theatre pub which more often than not would allow us to drink somewhat after closing time. When we got to Golders Green things were a little different as, being in north London, we frequently had mates drop in to see the show, who would join us in the pub afterwards. On one occasion, however, Annabel Barton had some friends come to the show and they were ensconced on the far side of the pub, obviously not wanting to join us. The next day I asked her why she hadn't brought her friends over to meet us and she reluctantly told me that they had been particularly unimpressed with my performance! Having had such wonderful personal reviews, I had lost sight of the fact that not all of the audience are of the same opinion and there is bound to be someone out there who does not like what you are doing: a salutary lesson.

To counterbalance this deflating experience: John Stride came to see the show and entered the dressing room afterwards preceded by a small dapper old man well into his sixties. Seeing Johnny over his shoulder and being somewhat surprised as I had no idea he was in, I exclaimed, 'Hello you old bastard, why didn't you tell me you were going to be out front?' At which point Johnny, indicating the old man, said, 'May I introduce you to your boss, Oscar Lewenstein?' Oscar was charming and the next day I learnt that he had asked Ray Kelly how much I was being paid and, on being told, said, 'That's not enough: give him another fiver a week!' That had never happened to me before, and hasn't since!

Billy Liar was to be the first of many provincial tours; and I must say that there was much to enjoy in those early days of travelling around the countryside, and staying in some really weird places. In later years I took to renting a little cottage or flat, but in those days each city seemed to have its own theatrical digs with many outlandish characters as landladies, some of them very famous in their own right and with their own special brand of hospitality. When I first stayed in Dolly Parrish's digs in Leeds, I was overwhelmed with the social whirl after the show when we were joined in the large kitchen by other theatricals from the variety theatre, all tucking in to improvised meals. On my first night I was warned that the house was haunted and that the ghost walked the corridors at night, so I was more or less prepared when the landlady's daughter knocked on my bedroom door in the early hours. I never have believed in ghosts, and thereafter became a very heavy sleeper that night!

On November 23rd 1962, my first son, James, was born at Lewisham Hospital in south London whilst I was playing Billy Liar in Blackpool; not unnaturally, we had a few drinks to celebrate after the show. The next morning was a dreary, rainy, windswept day and being in a hotel-cum-guesthouse on the front made it seem even worse. At breakfast, the waitress said she was going to the bookies and asked if I wanted any bets putting on. On looking at the newspaper, I discovered a horse called 'Paddy's Boy' and another called 'Lucky Jim'. Since we had already decided to call the boy James, I bet on both and they both came in first (in different races of course!). I was upset not to have been with Paddy at that time, and felt rather helpless. Tony Whelan, who once again had proved himself a thoughtful and considerate friend and was to become James's godfather, took my place at her bedside; I shot back home after the Saturday-night performance, driving through the night to find a little wrinkled red-faced infant looking not unlike Ena Sharples!

6

THE THEATRE ROYAL, Stratford East had carved out a very special place for itself in the history of British theatre under the reign of Joan Littlewood and Gerry Raffles. In a way it was home to the Anglicised version of the American 'method', which relied a lot upon improvisation and set great store in realism. The revolution in British theatre had already started with Osborne's *Look Back in Anger* opening the doors to plays about the working class and marking the death of the 'Anyone for tennis?' genre. Joan was a master of her art and had created her own Theatre Workshop company with its unique style; *The Hostage, Sparrows Can't Sing* and *Oh What a Lovely War* had all been spawned under Joan at the charismatic little theatre, rather cosily housed in the East End of London where it had been adopted by the Cockney market traders who inhabited the surrounding streets. Joan had moved on to other things, mainly on the continent, but her spirit lived on and Gerry Raffles still ran the theatre with productions that paid homage to Joan's style.

Thus it was that Brian Murphy, who had been one of Joan's stalwarts, had been invited to direct a new play by Robin Chapman and Richard Kane, called *High Street, China*. I was invited to go to Stratford East for what I thought was to be a casting interview; I arrived to chat with Brian and was then asked to join the company for a read-through, which I thought was part of the casting process. However, after the read-through, which took about two hours, they started to talk about the rehearsal schedule and, somewhat taken aback, I asked what was going on; had I got the part or what? They seemed surprised that I should ask and I was told they were expecting me to play the part! At this point, everything stopped as I insisted that they talk to my agent and sort out details like billing and money: nothing had been discussed!

I did join the company and rehearsals began but, to my dismay, I found the working method very different from what I was used to. All the time seemed to be taken up with improvisation and playing games, with no work on the script at all. By the start of the second week I was feeling very exposed and alone, so I told Brian Murphy I was unhappy and that perhaps it would be best if I were to leave. I liked, indeed still do like, Brian: he really is one of nature's 'gentle men', and I didn't want to let him down. However, I explained how uncomfortable I was with the improvisation and how worried I was that we hadn't touched the script yet.

A compromise was arrived at and I agreed to stay. Rehearsals continued, and although we did start work on the script they were still very free with the dialogue and ad libs seemed to be encouraged. I found this all most disconcerting and was very worried that by the time they had finished messing around, it was not going to be the play that I had agreed to do. The majority of the ad libs I found very puerile and unamusing and it was very difficult to time or shape a speech when you weren't sure of what the others were up to. I just wasn't used to this way of working and felt I didn't fit in. I was already, at the age of 26, old fashioned, and I'm afraid I didn't behave very well.

Living, as we were at that time, in south-east London was quite a bonus as I was based at home and was able to spend plenty of time with my newborn son. Shortly after the opening night, I received a telephone call one morning before I had really got myself into gear. An American female voice at the other end of the line introduced herself as Mr Orson Welles' secretary and asked to speak to Mr Farrington. I was suffering from a most dreadful cold and fighting it with medications galore, worried at the possibility of not being able to go on for the evening performance, so I was not in the best of humours and said, 'OK. Who is it?' The voice insisted, 'This is Mr Orson Welles' secretary…' at which point I said, 'Look, I'm tired, I've got a stinking cold and I'm in no mood to play games,' and rang off. A few seconds later the phone went again and we went through the same dialogue, more or less, and I rang off again. When the phone rang the next time a magnificent, deep and mellifluous all-male American voice said: 'My name is Orson Welles. I gather you're having some difficulty with my secretary.' He went on to say that he had been in to see the play, had liked my performance and could I come to see him!

That afternoon, sniffing and sneezing, I shot off up to an office in Regent Street to meet the great man. The first thing that struck me was his size: he was unbelievably imposing and towered above me as he rose from his desk to take my little hand in his immense fist. The second thing that struck me was his humility. He spent the first ten minutes apologising for calling me up from my sickbed and showing great concern about my health. He then explained that he was going to be directing the second location on a film of the Bible and had wanted to meet me with a possibility of finding me a part to play! On such a big project as the Bible, they were having two crews filming in tandem to cover the immensity of the task; I don't know who was directing the first location. Anyway, it didn't matter – I never heard another word about it!

My big break into Hollywood didn't materialise, and over the next six months I did a 'tele' more or less at the rate of one a month, starting with *The Avengers*: one of the early ones with Honor Blackman and Patrick Macnee. I was playing a promising young boxer and my role started with a strenuous training session in the gym, watched by Steed and Cathy Gale. For my opponent they called on the services of an ex-boxing champion of the paratroopers and simply told him to pull his punches! During the rehearsal period, they all knocked off an hour early and left us to practise our boxing bit on our own. I'm afraid the paratrooper found pulling his punches rather difficult and his instinct frequently got the better of him. I found myself driving home daily with a headache and cuts to the inside of my mouth!

That was in March; in April I played in an episode of *Moonstrike*, a series about the French Resistance, produced by Gerard Glaister. In May, I was recalled to Granada for an episode of *The Odd Man*, a series that starred Edwin Richfield, Sarah Lawson and Keith Barron. Alfred Burke, James Bolam and myself were the guests, and the show was produced by Stuart Latham who had been the producer on *Coronation Street* at its birth.

It was not unusual for a job with one of the larger companies to be followed by two or three different roles for the same management, so I was not altogether surprised when, in June, I was recalled to the BBC for another episode of *Moonstrike*. What did surprise me was being invited to play a different character in the same series! The director on this occasion was David Goddard, who had directed me at the start of my television career in *The Splendid Spur*. This I took to be a vote of confidence in my ability as a character actor; although to be honest, it was quite common in those days for an actor to appear in the same series in a variety of roles, though not usually so close together. I think they made a mistake!

In July I managed to fit in two televisions, although one of them was no more than one line in an episode of *Man of the World*, starring the American actor Craig Stevens. I can still remember the line! I was playing a helicopter pilot in the Amazon and only had to say, 'The Mission is just a short distance to the south,' which I delivered with a heavy Hispanic accent! The series was written by Ian Stuart Black, the father of Isobel Black whom I had known and been good friends with since she played my romantic opposite in *The Hostage* at the Library Theatre the previous year. She too was in the episode playing a quite large part, which may explain why I was invited and why I accepted such a minor role. Also in that episode was Paul Maxwell who had played Elsie Tanner's American boyfriend in some of the early episodes of *Coronation Street*.

My other role that month was in the *Suspense* series, a play called 'The White Hot Coal'. Although I had a good part, it was not a wonderful script or even believable; but it was a strong cast including Philip Voss, Frederick Jaeger and Edward Fox. However, I didn't seem to get on too well with the director, John Crockett. The rehearsal period was something of a battlefield.

My last television in this particular run was an ITV *Play of the Week* starring Leslie Sands, with George Woodbridge and Richard O'Sullivan, and called 'Nice Break for the Boys' by John Wiles. Once again it was not a large part, but I was getting valuable television experience and learning to be aware of the camera and then ignore it. There is something about that camera lens that allows it to see into the very soul. In the theatre after the curtain has risen, the actor has more or less complete control of his own performance; whereas in television, it is possible to be in a scene and never appear at all! The director sits in the control room with the vision mixer and they choose the shots from the four to six screens in front of them, each one linked to a camera. Thus, the actor is dependent upon the director choosing to transmit his or her particular contribution to the drama. An awareness of the camera is therefore, in my opinion, an important ingredient in television acting. There are those who believe that it is the cameraman and the director's job to film their performance and that it is better to ignore the camera. I have a lot of sympathy with this approach, but still feel that during the technical rehearsals it is of great value to keep an eye on the monitors and the red light on top of the camera in order to be aware of what is being shot and from what angle. All too often I have found that, by not being aware, I have reacted offscreen; by the time the camera has picked me up I have moved on, my reaction not having been registered, and look as if I had not been listening or not part of the scene. Simply delaying the reaction for a couple of beats often solves the problem. By being aware of the camera angle, too, one can often improve the shot or be seen at a more advantageous angle simply by transferring one's weight onto the other foot. Of course, you can wait for the message to come down from the control room, but in my experience directors are grateful for the contribution as time is always at a premium.

It also helps if the actors remain alert and focused on technical rehearsal days. There is a tendency for the concentration to wane as the cameras and sound take centre stage; the actors are shunted around like bits of furniture, and there is a grave danger of them amusing themselves with private conversations, gags and so on. I was myself very prone to 'mess about' on camera rehearsal days, until Paul Bernard, who was directing *Coronation Street* at the time, invited me to join him in the control room when I was not in the scenes. It was a revelation, and I think it would be a good idea for all actors to be sentenced to a spell in the control room! Apart from the bank of screens radiating on the wall with the distracting variety of their activities, there is the foldback of sound from the floor, the separate conversations of the cameras and sound intercommunicating, and when you add to that the incessant chatter of bored actors amusing themselves, it is almost impossible for a director to think straight. For this reason many directors have taken to directing from the floor and sending their instructions up to the control room, and there is a lot to be said for this method.

In advocating an awareness of the cameras and what they are doing, I must emphasise that, come the actual recording, it is imperative to forget them and concentrate on performance. Even then one must keep a certain percentage of the brain technically alert, but there is nothing more aggravating than an actor who is obviously 'camera aware'. Just as the learnt lines have to be made to seem spontaneous and natural, so the camera, having been taken into account, must be ignored. Therein lies the art.

Cinema acting poses many of the same problems to the actor. At this point I had little experience of filming proper, having only had one day's work on *Children of the Damned*, a sequel to *Village of the Damned*, in which I played a soldier (again in my own uniform that I had kept from National Service) with little more than one or two lines. However, I have subsequently learnt that the film actor has even less control over his own performance. Each scene is filmed multiple times, allowing the single camera to cover the action from all angles, and is then cut together in the editing room. Once again, the actor is at the mercy of the director and the editor as many a performance ends up on the cutting-room floor. In this regard, film acting comes at the end of the list of preferences for many actors and the theatre remains the first love.

It was therefore a great joy to be offered the lead in a new play at the Phoenix Theatre, Leicester, which was the start of a long relationship with its artistic director, Clive Perry. *Life Worth Living*, written by Robert Story and directed by Clive, was supposed to be a try-out for the West End, being sponsored by 'Binkie' Beaumont of H. M. Tennent, the giants among London's theatrical producers. It was only the second production in the Phoenix, which had opened in October 1963, and boasted a strong cast including Patricia Burke, who had an illustrious career on stage, film, and tele and then later became an agent, and John Sharp, a north country actor of Falstaffian proportions. Hilary Hardiman played my new young wife; Richard Kay, a promising young actor who sadly died at an early age, played the boy next door; and a young Anthony Hopkins played my sister's boyfriend, a relatively small part! Gillian Eddison who had been with me in *Billy Liar* played my sister. I played Jeff Cutler, and the play was in essence about his return, with his new wife, to his roots in the Midlands where he finds that, under the dominating influence of his overbearing mother, a stammer that he had conquered in his youth returns under stress. The curtain fell on the first act as I beat my thigh with the agonising effort of struggling to speak. I loved this moment, as I was aware of the audience straining forward in their seats in sympathy, trying to will the words out themselves.

Unfortunately Tony Hopkins, fresh from drama school and feeling very much out of place and inadequate, as he confesses in his autobiography, was finding the role difficult and had developed an uncertainty in his delivery that sounded not unlike the stammer that I was trying to effect and which was an integral part of the play. Patricia Burke and John Sharp found this very disconcerting and, a week or so before the play opened, came to me and suggested that we go to Clive Perry and ask for Tony to be replaced, as they felt the play had no chance of transferring to the West End with him in that role. I refused to back them in this, not because Tony was then a particular friend (although we did become pals in a later production) but because, as I said to them, 'This is rep and you can't expect every part to be cast perfectly when the company has to be assembled for the whole season; we are just guests.' In the words of Shakespeare, 'And this man is now become a god'! Although he was never happy in the role, Tony did manage to turn in a reasonable performance, despite his assessment in his autobiography. Indeed he got quite good notices, which is more than can be said of the play. The critics didn't really like it and it didn't make the West End anyway.

I spent that Christmas at home and started the New Year with little in prospect until my agent called to say that I had been asked to meet Peter Yates, the film director, for coffee in Soho. He was a delightful man and told me that he was doing a film of N. F. Simpson's *One Way Pendulum* for Woodfall Films, an offshoot of Oscar Lewenstein's company which had put on *Billy Liar*, and Oscar had asked him to consider me for the part of Stan, the boyfriend. I was extremely flattered and also excited, as the cast was very starry; plus it was a nice part, being pretty much the only 'normal' character in the film. I was to play Julia Foster's boyfriend, and had most of my other scenes with Eric Sykes. The film also boasted Mona Washbourne, Alison Leggatt and Dr Jonathan Miller playing the rest of the weird Groomkirby family, and George Cole and Douglas Wilmer in the court scenes, with Peggy Mount playing the woman brought in to eat up the family left-overs.

It was a strange, offbeat comedy, but I loved it and found it very funny; however, it was what was known as an 'art film' and although it did get a general release, I don't think it caught on with the general public. It was a connoisseur's film. I grew to admire enormously Eric Sykes, an exceedingly kind and generous actor, with whom I had my best scenes as he tried to build the Old Bailey in the living room with a do-it-yourself kit. Fairly early in the shooting schedule there was a scene when Eric had to make an entrance on a word cue from me; after a couple of false starts it was established that the difficulty was that Eric couldn't hear the cue, so I said simply that I would just speak louder. Eric took me aside and told me that he was a little deaf, but on no account was I to alter my performance to accommodate his lack of hearing: 'Let them deal with that.' We were having a drink after work one evening, in a local pub, when a couple of smart-alec louts recognised him and were taking the piss from afar. I was livid, and made to get up and go over to them; Eric just put his hand on my arm and said, 'Leave 'em, they're not worth it.' Another of nature's 'gentle men'.

Before returning to the Phoenix Theatre, Leicester, I went back to Granada again to appear in an episode of *The Villains*, written and produced by Harry Kershaw who had written my first episode of *Coronation Street*, and directed by Stuart Latham, the Street's first producer. Alan Rothwell, who had played Ken's younger brother, David Barlow, and myself were playing two young amateur soccer players and amateur embezzlers. The episode was called 'Amateurs'. It had been some few years since I had last played football and *The Villains* proved in this respect to be somewhat cathartic. We filmed the soccer scenes on a Saturday morning on the playing fields on the outskirts of south Manchester, which was seething with games of football. By the time we came to finish shooting, the teams were gathering for the afternoon games and since I was then free and dressed for a game, I wandered around the dressing rooms to see if there were any teams short of a player. My enthusiasm for the game was rekindled.

After the transmission Brian de Salvo, who was then writing a column for *The Stage*, approached me and asked if he could interview me. It transpired that he lived fairly near to my home in Forest Hill, and we arranged to meet in a local pub. During the course of the interview I discovered that he played in goal for Bromley FC Second Eleven, and hearing of my past football history he invited me to join the Bromley training session on a Thursday evening. All went quite well at first; I was feeling a little out of my class, but I was still moving. We came to the drill where the ball is played in to a spot equidistant from two players who then race to the ball and challenge for possession. I set off like a steam train and felt I did quite well to arrive at the same time as my younger adversary. However, the dash was uncontrolled and we clashed mightily. I had to have fourteen stitches over my right eye, and the young player had to have his ear stitched back on. I wasn't invited to training again, but Brian, who took me to Bromley Cottage Hospital and fussed around making sure that they were aware that I was an actor and couldn't afford to be scarred for life (which is why I had fourteen stitches instead of six and consequently there is no scar), remained a friend for many years. I was unable to play for some time, but my interest in soccer had been awakened and it was to prove somewhat of a problem in my marriage in future years.

Back up in Leicester, I had no time for football as rehearsals got into swing for *Edward II*. Clive Perry was directing, Richard Kay was playing Edward and I was playing the very showy part of Mortimer the Younger. Anthony Hopkins, who was still in the company, played Lancaster; John Quentin was Gaveston, and Hilary Hardiman played Edward's unfortunate wife.

Also in the company was Victor Henry, an excitingly promising young actor and a fireball of a character who courted danger on and off stage. Victor, Tony Hopkins and myself teamed up as a trio, spending much of our time together in the Bowling Green, the stage pub, where we became close friends of the landlord: not surprisingly since we were his greatest asset. During the rehearsal period we would spend most of our spare time in the Bowling Green, going on trips with the landlord to other pubs where we played the old-fashioned game of skittles in sheds 'out the back', and after the performances he would keep the bar open for us late into the night. After a heavy bout we would stagger back to Victor's digs where we drank scalding hot coffee from mess tins (as he had broken all of the mugs), and would turn up to rehearsals the next day with sore blistered lips!

Victor, or Alex as he was called then, in drink seemed to have something of a death wish and would frequently provoke some sort of altercation, more often than not with the largest person in the bar, and force Tony and I to leap to his defence. There was something about his character that couldn't resist testing the boundaries, seeing just how far he could go. His drinking led him to have many accidents, falling downstairs and suchlike, and it was generally accepted that he was unlikely to make 'old bones'. It was ironic therefore when, dead cold sober, he was standing at a bus stop and a woman drove into the concrete post which fell on his head; he was in a coma for many years, with his poor mother sitting daily at his side. He was a tragic loss: had he lived he would without doubt have been as exciting an actor as Anthony Hopkins, if like Tony he could have conquered his drink problem.

Rehearsals were very exciting and Tony and I had many scenes together. Tony's acting was developing into something mesmeric; he was very powerful and intense. I always described his acting as if he had ingrowing toenails; something else was going on inside, under the lines, and he really got under the skin of a character. He was too a marvellous mimic: his Richard Burton, Marlon Brando and Laurence Olivier were impeccable, and he had a wonderful voice in his own right.

Clive Perry's production of *Edward II* with Christopher Morley's set was highly praised by the local critics and transferred to the Arts Theatre in London for a six-week run. I also got very good personal reviews and had high hopes of it opening the door to a classical career, perhaps with the Royal Shakespeare Company. Every year since leaving drama school I had attempted to get into the company and usually presented myself at the annual auditions. As the years went by this was becoming increasingly embarrassing as I was turning up with kids fresh from drama school and I found it a little galling.

Just prior to the opening of *Edward II*, I had made my usual trip to the Old Vic where the RSC auditions were held and gone through the humiliating and by now familiar process. I say humiliating because auditions can be extremely nerve-racking experiences, dependent very much upon the attitude of the interviewer, who in this instance was John Barton. The routine was that, on cue, the next candidate was to walk out to the middle of the stage, state his name and the name of his agent, announce the source of his first piece, and go to it. This I did and, since the lights were in my eyes, I couldn't see anything out front. There was no reaction and I wasn't sure if anybody was there; so, shielding my eyes, I peered into the dark and asked if they wanted me to continue with the second piece. A rather weary, bored voice drawled, 'Ye-es,' and I delivered the second piece, turned on my heels and slunk out, depressed and humiliated.

I was now represented by Tim Williamson, a new agent who had approached me to ask if he could represent me, which is always very flattering. Since I was getting nowhere fast with Fraser and Dunlop, I had moved to him. On returning home deflated, I phoned Tim and asked him to register a complaint at the way they were treating people. I argued that many of them were fresh young nervous students and that there was no way they were going to get the best out of them without settling them down and chatting to them a bit. I was now a hardened old pro and I found the whole thing daunting; how must they feel? I wasn't really championing the inexperienced: I was just very upset at their indifference and cavalier attitude.

When, a few weeks later, Tim phoned to say that Bamber Gascoigne had told the RSC in glowing terms of my performance as Mortimer the Younger and that they wanted to see me, I therefore told him to tell them to take a running jump at themselves. Being less of a hothead than myself, he left me for a day or two before phoning back to say that he had fixed for me to see John Barton again! This time the attitude was very different; as I arrived on stage John Barton came down to the footlights and chatted to me about *Edward II* before I set off with my audition pieces again.

An offer did come through, but it was decidedly unattractive: little walk-ons and one-line parts with the possibility of something better later. Being aware of a number of disillusioned actors who toiled as spear-carriers for endless seasons with just such carrots dangled, I declined the offer and said I would love to come when they could sort out some decent parts for me.

In the gap before the London transfer of *Edward II*, I managed to fit in a nice little tele: an episode in Associated Television's *Love Story* series called 'Romance of Words'. It was quite a nice little tearjerker about a bedridden boy, paralysed from the waist down, who gets a wrong-number call from a plain retiring shy girl, and a relationship develops as they chat and then call each other back. She fantasises about her beauty and social attractiveness and he fantasises about his physical agility and prowess. They arrange to meet, but the girl's parents call on the boy to prevent the meeting because they don't want their daughter hurt. The girl was played by Meg Ritchie, and her parents by Warren Mitchell and Lila Kaye. Warren had not at that time won national acclaim for his Alf Garnett, but he was obviously an actor who had every intention of getting somewhere. His role, though admittedly very important, was not large; but we spent more rehearsal time on his part than the rest of the piece put together! He just kept picking at it and picking at it until he was satisfied enough to move on. I didn't get to know him very well, but I got the impression that he would be a difficult man to really get to know at the best of times; he was such a large, dominating character.

Christopher Morley's set for *Edward II* transferred so easily into the Arts Theatre, it might have been designed for it! There were two drawbridge-like constructions, one on each side of the stage. The doors could be up to form impregnable walls, half way down to form platforms or fully lowered as ramps. In one scene where the rebel army confront the army of the king's men, both doors were halfway down, and Tony and I as Lancaster and Mortimer stood with our army on one platform, facing the opposition on the other. At some time into the run at the Arts Theatre, I happened to notice David Ryall on the other side of the stage in the opposing army, sporting headgear that looked for all the world like a loose-knitted wool balaclava. It had got knocked a bit skew-whiff and looked decidedly unthreatening, and the more aggressive he tried to look the more amusingly incongruous he looked. I nudged Tony and signalled him with my eyes to 'clock' David Ryall. The laugh started inwardly, and gradually and silently built; I could feel him quaking with suppressed laughter at my side, which set me off silently and inwardly giggling. I don't think our surrounding army knew what we were laughing at, but it eventually got to them too and in no time at all the drawbridge was in danger of collapsing as it vibrated with mirth.

Until that point, I had not really seen Tony as a giggler, but from then onward we had quite a few onstage laughs. He had one little mannerism of pointing, not with his finger but with his thumb; and when I started to do this back to him and we stood together pointing at one another with our thumbs and twinkling at each other like mad, we were in danger of not being able to continue.

The question of 'corpsing', as it is known in the profession, is a tricky one. Some of our best, most dedicated and serious actors are well known as gigglers, Sir John Gielgud and Dame Judi Dench amongst them. It is essential that the spectators are not aware of these private gags, otherwise they can become very damaging and can alienate an audience; but they can have the effect of increasing the concentration, simply by lifting dialogue that was getting glib with repetition. At best, it increases the contact between the actors.

After *Edward II*, I had another run of television roles, starting with a return to Granada to play Patricia England's husband in a series called *It's a Woman's World*. The story, called 'Laura', was written by Margaret Drabble, and directed by Claude Whatham. Claude was a sort of director I had not come across since Mike Croft. He completely took over his cast. He became all-protective, all-controlling, and demanded total commitment: not only during the hours of rehearsal, but socially as well. Since we rehearsed and recorded in Manchester and I had to stay away from home, this was not a problem, and I quite enjoyed the total experience. Trevor Bannister played the milkman; not a large part, but he would later land the role of Mr Lucas in *Are You Being Served?* that was to make him a very recognisable face.

My next television was for the BBC: an episode in *The Indian Tales of Rudyard Kipling* called 'Love o' Women', in which I played a young soldier in India suffering from suspected syphilis. The cast included the distinguished actors John Paul and Joss Ackland, along with Harry Landis and David Burke. The episode was mainly on film, which was becoming more and more common, and we went on location – rather disappointingly not to India, but to north Wales.

Although I preferred the stage, I was happy for this little run of television as Paddy was expecting our second child and, while there was the odd spell 'out of town', I was able to spend quite a bit of time at home. In the gaps between engagements I signed on and collected the 'dole': a fact which seemed to upset my father, whose working-class attitude was that it was degrading and shaming. I can't say that I was myself delighted and would have much preferred to work; but although looking back it seems as if I was doing a TV a month, in many cases they were little more than a few days' work. With a family to feed and a mortgage to pay, I was keeping my head above water but not exactly living in the lap of luxury. I argued too that it was my own money that I had paid in and now I was drawing out; they didn't pay you anything when your benefit had run out.

There was also the argument that I had spent two years training and was now part of a profession that was bringing billions of pounds into the economy. Quite apart from the taxes on entertainment and the income from sales abroad, our television is the envy of the world, our theatre is known to be the best in the world and the tourist trade in London is very much based on the people who come from afar to see our West End productions. There are also the hotels and restaurants, taxis and public transport that all feed off the desire of foreigners to come to England to see the theatres. One reason for this is the standard of excellence of our actors; and one reason why we have such a plethora of good actors is the standard of our repertory theatres, which form the basis upon which the fabric of the entertainment industry sits. The reps cannot pay well; they just don't have the income, and in many instances they are dependant on the dedicated actor working for much less than he can expect to get elsewhere. It was my love of the theatre that had made me choose to turn my back on *Coronation Street* as a long-term employment. I did not become an actor to play the same part for the rest of my life, and in electing to join the rest of my profession with uncertainty of employment I felt I was doing my bit at the base of the triangle of excellence, contributing to the high standard of British theatre that was bringing so much into the national coffers. It was not therefore unreasonable to expect the state to support, in some small way, the less fortunate members of the profession that brought them in such wealth.

Signing on once a week was not a pleasant experience, although the pill was slightly sweetened by actors having their own special day and their own special Labour Exchange at Westminster. It was almost like being a member of an elite club, and one would often queue up behind some very recognisable and famous faces. On one occasion, I found myself ahead of Wilfrid Lawson in the queue; as I got to the desk, I stepped aside and invited him to go before me. I admired him greatly as an actor and felt slightly embarrassed for him being there. He was well known to have a very heavy drink problem, but despite that could turn in some wonderful performances and was much loved within the profession.

I had recently taken delivery of a brand-new car. I had bought a Singer Gazelle from Simon Ward's father's garage and had driven to the Labour Exchange in it that day, parking just around the corner to avoid attracting attention to myself. The one-way system forced me to drive back past the doors of the Labour Exchange where Wilfrid Lawson was in conversation with a couple of tramps; he appeared to be trading cigarette butts! On seeing me, he made the hitchhiker's sign with his thumb and I pulled up. He got in and I asked him where he wanted to go. In that wonderful drawling idiosyncratic voice of his, he said, 'Victoria will do me fine.' As we were driving there, he noticed that the plastic covers were still on the seats of the new car and he drawled, 'What have you got these covers for; did you think I was going to piss on your seats?'

It truly was sad that a man of his immense talent should be so dependent on booze. There are many theatrical stories of his drinking and, although many of them are amusing, drink not only ruined his health, it also lost him many a job. There was indeed a time in the theatre when the hell-raising drinker was almost honoured. At the time of *The Long and the Short and the Tall*, Peter O'Toole, Ronnie Fraser, Eddie Judd and Richard Harris led a sort of West End spree of heavy drinkers, and there was something attractive about their wild, dangerous lifestyles that caught the public imagination and fanned the flames. However, I think that escalating costs of production and the demand for a greater sense of reliability have rendered the alcoholic less acceptable. I say this with no sanctimonious undertones; I am myself very partial to the delights of alcohol, and have had to pay for the indulgence, more than once! I feel very much that it is a case of 'There, but for the grace of God...'

On September 20th 1964 our second son, Mark, was born at our home in Canonbie Road, Forest Hill, South London.

7

1964 to 1966 • Football • More television •
John Thaw • Jean Alexander • Barbara Knox •
Bryan Mosley • *Othello* • Phoenix Theatre •
Cy Grant • *The Great Train Robbery*

FOOTBALL WAS GRADUALLY creeping its way back into my life. My army soccer had virtually ceased when I went to Cyprus – I can only remember playing one game against a local village side – and, on returning to England, I was far too busy getting on with my chosen career. It wasn't until my role as the young soccer player in *The Villains* came along that I gave it another thought. I hadn't played seriously for about seven years, so it came as something of a shock to my poor wife, Paddy, when she found me getting more and more involved: first with a team of entertainers called the Northern All Stars, run by Freddie Pye, director of Altrincham FC, and later for Les Wise, cousin of Mike and Bernie Winters, who ran the London equivalent.

I think my interest was fuelled by my dissatisfaction with the way my career was going. Football burnt a little of that unused energy and took my mind off the feeling of not getting on as well as I would have wished. Although I was working fairly regularly, I was not getting the starring roles that my ambition required! I also convinced myself that it helped me to keep my feet on the ground, though I'm not sure where the danger of me getting carried away was coming from.

The showbiz team was called the TV All Stars, which was a bit of a misnomer since they struggled to get recognisable faces week after week. There were certain regulars: Jess Conrad, the sixties singer who's still going strong, in goal; Dick Richardson, the heavyweight boxer, at centre half; comedy duo Mike and Bernie Winters; Jimmy Tarbuck; Dave Dee, of Dave Dee, Dozy, Beaky, Mick and Tich; Junior Campbell, the lead singer from Marmalade; and actor Bernard Bresslaw. There were also a few doubtful characters who were perhaps known to the music industry but were new to me, and to the spectators; but the commentator, Johnny Cohen, who travelled with the team, was quite adept at bamboozling the crowds into thinking they were somebody they should have known. I say crowds, but we quite often played in pitifully half-empty stadiums.

We often picked up local star players on the way; in one of my first games in Skegness, I remember playing with one of my boyhood heroes, Tommy Lawton, the great England centre forward. I usually played in what used to be called the right half position, and probably would be the right side of the mid-field today. My ball skills were not to be wondered at, but I was a good ball-winner and a hard worker – a bit of a Nobby Stiles. In that particular match with Tommy Lawton, anxious to impress my hero, I won the ball just outside our area, carried it up the mid-field, and delicately lofted a long pass up the middle to Tommy who just had to turn and run onto the ball; he was free, alone in front of the goal with just the keeper to beat. As the ball, beautifully weighted, floated over his head, he didn't move; he turned to me, gave me the thumbs up and said, 'Good ball, son. At me feet next time!'

We were frequently joined by old pro footballers for one-off charity games: Malcolm Allison, George Cohen, Ron Atkinson, and Danny Blanchflower who I chatted to for ages in the dressing room believing him to be Val Doonican, not realising my mistake until I saw what he could do with the ball at his feet some half an hour later! Some quite starry showbiz personalities, labelled 'faces', also joined us from time to time: Tommy Steele, John Alderton, and Bill Oddie and Rod Stewart who were both very good ball players, but very greedy: after wasting my time calling for a pass, I spent the rest of the game refusing to pass to them as I never got it back! There was also the disc-jockey contingent: David Hamilton, Graham Dean and Ed Stewart were fairly regular, with Tony Blackburn and Pete Murray putting in the occasional appearance. The terrible trio of Jimmy Tarbuck, Kenny Lynch and Harry Fowler were also there in the early days, wreaking havoc wherever they went.

Since the games were all around the country, it was often difficult to persuade some of them to turn out, as it could take all day; indeed, once a year when we flew across to the Isle of Man, it was a whole weekend. The games were always for charity and although nobody was paid to play, any heavy travelling expenses were reimbursed and we were frequently treated to a good meal after the match. Sometimes, of course, the crowds were large enough to warrant the outlay, but frequently it was difficult to see where the money was coming from.

Besides the TV All Stars, there were also the Showbiz XI and the Entertainers XI; some of the more sought-after players turned out for whichever team had the best venue. The end result was that the recognisable 'faces' were sometimes a bit thin on the ground, and the charity soccer scene was getting a bad name. The games were often not good football; it was a bit difficult to tread the line between providing entertainment and playing a decent game.

We usually played the local team, and the games often got very edgy. The ex-pros sometimes found it difficult to subdue their competitive spirit. When we played at Wembley as a curtain raiser for the Youth Clubs' final, I was marked by Dave Mackay, the ex-Derby and Scottish player, in more ways than one. He seemed to spend most of the match picking me up off the floor and apologising for forgetting that he was playing in a charity game!

One would have expected the entertainers to take the games in a much more lighthearted manner; indeed we had one or two set gags when for instance I, as the smallest member of the team, would set about Big Dick Richardson and he would pick me up off the floor by my elbows. Some of them, however, took the whole thing very seriously. When I was visiting Coventry to see Paddy in a play at the Belgrade Theatre, Mike and Bernie Winters, hearing I was in town, invited me to play in the pantomime team against the local police. They had one or two 'ringers' in the side from Coventry City and we were winning 13-0, when Bernie got into an altercation with one of the opposition. He turned really quite ugly, and I said to Mike, 'If he's like this when we're 13-0 up, what's he like when he's losing?'

The charity games were on a Sunday, and for a more competitive game I returned to the Alleyn's Old Boys Club and played on Saturday afternoons. To add to this newfound interest in soccer, Brian de Salvo and I joined forces to write a football-based drama series for TV; in one storyline we used the incident when I had been injured in training with Bromley and had the stitches above my eye. We wrote about three episodes and synopses for a further dozen or so, and sent it to Granada and the BBC. The idea was rejected by both companies as being not feasible. The main objection seemed to be that it would be difficult to find enough actors who could play football convincingly enough. We were of course pretty deflated, but our disappointment turned to anger when a few months later the BBC started a series called *United*, and one of the storylines was remarkably close to one of ours!

In the September of 1964 (the same month that our second son was born) I did an episode of *Redcap*, a series about the military police starring John Thaw. John had been around at RADA when I returned from the army, but our paths didn't really cross until the early episodes of *Coronation Street* when John was also at Granada in a series of plays called *The Younger Generation*. Over a period of some weeks, I gave him a lift to London in my car on a Friday evening and back again on the Monday morning. There was no M6, and the M1 ended at Crick, so it was a long journey of some four hours; naturally we chatted for much of the journey and I got to know him, I thought, fairly well. He seemed obsessed by the fact that Tom Courtenay was doing so well, and very resentful since he obviously didn't think much of his work and thought he himself was much better. I also got the impression that John was very fussy about the work he was prepared to do; according to him, he turned down quite a bit of work if he thought it was not worthy of him, similar to the sort of work that I found I had to take.

I had no idea at that time that he didn't actually like me and was therefore very surprised at his attitude towards me when we met again in *Redcap*. I was expecting a warm welcome when I turned up for the first day's read-through; instead, he reserved his attention for Ian McShane. I had known Ian via the National Youth Theatre when he played Hotspur in *Henry IV Part 1* at the Scala Theatre and Mike Croft had asked me to call in and assist with the make-up. I had spent some considerable time helping Ian with his, and somehow expected a certain rapport. I don't think I'm being paranoiac when I say I had the feeling that the pair of them got together and decided that I was to be given the cold shoulder. There was no actual conflict and nothing was actually put into words. The only incident that somehow confirmed the feeling I had was when, in the middle of the camera rehearsal, John was chatting to Ian and I drew his attention to the fact that the floor manager was trying to convey a message from the director in the gallery, saying they wanted him to move. He was very unnecessarily unpleasant and more or less told me to mind my own business. It was as if he had been waiting for some time to show me what he really thought of me.

My agents Fraser and Dunlop also handled Ian Hendry, who was very much flavour of the month with the film industry but who, like so many, was finding it difficult to handle a predilection to drink. Prior to doing a film about the beauty contest industry, he was going into a drying-out clinic and would not be available for the camera tests for the female lead. I was offered the job of standing in for Ian to camera-test six beauties in three scenes over six days! The three scenes were, first, an argument in the apartment as the beauty stripped down to panties and bra; then, an evening scene in the apartment starting with drinks and ending in a smooch-type dance, followed by a scene in a bathing costume – the beauty that is, not me! They were directed by Val Guest, who had a reputation for being 'a bit of a lech'; and I was taken aside by the first assistant, who warned me against trying anything with any of the young ladies: 'They're Val's.'

Apart from the sheer delight of the task, it was a wonderful opportunity to get a better feel for filming as opposed to television. The six women were: Alexandra Bastedo, who was not at that time known as an actress but who had just won a beauty contest in Brighton (I believe Val Guest was one of the judges); Nyree Dawn Porter, who was already well known from *The Forsyte Saga*; Annette André; Shirley Anne Field; Janette Scott; and Susan Hampshire, also from *Forsyte Saga*. What a wonderful job! I kept my nose clean from the beginning, making sure I kept a very professional approach to the whole thing and never chatting with the girls about anything but the work, not that I felt the inclination to anyway; I found them all a bit intimidating, they were all so beautiful. At lunch break I never saw them – they would have lunch with Val in his caravan – and at the end of the day's work I would make myself scarce. They each had their one day of course, except Alexandra Bastedo who came in for a second try at the end; they were never in at the same time. They were all very different and each of them could have played the part well, in their own way. It was Janette Scott who eventually got the part, and she was the most technically sure and aware of the six girls. Annette André was the warmest, and the one that I found the most giving in performance, but perhaps that was because she was the one that didn't feel too tall for me! Alexandra Bastedo was the most stunning in underwear and swimming gear, and it was obvious that Val would have loved to give her the part, but she was very inexperienced and he couldn't take the risk. Susan Hampshire and Nyree Dawn Porter I was to work with later, but didn't get to know them well at the time. When they came to make the film some weeks later, I played the minute part of a newspaper reporter.

In November 1964, I returned for another brief visit to *Coronation Street*, just two weeks. Tim Aspinall had taken over from Harry Kershaw as producer, and had been brought in to axe a few of the original characters and give the show a bit of a facelift. He got rid of Harry and Concepta Hewitt, Martha Longhurst, Frank Barlow, Ken's dad, and also Florrie Lindley, played by Betty Alberge, who ran the corner shop; and he brought in the Ogdens and the then Barbara Mullaney to play Rita Littlewood. There was considerable concern and upheaval at the time with everybody in fear of the axe falling, and poor old Tim was not a popular lad. In retrospect, he did a good job, or rather an unpleasant job well. The characters that he brought in were to prove very successful and lasted for many years; indeed Rita, or rather Barbara, was still there the last time I looked.

I remember thinking at the time that she was a very accomplished actress, with absolute control and a comforting self-confidence. She was a joy to work with and one felt very secure when involved in scenes with her. I did not feel the same about Bernard Youens, however, who played the lazy layabout Stan Ogden. I don't know what his background was but I remember him being very dismissive and scathing about the theatre. I always felt that he would not have lasted long without Jean Alexander, who played his wife Hilda Ogden and who was to join the ranks of the matriarchal 'supremos'. Her character as the much-put-upon and long-suffering underdog really caught the imagination of not only the viewing public but also the scriptwriters. In a way this spoilt her characterisation for me, as I felt that they tended to accentuate the comic side of the character to such an extent that she was frequently in danger of descending into caricature. At every opportunity, they had her singing at her work in a voice that really set the teeth on edge and, to my mind, stretched the limits of believability.

However, I found her at her most impressive and formidable when she was allowed to be strong and aggressive in defence of her Stanley. I recall one scene I had with her when I had wrongfully accused her Stan of stealing from the Rovers till, and she came storming into the bar with a verbal assault on me that took my breath away. Jean and I got on very well when, at one of the Granada parties, we discovered that we were both able to do ballroom dancing, and proceeded to show off and give an exhibition of our 'steaming hot foxtrot'.

Tim Aspinall also brought Sandra Gough into the Street as the Ogdens' daughter Irma, and what an addition that proved to be! More of her later. Tim, having done the job, didn't stay; he was replaced by the producer/writer Peter Eckersley who later married Anne Reid and sadly died very young.

This was to be my last visit to the Street for six years, for a variety of reasons really. First, it seemed that they were always bringing me back with a dolly bird; while it had its bright side, this usually meant that in all of my scenes the camera, not unnaturally, always seemed to be focused on her. I could be acting my little cotton socks off in the background and out of focus; if I was lucky, most of the time I was out of shot. Being somewhat ambitious and arrogant, I found this very unsatisfying. Second, I found that people had the impression that I was in the Street as a regular, and I was afraid that this was preventing me from getting the sort of work that I would like to have been offered. There was too the news that Paddy was pregnant again and we had made the decision to move away from London.

My parents had moved from Peckham in south London to Ore, just outside Hastings. Paddy and I had found a large house in a sought-after area of Hastings, beautifully built in engineering brick just after the war. Apparently, it had been built for a local estate agent and all of the very best materials had been used. It stood in its own grounds with a tennis court; and, best of all, it was just behind the goal at Hastings United FC – hidden by trees, but it didn't take me long to put a gate in the fence so I could pop in to the social club for a drink in the evenings! Soon after we moved to Hastings, Paddy gave birth to our daughter Theresa, in the Buchanan Hospital. Tessa, as she prefers to be called now, was born on September 20th 1965, exactly one year to the day after our son Mark.

Having a large house in its own grounds meant that we could leave the door open without worrying about the children running out on to a busy road. It sounds grand, but property was a lot cheaper in Hastings than in London, and the cost of living was lower too. Although I never seemed to be long out of work compared to many of my fellow actors, I wasn't getting anything really well paid, apart from *Coronation Street* which I had decided not to return to. I had a one-day, one-line part in Dick Lester's film of *The Knack*; I played a guardsman, wearing just a bearskin. Since the scene was shot with me and a few other guardsmen looking out of a barrack-room window, my lack of inches and my lack of clothes didn't matter.

My next role was quite a nice one, in an *Armchair Theatre* for ABC TV at Teddington Lock. It was a remake of a previous success called 'The Last Reunion', by Kenneth Hyde. Starring the almost-blind Esmond Knight, it seems to be just a reunion dinner of a bomber crew. They decide to re-enact their last flight together, using the dining table and chairs as the plane; as the re-enactment unfolds, we mix to the interior of a real plane under attack, and we realise that they are all killed except for Esmond Knight, who is seen in the last scene sitting alone at the empty dining table. It was a very effective piece and I played the rear gunner, 'Ginger'. Also in the cast was Bryan Mosley, who played Alf Roberts in *Coronation Street*, which was a little unfortunate because he was one of those actors that I couldn't stand. It was almost a chemical reaction, and I am prepared to admit that it was quite unjustified on my part. He was just one of those actors – and he was by no means alone – that I took great exception to.

It had started in the early days of *Coronation Street* when he had been very dismissive of the Shakespeare series *An Age of Kings*; it wasn't a balanced critical assessment, it was just a dismissal of the whole thing as being intellectual rubbish. He had no time for Shakespeare. I don't know why, but I get very angry when I hear an actor show such little appreciation of the greatest genius of all time. In a profession based upon the understanding of human nature, storytelling and the magnificence of language, he is unparalleled and it upsets me to hear one of my fellow actors voicing objections to his greatness. By all means say that you don't understand him, or that you find him difficult to perform, or even that he is not your favourite playwright; but for a mediocre talent to deny him his true position is an indication of ignorance and extreme arrogance.

Having done a rather prestigious *Armchair Theatre* I was expecting things to brighten up a bit, but the next few months were very quiet. I did the awful feed for *The Joe Baker Show*, laughingly called a comedy; and I also had the first of a number of appearances in *Z Cars*, the overwhelmingly popular police series set in Liverpool and starring Brian Blessed, Colin Welland, Frank Windsor, Joe Brady, Jimmy Ellis and Stratford Johns. Although the show was still live, I was amazed at the way they messed around during transmission, right up until the last minute. In the scene I had with Brian Blessed in the police car, he let out a gigantic belch just before the cameras were due to come over to us – by all accounts I was lucky it was just a belch!

Next, I went back to Stratford East for a new play by Alun Owen, *A Little Winter Love*, directed by Gary O'Connor. By now the Littlewood influence had dissipated; although the theatre still had that wonderful atmosphere of belonging to the street market, it no longer felt that it was at the centre of something new and exciting.

However, I still found the theatre much more rewarding than television. As I have said before, you have greater control over your own performance; but also, as most actors say, the sense of contact with a live audience can be very exciting, and there is too a constant feeling of being able to improve, to dig deeper, to find something else, and the chance to do it again the next night and get it better.

Most rewarding of all, however, is the fact that, nine times out of ten, the scripts are much better. There is of course the odd TV play where the writer has rewritten draft after draft to hone the dialogue, and then had a decent rehearsal period with the final polish provided by the actors' and director's contributions. However, recent 'progress' in filming methods means that everything is now split into little parcels to rehearse and record, a process which is not conducive to that final polish, and the dialogue is not given the same intensive examination. Without that period of rehearsal to examine and test his characterisation, the actor does not have the confidence to question the dialogue, and frequently the most trite, inaccurate and puerile conversations are transmitted in the name of entertainment. Also, a long-running series eats up material, ever hungry for the next morsel, and in consequence the writers never get the time to do more than churn out the next episode. This is of course a generalisation, and there are certainly good writers amongst the many working on the weekly soaps; but the set-up is geared to speed and is not conducive to polishing and perfecting.

No complaints about my next author: back to the Phoenix Theatre, Leicester, to play Iago in Shakespeare's *Othello*. It was directed by Clive Perry and starred Cy Grant in the title role, with Wendy Gifford as Desdemona. Apparently, Iago is the largest of Shakespeare's roles in terms of lines, and I must say that if I were to be offered the chance to play again any Shakespearean role that I have played, it would be Iago. Unfortunately, Cy Grant was basically a singer, not an actor (England's answer to Harry Belafonte), and never quite managed to master the role. He didn't get a very good press and the hordes of young girls that came to see him in the flesh went away disappointed with Shakespeare, so in a way a lot of damage was done. I suppose the fact that Paul Robeson had 'got away with it' had made Clive think of Cy.

That apart, *Othello* was just the sort of work I longed to be doing, and I was very happy; however, something happened which was to have reverberations later, something so minor I gave it little thought at the time. We had two trainee directors who were not only helping Clive but also took part in the scene when Iago gets Claudio drunk. One was Carey Harrison, the son of Rex Harrison, and the other was the young Richard Eyre. I think they were a little self-conscious at being on stage, or felt that they were above playing such minor parts; or were just lulled into thinking that since the major actors were sometimes messing about, that they could have a go too. Whatever the reason, I found their activities became a bit distracting and asked them to stop. I didn't think too much of it at the time as it wasn't a row and I don't think I did it unpleasantly. However, nobody likes being told off or put down; and when Clive later took over the Lyceum, Edinburgh with Richard Eyre as his second in command, I was the only one of the Phoenix crowd who was not invited to play a part. I later learned from the casting director that whenever Clive had suggested me for a role, Richard had argued against it, saying that he found me too physical an actor.

I suppose this antipathy could also have been based upon the time that Clive had been unable to attend rehearsals as he was up in Edinburgh, negotiating his move, and Richard had, much to the dismay of Cy, taken rehearsals. Cy was livid and said he had no intention of being directed by an assistant, and to avoid an embarrassing drama I made it clear to Richard that he could concentrate on me. Rather like cows are inclined to go mad and become quite dangerous when they are let out in the spring after being indoors all winter, Richard started to give me note after note and confused me to such an extent that I lost confidence and was never again able to do that particular scene properly!

I must admit he showed no sign of animosity towards me when, some time later, I called in to Edinburgh and, Clive being unavailable at the time, Richard took me for a drink and we got on quite well together. A tragedy and a mystery really, since he is the sort of director that I would have loved to work with, in his later years, not just because he was so successful, but also because I felt very much at ease with him and in sympathy with most of his ideas.

I did work again with Clive at Leicester before he moved to Edinburgh; but before that I played two different parts in two episodes of *Softly Softly*, a spin-off from *Z Cars* starring Stratford Johns and Frank Windsor. Although there was a policy of not using actors twice in the same series in different roles within a year of one another, I had accepted and signed the contracts before the penny had dropped. They were neither of them such gigantic roles that the public were up in arms, and I took great pleasure in trying to make them unrecognisable. I was also grateful for the time at home as Theresa's arrival meant that we now had three children, all less than three years of age!

Paul Hill, who had been at Alleyn's and the Youth Theatre with me, was Mike Croft's right-hand man at the National Youth Theatre, now housed at the Shaw Theatre in Camden. It was there that Mike and Paul ran a professional company called the Dolphin Company. In February 1966, Paul asked me to play Romeo in a production of *Romeo and Juliet* he was producing and directing for the Sunderland Empire. Despite the fact that I was much more obvious casting for Mercutio, I jumped at the chance. I still had visions of myself as a romantic juvenile lead. Jennie Linden, who had already made her name in the wonderful film of *Women in Love*, was to play Juliet and Bernard Lloyd played Mercutio; Benvolio was played by Peter Ellis, who later went on to be a regular in *The Bill* for many years. We rehearsed in London, so I stayed up in town with my brother during the three weeks' rehearsal. Romeo is probably the greatest romantic role, but I was going to change all that and make him athletic, virile and earthy. As usual I worked very hard, arriving at rehearsals an hour before my first call, as was my wont, and concentrating hard all day, even taking myself off on my own during the lunch break to prepare for the afternoon rehearsal.

Towards the end of the rehearsal period – in fact, the night before our final run-through before going north to rehearse the play into the Sunderland Empire – Paul suggested we have a night out together and, much against my better judgement, I agreed but said I would not be out late. It was a conspiracy. Paul went out of his way to make sure that I had much more to drink than was good for me and that I didn't get to bed until the wee small hours. The next morning I was in a terrible state with a gigantic headache and mammoth hangover. I was very angry with Paul, and said I felt so rotten that I wasn't going to be able to do much more than walk through the run-through and that he was not to expect anything from me. I was as good as my word; I put no effort into the performance and merely went through the actions in second gear. Paul, plus the one or two visitors that he had smuggled in, and also my Juliet, were all of the unanimous opinion that it was the best I had ever done it!

Far from being happy about this reaction, I was more than a little dismayed. I was aware of the fact that it was in all probability accurate, but how do you go into a performance trying not to put everything you have got into it? It was an important lesson to learn but, having learnt it, it was not a sudden revelation that changed my performances for all time. I did, however, take on board that the skill is to make it look easy, not make it look like hard work. This is of course more easily said than done, and is also easier when playing the lead role. It is a well-known fact that the smaller parts are the most difficult: first because you have very little with which to make a statement, and second because, when playing the lead role, most of the work is done for you by the situation and by the actors around you who are directing their performance towards telling your story for you.

This is even truer of cinema acting where the leading man frequently gives minimal if any reaction to a bomb blowing up behind him while the minor parts are expected to 'mess their pants'. This is in part to give that macho image an extra fillip; it is also because the audience themselves will subconsciously fill in the expected reaction. I don't know how true it is, but I once heard of a Russian film director who stuck an actor in a room sitting on a chair and filmed him in close-up over several hours. He then cut the close-ups into a series of happenings and the general feeling was that the actor had given a wonderful performance! I'm not so sure that I go along wholeheartedly with this, but I do always say to myself when I embark on a television, as opposed to a stage play, 'Don't act it, think it.'

In Sunderland, we played mainly to school audiences and I was to find myself at the other end of the immature schoolboy reaction to some of the incidents. I had once been told of how Robert Donat, at the Old Vic, had wooed the school-children with simplicity and quiet authority; and when one night we had some sniggering on the first Romeo and Juliet kiss, I tried myself to just stop and wait, to embarrass them into submission. This in turn put the fear of God up my Juliet who thought I had dried and kept trying to prompt me with the line. My early sins at the schools matinees at the Old Vic were coming back to haunt me.

We tried to curry favour with the local Geordies by getting together our own soccer team and issued a challenge in the local paper. Our challenge was accepted by the Sunderland FC supporters club and the game was fixed for the first Sunday morning. Since Paul Hill and myself were the only owners of cars, we arranged to meet at the theatre and ferry the team and supporters to the playing fields. In the event, Paul didn't turn up and I was left to make the various trips with the company on my own. On my last trip I passed Paul, on the beach, strolling with Jennie Linden, my Juliet, and when he turned up in the dressing room before the match, he received the full brunt of my fury as I launched a verbal attack. I really was angry, and also keyed up for the game. When I went to toss the coin in the centre of the pitch with the referee and the opposing team captain I was warned, by the referee, that if he heard me using any of the language he had overheard in my tirade to Paul, I would be off the pitch!

This was not to be the last time that the Geordies' dislike of bad language was to surprise me. One night I was winding down after the performance, in a night-club as per usual. When time was called, I found myself with a nearly full pint of beer which the waitress was attempting to take away from me. When I told her to 'piss off', she walked away and threw the tray full of glasses to the floor, thus causing a scene and attracting the attention of the bouncers who ejected me from the club, which made interesting headlines in the local paper the next morning: 'Romeo Thrown Out Of Club'.

The hardships of the social scene aside, I found Romeo a particularly energetic part to play; and in the long period of banishment before the confrontation with Paris in the tomb, I would relax in my dressing room with a, strictly rationed, bottle of Newcastle Brown Ale. I would take off my sword and belt, put my feet up on the mantle over the fireplace and prepare myself for the death scene. On one particular occasion, my mind wandered and, on hearing my cue over the tannoy, I scooted downstairs and onto the stage, discovered Paris, and issued the challenge. However, on reaching for my sword, I discovered that in my haste I had forgotten to put the sword and belt on. In desperation, I lunged from the top of a flight of stairs and grabbed the bewildered Paris by the throat, grunting in his ear to die as quickly and as realistically as possible. This difficulty over, I set about the discovery of Juliet's body only to remember, when reaching for the phial of poison with which to take my own life, that that too was in my pouch, on my belt, in my dressing room; so I mimed taking an imaginary phial from inside my doublet and hastened to my death. When Juliet awoke and set about searching for the phial to take the last few drops and join me in death, I attempted to whisper, ventriloquist fashion, and explain the situation. Jennie was quick on the uptake and was soon to join me as she fell across my inert body, dead from the non-existent bottle of poison. As the Prince of Verona brought the evening's entertainment to an end with the epilogue over the bodies of the dead lovers, the ridiculousness of the last few moments started a chuckle in my stomach that was soon picked up by Juliet, and the Prince delivered the final oration to a pair of seemingly vibrating corpses, as we shuddered with suppressed laughter.

In April 1966 I returned to the Phoenix Theatre, Leicester, for a production, again by Clive Perry, of *The Rainmaker*. I had always wanted to play a cowboy; even as a kid I remember kicking open the swing doors of the cinema as I left a Western, as if I was entering the saloon bar! I had seen Sam Wanamaker playing the lead in the West End some years earlier and thought it a wonderful play, full of comedy and pathos. I loved it. Dressed in white from head to toe and wearing a large Stetson, it really was a play for an exhibitionist.

Shortly after we had opened, Clive approached me and asked if Paddy and I would like to head a company to perform five plays in repertoire over six months. The plays were to be *The Hollow Crown*, an anthology of prose and poems about the divine right of kings, to be directed by Joan Knight; *The Taming of the Shrew* with Paddy and I playing Kate and Petruchio, directed by Clive himself; *Little Malcolm and his Struggle Against the Eunuchs* by David Halliwell, in which I was not to play the lead, but to play Wick; *Portrait of a Queen* by William Francis with Paddy as Victoria and me as Gladstone; and finally George Bernard Shaw's *Man and Superman* in which Paddy and I were to play opposite each other again, as Ann Whitefield and Jack Tanner, and once again directed by Clive.

Since Theresa, already known solely as Tessa, was still only a baby of one year old, there were many problems to be resolved before we could accept. Paddy was very reluctant to leave the children so far away for so long; and after much persuasion and bartering, the theatre rented a house for us on the outskirts of Leicester, paid us enough to hire an *au pair*, and we moved the family up to the Midlands. Our first *au pair* was a disaster and didn't last more than a week or two. It was her first job and she was homesick. She was inept and also expensive: we returned home frequently to find her on the telephone and when we got our bill, we found that she had been doing little else. She was replaced by Françoise, a French *mademoiselle* of impressive proportions who turned out to be ideal: she loved the children, proved to be very capable and stayed with us for a long while. Nevertheless, it hadn't been a good start; Paddy was very worried, and it put a lot of pressure on the beginning of the season until it all settled down. The company were an extremely pleasant bunch and included William Simons (who was a regular in *Heartbeat* for many years), Christopher Cazenove, and Robert Booth, the brother of Tony Booth, our ex-Prime Minister's father-in-law.

The Hollow Crown got the season under way, and the company started to bind together. This was followed by *The Taming of the Shrew*, which I naturally revelled in. I liked Clive's interpretation of the play as being something akin to a pantomime, and we had a great romp which the audiences seemed to enjoy. *Little Malcolm* was another romp, but I didn't enjoy it so much as I wasn't playing the lead! Roger Croucher, who had the propensity to over-salivate, played Malcolm, and when in close conversation one was generously sprayed. I found this all a little unpleasant to take and played most of my scenes with him facing in the opposite direction. If I am honest, I think I overreacted a little out of jealousy, as I wanted to play his part. When the play had first been put on in the West End, by the Michael Codron management, I had been suggested for the role, but my agent said he had been told that I was too old.

Paddy was magnificent in *Portrait of a Queen* and I struggled with Gladstone, not unnaturally. I was also struggling with John Tanner in *Man and Superman* and it was obvious in rehearsals that Clive was disappointed and worried about my portrayal. The fact that I didn't really feel at home in the part had the effect of making it very difficult to learn the lines and I would spend all of my spare time, when not in rehearsal, wandering in the fields near the home we had rented, declaiming to the sheep and cows and trying to get a handle on the part. To say that it suddenly came to me would be arrogant; but I suddenly noticed a change in Clive's attitude towards me, and that gave me the confidence to think I was getting closer.

I had left it to the last minute, however, and it wasn't until the dress rehearsal that I finally had any idea of where I was going. In performance, I felt that I was growing with each repetition and discovering nightly more and more about the part. I think a lot of this has to do with Shaw, whose writing I had not really appreciated until I came to play in front of an audience, when it was they that showed me what gems there were in the text and made each night a joyous voyage of discovery. I think that part in that play stretched me more than any other up until then, and it had been quite a painful and unsettling journey. It was also the first part of a lesson that I was to learn the rest of later.

The season was a great success: the plays had been well chosen, well directed and the company had performed them well. The audience response too had been very encouraging and we had played to good houses. The local critic, however, had been less than exuberant in his reports and this had been really depressing and unhelpful. At the end of the season, the theatre supporters organised a ball for the company, supporters and local dignitaries. At one point Paddy was asked to dance by the critic, whom I had been consciously ignoring all night; when she returned to our table with him, saying that he wanted to be introduced to me, I said, 'No, thank you,' and walked away. He protested that he had always given me a personal good notice; which indeed he had, but the overall tenor of his criticisms was negative and unhelpful. At one point, he had even had the temerity to criticise the writing of George Bernard Shaw, who had become my new hero. I felt as if I had discovered him, and I objected to a provincial hack having such disrespect, and arrogance.

During a lean spell work-wise, I received a call from Peter Yates who had directed *One Way Pendulum*, asking me to come to London to meet Stanley Baker. They were making a film based on the story of the Great Train Robbery and Peter wanted me for a part, but Stanley had casting approval and wanted to meet me before anything was settled. This was to be quite a big number and I set off to London, very excited, not only at the prospect of a decent part in a decent film but also about meeting Stanley Baker who was at that time a film actor of international standing. I was greeted by Peter's secretary and asked to wait, which I did for what seemed an eternity but was in all probability no more than three quarters of an hour. Finally, Stanley Baker emerged from the office with Peter, putting on his overcoat; as he passed me on his way out, he gave Peter some sort of nod and left the building. Peter was delightful and explained that Stanley had to catch a plane to the US and that the nod had agreed my casting; we were back working together. He gave me a script to read and told me to telephone him that night if I wanted the part.

I was to play the driver of the getaway car for the robbery that was to provide the finance for the train heist; a cheeky cockney who took great delight in the thrillingly dangerous car chase, chuckling with glee as the rest of the gang were terrified at the wild driving through the streets of London. I told Peter there was no need for me to read the script; I accepted the part and set off back to Hastings to read the script and take Paddy out for a celebratory dinner. On our return home later that night, Françoise, the *au pair*, told me that Peter had telephoned and I was to return the call, no matter how late the hour. It took some time as the line seemed to be permanently engaged, but when I did eventually get through Peter was extremely distraught and told me that Joseph Levine, who was financing the picture, had already promised the part to Clinton Greyn, my old classmate from RADA! Apparently, Clinton had been under contract to do another film which had been cancelled, and as they had to honour the contract he was being given 'my part'. Peter couldn't have been nicer or more apologetic and he offered me another part as one of the train robbers, not such a juicy, eye-catching role but it was the best he could do; he understood my disappointment and said he didn't expect me to answer straight away, he would keep the part open for me until the last minute.

I was indeed gutted and my immediate reaction was to want nothing to do with the picture; but later, when I had time to calm down, get over the dis-appointment and realise that nothing else was on offer, I accepted the part of what was supposed to be 'The Weasel', one of the gang of robbers led by Stanley Baker. We were in fact about fifteen in number and most, apart from Frank Finlay and Barry Foster, had smallish unidentifiable roles, made all the more insignificant as we spent most of the time wearing balaclava helmets that we had to keep rolled down; only Stanley was allowed to continually reveal his identity!

We filmed in and around the Bury St Edmunds area and, as with all big films, for the small-part actors there was a lot of waiting around and hours and hours of not being used. The shooting took place mostly at night; and although there was a lovely little country pub not more than half a mile from the location, we were 'confined to barracks' and made to wait on standby in dreary caravans in the middle of the fields. One night, however, Barry Foster and I slipped away for a 'swift half'; on our return, finding that we had not been missed, we worked out a nice little routine, with safety back-ups, that considerably improved the dreary schedule. We ended up getting ourselves on night standby as often as possible.

8

1967 to 1970 • *Submarine X-1* • James Caan •
The Borderers • Michael Gambon • Glasgow •
K. D. Dufford • Grafton Square

THERE FOLLOWED ANOTHER run of television, at the rate of one a month for the next seven months. 1966 finished with a play in the *Seven Deadly Virtues* series: 'The Whole Truth' by John Bowen, directed by James Ormerod for Rediffusion. I didn't have much of a part again, and cannot remember anything about it except that, when we were sitting in the bar afterwards, James Ormerod was very derogatory about my performance. Since the recording was now in the can and since he had said nothing to me in the way of direction during the rehearsals, I was taken aback and very upset, slinking home to Hastings with my tail between my legs. One minute you're up and the next you're down!

After that, it was back to the BBC in an episode of *Champion House*, starring Edward Chapman and Virginia Stride (the wife of my old schoolmate Johnny Stride), and directed by Prue Fitzgerald. It was the first time I had worked with Prue, but would turn out to be by no means the last. Just a few weeks later she called me for another TV role; I was surprised to be working with her again so soon, and even more surprised when I learnt that the part was a gay yachtsman, in an episode of *The Revenue Men* to be rehearsed and recorded in Glasgow. I loved the idea of the challenge. Also in the cast was Isobel Black, whom I hadn't seen for some time and who was still as beautiful as ever. Since Isobel was of Scottish descent, she took great pride in showing me around Edinburgh when not called for rehearsals. She really did love that town and was a great guide.

It was in Edinburgh one evening that we ended up at the house of the Scottish actor John Cairney, who had such a 'thing' about Robert Burns that he seemed to think he was his reincarnation, or at least he did then. He started the proceedings with some recitations from Burns; this was taken up by others and the whole thing developed into a sort of Victorian *soirée* with everybody doing their somewhat upmarket party-piece. As the contributions went slowly around the room, I was horrified at the thought that it was obviously going to come to my turn and I was sadly ill equipped in such company. I considered the possibilities of becoming sick, of refusing point blank or just running from the room. Being something of a coward in this respect, I ended up singing 'Maybe It's Because I'm a Londoner' which was a poor contribution since I have never had much of a singing voice (when at infant school in Wales I was asked to just mime in the choral singing and not to vocalise!). I couldn't get out of there fast enough!

It is a strange coincidence that my next director, the following month, was James Gatward who later married Isobel. This was to play in a rather classy series called *The Troubleshooters*, starring Robert Hardy, whom I hadn't seen since *Henry V*, and Patrick Wymark, the almost permanent character actor with the RSC. Patrick and his wife, the writer Olwen Wymark, were great friends of Paddy's sister Maureen, and we had previously stayed with them at Stratford when visiting to see O'Toole's *Taming of the Shrew*.

This was followed by further televisions, starting with an episode of another series for Rediffusion, called *The Gamblers* and directed by Quentin Lawrence, fondly referred to as 'Q'. It wasn't much of a part, but I was in no position to pick and choose; in general at this time I just accepted whatever was offered. My ambition and arrogance were being tempered, but it still hurt. Nor did I have much of a part in my next television, an episode of *The Expert* with Marius Goring playing the lead role and directed by his partner, who was fast becoming my favourite director, or at any rate my most faithful: Prue Fitzgerald. In it, I played a young solicitor who was advising the lovely Rachel Kempson, a lady that I found impressively elegant and dignified. Then came an episode of *Detective*, directed by Anthea Browne-Wilkinson, and again I had very little to do.

It was about this time that I was called for the strangest of auditions. I was asked to go to Manor Place swimming baths, with my swimming costume, for an audition for a Mirisch Brothers film. It seemed that every young actor in London was there. For the first round we were required to swim one length of the pool, in batches of six. We were assured that this was not to take the form of a race: it was just to get an idea of our swimming style and ability. Nobody took much notice of that – it was a race! Luckily swimming had been one of my sports and I had represented the school at swimming and diving. Others were not so lucky; indeed, some just jumped in at the deep end with little or no hope of managing a full length and had to be fished out by the stuntmen who were acting as lifeguards.

Having survived the knockout first round, the next test was to jump in at the deep end and sit on the bottom for as long as possible, the idea being to see who could hold their breath the longest. Again, this was done in groups of six, and we were told that it was not a competition; and again, nobody believed this, and as I sat on the bottom of the pool I was aware that everybody was watching everybody else and waiting so as not to be the first to ascend. Seeing the situation, I started to go up and, as I moved, I saw at least two go to follow, at which point I settled again and sat it out to be the last. For the next round we were shown how to use breathing apparatus and had to swim a length under water, with bottles of air strapped to our backs, and take out and replace the mouthpiece while submerged; it was getting serious!

Alexis Kanner, a young French-Canadian actor who had recently made a name for himself playing Hamlet in a production where Hamlet spent most of his time hanging from a rope, and had also gained himself a reputation for being full of his own self-importance, at this point started to make a fuss about the amount of time this was taking and started to push to get himself at the top of the queue in order that he could get away for some important engagement that he had. I think there was also a touch of making sure that he was noticed, and stuck out from the crowd, which was a fairly well-known gambit. In this instance, however, it backfired on him as the stuntmen took an instant dislike to him, and he was provided with just one bottle and insufficient weight to take him to the bottom of the pool. He swam his length rather ridiculously with his flippered feet on the surface and his head about one metre below! We didn't see him again.

The film was to be *Submarine X-1* starring James Caan and directed by the American director, Billy Graham. The subject was the training of special teams of four-man submarine crews to go into a German port, cut their way through the defensive netting surrounding the ships and blow up the Germans' prize vessel. Although the top-secret venture proves terminal for all but one team, the mission is a success. It wasn't much of a script; it was rumoured that James Caan was under contract to do three films a year and had turned down so many scripts that he had been forced to accept this one. The whole thing was to be filmed on and around the Loch Ness area, and we were to be based in Inverness.

We were all being trained in the basics of scuba diving, and for the first few days did little in the way of filming but a lot in the way of swimming and diving in Loch Ness. The worst part was getting into and out of the drysuits that we were required to wear. Unlike the more modern wetsuits, the drysuits were one-piece rubber suits that could be worn over clothing, and were so tight that they were waterproof; by their very nature they were uncomfortable to wear and difficult to get on and off. There was considerable uproar when we had been sent off on second location to take instruction and were left all day without any provisions, in those suits and in the heat of the day. We were also going out socialising at night under the impression that we were not called for the next day, and waking up to find that a call-sheet had been pushed under the door in the night and we were required to work, having not been given time to prepare, and in many cases in no fit state to appear before a camera!

We were beginning to get very stroppy about the way we were being treated and a decision was made to approach the management and complain. We were demanding missed break payments, proper warning of daily calls, and payment for overtime. When I say 'we' were demanding, I should say 'I thought we' were demanding, because when I went to the administration caravan to complain, I found I was on my own! I then learnt a valuable lesson: never volunteer to be a spokesman – a lesson that I was to forget from time to time.

James Caan proved to be a very approachable star and, since he didn't seem to be taking the film too seriously, was happy to mix in with the rest of us, frequently joining us for our nights out on the town. Billy Graham, the director, likewise had a very laid-back attitude towards the film; nobody seemed at all dedicated or driven to create something special. That aside, we were a fairly happy band of actors and there were many laughs. It was also fascinating to learn scuba diving, especially in Loch Ness where the water is so black below the surface that it is said to be easy to get disoriented: with no light source from above, you can be swimming deeper thinking you are going towards the surface. There was one major scare when we were working from a raft and diving quite deep, without bottles, as a breath-holding exercise. On one take, an actor didn't resurface; after some considerable wait, things went very quiet, then there was a panic and two stuntmen were dispatched to go down and fetch him up. It turned out that he had surfaced beneath the raft and was alright, although considerably shaken!

A lasting memory was a day-off drive up through the lochs with Paul Young and Carl Rigg in Paul's little two-seater sports car, stopping off from time to time to wonder at the magnificent scenery; a trip that I have long promised myself to repeat, but next time not folded up in the back of an Austin Healey Sprite. My friendship with Carl extended long after the completion of filming and I would regularly thereafter stay with him in London whenever I was up in town for a job or an interview. He had a flatshare with Sandy Scott, a young trainee doctor from the Middlesex Hospital, who had a magnificent if somewhat run-down three-bedroom apartment above the bank opposite the George, the pub frequented by the BBC radio elite in Portland Place. It was like the student days that I had missed because I lived at home, and I enjoyed my frequent visits when I would join them at the George and simply cross the road and go upstairs to bed.

In contrast to *Submarine X-1*, my next job, which was an episode of *The Saint*, was again just a day or two on location, and I didn't get too much involved. I was playing an assistant detective with Ivor Dean playing the long-suffering Chief Inspector Teal. At one point we were to be discovered in a wood trussed up and tied to a tree in our underwear, a scene that was filmed somewhere in Sherwood Forest. Ivor and I had finished our contribution to the scene and had to wait whilst the rest of the scene was shot in that set-up; so we just sat down, out of earshot of the filming, and chatted while we waited. Some time must have passed before we became aware of the silence and stillness around us and, on looking around, discovered that we were on our own: the scene had been finished, and we had been left behind as the crew shot off to the next location. We had no idea where we were and Ivor seemed particularly unfazed, as if it was happening to him all the time. As soon as they got to the point where we were required on the next location, they discovered our absence and drove back for us, but I dread to think what would have happened if we hadn't been needed!

1968 began with another television for Rediffusion in an episode of *Sanctuary*, a series set in a nunnery, before what was to prove a traumatic production of Henry James' *The Outcry* at the Arts Theatre, London. *The Outcry* couldn't have started more disastrously. It was directed by Campbell Allen, who had been my voice production teacher at RADA, and who had approached me to play the part by telephoning me direct; I had said yes, I was interested, but insisted that he should contact my agent. It wasn't until I was already in rehearsal for *Sanctuary* that he called me back with a date for the start of rehearsals which overlapped by one week. When he learnt that I was unavailable, he went bananas; I thought he was going to cry! He was using his own money to mount this production and he accused me of all sorts of treachery and unprofessional behaviour; but when he had calmed down, I suggested a compromise. I told him that I had to honour my contract with Rediffusion but that, if I rehearsed with him in the evenings and whenever I was not wanted for *Sanctuary*, I could perhaps do both. Of course, he had to persuade the other actors, and they weren't at all happy, but it was agreed. I had quite a few scenes with Anna Barry (the daughter of Judith Gick, who had been my mime teacher at RADA), and so she was the most affected by the arrangement. After the initial and natural reaction of 'who the hell does he think he is', we got on very well and she helped to take the pressure off the rest of the cast by doing most of the out-of-hours work with me.

That, however, was just the start. I don't know if it was because he still thought of me as a student, or if he was intent on making this the performance of my life and felt that confrontation was the best way to inspire me, but Campbell proved to be a very aggravating director. We rehearsed in the rooms above the bar in a Soho pub; and, after one particular flare-up, I remember walking out of rehearsal and sitting in the bar below with George Coulouris telling me that I had usurped his position as the most difficult actor. As an emotional Greek, it was usually his province to flare up and walk out of rehearsals!

Part of my frustration was with poor old Murray Cash, who was married to the Canadian comedienne-cum-actress Libby Morris and was in essence a disc jockey. Again, as with Bryan Mosley and others before, it was almost a chemical reaction; I found acting with him like wading through porridge and couldn't understand, not only how he got the job, but why Campbell wasn't directing him in the way that he was directing me! I could see so much wrong around me; how could Campbell sit watching the rehearsals and not do something?

When we got into the theatre itself for the technical rehearsal, I could see that poor old Campbell was in love with the thought of being a director and was just sitting and enjoying the situation instead of concentrating on the play and the interpretations. I think he was even enjoying the drama of the outbursts as being part and parcel of true temperamental artistic creation. At the end of the dress rehearsal, he came into my dressing room and started to give me such insensitive and negative notes that I kicked him out and banned him from ever coming to me just before a show.

The production wasn't a success. For one thing, it wasn't a good choice of play at that time and we played to small houses, which was a disaster for poor old Campbell and I genuinely felt sorry for him despite our conflict. Usually actors are allowed a certain number of complimentary tickets, dependent on the generosity of the management. After having my allowance of two for the first night, I enquired at the box office if I could have any more and was told that there were to be no more 'comps'. Later that night when I was drinking after the show in the pub next door, a porter from Covent Garden, which was still a vegetable market at that time, offered me as many tickets as I wanted; he had a friend in the box office!

It would appear that I was 'flavour of the month' with Prue Fitzgerald who next employed me to play in a double episode of *The Expert*, which starred her long-term partner Marius Goring. Once again, she showed a confidence in my ability as a character actor (or was it a comment on my sexuality?) by casting me as the very 'poofy' partner of Anthony Valentine, who played the more masculine of the homosexual relationship. My costume and make-up were outrageous: I had my hair bleached blond and bouffant, I wore flowery scarves and rings and had a beauty spot. I also adopted a somewhat mincing gait and effete speech.

We filmed in Warwickshire, and after a day on Warwick station where I chatted up the stationmaster, in character, and nearly got the production kicked off the station, Prue and the crew decided to get their own back. The next day was market day in Warwick and we were staying at a hotel in the main street. After an early morning make-up call followed by breakfast I was told that I would not be needed for the first shot, so I was to stay and have coffee and they would send a car for me when I was needed. I sat in a quiet corner with my bouffant hair, scarves, rings and beauty spot, until the receptionist came to inform me that there was a telephone call for me. It was the first assistant to say that they had to change the schedule and I was now needed urgently; there was no car at the moment but they were just around the corner. I was to turn right out of the hotel, up the high street to the next traffic lights and then turn left.

Without thinking, I rang off and set out on the journey, becoming more and more aware of the fact that it was a busy crowded street and I was attracting a lot of attention in my outlandish get-up. I walked as butchly as I knew how; and I arrived at the traffic lights to find the entire crew laughing, pointing and whistling at me. The whole thing was a set-up!

Prue was always great fun to work with and was much loved by her crews. The only time I saw the smile wiped off her face was when I was riding pillion on the motorbike driven in the action by Anthony Valentine, who was a great motorbike fanatic; we overturned as we were cornering and my calf was badly burnt on the exhaust. Prue was distraught.

My next job was to return to Scotland again for an episode of *The Borderers*, directed by James Gatward who was now married to Isobel Black. I hadn't seen Isobel since we had starred together in a pilot for a proposed new series for ATV that never saw the light of day. Called *Scandal*, it was set in the production offices of a magazine. We rehearsed and recorded the pilot in the Teddington studios; at the end of the first week I asked if the Saturday rehearsal was for all day, or just the morning, as I was playing football in the afternoon if I had the time off. I was let off for the afternoon, and on coming in to work on the Monday morning I noticed a change in attitude towards me. It transpired that Charmian Eyre had been listening to her car radio on Saturday afternoon, on which there happened to be a commentary on the Leicester City game. At that time there was a winger playing for City called Trevor Farrington and he had had a great game, and was frequently referred to as just 'Farrington' during the commentary. Charmian had shared her information with the rest of the company and they were of the opinion that I was very cool and laid back about playing for a first-division side in my spare time!

It is a great pity that the series didn't get made; I would have got every Saturday afternoon off after that. The regular leads were to be Andrew Faulds (who later became a Labour Member of Parliament), Charmian Eyre, John Standing, and Isobel, with me as a young cub reporter on a Vespa. They had even bought the Vespa and my wardrobe; we had recorded the pilot; and a few days before we were due to start in earnest the director, Guy Verney, phoned me to say that they had pulled the plug on it and the dream was over!

As I say, I hadn't seen Isobel since that time, nor had I heard about her being with James. They invited me back to their cottage for lunch one day during the filming of *The Borderers*, and I was pleased to see that they were obviously very happy and well suited to each other.

The series, starring Michael Gambon, was about medieval border skirmishes and inter-clan conflicts, and involved horse riding and sword fights; I found my old mate Derek Ware, the accident-prone stuntman from *An Age of Kings*, was in charge of the stunts. He was also appearing as the odd soldier or horseman. In one particular sequence, he and I arrived on horseback, dismounted, and I left him to hold the horses' heads as I crawled on my stomach to lie between two bushes where I took aim with my pistol and fired. The arrival was filmed in long shot and then the camera was repositioned to cover me in close-up as I took aim and fired; Derek was in the background, holding the horses. After a couple of run-throughs without firing, we went for the 'take' and the pistol was loaded. All went well until I pulled the trigger, whereupon the horses, alarmed at the noise of the shot, reared up and took Derek with them. The final shot was of me in the foreground and two feet dangling in top of frame!

In conversation with one of the more conventional stuntmen, I learnt that not only were they all very fond of Derek, they also admired him greatly. As he explained to me, 'He's not an athlete, nor is he a tough guy; he can't stand horses and is in fact frightened of them. For him to do a stunt involves not only facing the danger of the stunt, but also overcoming his own fears and inadequacies. He's got more guts than most.'

I had quite a bit of time off between scenes and, being back in Glasgow, not unnaturally I found myself frequently in the BBC Club, where I was inclined to drink too much and too late. One morning, after a heavy session the previous evening which may have involved some singing on Queen Elizabeth Bridge, I awoke to find that I had lost my voice! I was due, that afternoon, to film a scene with admittedly only one line of dialogue, but I was still worried and decided not to tell anybody of my plight but to remain silent until I had to utter and then to pray for divine inspiration, or a cure.

I managed to get through the first part of the day without speaking, and came to my big moment. I listened intently to the instructions for the shot and nodded my understanding. I was to be picked up in the distance, approaching in haste on horseback; I would come closer and closer, riding like mad, to arrive in front of Michael Gambon and, in a commanding voice, demand that he release my brother (played by Alex Norton) from captivity. We were to go for a take straight away and I disappeared into the distance. On 'action' I set off at a gallop, appeared over the skyline and, somewhat like Omar Sharif in *Lawrence of Arabia*, got closer and closer until, arriving at Michael Gambon, I squeaked at him like Minnie Mouse, 'Gi' 'im tae us, Gavin!' He fell off his horse with laughter.

The situation was not all that amusing, though, because James Gatward had hired a Transatlantic crane (I think that's what it was called) for just a few days. It was a camera on a tall hoist that could get up above the action and look down; it was very expensive and the time allowance for its use was rationed. I was sent back to my digs to see the doctor and, after a consultation, it was decided to keep me there for a week and see if my voice returned.

In the event, my voice did come back; but the schedule was too tight to fit me in again and it was decided to shoot the scene in London during the rehearsal period. The usual routine at that time was to film all the exterior scenes and then rehearse the studio stuff and shoot for two days in the studio. This could throw up a number of problems as one often had to make a decision about character or costume which, on reflection and after rehearsal, one would have done otherwise. In this particular case, the problem was somewhat different; the bare trees of the Scottish borders became lush and verdant when the rest of the filmed insert was completed in Hampshire! I don't think Jimmy Gatward ever forgave me; I never saw him again, or Isobel!

I did, however, see Mike Gambon again. He was living in Forest Hill, not far from where Paddy and I had bought our first house. I had at some time boasted that I was born and bred in nearby Peckham, and Mike had expressed an interest in being shown around; so he and I, accompanied by big Iain Cuthbertson who had also been in *The Borderers*, set off one evening on a most entertaining pub crawl around the district. Mike has got the most expressive hands: I had noticed his use of them in rehearsals, when he had me in fits of laughter counting on his fingers to quite irrelevant dialogue. They were mesmeric, and I don't know how we got round to it but he started to mime the careers of well-known actors, with his fingers! It's almost impossible to explain, but it was brilliantly imaginative as he made his fingers dance, stumble, limp, skip, and run across the tabletop. We have often promised to repeat that night and whenever I happen to meet up with him he says, 'When are we going to do it again?'

This brings up a major problem that I have with friendship in the acting profession. In one respect, it is like one big family. When you work with somebody, it can be for just a few days on a film to perhaps a year or so in a long run or settled company. In general, however, I have found that with televisions and theatre plays, three to six weeks is a pretty fair average to take in rehearsal and performance. During that relatively short time, you sometimes have to get to know each other very closely, as you might be playing husband and wife, brother, lover or parent. Consequently there is a period of concentrated and intense learning about each other, and intimate relations are struck up at great speed. The play over, you all go your separate ways and may not meet again for some months or even years, but that intimacy is usually still there when you do meet up again. I cannot count the number of actors that I would class as my friends and yet haven't seen for some years.

It tends to make one feel that there is a degree of hypocrisy, which sometimes is undoubtedly so, but in other cases could not be further from the truth. There are of course those who feed off these meetings to insinuate themselves into the lives of the established or famous actor, for kudos or personal gain, and therein lies my problem. There have been a number of really close friends, like Johnny Stride, Albert Finney and Anthony Hopkins, and Mike Williams and Michael Gambon who felt like much more than just chance acquaintances, but who, on reaching a certain status, have disappeared from 'the Christmas card list'. To an extent in these cases I am partly to blame, in that I have made no effort myself. When I occasionally met up with Dame Judi, she would say, 'Why don't you give Mike a ring?' However, I have always felt that once they had attained the position that they had, it was more for them to phone me.

Whenever our paths do cross there is still a semblance of that friendship. I would sometimes meet up with Mike after seeing him perform at the National, and he was always delightful. When I was desperate to get to see Albert Finney's performance in *Art*, I left a message for him at the stage door and he not only phoned me back, but fixed tickets too; they were like gold dust. I have worked with Anthony Hopkins since those early Phoenix days, and he was needless to say quite wonderful. He took me to lunch during the filming of *A Married Man* and despite being unable to drink himself because of his well-publicised problem, he insisted that I should have wine with my meal. Sadly, however, when I recently took a holiday in California, I learnt that I would be staying very close to where he had just bought a house and I wrote to him via his agent suggesting that we could meet, and I got no reply. Of course, his agent could have failed to pass the letter on! I believe it was Eddie Judd who, when asked what it was like to be a star, replied: 'Very lonely!' Although he was sent up for this chance remark, there is a great deal of truth in it.

Towards the end of 1968 came an appearance in *Boy Meets Girl* for the BBC and an episode of *Crime Busters* for ATV. I also returned to *Coronation Street* for four weeks at Christmas, which gave us a bit of money for the festive season. I was becoming more than a little fed up with the size, or lack of size, of the parts I was getting on television; so I was more than relieved when I was offered a wonderful leading part in the theatre: as the detective, DS Johnson, in John Hopkins' *This Story of Yours*, with Rachel Herbert, John Rees and Brendan Barry and directed by Claude Whatham at the Citizen's Theatre, Glasgow.

We were in the little studio theatre, called the Close; meanwhile, in the main house, they were preparing for Adam Faith in *Billy Liar*. What a far cry that was from the particularly harrowing piece that we were doing. The play is in three acts, which rather cleverly go backwards. In the first scene, Detective Sergeant Johnson comes home drunk, obviously under some considerable stress, and has a violent and physical row with his wife. The second scene is a two-hander with his boss who is investigating the accusation that he beat up a prisoner; and the final act is the scene with the prisoner who is suspected of indecent assault, where the policeman makes an upsetting discovery about his own sexuality.

It really was a brilliant piece, but so disturbing that I had difficulty in learning the long speech in the first act where he describes the list of revolting duties that he is often called upon to perform; I found the speech so upsetting that my mind refused for a long time to take it in, and I also had difficulty sleeping. Claude Whatham, despite many requests by me to rehearse the end of the play, didn't touch the third act until the last moment, thus augmenting my insecurity. I found this exceedingly unsettling, in fact terrifying!

When everything was over, Claude admitted to me that he had deliberately put me on edge in this way to keep me working at the part, not settling on a performance until the last moment. I must say that, uncomfortable as I found it, it seemed to work and I was as happy as I have ever been with a performance. I don't want to give the impression that I was in the habit of feeling satisfied with my performances; I hope I was always striving to improve night after night, but I must say the rehearsal period had always seemed to me the process whereby one strove to make oneself comfortable and sure of what one was doing. Working with Claude taught me to live a little more dangerously, and in so doing I think helped me to improve as an actor.

Claude's intensive directing paid off: the play was a tremendous success in the little Close Theatre and had a powerful effect on the audience. At one early per-formance as I made my exit at the end of the first act after the long upsetting speech about the duties and sights seen as a police officer, I came across a young man being sick at the back of the bank of seats, so disturbed was he by the horror of the speech. That speech also had a long-term effect on me, and made me appreciate what a terrifyingly difficult and unpleasant job it is; I would advise anybody tempted to criticise our policemen to read that speech.

That was in March and April of 1969, and by now it appeared that television was drying up for me; I wasn't even getting offered the small parts. Perhaps it was that I had already appeared in most of the possible series. In any event, although I did much prefer the theatre, it didn't pay very well and I needed to earn more than I was doing. I even did a commercial, something I had sworn never to do. Attitudes were very different at that time; it was considered to be a retrograde step for an actor to appear in a commercial, almost like saying that he couldn't get a proper acting job. However, Brian de Salvo, who had become a close friend after the article that he wrote about me for *The Stage* and our abortive attempt to write a series together, was now producing commercials in Ireland and he sent for me to do a Worthington commercial. Since it wasn't to be shown in England I felt able to accept. Besides, I needed the money!

I flew to Dublin where I was met from the airport and taken to the location where Brian was shooting another Worthington commercial with Mark Kingston, who was an old soccer-playing chum. I arrived on set to find that they were about to film the close-up of the empty beer-glass, the contents having just been drunk. Apparently the 'cling', which is the term used by the trade to describe the way the froth sticks to the inside of the empty glass, was very important; and in order to get the authentic just-drunk look, I was volunteered, by Brian, to down a pint of Worthington on the cue for action. Needless to say, the shot was so important that it couldn't be done in one take… Some considerable number of pints later, they called a wrap and invited me to join them for a drink in the nearby pub!

Although I appeared to be working regularly, I seemed to be always short of money and was in dire need of regular well-paid employment. However, when David Halliwell offered me the lead in a play, I only had to read it to know that I couldn't turn it down, in spite of the fact that the money was terrible. It had the longest title I have ever heard of: *K. D. Dufford Hears K. D. Dufford Ask K. D. Dufford How K. D. Dufford'll Make K. D. Dufford*. Needless to say, the title got shortened to just *K. D. Dufford*.

It was the most remarkable play, which worked on many levels and was well ahead of its time. The dialogue was brilliant and a joy to learn and say; there were strong echoes of *Mein Kampf* in the conception, and I was urged to read as much as I could about Hitler. The play deals with a young man, a complete nonentity, who wants to make his name live forever. Since he can't do it as a hero, he decides to embark on committing an horrendous crime that will gain him the notoriety he so craves. Together with an accomplice, he kidnaps and murders a young girl and videos the whole process. On the surface, not exactly everybody's idea of a good night out! In reality, though, it was very funny as each scene was played five times from different viewpoints: first the view of K. D. Dufford, who saw himself as a hero; next the view of his sidekick, played by Tim Preece, who saw himself as the hero; then the father of the young girl who saw them both as a couple of clowns; then the mother who saw the whole thing in romantic slow motion; and lastly the media who take it and intellectualise and distort it.

In order to mount the production Halliwell had set up his own company called 'Quipu', and it was played in the theatre at LAMDA (London Academy of Music and Dramatic Art) in Earls Court. The hope was, of course, that it would be picked up and transferred into the West End. It had a large cast and was quite complicated set-wise so it didn't lend itself to touring or provincial rep, and unfortunately did not grab the imagination of a London management; so a wonderful play, although published, as far as I know has never been seen again. Nor did David Halliwell ever reach the heights that I believed he was capable of.

His *Little Malcolm and His Struggle Against the Eunuchs* was of course a great success and deservedly so, but it is disappointing that a writer with his ear for dialogue and the rhythms of speech plus his observation of the ridiculous didn't produce more than he did before his untimely death in 2006. He did write a number of one-act plays that I both acted in and directed at later times as I have always been something of a champion of his talent.

I was getting the odd job doing voice-overs, which can be quite lucrative, but I was not on the 'big boys' network. I had done a commentary for Hal Burton on a programme about Chopin and George Sand, a voice-over for Mars, and a number of commentaries on corporate videos. I had also played in corporate videos, which were good fun as they were always done at great speed and I enjoyed the pressure of getting it right in one go; but these were just means to keep my head above water.

Although still based in Ireland, Brian de Salvo was now also producing commercials on the Continent. I received a call from him, not only out of the blue but also out of the country, asking if I would get the next flight to Madrid to join him for one week for a Spanish commercial. The job turned out to be a peach. I was accommodated in a magnificent five-star hotel, and told that I had four days alone to learn the monologue and then two days in the studio. They hadn't even asked if I could speak Spanish, and assumed that I would need that time to learn it phonetically. Although my 'O' level Spanish was rusty, it didn't take me long and I had a wonderful time wandering around the capital. In those days, British actors and crews were considerably ahead of their European colleagues where the technicalities of television were concerned; when we came to shoot the commercial in the studio, I found the process exceedingly simple and managed to get the whole thing 'in the can' on the first morning, giving the rest of the crew a day and a half off. I was applauded from the set.

Next I was surprised to find myself in a Yorkshire Television series called *Parkin's Patch*, starring John Flanagan, and directed by Mike Apted. I had known John from Granada, where I had played football a few times with him; Mike had been a director on *Coronation Street*, and I had felt that he didn't like me. His attitude towards me during rehearsals did nothing to make me change that view: I found that he almost ignored me! Luckily, Jo Rowbottom, who was playing my wife, felt that he was pretty dismissive of her too, so we kept each other company; but it wasn't a job that I look back on with any fondness, compounded by the fact that Mike Apted has gone on to make quite a name for himself as a film maker.

1969 finished with four televisions at the rate of one a month. I had a small part in 'There is Also Tomorrow', an episode of BBC TV's *Wednesday Play* series; followed by another small part, this time in an *Armchair Theatre* called 'The

Prime Minister's Daughter', written by the Labour politician Maurice Edelman. I played an MP, the boyfriend of the Prime Minister's daughter, played by Sarah Badel. This was for Thames TV and was recorded at Teddington. On the final day of recording, I finished my last scene, which was set in the House of Commons, and after getting clearance from the floor manager I retired to my dressing room and showered, changed and went up to the club bar to await the rest of the cast, as we had all arranged to meet up for a farewell drink. Since they only had a couple of shots left to finish the scene, I was surprised by the length of time I sat up there waiting for them. When they did eventually come into the bar they expressed considerable surprise to find me sitting there. Apparently, they had been forced to take some extra shots of the House and had been looking for me and calling for me over the tannoy; getting no response, they had assumed that I had gone home. I can only surmise that I was in the process of putting my gear in the car before going to the club and didn't hear the message. The end result was that there are shots of the House of Commons where I appear, then miraculously disappear, before reappearing again as if by magic. It was too late to do anything about it, but I still come out in a cold sweat thinking about it, even though I had got clearance from the floor manager and that exonerated me.

Paddy and I were not too happy with the standard of primary-school education in Hastings and this, coupled with the fact that I was feeling a bit left behind by the profession, determined us to move back to London. I started to look in the south of the city, where my roots were, and eventually found a four-storey house in Grafton Square, Clapham. The square was extremely run down and was owned by a Mr Liebenthal, a very orthodox and wealthy Jew. The houses were being gradually emptied of their tenants and sold off one by one. This process had only just started and the square was in dire need of a facial; there was a lot of work to be done, but the prospects were that the square would eventually become very fashionable. We made an offer for a dilapidated house that had sitting tenants in the basement flat although the floors above were virtually derelict. The offer was accepted but we had to wait until the basement became vacant.

In the meantime I was offered *The Little Hut*, directed by Jeremy Burnham and with his wife Veronica Strong and Dermot Walsh, who had been a film star in the fifties, completing the cast. We were to rehearse in London and play in Westcliffe. Originally a French play by André Roussin, it had been adapted by Nancy Mitford. Three people – two male, one female – are shipwrecked on a desert island and set about surviving as comfortably as they can, and sharing those comforts, including the woman. A comedy with great possibilities for a creative imagination of the Flintstones variety, this is a play that I have often thought worth revisiting with another adaptation; but despite many efforts, I have been unable to get hold of the original French version. Our production, although fun to do, was not as successful as it might have been. I put that down mainly to the fact that Dermot, although he had been a handsome film star, was unable to do comedy. He just wasn't funny, and the play can come across as a rather nasty little piece if it's not funny. It had been made into a film with David Niven, Ava Gardner and Cary Grant; although it was quite successful, I still think it was better suited to the theatre.

Also not very funny at that time was the way we were treated by Mr Liebenthal and his company. After many weeks of waiting for the basement flat to be vacated, we were left in the situation where we had sold our house in Hastings and were due to move out. I even went to visit the residents in the basement to see what the problem was, and discovered that they were haggling about the amount of money that Liebenthal was offering to rehouse them. I must say I was very much on their side. The company were making huge profits and could well afford to be more generous to the tenants.

I told the tenants how much I had agreed to pay for the house and, armed with this information, they firmed their stand. Unfortunately they must have told Liebenthal because, when they did move, he said he was putting the house back on the market and raising the price from £16,000 to £26,000. We were caught in a cleft stick; there was nothing I could do but agree to the higher price, and immediately set about organising a return to *Coronation Street* in order to pay not only for the increase in purchase price, but also to cover the costs of renovation.

There was still a gap between sale and purchase, and Paddy had to move into digs in Wandsworth with the three children whilst I was commuting at weekends from Manchester. Paddy was on the verge of a breakdown; it wasn't an easy time for her. She was not happy in the digs and found it very difficult with the three kids. Of course, this also put a strain on our relationship, which wasn't eased when we did eventually move into the house in Grafton Square. The house was not habitable; there was so much to be done. The renovation was a massive task and, in order to get the maximum grant, I got planning permission and a grant to convert into four flats, one on each floor, with the intention of converting back into one unit on completion, leaving the option to reconvert to individual units as the kids grew up and left home in later years and we would need less room.

When the top flat was completed we moved in, but it was very cramped and necessitated coming up through the 'building site' in order to get home! My brother, who was at that time following in my father's footsteps as a builder and decorator, did most of the work, and any time off I had was spent with my sleeves rolled up and getting stuck in. Since I was still commuting to and from Manchester, having signed up to do the Street for one year, this was not a lot.

The kids, thanks to Ginny Stride, who was now divorced from John and living in that area, had managed to get into Macaulay School, a much sought-after church school nearby that had a deservedly good reputation. Her two girls from her marriage with Johnny Stride, and also the children of Tim West and Prunella Scales, were at the school at that time too. Ginny had to flutter her eyes and pull a few strings since my kids were baptised in the Catholic faith and Macaulay was a Church of England school, but she worked the miracle!

The whole move had been very traumatic and took its toll on Paddy, who was becoming more and more prone to bouts of depression. Although she had started to get very unpredictable in Hastings, I put a lot of it down to the fact that she felt out of it down there and I encouraged her as much as possible to accept work. I also hoped that when the house was finished the new home would help to settle her down; it really was magnificent. The semi-basement was a large kitchen and dining room opening out into a games room where we had a snooker table. The next floor was the lounge, which opened out onto a roof garden. Above that was our bedroom with a bathroom and sauna off, plus a large dressing room for Paddy. On the top floor were the three bedrooms for the children, with their own bathroom. Although I had been 'gazumped', the final result was stunning, and well worth the initial outlay and the subsequent tightening of the belt.

Some months after we had finished the whole conversion, we threw a party with about a hundred guests; amongst them were Cy Grant, Sinéad Cusack, and her then new boyfriend Jeremy Irons who seemed like a rather nice public schoolboy, out of his depth and very shy! When I met him again some years later all he could remember was that Sinéad had been very much taken by our quarry-tiled kitchen floor and had insisted on having the same. When Paddy and I split up, Paddy sold the house for £89,000; and some two years after that I learnt that it was on the market for £1,250,000. I don't like to think of what it's worth now!

9

CORONATION STREET WAS now in its tenth year. During the first ten years I had returned from time to time but, for fear of being permanently associated with the one character, I had restricted my returns to fleeting visits. The show's profile had risen to such an extent that there was little or no competition; there was no *EastEnders*, and although there were other soaps trying to follow in its footsteps, they couldn't compete. The Street was head and shoulders above the rest, mainly because of the original concept by Tony Warren and the wonderful team of writers that kept the standard going, with the same humorous undercurrent and love of the characters. Consequently, I was thwarted in my attempt to not get too associated with the role of Billy Walker. Each time I returned, I was rekindling the interest in the character; after a couple of appearances, it was as if I had never left. I was reaping the disadvantages of recognition but not getting the benefit, which was a regular handsome income!

In those early days, there were few who had played regular roles in a soap and left to do other things. Arthur Lowe had been one, but he had been the subject of a spin-off, in that he played the same part in his own situation comedy, and then developed into *Dad's Army*; but he was something of an exception. Philip Lowrie, who had played Dennis Tanner for about eight years, had left and was finding it difficult to shake off the association. It opened some doors, but at the same time it closed many more. As far as other television or serious classical theatre was concerned, the doors were closed. Understandable really, when the director, cast, designer and technicians have spent time, energy and expertise creating a make-believe world of times past, or a far-flung country or whatever, and the moment I appear the audience immediately think or say, 'Oo look, there's Billy Walker!'

On the other hand, repertory theatres and touring companies struggling to put bums on seats were grateful to have somebody recognisable, not only to pull in an audience but also to attract news coverage and additional publicity. Times have changed, however, and it now seems that television is also in the fight for recognisable faces to attract an audience, more often than not with disastrous consequences since not many soap stars are capable of portraying anything but their original character. There are a few notable exceptions like Sarah Lancashire and Tamzin Outhwaite, also Ross Kemp perhaps; but Martin Kemp, for example, is not.

It was with some degree of reluctance, then, that I returned to the Street; and this time I had decided to make it more financially worthwhile by coming back for a long stint as opposed to the usual two-week flying visit. The other reason for not returning for longer periods before was that I hadn't wanted to tie myself down for too long in case I missed that wonderful opportunity to join a company like the RSC, or a big film! So it was doubly sad for me to finally accept that it didn't look as if this was going to happen.

Much had changed since those early days. Most noticeably, the Street was now in colour. When it was still in black and white it had a documentary feel, and was slightly retrospective: it seemed ever so slightly to belong to a life now past. I have always felt that with the advent of colour it underwent a major change and has never been the same. The trouble with colour is that it is very difficult to show the drabness of life in the back streets. Colour takes away the nitty-gritty of life and glamorises it. The only film I have seen in colour that portrayed anything like the genuine drabness of backstreet life was Mike Leigh's *All or Nothing*. It was inevitable, I suppose, but I found it sad when *Coronation Street* changed direction so acutely; I would have loved to see it done in sepia.

With the colour came an awareness of glamour that had not been there before. It wasn't long before the actors cottoned on to the fact that light blue is a very flattering colour and a directive from above had to be issued to the wardrobe mistress to limit the number of actors wearing blue. This caused quite a few little tiffs and tantrums. The main actors too had grown in confidence and became aware of their power; correspondingly, the directors were losing their power as the actors rose. It was something of a vicious circle: as the actors started to flex their muscles, fewer established directors were eager to take the job, and Granada was also using it as a training step for young directors, which then diminished even further the respect of the actors for the director. The actors saw themselves, with some justification, as guardians of their characters; this occasionally led to conflict with writers and directors, which usually ended with the actor storming upstairs to the producer making threats of not signing a further contract et cetera et cetera. Pat Phoenix was probably the greatest culprit in this respect; she was enjoying her reputation as an earthy sex symbol and, to my mind, had lost the division between herself and her character. She was not alone, however; there were stories of little Minnie Caldwell sitting in the snug at the Rovers Return in a mink coat – not at rehearsals, but on transmission!

On January 12th we were all invited to a celebratory dinner at the Savoy Hotel, given by the Variety Club of Great Britain to mark the Street's first ten years. We were all taken on the outing to London, travelling by train in a special reserved coach. Granada decided to make a long weekend of it and we were all put up in a top London hotel, together with our partners, who were unfortunately not invited to the dinner but were fed in the hotel when we were at the Savoy. It was all rather grand and star-studded, and we were wined and dined royally.

During the pre-dinner drink session, I slipped into the banquet room to look at the seating plan, to find that we were all on the top table, alternating with prominent members of the Variety Club. To my dismay, I found that I was sitting next to Hughie Green; I didn't know him, but I knew that I couldn't stand him, so I switched the table cards to put him on the other side of Sandra Gough, who I wanted to sit next to anyway. When I got back to the drink session Sandra asked me who she was sitting next to and when I told her, she made me go back in and put Hughie Green further away from her, as she couldn't stand him either. He was gradually getting nearer and nearer to the head of the table! He also missed out on the wine because when our bottle of red ran out Sandra switched our empty bottle for his full bottle that he was saving for later!

The second night we all went to see *Hair*, the new musical, which stretched the barriers of nudity for the first time in a London theatre; and afterwards Pat Phoenix took some of us to Danny La Rue's club just off Regent Street where after the show we all went backstage for drinks in Danny's dressing room. When I say all, not everybody came: some of the older members of the cast slid off to bed and sadly Paddy, who for some reason that I can't recall was in a bit of a mood, went off to the hotel too. I carried on with Neville Buswell and his wife Sue, arriving back at the hotel having had a little too much to drink; on getting into the lift I tripped, and since I had my hands in my pockets at the time I fell forward and met the far wall of the lift with my nose. Paddy was not very sympathetic the next morning! I must confess that I was getting into a rather heavy dependence on drink. No, that's not quite right: I wasn't dependent on it, I just seemed to be using it a bit too much and too often. I wasn't what you could call alcoholic; I just didn't have enough to do to keep me centred.

Granada was obviously well aware of the jewel they had; the Street was proving a great source of income and was here to stay. A real street had been built on the lot at the back of the studios, with the corner shop, the warehouse, and the Rovers Return. The houses, however, were just façades; as you went through the doors on film, the scene would be picked up internally in the studio. The outside filming was done a week in advance, and the studio scenes would then be rehearsed and recorded at the end of the week.

The rehearsal room, which was the permanent home of the cast, was now on the fourth floor of the main building and the area was becoming adapted, with little corners becoming the domain of different members of the cast. Windows ran the full length of either side of the room, and there was a deep ledge or

My first ever speaking role – in French!
Le Médecin Malgré Lui at Alleyn's School, 1953

The first NYT production: *Henry V* at
Toynbee Hall in 1956. David Weston as
Pistol being menaced by me as Fluellen,
with Dave Fournel as Gower

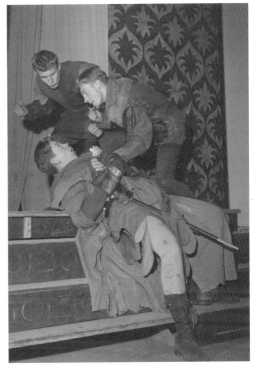

The 1957 NYT production of *Henry IV Part 2*.
Poins (me), Prince Hal (Derek Jacobi), Falstaff
(David Weston) and Doll Tearsheet (Paul Hill)

My RADA class in 1956. I'm wearing the boater; Diana Rigg is standing directly behind me

1960: BBC TV's *The Splendid Spur* with Victoria Watts

The NYT's *Hamlet* at the Sarah Bernhardt Theatre, Paris, 1960. Myself as Claudius, with Neil Stacey as Polonius and Hywel Bennett playing Ophelia

The original Walker family in *Coronation Street*: Jack and Annie (Arthur Leslie and Doris Speed), Billy, sister Joan (June Barry) and Joan's husband Gordon (Cavan Malone)

With my mate Graham Haberfield

With Anne Kirkbride

With my screen mum Annie, played by Doris Speed

A cheeky moment with Bernard Youens and Alan Howard

Brendan Behan's *The Hostage* at the Library
Theatre, Manchester with Isobel Black, 1961

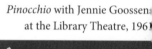

Pinocchio with Jennie Goossens
at the Library Theatre, 196

Billy Liar with Frank Pettitt,
Eileen Dale and Nan
Marriott-Watson, 1962

On the ropes with Honor Blackman
in *The Avengers*, 1962

(Photo © Studiocanal Films/
REX/Shutterstock)

As Mike Langley in 'Romance of Words', a 1964 play in the ATV series *Love Story*
(Photo © ITV/REX/Shutterstock)

The film *One Way Pendulum* with Eric Sykes, 1965

As Mortimer the Younger in
Edward II at the Phoenix Theatre,
Leicester, with Anthony Hopkins
as Lancaster, 1964

Playing Iago in *Othello*
at the Leicester Phoenix
with Cy Grant, 1965

Romeo and Juliet at the
Sunderland Empire with
Jennie Linden, 1966

The Taming of the Shrew at the
Leicester Phoenix in 1966 with
my ex-wife Patricia Heneghan

The Little Hut at the
Palace Theatre, Westcliff-on-Sea,
with Veronica Strong and
Dermot Walsh, 1970

With Paul Moriarty in *Waiting
for Godot* at the Library Theatre,
Manchester, 1971

With Richard Frost in
The Norman Conquests at
the Liverpool Playhouse,
1977

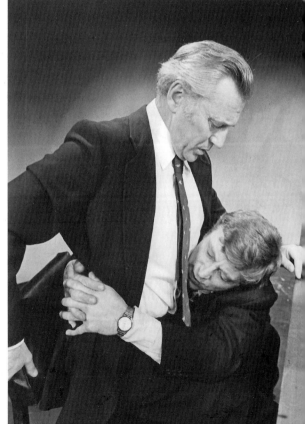

With William Lucas in
This Story of Yours at the
Liverpool Playhouse, 1977

The Front Page at the Liverpool Playhouse with John Hart Dyke and Lesley Grayburn, 1977

With Patrick Mower in Tom Stoppard's *Night and Day* at the Phoenix Theatre in London's West End, 1979

Jane Lowe playing my wife (again) in *Death of a Salesman*, Liverpool Playhouse, 1982

With Tina Marian in *Educating Rita*, 1982

Playing Sir Thomas More in *A Man For All Seasons* at the Nottingham Playhouse with Jenny Michelmore, 1985

As Pastor Manders in Ibsen's *Ghosts* with Rosemary Leach at the Leeds Playhouse, 1990

With Sir Stanley Matthews (front row, second from left) on his 80th birthday

As the Old Man in *Bingo* with Paul Jesson as Shakespeare, Royal Shakespeare Company, 1995

Jack Gates up to no good in
Family Affairs
(Photo © FremantleMedia Ltd/
REX/Shutterstock)

As Tom King in *Emmerdale*
with my three sons: Tom Lister,
Matt Healy and Nick Miles
(Photo © ITV/REX/Shutterstock)

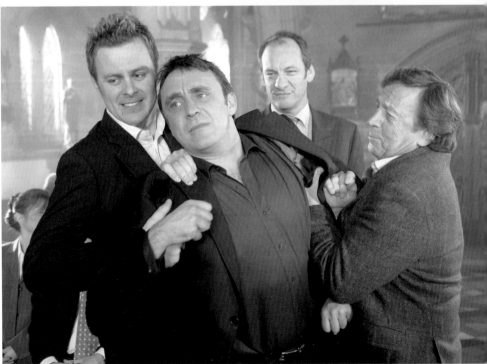

windowsill at desk height where those who preferred not to sit in the green room all day marked out their province. I staked out my claim beside Doris Speed and we would meet and chat first thing every morning. One bitterly cold November day she asked if my hands were warm; when I replied in the affirmative she asked me to do up her stocking suspender, to which I replied, 'Good God Doris, I'm not made of stone!'

At one end of the rehearsal room was the green room where Violet Carson held sway (which is, I suspect, why Doris was outside). Here Violet tended the houseplant she had brought in, until it completely covered one wall. The legend grew up that *Coronation Street* would last for as long as the plant survived; just like the ravens at the Tower of London. As far as I know it is still going and has moved from home to home as the cast have been rehoused from time to time. Next to the green room was another hideaway for the cast, where the younger members often joined for card games. In the old days, poker was the game, but had to be banned because it began to interfere with work. Despite limits, the pot would sometimes get to as much as £80, which was worth, in the sixties, quite a lot more than today; and there was the infamous occasion when young Jennifer Moss, who couldn't have been more than about 16 at the time, had a good hand and the pot was decidedly healthy when she was called to the studio for a scene, and declined to go until the hand was resolved!

Now, however, I found the scene had changed and bridge was the game. Bill Roache had taught a number of us how to play, and the enthusiasm was so strong that we had the odd evening session when we would stay behind after work and continue to play in the silence of the rehearsal room. I arranged for the Town Hall Tavern, an upmarket pub run by George Best's ex-partner Malcolm Wagstaff, to set a little corner aside for us; and sometimes Bill Roache, Neville Buswell, myself and Graham Haberfield would go to Graham's house and play into the early hours. Bridge became a serious business, and it wasn't only the young ones: Doris Speed and Irene Sutcliffe were just as enthusiastic, and Diana Davies too.

The weekly schedule was still very much the same, starting with blocking of the two episodes on Monday afternoon, then rehearsals Tuesday and Wednesday, with the technical run-through on Wednesday afternoon. Thursday morning off was followed by the afternoon in the studio, and recording of the two episodes on Friday afternoon. A number of the cast were still based in London, and the Friday journey down became a ritual with the taxi dash to catch the 6.30, and the relaxation with a bottle of wine and a meal after the trauma of the recording. In my Hastings days I would then have to continue from Victoria and would spend most of the journey in the bar, arriving at Hastings very much the worse for wear! Now in London, it became a much less traumatic journey; and Paddy would meet me in the Rose and Crown, in Clapham Old Town, where Jim the landlord would always keep the bar open for me no matter what time I arrived. This concession became very valuable in the ensuing years when I would often arrive home in the early hours of the morning after long and stressful car journeys.

A great number of the old characters were still there, together with a few new faces, at least to me. Jack Howarth was still going strong as Albert Tatlock. He was amazingly reliable and was a great asset to the show even at the age of what must have been about 80! He was by now quite a wealthy man and lived during the week in a suite at the Midland Hotel with his wife Betty who, it was rumoured, came from a wealthy background. It was also rumoured that they had inherited a country mansion in Wales. Many entertainers of that era had a reputation for meanness (Wilfred Pickles, Ken Dodd, Hughie Greene to name but a few), and Jack was no exception. He had been in the business for many, many years, and the insecurity of the profession coupled with the hardship of the early days no doubt coloured his attitude towards his new-found wealth. It became so much part of his character that most of his colleagues regarded it as merely amusing and took it on board without any real antipathy – apart from Margot Bryant, that is, who couldn't stand him.

When I was asked to collect for the staff Christmas box that year, I considered that the previous sum of £3 per head was not much when you considered how much we were being paid and how many it had to be divided between. There were all the canteen staff, and the commissionaires who manned the car park and the reception at Granada. I therefore raised the sum, after consultation with those of the cast that were present, to £5 per head. It was also easier to collect a five-pound note! When I approached Jack, he first of all questioned the rise, as he hadn't been present at the discussion; and then, grumbling that it was 'under protest', reluctantly started to get his money out. Pointing out that it was purely a voluntary gesture, I refused to take his money and made him chase me for a week and say 'Happy Christmas' before I would accept it.

Perhaps he got his own back shortly afterwards when we were all trying to get away for the Christmas holiday and found there were no taxis, due to the rush, coupled with the foul weather. We were all waiting in reception getting more and more frustrated when I discovered that Jack had a private car coming to take him to the station. He had been forced to hire a private firm to take him whenever he wanted because of his reputation: first, he had been in the habit of taking a black cab to travel some five hundred yards from Granada up the road to the Midland Hotel and not tipping; and second, he had been inclined to tap on the roof of the cab with his silver-headed cane, until a driver once got out of his cab and accosted him! On this occasion, there were four of us and I bullied him into taking us in the car with him. He had frequently joined us in our cab when he was stuck. On arrival at Piccadilly Station, I was getting the cases from the boot when I heard the driver tell Jack that the fare was sixty pence (it was 1970 don't forget!). When we got onto the train Jack collected twenty pence from each of us, thus not only travelling free himself, but making twenty pence profit!

During Pat Phoenix's *This is Your Life*, the producers noticed that Jack was very susceptible to bursting into tears; they love all that public show of emotion, so they set him up to do his life story. Jack was surprised by Eamonn Andrews with the 'big red book' on the set at Granada before being whisked away by train to London for the live show that evening at Thames TV's studios in Euston Road. At the hospitality reception afterwards they made the mistake of telling Jack to visit any time he was passing. Taking them at their word, he and Betty would call in to sample the hospitality whenever he was in town, and since he had a flat somewhere near Regent's Park, that was quite frequent. When I did another *This is Your Life* later, they told me that Jack was there almost every week!

Granada looked after us all very well, and apart from the sumptuous free meal in one of the committee rooms on transmission day, they also sent up a tea trolley from the canteen every day at teatime with a variety of beverages and a selection of cakes. Jack was always first at the door to greet the trolley and quickly whip the Eccles cakes which he would put in his pocket and take with him to have with Betty in their suite at the Midland Hotel. This would infuriate a number of the cast who were also partial to Eccles cakes; and Neville Buswell and I became quite popular when we devised a method of jostling him at the trolley, not too violently, but enough to reduce the Eccles cakes to crumbs in his pocket. This may sound callous but was, at the time, hilarious; and it didn't stop him anyway.

Eileen Derbyshire, who had been Arthur Lowe's (or rather Leonard Swindley's) sidekick in the early days of 1962, was still there, keeping a very low profile. Eileen is the epitome of discretion and good sense. She shuns the limelight and, unless forced, will not go to any of the social functions. She was a very good friend of Doris Speed and, as Doris and I were such pals, she became a pal of mine as well; I sometimes phone her if I need news of what is happening. Another of Doris's pals who more or less inherited me too was Irene Sutcliffe, another of our bridge school. Irene played Maggie Clegg who had taken over the corner shop from Florrie Lindley, with her son Gordon Clegg, played by Bill Kenwright.

I first heard of Bill some year or so before I met him. He had been in the National Youth Theatre, but long after I had left. When I was on tour with *Billy Liar*, Des O'Connor came to see the show in Chester and invited us all to join him at the Gorsey Cop Country Club where there was some sort of party. It turned out to be a Kenwright family 'do' and Des O'Connor and I were invited to say a few words and cut the cake together. (There are those who thought Des and I were brothers!) During the course of the evening I met Bill Kenwright's mother who informed me that her son was a better actor than I was and that we would all hear great things of him one day. Not exactly a sensitive thing to say, and not a good start to a relationship; but on regular train trips down south I got to quite like him, and since he was now living with Virginia Stride near Battersea Park, we were to meet up socially from time to time.

In June of 1970, Arthur Leslie who played my father Jack died; and although the Rovers bar staff had just been joined by Betty Turpin (played by Betty Driver who had been a variety artist, singing Tessie O'Shea numbers at a piano with a couple of poodles), it was thought necessary to bring in another barmaid. The then producer June Howson decided to bring back the character of Bet Lynch, who had been one of the machinists in the factory; and it was my character, Billy, who had the task of recruiting her to the Rovers, much to the consternation of Annie. At first I quite got on with Julie Goodyear; she could be amusing and had a quick wit. It was not until some time later, when I realised just how devious and manipulative she could be, that I grew to dislike her intensely.

On the other hand there was Sandra Gough, who played the Ogdens' daughter Irma who later married David Barlow. At first I was very wary of her since she had been acting at the Library Theatre and had left under something of a cloud, having had some sort of contretemps with David Scase, and I found it difficult to imagine anybody not getting on with David. Eventually, however, although she was something of a law unto herself I became very fond of her and she became a good pal; she was much conspired against by Julie Goodyear who was obviously jealous of her and her position in the Street and set about undermining her. This was all in the future and there was no hint of the upsets to come.

I think this was my happiest period in the Street, mainly because I struck up a real friendship with Graham Haberfield and Neville Buswell. They had both been in the show for some time, so the early euphoria of being in a high-profile tele had worn off and they were having to deal with the nitty-gritty of churning it out day after day. When you have the main storyline it's no problem, but there are often weeks on end when the part makes few demands on you, and it can be very boring when you have no more than a couple of lines to rehearse all week. Graham had already tried, as I had, to get out and do other things, and indeed had been wonderful in *The Dustbinmen* and in *Germinal*; but, having a young family, he had been forced back into the Street for financial reasons.

Mainly inspired by Graham's immense imagination, we had a sort of naughty schoolboy trio: that is, Neville Buswell, Graham and myself, often joined in our silliness by Anne Kirkbride, who had a similar sense of humour. It took the form of a lot of giggling and an almost private language. Graham had the wonderful knack of summing up personalities in one phrase, or a couple of words. Doris Speed was 'Old Yellow', which was inspired by her thin wispy bleached hair. Neville was 'Side Swerving Tovey', which reflected the fact that it was difficult to pin him down; he would frequently be in your company and then disappear and you wouldn't see him until the next day. I was 'The Mancunian Candidate With the Eyes that Died of Shame', on account of the fact that my eyes were beginning to reflect the strain of the frequent late nights out in Manchester city centre. Anne Kirkbride was 'Dirty Black Annie', Jennifer Moss was 'The Wart', and when she later gave birth to her child, it was labelled 'The Pimple'.

His fertile imagination also led him to conjure up improvisations in the green room. He would, for example, take a couple of handkerchiefs and a stick and do a hilarious morris dance. He could weave a good ten minutes of improvisation around a random hat or prop, in the most wonderful and amusing way. He also had a pretty hilarious Wilfrid Lawson impression; as the countdown to recording started in the studio, he would screw up his little face and the angst-ridden, high, drawled voice would ring out from behind a flat with the pitiful cry, 'Farewell, real world!'

This levity and irreverent attitude was not appreciated by all of the people all of the time. At one point during a camera rehearsal the director, Bill Gilmore, was sending messages from the control room down to the floor, via the floor manager, to adjust the position of Neville Buswell, myself and Anne Kirkbride in the Rovers bar. Finding ourselves rather unnaturally repositioned to be all three facing in the same direction in a line and very close together, we broke into a chorus of 'Chattanooga Choo-Choo' and a soft-shoe shuffle; at which point Bill left the control room in a fit of uncontrollable Scottish anger, descended the iron staircase without touching the steps, and launched himself at the three of us. Neville walked away, Annie just smiled pleasantly, and true to type I stayed and fronted him, exacerbated his anger and got myself into a bit of a state as well!

On another occasion during a fairly slack rehearsal Neville was sitting alone in the card room, playing patience, and I was kicking my heels outside waiting to be called. I started to collect odd tables and chairs and other bits of miscellaneous furniture from around the rehearsal room and stack them up to barricade the card-room door, and then got a collection of bowls and other receptacles, filled them with water and balanced them as precariously as possible on the barricade. When Neville was called, he opened the door, which opened inwards, saw the assault course I had set up for him, closed the door and went back to his game of patience. The director then turned his ire on me and I was ignominiously set to dismantle the barricade.

These childish schoolboy pranks were an indication of our boredom, and just a way of keeping ourselves sane when we had little to do. When it came to the crunch, and demands were made upon our character, I would like to feel that we knuckled down and took the job very seriously, but there really is a problem for the imaginative actor in reproducing week after week the same undemanding performance.

I stayed a number of times with Graham Haberfield, sometimes when his wife and two boys were there. On each occasion I was appalled by the way he would cough endlessly at the start of the day. I called it 'the dawn chorus'; it was a full half-hour of very heavy coughing, and was obviously putting a heavy strain on his heart, because some few years later his wife came into the bedroom with a cup of early-morning tea and found him dead. He was an immense loss, not only to *Coronation Street*, but to the acting profession. To my mind he was the most gifted of all of the actors that have appeared in the Street; had he lived he would without doubt, on the demise of Wilfrid Lawson, have been a successor to the crown of character actor, now worn, in my opinion, by Freddie Jones; they were all very similar in their tortured dedication and compulsion to act. Graham smoked and drank to excess – he did everything to excess – but he was adored by all who knew him. He had a heart of gold and an immense talent.

The other member of the trio, Neville Buswell, who played Ray Langton, was a much more glamorous figure. Although his sense of humour was very much in tune with Graham's and mine, he was an enigmatic man who kept himself very much to himself. He too had a great affection for Graham, but he also had a very young and attractive wife, and would frequently just slide away to go home early to her. Hence the tag 'Side Swerving Tovey'; he never said anything, he just disappeared. Neville was never as dedicated to the concept of acting as Graham and I were. To him, it was a means to an end and he had a very laid-back attitude to the whole circus. Nothing ever mattered too much to him; he was in it to make money and have a good time.

His final disappearance was a mystery; one minute he was there, I left the Street for a spell and, when I returned, he had gone! Nobody knew where he was. There were a number of rumours, the most predominant being that he had gone to Las Vegas as a croupier, and shortly before disappearing he had been hounded by the Inland Revenue. There were even stories of the Inland Revenue waiting at the main reception of Granada and Neville disappearing through the car park! When I returned to find him missing, I even phoned his mother who was very evasive and I rang off none the wiser.

Many years later I was appearing as a guest on *This is Your Life* when Anne Kirkbride was the victim, and Neville was the surprise guest at the end! We had quite a long and pleasant chat in hospitality that evening; when I tackled him about his disappearance, he just shook his head disbelievingly and smiled in that 'side swerving' way of his and I was still none the wiser. Many more years after that I got a little nearer the truth when I managed to get hold of his address in Las Vegas and, when I was on holiday, we met up for a few days. He was still with his very pretty wife, Sue, and part of the story was confirmed. He had started in Las Vegas working on the gaming tables, but was now in the mortgage and real estate business; still a bit vague, and when I mentioned the Inland Revenue, he still just smiled and shook his head in disbelief. 'Side Swerving Tovey' to the last! Graham had a wonderful way of getting to the nub.

As the son of a doctor, Bill Roache had a classier image than us working-class lads and in a way we looked up to him; he became the sort of spokesman for the younger set and, of course, with age he has now become more or less the 'head boy' of the Street. He certainly didn't deserve the epithet of 'boring' that was given him by the journalist Ken Irwin, and I was delighted when Bill took him to court, but saddened when the anomaly of our judicial system meant that it cost him dearly, financially. Irwin was one of the rather parasitic little gang of gossipy-type journalists that hung around the cast hoovering up little quotes and snippets to weave into some sort of sensational story. I remember him sidling up to me at Violet Carson's memorial service and trying to get me to say something. I even remember his oily little phrase when I refused to give him anything; he said, 'Oh come on, Ken, we go back a long way, you and I.' By then, of course, I had learnt just how much a simple little quote could be twisted out of context to prove an embarrassment!

I also learnt a valuable lesson from Bill Roache, in one of my early returns to the Street. I noticed that Bill seemed not to spend too much time learning his lines, and he admitted to me that he intentionally left them unsure in his mind. Not only did this give his words the appearance of spontaneity, it also looked as if he was thinking deeply, which indeed he was: 'What the hell do I say next?' I found this extremely impressive, not to say dangerous, but I did take it on board, and never in fact from that day learnt the exact lines myself. I spent quite a bit of time learning the thoughts but not, parrot fashion, the lines; I found it invaluable in my approach to soap acting, which requires a style of its own.

Most of the regulars had now settled down in Manchester and bought themselves property in and around the city; I was more or less the only one of the main cast that still travelled to London each weekend. This of course also meant that, at the end of the day's rehearsal, they all had homes to go to. For a while, I stayed at the pub, the infamous Brown Bull, and later I rented a flat in Whalley Range before buying a house in the same area. Coming from a family of builders and decorators, I bought a terraced house in dire need of renovation with the hope that cosmetics and time would make it a good investment. It really was a rough area and I doubt if, even now, it has improved in any way enough to be called desirable! It only cost £1,000 and the vendor wanted cash before he would move out. I was strongly advised against this by my solicitor, but I wanted so much to get my teeth into a project that would give me something to do and also make me some money that I agreed. I turned up at the house on completion day with £1,000 in used notes, and watched the man that I had bought it from walk off down the street with a fridge on his head and for some reason a saw in his hand!

Externally there wasn't much I could do about the house other than give it a lick of paint. Internally, however, it was a different matter. Having gutted the place and thrown out all of the left-behind rubbish, I made one large bedroom on the ground floor, with a dining room and kitchen, and upstairs a lounge and bathroom and one bedroom with a further large bedroom on the top floor. I let out rooms to the Library Theatre actors and continued to do so after leaving the Street. I kept the ground-floor bedroom for myself, and would sometimes stay there when I was touring in the area or directing at the Manchester Youth Theatre as I did for some seven years.

Over the years, the house became very tired and the furniture suffered from a lack of tender loving care. When I was not there, I got the impression that the theatre personnel were using it for all manner of activities, such as when they wanted to rehearse scenes together on their own. I also learnt that when Corin Redgrave was at the Library he used the sitting room for meetings of the Workers Revolutionary Party. I once arrived at two o'clock in the morning, stopping off en route for a tour date, to find somebody in my bed!

On one occasion when I was still staying at the Brown Bull I went up to bed as they gave the first call for time, and as I lay in bed I heard low conversation in the passage outside my room. On opening the door to complain, I found George Best sitting on the floor with Malcolm Wagstaff, his business partner in the Village Barber shop, waiting for Texan Bill the landlord to get rid of the punters so that they could go downstairs again for the 'lock in'. I knew Malcolm fairly well as I always had my hair cut at his establishment, and George a little; I invited them in and we opened a bottle of whiskey.

I had previously found myself in the same company as George but, until now, had not really had a one-to-one conversation with him. A few days before, I had been in the bar of the Brown Bull when George had come in having just bought a pair of trousers; he went into the gents' and changed into them, throwing the pair he had just taken off into the corner. A minute or so later I went to the loo to find a rather overweight United fan who, having found them, had put them on; and despite the fact that he was unable to do them up, danced excitedly into the bar, delightedly announcing to the assembled company that he was wearing George Best's trousers!

I frequently bumped into George as we seemed to be using the same clubs and pubs and to know the same people. I had first met him in Annabelle's disco when Malcolm had offered me a lift home in George's car with George and his chauffeur. We had only gone a few yards down the road when George told the driver to stop at another nightclub, left us in the car and went downstairs into the club which had closed and was in the process of counting up the takings. A few seconds later the club doorman came to the car and told the driver George had said to go on without him, and would the gentleman in the back care to join him? Star-struck, I couldn't believe my luck, and I joined him downstairs where he was chatting up one of the waitresses, which was the reason for his change of plans.

One to one with George wasn't easy; my fault, not his, as I think I was too overawed to be able to completely relax. In my effort to keep the conversation going, and also give myself a little macho credibility in such company, I am sure I said some pretty stupid things that were later to come back and haunt me, or at least cause me some concern. On the whole, however, I found George pleasant and friendly enough and felt privileged to be able to talk football to him when I felt it was acceptable; there was always the fear that he was fed up with talking football. One Friday evening in the Brown Bull he showed me his ankle which was badly swollen, so badly in fact that the swelling was hanging over his slip-on shoe, and told me that despite this he had been told that he had to play the next day; come what may, he was expected to turn out.

Even amongst his friends, George had a reputation for not being reliable, and they just laughed and shrugged it off; they were obviously as impressed as I was with his star status. But if it is true that you can tell a man by the company he keeps, George was obviously a nice enough lad. He was surrounded by the usual sycophants, but they were not the ones he gave much time to; his real friends were pretty solid and decent. Nevertheless, he really did get himself into one hell of a mess.

He nearly got me into one hell of a mess too! At one time during his more wayward period at Old Trafford, he had disappeared for days on end and had been discovered 'shacked up' with Sinéad Cusack, giving the press a field day. Some time after, Sinéad happened to be in Manchester recording a play for Granada. She really was a very special lady; not only was she good to look at but she was great fun to be with and was very popular. I had met up with her in the Stables, a bar at the rear of the Granada studios where the actors from the various productions met up for a drink after the day's work.

One weekend I had to stay up in Manchester as I was playing in a charity soccer match on the Sunday, and George had got me two tickets to see the United game on the Saturday afternoon; I was taking my mate Geoff Sykes. When Sinéad, in conversation, said that she had never been to a soccer match and she would love to come with us, but was fearful of George finding out since she had always refused to go with him, I pointed out that there would be about sixty thousand people there and that George was hardly likely to be able to spot her in that sort of crowd. She agreed to come and I phoned George for another ticket, but didn't, of course, tell him who it was for.

Since I only had a two-seater sports car at that time, I arranged to pick up Sinéad from the Midland Hotel and to meet Geoff at the ground. All went well until after the game when, stuck in traffic with Sinéad in the passenger seat, I found we were alongside Malcolm Wagstaff's car, with 'Waggie' and George staring unbelievingly at us. Sinéad was a little distraught; but after a drink or two in the Grapes with Geoff, who had made his own way there, she calmed down and expressed the desire to join us on our evening trip around the nightclubs of Manchester.

I suppose it was inevitable that George should turn up at Annabelle's, and Sinéad decided she felt uncomfortable with him there, so we slipped out to another late-night fun-spot just up the road. When George and his entourage turned up there later that evening, Sinéad said it was pointless dodging around like this and went to talk to him. Geoff had gone home earlier, and I felt a bit of a lemon standing at the bar on my own, waiting for what seemed like an eternity; I was also mindful of having to get up the next morning to play football, so at about two o'clock I went over to George and Sinéad and told her that I had to go, but I would see her at the match the next morning. I truly didn't mind; I wasn't in any way whatsoever involved with Sinéad, but I was a little worried about leaving her since she had been so fearful of meeting up with George earlier. She asked me to wait, but I could see that she was enjoying herself with George and in all probability wanted to stay. I said I would wait below in the car, and if she decided to stay, not to worry: I would wait until two thirty and then I would go. When she didn't come down at half past two I wasn't at all surprised and went home to bed.

The next day she didn't turn up at the soccer match, but on Monday morning she telephoned me in the rehearsal room and said that she had come down only to see me driving off and had taken a cab back to the hotel, where George had turned up later and conned his way past the night porter, and got up to her room. She had had a lot of trouble with him, and had been in no fit state to come to the charity soccer match.

I wasn't miffed, jealous, upset, or angry, but I was extremely worried when I was informed by the press office that the *Daily Mirror* was on the phone and wanted to speak with me. They were asking for my comments on a story they had received that I had been out with George Best's ex-girlfriend, and that I had been thrown out of one club and barred from another! I affected complete and utter bewilderment, asked who George Best's ex-girlfriend was, and then professed to have heard of Sinéad but to have never met her; they rang off convinced that it was an unlikely match and that they had received a hoax call. I don't know who tipped off the papers but from that moment I stayed clear of that little set-up, not wishing to get caught up in George's love of being in the public eye.

I had begun to weave myself a double existence. During the week, I was the 'gay young blade' of the Manchester nightlife; and at the weekend, I returned to the bosom of my family. Julie Goodyear, in the days when I was still talking to her, rather amusingly fantasised about my arriving at Euston Station on a Friday night, going to the left-luggage lockers and changing out of trendy gear into a cardigan and brogues! None of this was conscious behaviour on my part; it just so happened that I was alone and bored in a city that had much to offer in the way of social life.

I found myself regarded as something of a celebrity and seemed to be made welcome wherever I went. The clubs were keen to have me; I not only got in free, but I was treated to hospitality by the management and made to feel very important. At the Hunting Lodge, I became the personal friend of Ray Williams, the owner, even being taken by him to south Wales one weekend to be made president of Neath Rugby Club. I was driven through the streets of Neath in an open landau, and the bride and bridesmaids of a church wedding left the group photograph outside the church to come over and follow the car. When we got back to the hotel, I was told that the management had to eject two young ladies who had broken into my room via the bathroom window! I was getting paid to read the numbers at bingo, open fetes and shops in my spare time and I was recognised wherever I went. It struck me as ironic that when I had no money and would sometimes have to check all my pockets to rustle up the price of a pint, I would drink alone at the bar, hoping that nobody would come in whom I would feel obliged to offer a drink. Now, when I was given not only the weekly wage but also a little envelope of cash each Monday morning as subsistence, I rarely had to buy myself a drink as people would be only too eager to join me at the bar and ask what I was having.

I am, of course, trying to make excuses for myself. In essence, I fell into the trap that so many young men have done, faced with exposure to the sort of temptations I was faced with. I was young, I was famous, and I was away from home. The fact that the character I was playing was a bit of a lad with the girls only served to fuel the imagination and increase the temptation. Not much of an excuse really!

There were many aspects of being a well-known face that were not in any way pleasurable. The first flush of enjoyment in being recognised and feted was by now long past. After being shouted at in the street thirteen times a day, year after year, with the same cry of 'Hello Billy! Where's Annie?' usually accompanied by a raucous and self-congratulatory laugh as they enjoy the unamusing joke with their mates, it becomes difficult even to smile in recognition, and I started to avoid situations where I might be subjected to this.

I also found it embarrassingly galling to be followed around the supermarket when I went shopping with the kids, with gawping customers who just pushed their trolleys and smiled vacuously. I found it difficult too, when I was sometimes dragged across a saloon bar to be presented to a tableload of grinning nodding 'Corrie' fans with the proclamation 'See, it is 'im, ennit?' I don't know why but my character seemed to invite people to be matey, and they assumed a degree of intimacy that allowed them even to join me at my table if I happened to be in company, and treat me as a long-lost friend. They would then frequently tell me who I was and proceed to recount to me my exploits in the last episode!

They weren't always admiring fans either; sometimes it would be the resentful, who were quick to tell you that they never watched the show, and thought it was just crap anyway. This without being asked for an opinion, and apparently oblivious to the illogicality of reaching such a conclusion without watching the show. Not surprisingly, I did not encourage this sort of approach; but if I reacted frostily, I was in danger of being told that if it weren't for them I wouldn't be where I was!

Of course, when done quietly and respectfully, as it often is, it can be a pleasure; but I have never really understood the celebrities who curry favour with the public by announcing that they love being recognised and would be worried if it stopped. Now that I am no longer so obviously in the show, it doesn't happen anywhere near as much and I find it acceptable; but at its height I found the loss of privacy was too high a price to pay, and when my contract was coming to an end, I decided not to stay on.

In all probability, they weren't going to ask me anyway as I had somewhat blotted my copybook when we had gone to the Preston Guild to film the Street on a day out. I only had one scene to do, which was coming from a tent with Bet Lynch, and unfortunately the scene was not scheduled until very late in the day. By this time I had more than had my fill of hospitality champagne in a variety of marquees where Neville Buswell and I had done the rounds throughout the day.

By the time we came to the scene I was finding it very tricky to walk in a straight line, and Eric 'Taffy' Prytherch, who had just taken over as producer having previously been one of the directors, was absolutely livid. As I sat on the coach ready to go home, he came aboard and delivered a verbal assault that was wasted on my ears as I fell asleep during the tirade and woke up the next day sleeping on the floor of one of the dressing rooms, where I had been dumped. Until that point I had got on very well with Taffy and, of course, I was very contrite and apologetic. In the long run, I think it was about time that I left. I had been back in the Street for nearly a year.

10

1971 to 1973 • Library Theatre • *Coronation Street* •
Julie Goodyear • Manchester City •
Mike Summerbee • Freddie Griffiths •
Manchester Youth Theatre

I DIDN'T GO VERY far: just up the road to the Library Theatre to work again with David Scase, although my first production, Samuel Beckett's *Waiting for Godot*, was directed by John Blackmore. I played Vladimir, and Paul Moriarty (who was later to go via the National Theatre to *EastEnders*) played Estragon. I had seen the original production when I was a RADA student; I hadn't managed to get a seat but stood all the way through.

When the play was first performed at the Royal Court Theatre there was uproar with some people walking out during the performance and others saying that it was the greatest theatre they had ever seen. I belonged to the second group and I loved the play. I found it just pure theatre: amusing and fascinating to watch, and stimulating to the mind as its meaning is many-faceted. Rather like a painting, it can mean different things to different people; and rather like a painter, Beckett refused to explain it. I saw it as Life, with a capital L, in microcosm, with Vladimir and Estragon searching, waiting and suffering the ups and downs of existence, and Lucky and Pozzo coming in as representatives of money and possession and demonstrating the influences of power and dependence. This is obviously very simplistic and would need more study to support it, but it is roughly what I remember as being the basis upon which I built my performance.

We played the whole thing in a great bowl of sand and were lucky enough to have the set for rehearsal, as it was the first play of the season. When I say lucky, in one way it was not so lucky; the bowl of sand was set on the rake and I had lots of movement up and down stage. I would go home knackered. Paul and I played with Irish accents, which we found complemented the complex rhythms; when we got them right they were a joy to play.

John Blackmore proved to be a very demanding director and insisted on us playing the pauses until we felt the audience would take no more, and then extending them further. I found this very difficult, as I felt we were in danger of antagonising the audience who were already struggling to make some sense of the play, which is by no means an easy one. He also had acquired the popular idea of early-morning warm-ups and game-playing. This too I found difficult to take on board as I was in the habit of getting into the theatre early and warming up myself to be ready to start work when rehearsal began.

At first, we joined in with the game-playing, which frequently took the form of some kind of improvisation. We were given characters to play, and a situation. John had a whistle and a rattle: when he blew the whistle the situation stayed the same and we were to change our characters, and when he rattled the rattle the character stayed the same and the situation changed. Luckily Paul felt the same as I did and found this all a waste of valuable rehearsal time, so we buried the rattle and the whistle in the sand and we didn't play it again.

John then tried another game called 'Trust', when one person stood in the middle of a circle with his eyes closed, fell backwards and trusted for the others to catch him before he hit the floor. After persuading John to get into the middle and failing to catch him a couple of times, that game too was withdrawn and we gradually got rid of the game-playing!

The rehearsals, though, were very rewarding; and when we opened at the Library Theatre we played to maximum capacity, even turning people away. Therefore, it was very puzzling and disappointing when we transferred to the Forum Theatre in Wythenshawe and played to half-empty houses. The Forum was a new venture for the Library: a brand-new venue which had been built in a cultural wasteland south of Manchester. Paddy had been in the first play, *Laura*, with Brian Blessed and Mike Pratt, which opened the Forum at the same time as we opened with *Godot*, and after a three-week run we changed places. My parents were looking after the kids and we got home at weekends. Many years later, I met Paul Moriarty at a casting in London and as we reminisced, he told me that *Godot* was one of his most treasured memories and he had loved the whole experience as much as I had.

I stayed with the Library Theatre for the next two productions, the first being *After Haggerty* by David Mercer with David Scase directing and with Sue Brown playing opposite me. Also in the cast was a young Paul Seed, who had been a student of Geoff Sykes and went on to be a TV director of some note.

I was due to leave the Library and return to Granada for another spell in the Street. I had decided that it would be better for me to make use of the fact that I could earn good money to finance what I really wanted to do, and just not to stay too long and get frustrated, instead of trying to resist it altogether. David Scase meanwhile was directing *Say Goodnight to Grandma*, the first play written by Colin Welland; the last act was a party scene with four or five rugby players, and he was having trouble casting the players as they were not big enough parts to attract the sort of actors that he wanted. It was found that with a bit of juggling of rehearsal times and a little goodwill from Granada, I could play one of the rugby players, doing the Street in the daytime and the play in the evening. *Grandma* was only to play at Wythenshawe for three weeks and was to star Colin

Welland and Sue Jameson, who had also been in the Street as wife to Graham Haberfield. As an added incentive, we were to have a cask of real beer for the final scene: no cold tea!

One of the other rugby players was Paul Luty, a lovable ex-wrestler who, much to David's consternation, dropped me on the top of my head at one rehearsal when he was demonstrating a wrestling trick. He was trying to show me how it didn't hurt and was supposed to have stopped just before my head hit the stage. Perhaps I was a bit taller than he thought, because there was a resounding thud as my head struck the ground and David rushed from his seat in the stalls calling Paul all sorts of names. Paul was absolutely distraught and so apologetic that I had to pretend it hadn't hurt, to save him embarrassment. In reality, it was bloody agony and I had a pain in my neck for days. Paul became a good friend, and eventually also played in *Coronation Street* as a window cleaner. He was such a likeable guy that I was not surprised to find that he numbered amongst his friends Bobby Charlton; but I was surprised when I went out with him one night and he just happened to call in at the Charlton household, where Bobby greeted him as if he was a permanent fixture there. I, of course, was just delighted to meet another of my footballer heroes!

Football had taken on an even bigger role in my life, despite the fact that I was working so consistently. I had become involved with the 'Arnold Berlin Pennies for the Blind' fundraising. Piles of pennies were stacked up in pubs, and once a year Arnold Berlin would organise a fortnight of 'celebrity knock downs' which involved television personalities, football stars from Manchester United and Manchester City, and bunny girls or models. We would meet up at Arnold's club, Milverton Lodge, and split up into about four teams consisting of one from each group. Then the teams would set off in small coaches and each visit four or five pubs to knock over the piles of pennies, gather them up into a big blanket and cart them off to buy guide dogs for the blind. At the end of the evening, we would sometimes all meet up again at the club for a buffet snack and a few drinks.

I was in seventh heaven, rubbing shoulders with players from Manchester's two great clubs. We visited quite a mixed choice of pubs, from the upmarket drinking of south Manchester in Knutsford and Cheadle, to the more 'spit and sawdust' of Moss Side and Whalley Range. It was, however, more or less guaranteed that the more deprived the area, the more generous were the donations. In the really rough areas the piles of pennies were gargantuan and the pubs crowded; in the smarter areas there was much less enthusiasm.

I think it was Eileen Derbyshire who had first introduced me to this set-up, in order to take her place on the team. She had a good heart and felt that she should do something, but she hated the traipsing around the pubs: it just wasn't her scene. However, it suited me just fine and I soon became a regular member of the Pennies team; and George Sheppard, who organised the evenings on behalf of the RNIB, was to eventually use me as his Granada contact, supplying him with 'faces' to make up the TV contingent. Besides *Coronation Street*, where my main recruit was Anne Kirkbride (the rest being mostly not interested, or not interested unless they were paid), I also brought in people from other shows like *A Family at War*, including Diana Davies who later joined the cast of the Street.

It was through these evenings that I met Mike Summerbee, who played on the wing for Manchester City and England, and we became great friends, often going off together to judge beauty contests and the like. He also had a bespoke shirt-making business and I became his Granada contact for that too! I had picked up a soccer injury playing for the old boys of my school and Mike arranged for me to see the club physio, Freddie Griffiths. This was to be the start of a long relationship with Manchester City, and with Mike and Freddie in particular.

Freddie invited me to join him on his Thursday-morning session training the players that were recovering from injury, and sometimes he also invited me to join the fit City players for a morning training session. When the Granada press office got hold of the news, they arranged with City for a photographer to come and take pictures. The manager was Joe Mercer, with Malcolm Allison as his assistant. City was riding high at that time with Franny Lee, Colin Bell, Tommy Booth, Joe Corrigan, Alan Oakes, Will Donachie, Asa Hartford, as well as Mike Summerbee, and Tony Book who eventually became manager.

I gloried in my privileged position, turning up regularly for Thursday-morning training, whatever the weather and whatever I had been doing the previous night. Mike insisted that I was simply training to stay fit to keep myself going in my role of Manchester playboy; he used to introduce me at the various functions that we attended together as 'The King of Manchester'! I became a regular fixture at Maine Road, going to the mid-week matches, and the Saturday games if I was in town. Not only did I get invited into the directors' box, I also joined the team in the players' lounge after the game and once even sat on the bench with Freddie Griffiths. When City reached the League Cup final in 1970, Joe Corrigan phoned me up a week before the game and asked if I had tickets for Wembley; when I told him I hadn't, he asked if I would come as his guest and look after the players' wives during the game. So there I was at Wembley sitting in the best of seats in the middle of a dozen very attractive young ladies. I later joined the victorious team at their celebrations in the Dorchester hotel and drank from the Cup!

Obviously the line-up changed from time to time and the squad was joined by players like Joe Royal, Rodney Marsh, and Peter Barnes, whose father Ken I had got to know through the Northern All Stars celebrity team and who was on the training staff at City. Peter was a very promising young player and although he played a few times for England, he never really achieved his full potential. During the training sessions with the recovering players, Freddie would often push me harder to demonstrate to them the degree of commitment and effort that he was looking for; and although even when injured they were infinitely more capable than I, my enthusiasm and desire to not look too big a 'wally' meant that I would frequently put more effort than they would into Freddie's training routine. Peter Barnes was one such player who took things at his own pace, and perhaps that would be the reason for him never achieving the career that he looked destined for.

Another player who took things at his own pace was Rodney Marsh. On one rare occasion when I was training with the main squad at Maine Road, I was sitting in the dug-out with Rodney when Freddie descended and ordered us to start 'lapping', which was a strenuous sequence of sprinting the long side of the pitch, jogging to recover along the short side, then sprinting the long side again et cetera. I immediately jumped to obey the order, but Rodney stayed sitting and calmly said, 'No, I'm a ball player. Ball players don't do lapping.' Freddie was not a man to argue with; I set off lapping and left them to it. Rodney did join me on the lapping: he had only been joking, but nevertheless his heart wasn't really in it. I think the most gruelling of all Freddie's exercises was to sprint up and down the stairs in the main stand; he would then check the pulse for recovery and send you off again.

Apart from the large bath that was capable of taking the whole team, and was a welcome relief as you came in and saw it steaming, there was also a sauna and a bath full of iced water, together with a very powerful Jacuzzi and of course showers. Much of the pleasure was in toning myself up ready for the pressures of the next week and getting ready for the two days in the studio. It also meant that I was getting fitter and more and more eager to play.

At weekends when I returned home I was still playing for the old boys of my school on the Saturday afternoon, and on Sunday for the TV All Stars. When in the north I would play for the Granada team, which consisted mainly of Granada employees, amongst them Jack Rosenthal, who often brought Maureen Lipman, whom he later married, to kick off; Alan Grint, the cameraman, who later became a director; Richard Beckinsale; Chris Quinten, who was then in the Street and had not yet risen to be Peter Stringfellow's right-hand man; and a variety of guest stars.

My favourite team to play for, though, was the Northern All Stars, which was full of former professionals like Charlie Mitten, Ken Barnes, and sometimes the more recent stars like Bobby Charlton and Nobby Stiles; I was rather honoured to be more often than not the only non-ex-pro, apart from the occasional appearance of Stuart Hall. I had moved up to inside right, alongside ex-Everton player Tony Kay. Tony had been banned from professional football when he was found guilty, along with two other players, of taking bribes to throw a game. When we played at Leeds, we changed in the dressing rooms at Elland Road as the pitch was nearby, but Tony had to change in the coach as he wasn't allowed inside the ground. He had ruined a fantastic career; he had already played for England and would most certainly have featured strongly in the England side for many years to come. His skill with a ball was amazing. I remember the referee calling for the game ball that Tony had been kicking around before the game had started; he just chipped the ball so that it floated to the referee's feet, and as he bent down to pick it up the ball bounced and spun back to Tony.

With him beside me and feeding me the most amazing balls I became quite a prolific goal-scorer, to such an extent that our sponge man, who was also the sponge man for Mossley in the Cheshire League, came with an offer to play for the professional side! In all honesty, I think they were having trouble with very low gates and the main idea was to get publicity and perhaps attract a few more spectators. In any event, I didn't pursue the matter and neither did they.

I must say that the charity soccer that I played up north was considerably more enjoyable than the charity soccer that I played down south. Somehow, it was more honest and the participants were more genuine and less egotistical. I met many old heroes and even got to play against the great Tom Finney, who must have been in his late sixties and still bamboozled me; as I chased him down the wing, he appeared to overrun the ball and I stopped to gather it and set off in the other direction, only to find that he had scooped the ball up with his trailing foot and left me standing and bemused!

As you may have gathered, football was playing a more and more prominent part in my life, partly to cope with the lack of artistic stimulus that I was getting from the Street. Apart from the weekend games and the Thursday training sessions with City, I would also frequently arrange a six-a-side or five-a-side game with some of my colleagues at Granada. We also had an interdepartmental six-a-side tournament on a yearly Granada Day when family and friends all joined in, and I was asked to train up a girls' team: asked by the girls, I might add. Which also served to take my mind off the lack of impetus at work!

After my last spell at the Library Theatre, from September to December 1971, I had returned for another longish spell in the Street from November 1971 to May 1973. Since this overlapped by a month, it was to be the longest continuous spell that I had played in the Street. Neville Buswell and Graham Haberfield were still there and just as mad; Peter Adamson was also still there and still on the wagon. Eric Prytherch appeared to have forgiven me because he allowed me time out to go back to the Library to play in Bill Naughton's *Alfie*, again directed by my favourite David Scase, for the month of September 1972.

The Street character of Elsie Tanner had remarried in the storyline and was now married to Alan Howard, played by Alan Browning, and Pat Phoenix as usual carried the whole thing further and married Alan Browning in real life. I got on very well with Alan, although he seemed to be a bit wary of getting too pally with me, as Pat and I didn't exactly hit it off. We happened to do a personal appearance together for some charity or other one night, and after the event I took him with me to the Explosion, a nightclub that was later closed down when Jackie the owner was sent to jail. The next day Pat gave me an ear-bashing for leading her husband astray. It was the first time she'd spoken to me for ages!

It was another personal appearance that brought home to me just how dangerous a lady was Julie Goodyear. It was more or less the same scenario; we had been at some sort of charity do together, and afterwards I said that I was going to the Explosion and she asked if she could join me, which she did. It was of course very late at night, or rather early in the morning, when I drove her back to Granada where she had left her car. The next day she came to me at rehearsals in a state of apparent anxiety and dramatically said that her then boyfriend had been waiting for her, and it was obvious from what she told me that she had fed him some sort of story that had wound him up. Not only was he furious, he was allegedly dangerous and had already served a term in prison for grievous bodily harm. I was not in the least bit worried as we hadn't done anything, and I was under the impression that she was exaggerating and being dramatic; she certainly loved to attract attention to herself in any way that she could.

A little later that morning I received a phone call from Granada reception to say that Julie's boyfriend was downstairs and wanted to see me. My first reaction was to tell him that he could wait, and I went to Julie to ask exactly what she had said to him; she was loving it! I then went downstairs and met this wildly dangerous man. His opening gambit was to say to me, 'I don't like what happened last night.' When I asked him to expand on that, he said that he didn't like his girlfriend being seen in a joint like the Explosion.

At this point, feeling somewhat affronted, I decided to take a chance on Julie having lied to me about his past form, which was not all that big a risk as she was renowned as a liar. I told him that he should take the matter up with Julie, not me; she was quite capable of saying no, and in fact she had asked me to take her. I was not interested in their little lovers' tiff, I said, '…so piss off'. Whereupon I turned on my heels and went upstairs where Julie was enjoying the drama that she had woven so maliciously!

That wasn't the terminal moment in my relationship with Julie; that came later, but not much later. I had struck up a very comfortable relationship with Sandra Gough who, although she could be somewhat volatile and unpredictable, I found extremely talented and lively to be with. We would go out together on a Wednesday night after rehearsals, given that we had Thursday morning off. We would typically start with a drink in the Bier Keller and then go to a club, where we would usually part company as one or other of us would slip off at some time during the evening. On one particular evening, the clubs were unusually dead; we were neither of us enjoying ourselves, and decided to call it a day. Sandra wanted me to go back with her to her home, but I was not only very wary about changing our relationship, which was platonic and meant a lot to me, I was also due to train at Maine Road the next morning; so after a long discussion when she tried to persuade me, I dropped her back at her car.

The next day when I went in to the studios, I went first of all to the set where Sandra was in the Rovers bar, having been called earlier than me, to say hello to her. She refused to look at me, pointedly turning her head away when I tried to attract her attention. I was then told that Sandra had told everybody that she had made advances to me and that I was a homosexual! This little game continued for the afternoon and none of us were taking it too seriously; it was just one of Sandra's games. In fact I found it hilarious and I could see that she was joking.

During a scene that I had with Julie, there was quite a bit of hanging around on set, waiting for lighting, camera, or sound to sort something out, and as usual we just got to chat as we waited. Julie happened to ask me what was going on; and I stupidly, not being then as aware of her guile, happened to tell her about the previous evening and how I had declined an invitation to take Sandra home because I didn't want to change our relationship.

It wasn't until the next Monday that I realised that something had changed. Sandra was no longer playing at the ignoring; it had now taken on a much more sinister feel. She was obviously very angry with me and ignoring me in earnest. I managed to get her on one side and forced her to tell me what was wrong. Apparently, Julie had made a point of calling on her over the weekend and told her that I had said I wouldn't 'go with' Sandra if she were the last woman on earth! I was absolutely flabbergasted and simply said, 'I'm not going to say anything; if you really believe I could have said such a thing then there is no point.' We were friends again. I don't think she had believed it anyway; she was aware of what a liar and troublemaker Julie could be.

However, that was the end, as far as I was concerned, with Julie. I confronted her and said that I wanted nothing more to do with her. I would work with her, when I had to, but since she was such a twister of conversations and such a vicious mischief-maker, I would not have any more dealings with her. Looking back on that time it occurs to me that it was all part of Julie's plan to get rid of Sandra. There was much about the characters they were playing that meant they were in competition, and Sandra was considerably more gifted. Julie set about making her miserable, and I think it highly probable that this was to get her to feel so unhappy that she couldn't stay, which is what eventually happened.

I wasn't alone in my attitude towards Julie and most people gave her a wide berth, but she was a very strident personality and, I have to admit, could be very witty, so she was pretty hard to ignore. By virtue of the fact that she was a barmaid at the Rovers, I found it difficult to avoid her altogether, but I made my feelings as clear as I could. Doris was a little bewildered and often asked me why I disliked her so much; it wasn't until much later when she had retired that she admitted that she too had come to the same conclusion that I had.

Before I took my time out to play Alfie, I had a little hiccough: I was charged with drink driving! It is ironic that it came at a time when I was not drinking as much as I had been, and doubly ironic when I hadn't had much to drink. I had left a pub in Deansgate after a couple of glasses of wine, three at the most, which was nothing for me at that time, and forgot to switch on my sidelights. Although the street was well lit and it wasn't that late, I was flagged down by a police car and given a breathalyser test, which was positive – just. I accompanied the officer to the station for a second test, which was again marginal, so I had to wait for the police doctor to come and take a blood test; and then I joined my friends in the club and had a proper drink.

The next day at rehearsals I received a telephone call from David Scase to say he had heard that I had been arrested; what had happened? Since I had not had the time or even the inclination to tell anybody, I asked how he had heard. Apparently, some of the present cast at the Library Theatre had been drinking that lunchtime in the Bootle Street pub which the police themselves used a lot, as it was next door to the station. They had been accosted there by a policeman who was boasting about who they had caught last night! I assured David that it wasn't going to be a custodial sentence and that I would still be able to do the play. I was fined £15 and disqualified from driving for one year.

The first thing I did was to find a second-hand bike in the newspaper. On my first night out after the ban I cycled to the Portland Lodge, and at the end of the night, despite many offers to put the bike in the boot and give me a lift home, I insisted on going home on my own two wheels: a decision that I regretted as I set off as it was raining quite hard. The rain on my glasses made it impossible to see, so I cycled with my head down and attempted to follow the line of the kerb, coming off with a crunch as I rode into the back of parked cars – twice!

At the risk of stating the obvious, Alfie suited me well as a part and I loved playing the role. As a Londoner I have always considered myself as something of a cockney, or at least possessing the same sort of humour. I remember David Scase, on the first day of rehearsals, giving an example of cockney wit. Apparently as a young man he had been riding pillion behind a somewhat over-exuberant cockney motorcyclist who, when he had to brake violently behind a London bus and it was obvious they were going to crash into the back of it, yelled out, 'You go upstairs and I'll go inside!'

The cast included Maggie Shevlin, a delightful little Irish actress who was later to come for a brief visit to *Coronation Street* and whom I was to use in one of my lunchtime productions; Marlene Sidaway, whom I would come across frequently in the future as she often turned up playing my wife in corporate videos; and Peter Theedom, playing the abortionist, who despite the awful nature of the scene played it in such a way that I had great trouble in keeping my face straight. It had nothing to do with his interpretation: I had a great respect for his acting, and I am surprised that I haven't heard much of him since; he was very talented and had a mesmeric quality. In fact, I found the play often so awful in the terrible way that Alfie rode roughshod over his women that I felt a frequent tendency to giggle.

During the Wythenshawe performances, I was once again overlapping with *Coronation Street*; in the studios during the day and in the theatre at night. Apart from the financial advantages of having two jobs at the same time I enjoyed very much the pressure of dashing from one to the other and I was sorry when it stopped and I was back to doing just the Street. When I left in May 1973, I had no idea that it would only be about seven months before my return.

The fact that I was becoming permanently associated with the part of Billy Walker was borne out in my next job. I was playing a very unsavoury fairground attendant in *The Tomorrow People* for Paul Bernard who had written the three episodes that I was involved in and was also directing. I was dressed as a scruff, with my hair dyed black, a moustache, a week's beard growth, an earring and a scar on my darkened face. We were filming on Clacton pier, and I was sitting on a bench some way from the filming when two middle-aged ladies passed and, hardly bothering to look, said, 'Hello Billy,' and walked on!

By now the Youth Theatre had developed beyond all of our wildest dreams. Michael Croft was still battling but had achieved national recognition, received sponsorship from a variety of commercial firms and had earned himself an MBE. I had never lost touch with Mike and the Youth Theatre; I would often call in to see them, and made a point of trying to see all of the summer productions. I would also help out, whenever I was free, with the auditions which were now held all over the country. Kids would travel to their nearest big town for the preliminary auditions, which were taken by past members such as myself who knew what to look for; if they were successful, they would then travel to London to meet Mike himself. It was Paul Hill and I who first auditioned Helen Mirren as a very confident and well-endowed schoolgirl, who left Paul open-mouthed at her brazen assertion that she would do absolutely anything to get into the Youth Theatre. She was indeed very striking, and not only physically: she did a very impressive audition and I remember writing on her audition form, 'Mike must see!'

I also did a great deal of fundraising for the Youth Theatre. I organised a sponsored walk of twenty-six miles around London, when hundreds of us set off from the headquarters in Eccleston Square and called on all the people and places who had helped the Youth Theatre: Sir Ralph Richardson's home in Regent's Park, the Veever sisters, Alleyn's school, Toynbee Hall. Apart from raising a deal of money, it served to draw attention to the Youth Theatre and showed young people prepared to put some effort into doing something for themselves. Dicky Hampton and I also put on an evening of poetry and prose, with Judi Dench and Edward Woodward who proved able to do a hilarious and realistic replication of a trumpet! Mike also called upon me to organise a march on the Arts Council, to protest at not getting a grant; or was it to protest at the cutting of the grant, I'm not quite sure.

My final fundraising effort was a hugely successful charity soccer match at Crystal Palace. I used my contacts with the charity football scene and organised both teams myself, not wishing to end up with the usual collection of nobodies. Graham Haberfield turned out with Bryan Pringle, his co-star from *The Dustbinmen*; along with Terry Spinks, the ex-Olympic boxing champion whom I had met in a sports shop in Brixton, Brian Glanville the sports writer, Dennis Waterman, and Jimmy Tarbuck who had flown back from Spain early in order to play. I had invited so many 'names' that I didn't feel I could play myself and leave one of them out. Many of them had said they were unfit and only wanted to play half a game, but when it came to the crunch at half time, they didn't want to come off. They were enjoying it that much; loving the limelight. At half time in the dressing room, Jimmy Tarbuck said, 'Here, take my shirt and get on.' On hearing of this, the opposing side asked him to play for them and he got a full game anyway, but it was a generous gesture on his part.

After the game, I stayed behind to help clear up and pay the various bills, so I got back to Eccleston Square late for the little celebration that had been laid on. When I arrived, the place was heaving. There were people I had never seen before; they certainly hadn't helped with the game. There were also such luminaries as Vanessa Redgrave, who hadn't even been at the game. They were all swigging wine and getting stuck in to crab salad. I was at first a little put out, but when I asked who was paying for it and was told that it was being paid for out of the match profit, I was livid and had a big row with Mike, telling him I would no longer be involved in fundraising for the Youth Theatre. Instead, I turned my attention to the Manchester Youth Theatre where I had been invited by Geoff Sykes to direct *Antony and Cleopatra*.

In reality, I couldn't deny Mike for long and I was prevailed upon to get involved once again in fundraising when the playwright Alan Plater approached me to set up a soccer game in Hull to raise money for the theatre there, as well as for the National Youth Theatre. To make it an attractive proposition, I hired a luxury coach with TV, bar, toilets et cetera on board, and set about getting some well-known faces. Tom Courtenay, John Alderton, Barrie Rutter and a number of others agreed to play, but come the day they all opted to make their own way north and make a weekend of it as they mostly originated from that area. In the end Michael Parkinson, whom I had known as a drinking companion in the Film Exchange in Manchester, travelled in lonely splendour, accompanied solely by a couple of Youth Theatre volunteers who had agreed to act as stewards and run the bar, arriving at the game in what appeared to be the next stage up from a stretch limo. Since I had also made my own way there in order to make sure that everything was all right, he travelled back in solitary splendour too, but I received a phone call from him early the next morning to say that the coach had broken down on the return trip and he had only just arrived home!

The success of the National Youth Theatre was changing its face. It was now a recognised way of becoming an actor and as such was putting the emphasis more on talent, which was inevitable really. In Manchester, the original principles were more in evidence. There were three ways to get acceptance in the company. First, of course, there was talent; second, we would accept kids who we thought had the right attitude and would be good to have around; and then there were those who were somewhat deprived and who we felt would get some benefit from the experience. In the first week of the summer session the whole company of about eighty kids met up for a few days of workshops, movement classes, improvisations and games. Meanwhile, one by one, Geoff, myself and his new wife Hazel held auditions and interviews and sorted through the whole bunch, culminating in the weekend session when we would meet up at Geoff's house and cast the plays, vying with each other for the talent available.

Also in that first week I organised another of my sponsored walks starting at the Forum, Wythenshawe where we were to play *Antony and Cleopatra* and culminating at the Library Theatre. I managed to get Mike Summerbee to start us off and he walked with us for the first few miles. It was about this time that we managed to get the pharmaceutical company Ciba-Geigy to sponsor the Youth

Theatre, and they did so for the next seven years. I like to think that it was my involvement that persuaded them to invest; I had managed to raise the profile of the MYT, getting more press coverage and stimulating interest simply because I had been in *Coronation Street*.

Choosing to do *Antony and Cleopatra*, I was throwing myself in at the deep end, but I felt that I could use much of my experience from Croft's production at Alleyn's. I was lucky enough to get a very good Cleopatra, who was not only very capable but also very attractive. Enobarbus too was an excellent actor, Chris Fox, who eventually went on to become professional, as did David Threlfall who played Mardian, the eunuch.

The rehearsal period was exceedingly traumatic and I realised why Mike was so successful: it doesn't do to be married! I had persuaded Paddy to come up with the kids and they were to get involved in the productions, working in Geoff Sykes' production of *Troilus and Cressida*. We were staying at the house in Whalley Range, which Paddy understandably found a bit of a rough area. I tried to get her involved with helping me by taking some of the kids aside and helping them with their speeches, but it didn't work; towards the end of the rehearsal period she 'threw a wobbler' and returned home, leaving me with the kids!

To cap it all, just before the MYT season, I had been working on a one-man play called *The Man Who Almost Knew Eamonn Andrews*, by John Heilpern. The play, about a young man dying of cancer and writing a letter to Eamonn Andrews as he sits in his bedroom playing occasionally with a yo-yo, was directed by Stephen Butcher, a floor manager at Granada who wanted to and indeed did become a director. I performed the piece at the Swinton and Pendlebury Festival in the early days of rehearsing *Antony and Cleopatra* and was seriously brought down to earth by playing to a mere handful of people on the two nights that we ran for. I remember on the last night seeing Doris Speed sitting in the front row with her handbag clasped on her lap, looking very proud and pleased with her son; she was almost alone! I was still very raw from this levelling experience.

This was my first attempt at directing and it was traumatic to the extreme. The biggest problem was the set. The designer appeared to have bitten off more than he could chew and, when under pressure, was inclined to bury his head in the sand and start fiddling around with something completely unimportant, which increased my frustration and consequently my fury. I had rows with him daily which only seemed to make things worse. Despite all of this, the production was a great success and was the start of my seven-year involvement with the Manchester Youth Theatre.

11

1973 to 1975 • *Getting On* • Liverpool Playhouse •
Peter Stringfellow • *Coronation Street* •
Anne Kirkbride • Lunchtime theatre •
Harrogate • Ted Edgar

ONCE *ANTONY AND CLEOPATRA* had opened, I was commuting between Liverpool and Manchester as I had been invited to play the lead in Alan Bennett's *Getting On*. This was to be the start of a long relationship, in fact the start of two long relationships: the first with Liverpool Playhouse and the second with Anthony Tuckey, for some reason known as Dick Tuckey. In fact, now I come to think of it, it was the start too of a long-running relationship with Jane Lowe who was to play my wife, over the next few years, on many occasions.

I loved Liverpool. I knew it slightly as I had visited socially from time to time when in Manchester; and just as Manchester had a well-deserved reputation for its vibrant nightlife, so did Liverpool. This first visit, though, at the end of 1973 was to be just a taster; I didn't come back until April 1975, after another lengthy return to the Street and when Leslie Lawton had taken over the Playhouse, Dick Tuckey having gone to Ipswich. I also loved Alan Bennett's play; there is one speech when the middle-aged MP stands alone, looking out of the window, and eulogises about autumn, which for some reason I have always found very moving.

Before heading back to *Coronation Street* for another eighteen-month stint, starting that December, I fitted in a radio play from the BBC studios in Leeds, where Alfred Bradley and Tony Cliff frequently called me for the odd weekend to play in their BBC Radio 4 dramas. On one of these visits to Leeds I was cast alongside Robert Powell; and after the first day's rehearsal and a few ales in the pub with Alfred Bradley, we found ourselves on our own and not yet ready for bed. Robert took me to a club that was fast becoming the 'in place' to go, Cinderella Rockerfella's, where the DJ was the very upwardly mobile and ambitious Peter Stringfellow. Robert appeared to be 'in the know' there, and we were shown to a side table overlooking the dance floor. After getting a drink, Robert excused himself and went to the loo; I saw him having a word with Stringfellow on his way out. When he returned, Stringfellow, who was somewhat of a live wire on the microphone, announced that Robert Powell and Billy Walker were in the club, a light came up on our table, and a few moments later a bottle of champagne came in an ice bucket.

When Peter and his family moved to Manchester some year or so later, I was invited to their house in Cheadle and he asked me to help him get a licence to open a club in Manchester. He apparently needed a reference from a responsible member of the community and I provided him with Geoff Sykes, who was head of English at a respected school and also, because of his position as director of the Manchester Youth Theatre, was rubbing shoulders with local councillors in his attempt to get local funding. Peter got his licence, and Geoff and his wife Hazel were given a good night out at Peter's new club, the Millionaire.

I too had gained some brownie points and was made a VIP member of the club, the validity of which was stretched some year or so later when I took Hywel Bennett (who had played Ophelia in the NYT production of *Hamlet*) late one night, only to be told that Hywel was banned. Apparently, he had disgraced himself on a previous occasion, but he wouldn't tell me what he had done. Peter came to the door and, as a special favour to me, he allowed Hywel in, but I was to be held responsible. Later in the evening when Hywel had taken enough on board to forget himself again, he went missing. I discovered him in altercation with a waitress, and found out why he had been banned; he could get a bit violent when he was in drink and didn't get his way. I got him out of there as fast as I could. What had happened to the little boy who had played Ophelia!

When I returned to *Coronation Street* at the end of December 1973, I had only been away for some seven months, so little had changed except that the Street now had a new producer, Susie Hush. I had long argued that it was beneficial to the Street for its actors to get out and do other things, to charge their batteries and to improve their craft, and in general I had not encountered much resistance to me doing things, as it were, extramurally. Since I was now more or less committing myself to being a regular in the Street I was open to any suggestions; so when I was approached by Richard Guinea, who was a director at Granada, and asked to do lunchtime theatre at the beginning of December before my return, I jumped at the chance. London had already experimented with the idea of taking over a room in a pub and putting on half-hour dramas, mostly comedy, which people could enjoy while they took their lunch. John Stevenson, who was on the team of Street writers, wrote a little piece called *England Swings*, with three actors: myself, Diana Davies and André Van Gyseghem. Upstairs in the Nag's Head, it proved to be a great success and the place was packed, so much so that the pub found it difficult to cope and wasn't too keen on doing it again.

Tommy Mann, the wrestler, who had been fight advisor for *This Story of Yours* in Glasgow, took up the fight from there and managed to get a brewery to promise sponsorship; he then approached me and asked if I would put together a production for another pub: the Grapes. Buoyed by my first and recent success at directing the MYT, and anxious to get some sort of stimulation from outside the Street, I started searching for a playlet to perform.

I didn't have to look far. I found a book of three short plays by David Halliwell, whom I had admired ever since *K. D. Dufford*, and wrote off for the right to produce *Muck from Three Angles*. It was a very funny three-hander, where the action is played three times, each time the same scene but from the viewpoint of a different character. In reality, there was much of the K. D. Dufford in embryo about it.

My first thought when it came to casting was my mate Graham Haberfield, whom I admired greatly, and Anne Kirkbride whom I also had great admiration for, so much so that I kept trying to persuade her to leave the Street and get out to do other things; I felt she was wasted. Once she had settled into her character of Deirdre, she was not going to move. I tried on a number of occasions to get her to take a chance and get out; I was certain that she had qualities that could have taken her to the top of the acting profession, but after one such attempt when she told me to f--k off, mind my own business and leave her alone, I didn't mention it again. But I still feel that she was wasted and when I worked with her on *Muck from Three Angles*, I was convinced that I was right.

I had also persuaded Maggie Shevlin, who had been one of Alfie's conquests, to come and rehearse for two weeks and play for one. The money of course was not good, but because the brewery was sponsoring us I could at least offer something. No sooner had I got the whole thing set up when Tommy Mann informed me that the brewery had reneged on its sponsorship and there was no money forthcoming! By now I had really got my mind set on the production and felt I was in too deep to back out, so I decided to use my own money to pay the cast and try and recoup on the takings. Graham, when he heard, said he would split it with me and we went into our first venture together!

Muck from Three Angles was an even greater success than *England Swings*. The Grapes had never before been so jammed full; they were queuing to get in and we played to standing room only. Unfortunately, we had only arranged to do four performances and when we asked if we could extend the run, again the pub was still reeling from the disruption of their normal trade and said no. By the time Graham and I had paid the girls and bought the odd prop, we split the profit between us and got sixpence each! I gave Graham a cheque, which he said he was going to frame.

Working with Graham as a director was, on one level, wonderfully stimulating and rewarding. He had such a creative imagination that it was mainly a matter of keeping it in check and being selective; allowing him to fantasise in a particular direction and then helping him to choose what to keep and what to leave out. On another level, however, we had a falling-out. On the day of the last performance, when we had not been rehearsing at Granada in the morning, Graham turned up pissed; and although he managed the performance, he was all over the place and let the girls down badly as they had to bail him out time after time. I was livid, but said nothing until we were walking back to Granada after the show and I gave him a verbal assault. I lectured him at some length about how he had not only let the girls and me down, but how he was letting himself down too. He was outraged that I should talk to him in that way, but I think he knew he was at fault, because he turned quite violent. Not with me: although it was directed at me, I'm sure he was angrier with himself. As we walked down Quay Street, he started to punch the wall until his knuckles were bleeding. I was quite frightened by the intensity of his anger; but when he had sobered up we were friends once more, and it wasn't long before we were again to try our hand outside of Granada.

That summer I took the month of August off to direct the Manchester Youth Theatre once more. This time it was *Henry IV Part 2*; and, remembering the general chaos in the set-building department, I persuaded my brother Brian and an enterprising young man from Alleyn's, Graham Budden, who had just left school and was waiting to go into the air force, to come up from 'the smoke' and join us. My brother was at that time a self-employed builder and decorator, whose marriage had broken up. He had always had a soft spot for the Youth Theatre, having joined the crowd in *Henry V* at Toynbee Hall, and had the time of his life. I'm afraid my brother had none of my advantages. At an important time in his development, he was very ill with osteomyelitis, and almost died. Although now very strong, it had badly interrupted his schooling; and, whereas I had won a scholarship to a direct-grant school, he had had to make do with a state education, which in those days in the Peckham district was disaster.

Graham and Brian worked together well and the set-building department became one of the strong areas of the MYT. One of the great things about the Youth Theatre movement was that it provided the opportunity for kids not only to act, but also to take part in the many other aspects of the theatre such as design, wardrobe, set building and stage management. Having had a rather traumatic time with the designer of *Antony and Cleopatra* the previous year, I was trying to get Geoff to get some kids in to try their hand at designing too. Hitherto, they had an art teacher who more or less did it all single-handed. If I had any criticism of the Youth Theatre (which of course I did), it was that there were too many teachers involved and their method of maintaining order was too much like still being at school. There was of course the difficulty that teachers were the only ones who were available during the summer holidays; a good argument.

I also managed to get Gordon McKellar involved with the MYT, as a 'Mr Fix-It'. He was a sort of troubleshooter-cum-assistant-producer for *Coronation Street*, and was invaluable as he knew all the right contacts and was able to pull in many favours for us. He persuaded Granada to let us have the old sets that were due to be demolished, so we were able to cut costs on materials. I learnt that the union rules meant that when a set had been finished with, it could not be adapted or used again by Granada. In order to keep the carpenters and set builders in work it had to be destroyed, and a firm was paid to take the stuff away and burn it! Before the season started I did a tour of the scene dock at Granada and, seeing what was available, designed my set accordingly.

Henry IV Part 2 has always been one of my favourite plays with its wonderful mixture of historic drama and low-life comedy. It was also ideal for the MYT as it called for a large cast, with a wonderful selection of good meaty parts to share out. I was lucky enough to have one of the more mature of the old members, Alan Williams, to play Falstaff. He proved to be not only a good actor, but also a budding playwright when, some years later, he was to write a play for the MYT that I was to direct. Alan had a good presence and a very rich voice, which was ideal. He was, however, very thin, and Falstaff should not look exactly under-nourished, as Alan not only looked, but was! I had no idea until he collapsed between shows at the Forum Wythenshawe, and I discovered that he hadn't eaten for some days. Alan was one of my students, as I like to call them, who eventually went on to a career in the theatre, not only as an actor but also as a writer. I still see him cropping up from time to time, and he never looks well to me!

Once again, in the production of *Henry IV Part 2*, I borrowed much from my early days with Mike Croft. I did, however, have what I considered a bright original idea for the ostlers scene, which is quite often cut. I had the prop department construct a basket with a turkey's head sticking out of it and a false hand, so that the actor could animate the turkey, somewhat like Rod Hull and his Emu. This give some point to the line 'The turkeys in my pannier are quite starved'; the actor was able to manipulate the turkey to be continually attempting to bite his neck, thus giving the opportunity for some Rod-Hull-type comedy. A bit pantomimic, I suppose, but I was trying to make the comedy scenes a bit of a romp.

After the play opened, I was back in the Street and of course kept an eye on the production in the evening. I turned up one night to find that one of the actors, who as a child had lost his hand in an accident and wore a false one, had built in his own comedy moment when he shook hands with another actor and walked away, leaving him holding his false hand! They were a great bunch of kids and I was really getting into the Youth Theatre movement again with a vengeance.

I was due to leave the Street in April 1975, round about the time when, each year, the producers liked to get some sort of spring wedding into the storyline. As I understood it, Peter Adamson and Neville Buswell were each approached and asked if they fancied their characters getting married, but they both declined. This was understandable as unmarried characters tended to get more attention, more fan mail, and also more interesting storylines. Susie Hush then asked me if I would be prepared to marry Deirdre, and I said I didn't mind at all; I loved working with Annie. It was then that Susie became aware that my contract was due for renewal in mid April and said that it would not be right to marry me off to Deirdre if I was going to leave just after the wedding, so would I be prepared to sign another contract to stay for at least six months? At this point, I thought it time to bring my agent into the equation. By now, I was with Richard Eastham, who had been with the American William Morris agency and had also been Michael Codron's right-hand man; he was therefore extremely experienced and capable and I arranged for him to meet Susie for lunch.

We weren't looking for more money, as I gather I was already being paid the same as all of the top artists like Doris Speed and Bill Roache (I was told that there were six of us on the top money), but we were looking to negotiate for more weeks out, with pay, as I knew others had done. I understood that at the lunch there had been no problem and Susie had agreed with Richard; I was to sign for another six months and was to get an extra fortnight of paid holidays.

The storylines started; Deirdre and Billy got it together and in due course became engaged. When the contract eventually came for me to sign, I noticed that there was no mention of the extra holiday weeks and set my agent to work to find out what was happening. The contract department told him that Susie had no authority to agree to my extra weeks and they were not going to allow it, so I refused to sign. As the day for the marriage drew near, Susie happened to mention that they had booked the church and the day was set for something like April 11th; I said, 'That's good, 'cos I leave on the 18th.' She was distraught and surprised, as the contract department hadn't even told her.

There followed a number of frantic telephone calls and pleas, but Artists' Contracts refused to budge and I refused to sign. I was quite angry that some accountant in the pay department should have the power to dictate policy to the department that created the entertainment that provided him with his wages. However, I was also aware that I, or rather they, had given Susie and the casting department, Judi Hayfield in particular, a problem, as the scripts had already been written and there was not much time to get me out of the engagement, so I agreed to stay on for a further three weeks to give them time to rewrite. The engagement was broken off, and Deirdre married Ray Langton! The church had been booked and they had to have a wedding!

Peter Ellis, the brother of Robin Ellis who had played the lead in *Poldark*, was a floor manager who wanted to be a director; just before I left, he asked me if there was anything I would like to do with him. Once again David Halliwell came up trumps and I suggested we did *Who's Who of Flapland*, a two-hander that was too long for lunchtime, but would make an ideal evening in the Stables Theatre. Above all, I wanted to do it with Graham; I wanted to see if I could live on stage with him. I had such an admiration for his acting, and I wanted to measure myself up against him.

I had always wanted to direct the play myself, so I had a fairly firm view of how it should be done, which was unfortunate for Peter who had rather a baptism of fire. Graham and I more or less had our heads, and it became a contest of imagination; we were both playing tramps and tried to outdo each other in awfulness, dressed in rags with our possessions hanging from our waists, covered in sores and smelling awful. I blacked out my teeth and Graham topped it by taking his out! He also had the brainwave of wearing glasses with one frosted lens; I wore glasses with no lenses at all. To test our make-up, we got dressed and wandered into the Granada car park one lunchtime, scrabbling around in the waste bins until we were kicked out by Granada security, who knew us both well but were, for a time, completely fooled. The moment of truth was actually caught on camera as Stuart the Granada press office photographer was standing by.

We didn't perform on a stage; the Stables was set up with tables for drinking and eating, and when everybody was settled we ad-libbed our entrance in all our awfulness, took up our position on a vacant table and started the scene, which is a wonderful exercise in verbal gymnastics and very funny. We played for a week to absolute capacity and were then invited to take it to the Shore Theatre in Oldham, where we played for a further week to full houses.

All went well again until the last night. I was no longer in the Street at that time and since I was still banned from driving, I was waiting at home in Whalley Range for Graham to pick me up. He was late, and I was beginning to get worried when the car arrived with Graham in the back seat and Valerie, his wife, driving. There was a terrible atmosphere and it was obvious within a few seconds that Graham was pissed and they had had a great row. I got into the back seat and said nothing. I had seen how violent he could get when in drink and decided that it wasn't worth risking an outburst and the possible cancelling of the show.

That last show was a nightmare. Graham was all over the place and although we got through it, it was not a good show and we only just made it. Since we were both heavily made up and smelly, after a glass of champagne that Peter Ellis had sweetly brought backstage for us, we took a shower. Nothing was said until we were alone together under the shower. I wasn't talking to him, and Graham knew something was wrong. He opened the subject by saying, 'You thought I was pissed, didn't you?' at which point I let rip and told him just how stupid I thought he was. I told him that I really envied him his talent and would give my right arm to be as talented as him; I found it so sad to see him wasting it in such a way, and he should get out of the Street and back to acting in plays that would stretch him and develop his talent instead of restricting it to the limited demands of a twice-weekly soap. He also did himself no favours with his drinking which was perhaps a symptom of his frustration. Strangely, he didn't get violent; he started to cry, and so did I. We stood together under the shower crying!

That summer I came back up to Manchester for the Youth Theatre season, this time directing a play that the kids had constructed for themselves, called *Who Do You Think You're Talking To?* and performed at the Library Theatre. I must say I wasn't as happy doing this sort of thing as I was when directing the classics, although it was quite a good exercise in trying to get mediocre scripts to work.

I returned to Liverpool Playhouse for a new play by Hugh Leonard, called *Da* and directed by Leslie Lawton, who had just taken over as artistic director from Dick Tuckey and was making quite a name for himself. There is always a great thrill in being the first to play a character, and it is doubly rewarding when the author is around from time to time to give his support and help to build the confidence. Since *Da* is an autobiographical piece, being very much about Hugh's relationship with his father and dealing with his return to his home in Ireland for his father's funeral, it was invaluable having him there, and I must say he didn't interfere much. Leslie proved to be very good for me to work with; we got on well, and I was to work a lot for him in the future. My father, or rather the spirit of my father who appeared from time to time, was played by Denis Carey and I was warned at the start of rehearsals not to take him out for a drink. Apparently, he had a big drink problem and was on a promise not to touch a drop. I spent most of the play watching the younger me with my father in flashbacks. It really was a touching piece and I am surprised that it has not been done more often.

It was on this trip to Liverpool when I first came across Alan Rudkin, who was a gutsy little Welsh boxer, who should have been a world champ, but was cheated from the title. I discovered him running a pub in the centre of Liverpool and when I was offered the chance of drinking there after the show it became a favourite haunt of mine! At some time, I think in Alan Rudkin's pub, I had met and become friendly with Brian Labone, the ex-captain of Everton and England centre half. He had come with his beautiful wife Pat, who had been Miss United Kingdom, to see the show, and thereafter I had occasionally been invited to join them at a cabaret club where they sometimes went in the evenings.

One weekend when Brian and Pat learnt that I was not going home, they invited me to Sunday lunch; it was arranged for me to meet Brian in his local pub and then go back home with him. I thought I could hold my own, but I found I was really out of my depth. There were six of us in the round and everybody had a whiskey and chaser each round; that is, six times! By the time we got home to lunch I was well and truly oiled; and after lunch, with wine, I wandered out into the garden and played with Rachel, their daughter. Maudlin with drink, I was getting homesick and missing my own kids. I pushed her on the swing and then she asked if I would like to see her horse, and took me to a field with two horses, a small pony and a large magnificent-looking animal.

I have always had a soft spot for horses and ever since the days of *The Splendid Spur* have wanted to have one of my own. Encouraged by the little girl and emboldened by the drink I managed to mount 'the magnificent beast', but not for long. I had never fallen from a horse before; in fact I didn't exactly fall from this one, I was thrown; then again, not just thrown – I was flung upwards into the air and landed some distance away. As I lay on the ground, I was aware that my left arm was bending the wrong way from the elbow. I wasn't in pain, and I wasn't drunk any more. I rose in a daze and seeing my left arm now just dangling at my side, I took the elbow and forced it back into its joint, got the little girl to pick up my glasses and trudged back to the house.

When Brian saw me, he said my face looked like a 'boiled shite'. At this point he informed me that the smaller horse belonged to his daughter, and the larger horse had not been broken in yet. He and Pat took me to the local hospital where a doctor put my arm in a sling and said there was nothing he could do. By now, the pain had set in and I was living on painkillers.

That night I stayed with Pat and Brian and, having phoned Leslie Lawton, arrived early at the theatre to work out how I was going to perform with one arm in a sling. We changed the sling for a black one to make it look more attractive and the show went on. So did the pain; it persisted for some weeks and I eventually took myself to see Freddie Griffiths at Manchester City, who told me that the sling had been too low and loose and if I hadn't come to him, my elbow could have locked at half cock and I would have had to have an operation. I was also told that I had been lucky to 'reduce' the dislocation immediately; if I had waited the swelling would have made it impossible! I still have trouble with that elbow: its movement is quite restricted.

The first time I had played Liverpool in *Getting On*, I had stayed with Alan and Beryl Williams – not the Manchester Youth Theatre Alan Williams, but the one whose claim to fame had been that he was the man who gave away the Beatles, and now made a living by lecturing on what a bloody fool he had been! He and his wife Beryl had a large house with rooms let out mainly to theatricals. I was in a room on the ground floor and was woken one night, or rather in the early hours of the morning, by somebody in the garden tapping on the window and calling my name, Ken. On opening the French doors, I discovered a complete stranger who, on seeing me, explained that he was looking for Ken Campbell, who apparently usually had that room. It was a pretty mad household.

On this, my second trip to Liverpool, I managed to get into the theatre house, 8 Huskisson Street, also owned by the Williamses and occupied solely by the Playhouse actors. Each tenant had a bedsitting room, and there was a communal kitchen and lounge in the basement. The house was early Victorian and five storeys high. The whole thing was very tacky and dilapidated; all of the furniture had seen better days, and although Beryl came in to clean the communal areas and collect the rent once a week (we left the cash under the pillow), it never really felt clean. Somehow, though, it was home and after a few weeks there I became as fond of the place as all of the regulars.

Huskisson Street itself was also a very dodgy area, within walking distance from the theatre and, so I was told, home to many of the local prostitutes. Every morning the man in the house opposite would get up at 6.30 and take his two Alsatian dogs, barking madly, down the front steps and put them into his Land Rover, leaving them there for some few minutes to make sure that nobody in the street was still asleep before driving off. I determined to get up one morning and do something about it, until I looked out of the window and saw just how unsavoury a character he was! Our nearest pub, luckily, was the Vine, run by John and his wife. The Vine was not only a good well-run pub, it was a beautiful old Victorian place with the original tiles and many nooks and crannies. It was only challenged for beauty by the Philharmonic which was nearer to the theatre and boasted the most magnificent Victorian gents, which people would come from far and wide to see; it was not unusual to be interrupted when 'taking a leak' by somebody showing his wife around the urinal!

For many years I loved Liverpool and had many happy times there; but in later years when I returned, I was saddened to find how it seemed to have lost its soul. Liverpool suffered more than most from the unemployment that struck the country during Thatcher's crusade to stifle the power of the unions. Not only did it lose its resilience and humour, many of its unemployed left the city ostensibly to try and find work elsewhere but in reality to live off the dole and steal in more affluent areas, and ended up giving a very bad name to the Scouser.

In many ways my relationship with Liverpool was mirrored in my relationship with David Clapham. I met David very early on in my first visit to Liverpool. He was a lecturer in the art department at the polytechnic, specialising I believe in animation. He was to be very helpful in later years when my eldest son was starting out in that field and David let him loose in the studios. I think I first met David in the Philharmonic when he asked me to play in a cricket match at the polytechnic. The friendship developed and we met regularly for a drink. I did the odd voice-over on videos that he did privately, and when he opened up his own studio in an ex-police station called the Bridewell I even appeared in the odd video. I enjoyed doing them, and he would fit them in around my availability. There wasn't much money involved; I did them mainly because I liked him and enjoyed his company.

As the years passed, he either left or was pushed from the polytechnic; he set up more permanently in his video business, and I worked quite frequently for him. When I was no longer working in Liverpool I would stay with him and his wife. The final job for him was for a self-defence video, which I not only rewrote and directed, but appeared in and also got my then partner to play a leading role. The money was all agreed but never arrived; after much pressure, I got him to pay her, but without consultation he unilaterally decided to reduce her payment. I waited some years before I got paid and then only after getting Equity to take legal action. The money wasn't much and I was sad to have to go to those lengths, but I was angry and hurt that he did not simply write or come to me and explain the problem. I later learnt that his marriage had broken up; I have not heard of him since. In the same way, my relationship with Liverpool died over the years and in the end there is sadness at what has become of that once vibrant and exciting city.

But in the early days at the Playhouse I couldn't have been more contented. Not only was I happy with the plays, I was also delighted to find myself in a provincial theatre that was doing good work and was appreciated by the general populace. I was to return there often in the future.

It was while I was at Liverpool that I heard of Graham Haberfield's death on October 17th 1975. I was of course completely distraught and was glad to be able to get away for the funeral in Knutsford, even though I had to get back to Liverpool for the evening show. The place where he is buried is a typical old English country churchyard way out in the country, with old and mossy leaning headstones, a yew tree and hedgerows full of birds' nests. For some years afterwards I made a point of calling in to the churchyard whenever I was in that area. It is now more than forty years since his death and I still miss him. I not only admired him: I loved him.

It must have been something like two years later, during my next return to the Street, that Bill Roache gave me the exercise book that had belonged to Graham and was supposed to be the start of a play he was writing. Bill at that time was dabbling with the occult – he was I believe a Druid at one time – and told me he had had a visitation from Graham who had asked him to give me the exercise book and tell me to take up the writing of his play. When I looked inside the book, there was just one page of dialogue, set in a newspaper office, and not very good dialogue at that! He really was 'off the wall'!

I have frequently been advised to take a job because the director was a promising young talent and working for them could supposedly pay dividends in the future. Sadly, those early favours are so often forgotten when the young hopeful does eventually 'get his spurs'. Stephen Butcher, who had been a floor manager and was now a director at Granada, had made considerable progress since he had directed me in the one-man show for the Swinton and Pendlebury Festival, and proved an exception to the rule by not only offering me a job, but also in going to some considerable lengths to make sure that I got it.

Apparently, the general policy at Granada was to not encourage regular Street actors to leave and seek other work. The reasons I gather were twofold. Obviously they wanted to keep their actors wherever possible and not have them coming and going; they also wanted to maintain that perception of them in the public's mind as being real people and not actors, which seeing them in something else would undermine. Thus it was that Stephen asked me if I would play a character in the dock for three episodes of *Crown Court*, but not to mention it to anybody. I could tell my agent, so that he didn't find me something else, but I wasn't to expect a contract until the very last minute. By the time the casting office were aware of what had happened, it would be too late.

The show was rehearsed without the jury for one week and the prosecution and the defence were prepared. On recording day the jury was brought in; they were not actors but genuine members of the public, who were sworn in and heard the cross examinations before being taken aside and, under the auspices of the floor manager, would debate the case and come up with a verdict.

I was later told that they were all expecting at least one of the jury to recognise the fact that I was, or had been, Billy Walker in *Coronation Street*; but when it came to it, it was never mentioned once in the discussion and they weren't aware until somebody asked them afterwards if they had noticed and none of them had. I had last appeared in the Street at the end of April and this was now November, so it wasn't all that long a gap. Which obviously says one of two things: either I was very good at appearing different, or I was pretty insignificant in the Street!

12

TOWARDS THE END of 1975, discussions began with Marilyn Davis of Mansion Plays for a tour of a thriller that was to have a dramatic effect on my private life thereafter. As far as I could gather, the management was new and had no track record. Marilyn was a 'Little Miss Rich Girl' (or rather a Big Miss Rich Girl) who had been given money by her father and wanted to 'have a go' at theatre management. The money was very good, but the play was dreadful. They planned to do Jack Popplewell's *Dead on Nine*; I accepted the job because of the money, and begged them to try and find another play, but Marilyn said it was impossible: they had already paid for the rights.

Since I was the first actor to be cast, I was on the highest money, their plan being to get some sort of recognised name or face to accept and then, with that bait on the hook, to put together the rest of the cast. Consequently, I was on more money than Maxine Audley who was the next poor fish to put her name to this terrible play. I don't think she took the job because my name was on the cast list, but because she was able to do a double deal and get her partner Leo Maguire into the play so they were on two wages. We started rehearsals in February 1976 in a church hall in Pimlico with a press meeting, when the cast and writer were presented to the press and we all met each other for the first time.

My first meeting with Sandra was when, just prior to the arrival of the press, I asked her if she was related to Dinsdale Landen's wife, who happened to share the same surname. Her reply was something of a put-down: 'I can't stand it when people tell me I look like someone else!' Since I hadn't said anything of the sort, I was a little taken aback. With hindsight, I'm even more taken aback since that is exactly what she is constantly doing; whenever she meets or sees anybody for the first time, she always tries to find some reference to somebody she already knows. She was, however, very attractive and I soon forgave her, although it made me a little wary.

After meeting the press, Marilyn treated us all to lunch in a nearby pub; and it was when we were walking back from the pub to the rehearsal room that Sandra said to me, 'This is the first acting job I've had for ten years.' I found the candour very disarming, but since she was playing my secretary with whom I was to have an affair and for whom I murder my wife, I was also a little alarmed: it was an important part! I told her that I was not the person to whom she should be confessing this as I could easily go to the management and ask for her to be replaced with someone with more up-to-date credentials; but I guess I must have been already a little smitten as I just found her candour truly refreshing – and she was very beautiful, or have I said that before?

During rehearsals, I found that she not only looked great, she had an intoxicating personality too. My first surprise was to hear her laugh, which was a bit like a fishwife's cackle, and was all the more surprising since she looked so much like a very well-heeled and upper-class lady. She was married, and I imagined her as the wife of a successful and wealthy architect or lawyer. She had apparently been trained at Central School and had started her career promisingly, having played in the West End and made a film, in which she had played the juvenile lead. At her mother's insistence, she then trained as a teacher to provide her with something to fall back on, and had risen as a teacher to lecturer where she was teaching teachers to teach. From there she had somehow been seen by a photographer and persuaded to go into modelling as a sideline, which eventually took over and she seemed to get every job she went for, ending up in almost every commercial. She was then advised to get a theatrical agent and get back on stage. Her career had come full circle and she was back to acting, although she still did the occasional modelling job.

At one point during the rehearsals, she asked me to cover for her when she slipped off to Spain for a few days to do a commercial for fruit juice. She had a smile that she could just switch on to order, and it was genuine – it hadn't got that fixed look. She was exceedingly photogenic: the cameras loved her, and she returned the compliment. I found her beauty rather daunting and although I flirted, I had no pretensions; I thought her a little difficult. At one point when we were line-learning in the rehearsal-room kitchen, just running through the scene to check the lines, I crouched beside her chair in order to hear her better and not to have to speak too loudly and disturb the others; she told me to go back to my chair, she could hear me from there!

As was my wont, I spent the rehearsal period completely and totally immersed in the play, even though I thought it was crap. There is some sort of protective instinct in an actor that subconsciously persuades him to have a belief in what he is doing; it is often not until well after the event that he realises just how awful it was! I remember once making the mistake of going backstage to see Mike Williams and Judi Dench after a performance of *Pack of Lies* and telling them that their talent was wasted in the play which I thought very trite and badly written; I watched Mike's face fall and he went a bit frosty!

Since the rehearsal hall was not far from my home, I walked to and from work every day, using the walk to learn my lines and work on the part. Sometimes, if we finished at the same time, Sandra would give me a lift home to Clapham; and in the morning, if she saw me walking in, she would pull over. I would sometimes accept the lift, and sometimes wave her on if I was too caught up in my work. I was completely committed to the play and had no room, even in my thoughts, for anything but the production. We were being directed by Royce Mills, a very established and accomplished actor himself, who was demanding and rewarding. I liked being directed by an actor with his sort of technical ability; I had great faith in what he had to offer and loved the challenge. Although I hated the play, he helped me to get some sort of belief in it to make me want to make it work.

We opened at the King's Theatre, Southsea in February 1976. The tour started, and so did the affair that was to bring such grief to people that we loved.

The tour and the affair continued and about half way through the ten weeks, we had a week out, as Mansion Plays had been unable to find a booking. We were playing Birmingham just before breaking up for the week out when, on the last night, there was a knock on my dressing-room door. I called out, 'Who is it?' and Sandra's voice answered, 'Trouble.' That seems to have summed up the whole affair in one word. I was distraught at the thought of losing her and didn't know what the hell was going to happen. I had been 'hoist with mine own petard'; I was in love with her and I didn't know where it was going to lead.

It was during the week out that she phoned me and told me that her husband knew all and wanted her to leave the tour, but she knew she couldn't do that; the legal ramifications would have been horrendous. She was to continue in the play, but we were to terminate the affair. We were not to stay together, but he was allowing her to travel with me in the car. I didn't know how she managed that one, but I was to learn later that she had a tremendous hold over her husband and could get him to agree to almost anything.

I think we both felt that once the tour was over we could just go back to where we were, pick up the broken pieces and put them back together again. In my case, Paddy was not aware of what was going on so I had the easier task. We continued to enjoy the relationship, even if riddled with guilt. It just felt so right that we should be together: we enjoyed the travel, the eating out, the dancing in discos after the show and stayed together more or less openly as far as the rest of the cast were concerned.

We neither of us liked what we were doing. Although Paddy didn't know, I was very aware that I was betraying her and I still loved her. Our relationship was going through a dodgy period and we had not been happy together for some time. I don't know what was wrong; she would just get depressions that I could do nothing about. They didn't seem related to anything that I was doing or not doing, and they seemed to have no logical cause. They could arrive at any given time, and I found that I was not very sympathetic; I couldn't stand the negative attitude towards everything. They had started way back in the Hastings days and I had frequently arrived home after the long journey from Manchester, looking forward to a warm reception and a fun family weekend, to be treated to days of unexplained silence that I could do nothing to alleviate. I felt frustrated and helpless and, after a number of attempts to brighten the atmosphere, I became angry and felt cheated.

I also felt guilty about Brian, Sandra's husband; I didn't know him, but I felt that he would have been the sort of guy I would get on with, and many of Sandra's friends observed that he was not terribly unlike me, though more handsome. He made quite a living as a male model, mainly with Sandra; they did a lot together. He had been a sportsman, rugby and the pole vault, and had then become a teacher before giving it up to join Sandra in modelling. She too was unhappy about what she was doing to him; she still loved him. It was all a bit of a mess. At the end of the tour, we parted, or at least we tried.

One weekend after the tour, we had grabbed a few days together in the house of her friend Nicky Glenn, who lived in Catford with her then husband Steve Glenn, a musician. Nicky was later to remarry and, together with her new husband, started Bucks Fizz. She's now a very wealthy lady. At this time, however, she acted as go-between; in the early days I would call her to find out what was happening to Sandra, and later she became a 'postie', receiving and delivering mail between us. I didn't like the clandestine way the affair now had to be continued. On the tour we had been able to be more open about it since we were away from the people who could be hurt, in areas where they were not known; in a way I felt it was happening to someone else, my other self, not me. Back home and making devious arrangements made it all seem very different.

A month after the tour, I was offered a part in *General Hospital*, at ATV in Elstree. I was playing a man who had been beaten up and thrown from a car at the door of the hospital and who eventually dies in bed. The whole thing was being filmed in the studios in separate scenes much like a film. At the end of the first day, we had arrived at the scene in which I died. It was a difficult scene; I had a longish speech, and gradually got weaker and weaker, then died. We had done it once and the director, not being too happy with it, decided to go for another take. This time it was going well until, just six seconds from the end of the scene, the lights in the studio went out and everything came to a grinding halt. I was lying in bed in my pyjamas and asked what had happened. A rather large (in fact, fat) electrician, who was obviously the chief electrician as he had done nothing all day but sit around watching others work, had risen from his chair and said, 'It's eight o'clock, brother: knocking off!'

I blew my stack. I leapt out of bed in my pyjamas, threw my script (which I kept under the blankets for security) to the floor and gave the fat man a verbal assault, saying more or less that he was a parasite on the profession; they had been late back from tea breaks and from lunch, they had ruined the film industry with their indolent attitude, and were now about to ruin the television industry et cetera et cetera.

The next morning I had to come in early to retake the scene, none too happy as it would have been so much better to have done it at the end of the previous day when I had warmed up to it instead of having to do it now, cold. I seemed to have been waiting in my dressing room an awfully long time when the director and the producer came in and said, 'There's a problem.' The electricians were refusing to go to work until I apologised! They both agreed with me that I was right; the electricians were a particularly bolshie lot and were undermining a lot of the work done in those studios. They told me a story of a generator breaking down when out on location; they managed to come to an arrangement with a nearby house to plug in to their mains and continue work, but the electricians said they had to get another electrician to come out from base as it was not within their remit to plug in. They had to wait two hours for another electrician to arrive and plug in; he then sat around for the rest of the day, doing nothing but waiting to unplug at the end of the day!

I refused point blank to apologise. Shortly afterwards we started work; I was under the impression that I had won, but learnt later that the electricians had gone back to work on condition that I was not employed again for ATV. Much as I disliked Thatcher, I applaud the fact that she broke the power of the union movement that was capable of behaving in that way.

Via Nicky Glenn, I invited Sandra to come for lunch at the studios; I couldn't stop thinking about her, and couldn't bear the thought of not seeing her again. I was finding the deceit and the hurt, plus the danger to my own situation, was spoiling the wonderful feeling that we had had. It was different on tour, when we seemed to have been two separate people; now, back home, it all took on a nasty, self-indulgent and seedy aspect. The time was approaching when we had to either go for it or split up.

On my last day in the studios I got Sandra to come in by herself, in her own car, and after my last shot we went off to a little country pub, where I broke the news that we had to stop. I had three young kids and I was not prepared to sacrifice them at that age. James was 13, Mark 11 and Tessa 10 and I felt that educationally it could have been disastrous for them; I was also very torn about the pain I would be inflicting on Paddy. I had already received a letter from Brian, asking me to find some way to make Sandra hate me and give her up. In all honesty, I didn't know if I would be able to do it, and deep in the recesses of my mind was the thought that perhaps later… At that time, though, I had to make it sound terminal. In all fairness I couldn't say I was making a genuine effort and probably gave out uncertain signals. As I drove back to London, she followed in her car and I could see in my mirror that she was crying her eyes out all the way. We arrived at the point of parting, I pulled over to the side of the road, and we said goodbye for what was supposedly the last time.

It didn't last long, however. I was soon making contact again via Nicky and we met up from time to time. It was summer and I would drive out to Surrey where we would spend the day together, but the whole thing was very unsatisfactory; the guilt and subterfuge were taking most of the pleasure out of it. But it was all we could get, except the one trip I made to Manchester for a pre-season meeting for the MYT; I took Sandra with me and, after the meeting, we went to the Royal Exchange Theatre. On returning home, Paddy and I took the kids for a day out to Cobham and a walk along the banks of the river. Paddy was very silent and uncommunicative all day, making no contribution whatsoever to the occasion, but I didn't think too much of it; it was fairly characteristic and I thought it was just another of her moods.

However, on getting back home to Grafton Square she gave me a letter she had received that morning, from a well-wisher; unsigned! It purported to be from someone who had seen me at the Royal Exchange with a pretty blonde lady. The letter-writer claimed they had a husband who had done something similar and, having been told, were able to nip the affair in the bud, so they felt duty bound to let Paddy know what was going on! There was little I could do but confess and admit that it was true; and in a way there was an element of relief, in that I really hated the deception.

There was something about that letter that didn't ring true; the writing was obviously disguised. I have come to the conclusion, and I'm sure I am right, that it was Sandra's husband who had written it as a last-ditch effort. He knew Paddy was unaware of what was going on, and had previously told Sandra he thought it unfair that I shouldn't suffer. Initially the letter had the desired effect; after much soul-searching and sleepless discussion, I accepted that I couldn't leave Paddy with the kids at that stage of their development. I was very aware of my responsibilities, and agreed to not see Sandra again.

That summer I threw myself into the MYT production of *The Duchess of Malfi*. Once again, I took my kids with me and they all got involved in the various productions: Tessa on stage, Mark with my brother in the workshop and James went off almost daily to Liverpool to try his animation with David Clapham. For the first time I was doing a classic play that I hadn't done previously in some way or another; I was lucky to have Paul Mitchell and Sue Mitchell (they were not related) in the lead roles, and I threw myself into the production. Paddy came with me from time to time, partly I am aware to keep an eye on me. She was understandably in an unhappy mental state, and apparently had at some point spoken to Harry Secombe, with whom she had worked in *Schippel*, who advised her to get a divorce! She had then been to see a solicitor, who told her to start collecting evidence. I really have a hatred for this vocation that makes money by exacerbating the misery of the less fortunate, with their extortionate charges for a letter or phone call, their inflated hourly rates and the elaborate and intricate language designed to heighten the mystery of their profession.

The result was that one night, in the middle of the rehearsal period, I was woken by Paddy attacking me and beating me about the head as I lay in bed. In order not to wake the kids, I took some bedding into the lounge and was trying to get some sleep on the floor when she let the police in and accused me of attacking her! I guess they were quite used to incidents of this nature, and I pointed out that there wasn't a mark on Paddy, I was the one with the bruised face and the bleeding lip, and told them to piss off. I don't think they recognised me, but I was grossly embarrassed. At the time, I was not aware that she had seen a solicitor and put the incident down to a natural pent-up anger, and part of the price I had to pay. I also took it on the chin when, dining in a quite upmarket restaurant with Geoff and Hazel, she made a very public exit, loudly declaiming to the whole room that I was having an affair with a blonde tart!

It wasn't always like this – these were just manic outbursts – so when we were invited to do Noël Coward's *Blithe Spirit* by David Sumner, who had been in my class at RADA and was now artistic director at Crewe Repertory Theatre, I thought it might help to get us back on a more even keel and we accepted. The money was not good and, to make the job more attractive financially, David offered to put us up free in his house where he had a spare room, with bunk beds!

I didn't find David's direction too inspirational and found his casting of a black actress as Elvira, the ghost, to be somewhat perverse. Paddy was superb, though, despite her mental state, and I enjoyed acting with her. Offstage, however, she was very raw and I was still having to pay for my betrayal. I don't think David quite knew what he had landed himself with; he must have been aware of the many outbursts. I was subjected to another nocturnal beating, in the bunk bed; and once, when I raised my knees to protect myself, I happened to catch Paddy on the nose and made her nose bleed. I was very apologetic and tried to comfort her, but in the middle of the night she took herself off to the local hospital and registered herself as a battered wife! She was of course collecting ammunition for the solicitor. Nevertheless, I was resolute in my attempt to make the marriage work. I was quite relieved when after *Blithe Spirit* I was invited back to Liverpool by Leslie Lawton with a wonderful series of parts, starting with Henry II in James Goldman's *The Lion in Winter*, directed by Robert Cartland.

Back in Liverpool and ensconced in Huskisson Street, I worked hard and played hard. There were many places in Liverpool that reminded me of my time there with Sandra when we had played there on tour and frequented Kirklands, a wine bar, almost daily, and Chauffeurs nightclub after the show. It wasn't long before I fell back into my old routine of late nights and too much to drink. Bob Cartland admitted some years later that he was very worried about the way I was burning the candle at both ends. He said he was just waiting for the time when he could catch me out with not knowing my lines or missing an entrance because I was sleeping at the side of the stage. I would frequently lie down between scenes and be apparently asleep, but I was simply conserving my energy and would leap to my feet when I heard my cue coming up. Bob admitted that he was never able to catch me out, but I couldn't have been doing myself any good.

Somehow, the unruly existence that I was leading lent itself to the sort of parts I was getting. Leslie Lawton was the artistic director of the Playhouse and was really putting the place on the map. He certainly had a good eye for what would attract attention and put bums on seats. In the first play of the season, he had managed to get Rachel Herbert to appear nude, and he was looking for a similar headline-grabbing event to include in *The Lion in Winter*, which was to be the second play. During early rehearsals, it was suggested that I should start the play by appearing nude from under a pile of furs and, as the scene progressed, slowly dress as I collected my garments which had been discarded in a fit of sensual indulgence! Much to their dismay I refused, and compromised by emerging in my period underpants which looked not unlike a large nappy. They still were intent on getting their nude bit and eventually persuaded Peter Wight, who was playing the Dauphin, to appear naked with Prince Richard in a later scene; but after some rather belittling press coverage, he changed his mind and got dressed!

Leslie himself directed the next play, *Saturday Sunday Monday* by Eduardo de Filippo; I played Don Pepino, with Jane Lowe, whom I loved working with, as my wife for the second time. At first, we tried it without the Italian accent, but it seemed a bit laboured. However, the moment we all tried the Italian it not only came to life, it became immensely amusing and rewarding to play. It had a large cast and Leslie gathered together the most exciting company I have ever worked with. Apart from Jane there was Brian Miller and his wife Lis Sladen who had been Sarah Jane Smith in *Doctor Who*, a very talented pair. Robert Cartland, who had just directed me, and Lesley Grayburn, who later became a casting director, were also in the company. Vanda Godsell was a very well-known veteran actress who, I later learnt, died penniless in a council flat with no furniture but a mattress and a tea chest and with her little dog that never left her side: it was always in the wings and even got directed into the action. Leslie had worked with most of them before when he was artistic director at Westcliffe, and on getting the prize job of artistic director at Liverpool was one of the rare people who retained a sense of loyalty that prompted him to take them with him. They in their turn were very loyal to him and, despite the fact that he could often be very difficult, they all loved him; there was a wonderful sense of teamwork about that whole season.

Leslie was able to be quite bold and ambitious with his choice of plays and seemed to be winning everything; the more ambitious he was, the greater his success. His next play, *The Front Page* by Hecht and MacArthur, was another large cast with many of the same company, joined by John Hart Dyke (who played Walter Matthau to my Jack Lemmon), Jenny Tarren and Hugh Ross. I loved working with John, which was fortunate because we were next to do all three of Ayckbourn's *The Norman Conquests* together, directed by Bob Cartland; Jane Lowe came back to play my wife for the third time, with Lesley Grayburn, Hugh Ross and Jennifer Piercey also in the cast.

The three plays of *The Norman Conquests* were to bring to an end the six-play run of this particular return to the Liverpool Playhouse. I was missing Sandra desperately, and kept peering through the curtains before the show each night to see if she might be in the audience. She had recently done a photographic modelling job and in Williamson Square outside the theatre there was a large life-size poster featuring her, which I made a point of going to see each night.

Apart from the misery of not being with Sandra, I was very happy in Liverpool; they were a great company and there was a wonderful atmosphere around the theatre. Not only were the plays a great success, but the cross-section of people they appealed to went right across the board. The theatre was not just for the enlightened middle class, it was supported by all and it was a joy to be recognised in the street for something that I regarded as of more quality than *Coronation Street*. I loved the buzz of the city; and I made many wonderful friends, among them Carl Hawkins, Alan Rudkin, Brian and Pat Labone and David Clapham. I think it was probably my most productive period to date, artistically.

The season finished in July and I made my now yearly return to Manchester to direct the MYT, tying it in with a return visit to *Coronation Street*, but this time only for two weeks after I had finished directing *The Devils* by John Whiting.

There were one or two new faces that had arrived in the Street during my absence. Johnny Briggs was playing Mike Baldwin, seemingly the kind of lovable rogue that Billy Walker had hitherto been; and Cheryl Murray was brought in as Suzie Birchall, the sort of character that Pat Phoenix had been playing, but was getting a little old for. Since Julie Goodyear saw herself as fulfilling that role, there was a certain amount of tension as Julie saw her position challenged and tried to undermine Cheryl, just as she had done with Sandra Gough. There was also a delightful little actress, Helen Worth, playing Gail Potter; and Geoffrey Hughes as Eddie Yeats, who was to fill the gap left by Bernard Youens, who wasn't getting younger. It seemed that there were certain character types that the writers wanted to keep going, and as the Street was now in its seventeenth year they were looking to train up the replacements. There were of course new characters like Fred Gee, played by Fred Feast, who was to be built up as the Rovers' devious potman.

There was also a new producer, Bill Podmore, who was to be there for longer than anybody else in that position. Bill was a well-known face at Granada having been deeply involved with the Hylda Baker series *Nearest and Dearest*; and he had brought with him Madge Hindle, to take over the corner shop. Margot Bryant had been written out and was to end her days alone in a mental hospital. I did hear that in moments of lucidity she was apparently rather bitter about Granada and spoke out against them, but in reality the Bernstein brothers had been very good to her and were picking up the tab for her treatment in the Cheadle Royal. Doris was still going strong and the Street was unchallenged in its position of number one. Doris was awarded the MBE, and rather sweetly offered to share it with me as she said I had helped her to get it.

Doris was renowned for her quiet, dry wit. She was getting older and needed to be looked after and handled with kid gloves. Gordon McKellar, the trouble-shooter-cum-assistant-producer, often looked after her far beyond the remit of his job; in fact, he was very much on hand to help out anybody. He drove Doris to various functions and looked after her like her personal valet. Doris was very fond of the theatre, very loyal to her friends and would travel great distances to see them if they were in a play somewhere. She had been to see Irene Sutcliffe in *Vanity Fair* at Westcliffe, way down south, and Gordon had driven her there. The show had gone very well, and afterwards Doris and Gordon were in Irene's dressing room (I believe it was the first night) surrounded by Irene's friends and toasting her success in the show, when Doris asked Gordon to get her fur coat which she had left in the car. Gordon pointed out that the car was parked some way away and by the time he had come back with it, it would be time to go. Doris replied, 'I know dear, but I really do need it now; other people's success always makes me feel rather chilly!'

Of course on the surface the remark could be taken as somewhat mean and small-minded; but knowing Doris, she was setting herself up to be laughed at. She had a wonderfully self-deprecating sense of humour and was always ready to poke fun at herself. After her death I remember seeing Betty Driver, who had played Betty Turpin since 1969 and spent most of her time with Annie behind the Rovers bar, being interviewed by Richard and Judy; on being asked if Doris was as big a snob as her character, she nodded and said, 'Oh yes.' It was during the forty-year celebratory show and both Daphne Oxenford and myself, who were watching the interview together in the green room, said aloud, 'Oh no!' I can only surmise that it was the way the question was put that caused Betty to reply without really thinking. Doris was in many ways exactly like her portrayal of Annie, but with a wicked sense of humour and genuine humility; she worked like a Trojan and cared very much about the Street, and protected her character with a professionalism that was far greater than anybody else's in the show.

I wasn't long away from Liverpool, as I was invited back to play 'The Common Man' in *A Man For All Seasons* by Robert Bolt, directed by Leslie Lawton. William Lucas played Thomas More and there were many of my old friends still in the company. Unfortunately, Leslie had himself played the Common Man in a previous production and had obviously been very successful. I say unfortunately because it proved to be disaster in that whenever we came in rehearsals to my bits, which were often soliloquies to the audience, he said, 'Right, let's skip that boring bit,' and I got very little rehearsal and almost nil direction from him. It wasn't done maliciously; it was very funny and I think that perhaps he thought I should be able to play the part standing on my head. It certainly is the sort of part I should have thought I could do, but in reality my performance was very disappointing.

13

1978 to 1980 • Rose Bruford • *Danger UXB* •
Crewe: *The Odd Couple* and *Bedroom Farce* •
Last MYT • West End: *Night and Day* •
Patrick Mower • Guildford: *Getting On*

ON LOOKING BACK over the years and writing this, it would seem that I was rarely out of work. I was indeed very lucky in that I was able to at least earn a living in the theatre (which is in itself some sort of achievement); but in reality a lot of the work I was doing was not very well paid, and there were many periods of unemployment. While these were not long compared with most actors, they were still enough to dissipate my earnings which I found frustrating.

In July 1975 my old mate David Weston had got me to join him as a guest director at Rose Bruford College of Speech and Drama. Not many actors would have been willing to share such an introduction – they are usually inclined to guard anything like that in case their position should be usurped – but David has always had a wonderfully generous nature. Indeed, he has gone even further, from time to time phoning me up to tell me of an audition that he has just had and, if he felt I was right for the part, suggesting I follow it up!

Strangely, considering my resistance in the past, I had started at Rose Bruford with an improvisation workshop. Although initially unsure of my ground, I took the story of Antony and Cleopatra, gave it a modern setting and got the students to improvise around the scenario of a prominent surgeon having an affair abroad and facing up to the censure of his superiors and his wife. I can't have done as badly as I had thought, as I was invited back again in 1978 to direct excerpts from *The Norman Conquests* and then, the next term, *Billy Liar*. Both were plays that I had done and knew well, so this time I felt much more confident.

I got myself something of a reputation as a stickler for punctuality. When I was directing *Norman Conquests*, I noticed that a student from the production rehearsing next door was continually badly late (he had to pass through my rehearsal room to get to his). When I found that he was playing Billy in *Billy Liar* I was understandably on my guard, so I laid down the ground rules on the first day of rehearsals, for which he was late. Once I had the entire cast together I told them that I was not going to accept any excuses for lateness; quite apart from being rude and an arrogant waste of other people's time, it destroyed the other students' enthusiasm and passion, and mine too. I couldn't believe it when the same student was half an hour late the very next day! Luckily, the part of Billy was double cast, so I told the other Billy that he would be playing the part alone; when the errant student turned up, I informed him he had been replaced. He was naturally taken aback and asked if I wasn't even going to listen to his excuse. I told him that I was fully aware of his record of lateness and had no doubt that he had a good excuse, but I was already behind schedule and had no time to listen to it.

I was later called in to see the college principal and asked if I would reconsider; I refused and said, 'It's him or me.' The principal at that time was Jean Benedetti (previously known as Norman Bennett, I believe) and he reluctantly supported my decision. He was reluctant because the offender was one of the few paying students – that is, not on a grant – and Jean (or Norman) did not want to risk losing him. In the end, he didn't leave, and even came to me at the end of term and thanked me for teaching him a lesson. I don't think he ever made an actor; I have never seen him since.

Two of my students have done well though: Janet Dibley, who played the Granny in *Billy*, and Robert Pugh who has turned in some wonderful perform-ances on the box. I liked teaching; it seemed to be the next step on from the MYT. Unfortunately the openings for guest directors dried up when the college found itself in need of funds and had to cut back. I believe this to have been a short-sighted policy, since I remember from my own student days just how valuable it is to have a working actor, in my case Peter Barkworth, to remind the students that they are part of something living and not just an extension of school.

After my terms as a teacher-cum-director at Rose Bruford, I went back again for what was becoming my yearly fortnight in *Coronation Street*. In the storyline I was returning with my sister Joan, who had originally been played by June Barry, a blonde of about five foot six. Apparently June had been unwilling to come back into the Street so they had been obliged to recast; I was amazed to find that they had chosen an actress called Dorothy White (whom I had first met in *A Splendid Spur*), who was nearly six foot with dark hair! Normally, I would have said that the casting department was brilliant, one of the main strengths of *Coronation Street*, but I couldn't understand their reasoning on this one.

Neville Buswell was still in the cast, but I didn't meet up with him again on this trip and the next time I came back, he would be gone. Stephen Hancock, meanwhile, had already gone; Bill Podmore was still the producer, and when Stephen tried to negotiate more money by threatening to leave, Bill called his bluff and didn't renew his contract. Stephen, so I was told, tried to get them to leave the door open for his return, but probably as an example to the others he was killed off!

Before returning to Manchester later in the year for the MYT summer season, I managed to fit in a film for the Children's Film Foundation. It was a sad affair: a trite story, poorly written and with action that was very difficult to make believable. The director was in sympathy with our problem as actors and allowed us to find ways of altering some of the less believable moments to make the thing a little less 'naff'. After the shoot was finished, the producer, who was also the writer, wanted us to return and refilm certain sections because he was unhappy with the changes. At first I refused but, after pressure from my agent, agreed to reshoot certain scenes with reservations. The end result was childish: an insult to children. My co-star on that sad little venture was Jonathan Burn who had been in *Crossroads* as the head waiter, Max. We were to meet up again a few years later under very different circumstances.

I was still playing football as regularly as I could: for the various showbiz sides on Sunday, and for the old boys of my school on Saturday afternoons in the Southern Amateur League. I was also heavily into fundraising, not only for the National Youth Theatre, but also for the Alleyn's Old Boys, who were in dire need of money to rebuild their pavilion which had burnt down. Kit Miller, son of Gary Miller the sixties singer, together with Bob Joyce, my solicitor, and myself, organised an evening of boxing at the school in the old Buttery, with a dinner, to raise money. A number of professional boxers had been persuaded to give their services free; amongst them was my friend Pat Brogan, who had been the British Lightweight Champion and whom I had met at Leicester, his stamping ground.

Kit was a journalist for the *Sun*, I think, at the time and had some good, if doubtful, connections. I was also persuaded to step into the ring against Jonathan Burn, who was a full stone heavier and a good deal taller. The fight was to be billed as *Coronation Street* versus *Crossroads*. In the makeshift changing room beforehand, the professionals were discussing how their fights were to go. They weren't being paid, so they regarded them more as exhibition matches, which is understandable I suppose. Jonathan came to me and said, 'How are we going to do this?' to which I replied, 'I'm going to f---ing kill yer!'

I think the fight was very nearly the end of us both. I realised that he had the weight and the extra reach, but I was southpaw and he was slower so if I kept moving to the left, he would find it difficult to hit me. This worked quite well for the first round; I even knocked him down, although he claimed he had slipped. Sadly, I got a little over-confident in the second round and, in order to get at him a bit more, I forgot to keep moving to my left and walked into some pretty heavy punishment. In the third round, I don't know what was keeping me up!

Of all sports, boxing must be the most gruelling. Not only have you to contend with the physical exhaustion of your own effort, which believe me is considerably more draining than one would think, but you have also to put up with someone knocking the breath and resilience out of you. Because the professionals were soft-pedalling in their 'fixed' bouts, ours was the only fight that brought the place alight; inspired by the reaction we were getting, we pulled out even more stops, and were nearly dead after the three rounds. I think the fact that I was one of the organisers must have influenced the result, as I was given the decision. Also, of course, I was on home territory and it was a popular win.

My victory was somewhat tarnished, however. I had not been able to enjoy the entertainment before the fight (I didn't trust myself to eat, let alone drink), but I made up for it afterwards; and, when helping to dismantle the ring and clear away the tables and chairs, I wasn't as 'in control' as I should have been, tripped when carrying a bench, broke my glasses and gave myself a black eye! There was another reaction later: I developed a terrible pain between my shoulder blades. Luckily, I was on my way north to Manchester and went to see my mate Freddie Griffiths, the physiotherapist for Manchester City, at Maine Road. He sent me for an X-ray and, while he was studying the negatives, I asked if it was perhaps because I had hit too hard and dislocated something in my back. He replied, 'No, it's more the damage that was done when your head was being struck; it jarred your upper spine, crushing some of the discs between the vertebrae.' That was my last fight, at the age of 42.

I was relieved to get off to the MYT for the summer. The previous year, at the first two days of auditions, I had seen a young actor who had impressed me greatly; not only could he speak verse with a natural sense of the rhythms and meaning, he also had great stage presence. At the auditions I had expressed the desire to do Shakespeare with him, and specifically *Hamlet*. I was a little miffed when Geoff, on being asked to do a production for the MYT's first appearance at the Royal Exchange Theatre, had pulled rank on me and decided to do *Hamlet* with the young actor concerned, Tim Walker, and himself directing! I was still smarting a bit; it was not really like Geoff to do that sort of thing and I put it down to Hazel, his wife and secretary to the MYT, who was far more ambitious for Geoff than he was for himself. I can understand that she felt it was for him to do the first production at the Royal Exchange, and I am sure it was she who persuaded him to do *Hamlet*; I understood it, but was a little upset. This year by way of appeasement I was given Tim Walker and a new play (written by Alan Williams, who had played Falstaff for me) about Billy Meredith, the great Welsh footballer who had played for Manchester City and Manchester United, and also started the Players' Union at great sacrifice to himself. Tim played Billy Meredith with a great deal of charisma, intelligence and obvious talent and I wanted even more to do a Shakespeare with him.

Back in London after the MYT season, I was still thinking often of Sandra but had got back into a daily family life. Euston Films had taken over a school on the north side of Clapham Common, not much more than four hundred yards from my house in Grafton Square, and were well into a series about the bomb disposal units of the Second World War. Titled *Danger UXB* (*UneXploded Bomb*), the series starred Anthony Andrews as the officer. Robert Pugh, my ex-pupil from Rose Bruford, was one of the squaddies, as was Ken Cranham, whom I knew as a member of the Youth Theatre; also, his parents lived in Hastings and had been occasional drinking partners of mine when I lived on the south coast. I went in to join the cast as Major Francis, a strict disciplinarian who makes himself very unpopular and then, in his last episode, reveals that his somewhat callous attitude toward the junior subalterns is based upon the fact that his wife had had an affair with a second lieutenant and left him. The scene when this was revealed was very well written, and I was able to summon up a deal of emotion that probably had much to do with Sandra and my pent-up frustration over the situation. It wasn't a large part, but it was quite showy, and my performance in that final scene in particular earnt me a deal of attention.

I found it strange that, because I was playing an officer and a gentleman and in uniform most of the day, I was treated by the crew as if I was that bit more special than the non-commissioned ranks. Someone would invariably bring me my tea whilst the privates, sergeants and corporals queued for theirs, in spite of the fact that they were regulars in the series and with far more important roles than myself! Ferdinand Fairfax, the director, seemed particularly pleased and after the series we met up for a drink when he told me he wanted me in his next production; I was a little hurt though when the offer came through and it was only one line! I turned it down and that was the last I ever heard from him.

On the positive side I got a fan letter after the transmission signed 'Derek Hilton', which was the name of the resident musical director at Granada. When I met Derek some year or so later I mentioned that I had received a fan letter from somebody with the same name as his; he told me that it was indeed him and that he had been very moved by my portrayal. That's the sort of compliment I like: from someone in the same game and with knowledge of what they are talking about. I am not prone to writing fan letters myself, but I have from time to time taken heart from the way I felt about Derek's letter and I have written a few – well, three to be exact.

Things were still fairly quiet when I was offered a small part in an episode of a TV series called *Tycoon*, directed by Stephen Butcher who was now freelance, and recorded at the BBC's Pebble Mill Studios in Birmingham. Among the cast was Eddie Judd whom I had bumped into in various 'watering holes' over the years, the last such occasion having been after work one day at Elstree Studios in the days of ATV. I had finished late and gone into the bar for a drink before driving home, to find Eddie already far gone. He could hardly stand and was talking rather loudly to no one in particular. I managed to quieten him down a little by giving him some attention; and things were not too bad until he went to get us both a refill and joined the crowd at the bar, where he stood apparently chatting to Billy Eckstine, the by now somewhat aged American singer. Voices began to get a little raised as Eddie tugged at Billy's hairpiece and said something like, 'You can't see the join.' At this point Billy's PA tried to alleviate the situation by stepping between them, and Eddie told her to 'f--k off'. Thereupon, Billy Eckstine thumped Eddie, who fell to the floor and slunk back to me, nursing his bruised chin and trying to mend his gold neck-chain which had been broken in the scuffle. I felt as if everybody was looking at me and aligning me with the embarrassing occurrence they had just witnessed.

Rather unsurprisingly, Eddie appeared not to have any recall of our previous meeting and was quite friendly. I was playing a detective and, in an attempt to make the part slightly more interesting, with the acquiescence of the director I gave him a Welsh accent, which I felt comfortable with following my early success with Fluellen. However, I was brought down to earth by the Welsh make-up girl who, just before the recording, was touching up my make-up and said, 'What accent is that you're supposed to be doing?' She ruined my performance! Also in the series playing a secretary was Denise Buckley, Denise Marshall as she is now, who was later to become my agent as the other half of Scott Marshall.

My somewhat traumatic time at Crewe in *Blithe Spirit* with Paddy can't have been too horrific because David Sumner invited me back to do *The Odd Couple* by Neil Simon. I used the fact that he wanted me rather badly to say that I would do it if he allowed me to direct the next play, and it was agreed that I should direct *Bedroom Farce* by Alan Ayckbourn. Another of the conditions was that he should get Alan Moore to play Oscar to my Felix. Alan had played with me in *Getting On* in Liverpool and I had become quite impressed with his comedy. He often worked as a stand-up comic and had a very good line in improvisations, plus we got on well together. About a week before the rehearsals were due to start David informed me that he couldn't get Alan, but said that it was all right as he himself would play the part. This put me in a very tricky position; I didn't want to do it with David, and I told him so, but when he asked me for a reason I told him that I couldn't tell him, but to try again for Alan.

In the end, Alan agreed to do it and I learnt that it was more to do with money than anything else. David was curious to know why I hadn't wanted him to play the part and I agreed to tell him after the production had finished. The play did well; the Lyceum Theatre at Crewe was going through a difficult time, in that it was struggling for an audience, but we played to good and appreciative houses. Alan and I worked together well and, as I had expected, I learnt a lot from him about comedy. When I eventually had to face David and tell him why I hadn't wanted to play with him, I had to break it to him that I didn't think he could do comedy. He found this a bit unbelievable, but my opinion was vindicated in the way he directed the play. David and I didn't at all have the same approach to humour, and I was fortunate that Alan was so good at comedy and frequently rescued the situation. Also in the cast were Dillie Keane and Phyllis Logan, and I was lucky enough to have them stay on to be in *Bedroom Farce*, my first attempt at directing a fully professional company in a professional theatre.

It was a good choice for me: I was much more creative when it came to comedy, and I am a great admirer of Ayckbourn, who is considerably deeper than it appears on the surface; he reflects the mores and neuroses of our time in the most subtle and amusing manner. I spent most of the day in rehearsal laughing. It was a great shame that Crewe was so strapped for cash; there were shades of Stratford East about the atmosphere surrounding the theatre, mainly because the Market was on the doorstep, and we managed to stir a certain amount of interest, partly because of my Street connection. I'm sure that with a bit of money spent on the theatre it could have proved a bigger attraction in that catchment area.

After the opening night of *Bedroom Farce*, I spent the next four months without much work, apart from a brief part in a play directed by Alastair Reid for ATV, called *New Girl in Town*, in which I played an Australian. Things were pretty grim at home with the lack of work, the lack of money and still thinking constantly of Sandra, so I opted to return to *Coronation Street* for the month of May. Graham was dead, Neville had gone, and so that was the end of the trio. Doris was still there, but she was tired and wanted to get out. However, the writers found her too attractive a character to write for to leave her alone, and she was always grumbling about having too much to do. She had also come round to my way of thinking about Julie Goodyear, and found that she couldn't stand her either. She didn't say much at this point; she simply said, 'Oh, by the way, you were right about Julie.' I have to reluctantly admit that she was very good at the one-liners, but even after all these years she had no feel for shaping a scene, and working with her was pretty unrewarding. Sue Nicholls had just joined the cast and it was a joy to have a properly trained actress. The casting department were inclined to look for offbeat and unusual 'characters' rather than experienced actors, and working with them was an uphill grind.

Of course, sometimes the gamble works, and after a while as they get more confidence they develop into very good actors. Lynne Perrie was one such; she started life, or rather her entertaining life, as a club entertainer, like her brother, the comedian Tom O'Connor. To make the change from solo performer to being part of a team is not an easy one; and although many comedians attempt the switch, there is always something of the solo performer in them and they never really make the change totally convincingly. Max Bygraves was dreadful in the film of *Spare the Rod*, Mike Reid was teeth-curlingly bad in *EastEnders*, Bill Maynard was eccentric and egocentric in *Heartbeat*, but Lynne Perrie was to me one of the best actresses that had graced the screen in the Street. She was totally believable and realistic, and not just in the easy bit, portraying the everyday-nothing-happening-drink-in-the-Rovers-type dialogue: she could also turn on the dramatics without losing the reality.

There is a style of acting that is peculiar to soaps and is fairly easy to do. It consists mainly of being able to not be fazed by the camera and to appear natural and relaxed, something that seems to come easily to quite a few of today's confident youngsters; but put that youngster under pressure to emote on a theme that is not able to be thrown away and many will be unable to cope with portraying the emotion in a believable manner. Probably the best exponent of the art of soap acting, to my mind, was Patsy Palmer from *EastEnders*; I found her acting mesmeric and a constant surprise. She was certainly able to teach her elders a thing or two; she was superb.

What proved to be my last production with the Manchester Youth Theatre was *Henry V* at the Royal Exchange Theatre with, at last, Tim Walker playing Henry. This was 1979, my seventh year with the MYT, and I wanted to graduate to the National Youth Theatre. Geoff and Hazel seemed to be quite happy with the MYT and were not busting with the same ambition to take it further that I was. I was all for getting a home of our own, and I was frequently badgering them to try and get Ciba-Geigy to finance the buying of an old theatre in All Saints that had been turned into a snooker hall. Its position was ideal, just off the centre with fairly easy parking. I saw it as a permanent theatre club for young people, with the main auditorium and a studio space that could both be rented out for all sorts of functions. I saw the establishing of a permanent wardrobe that would be able to pay for itself by hiring out, and also a set-building workshop with similar prospects. I tried to get Geoff to at least approach Ciba-Geigy and offer them the idea – they would hold the freehold of the building which would be improved with use by the MYT, and they would always have an investment that would be increasing in value – but I don't think he ever did; and since the MYT was his baby I decided to move off south after *Henry V*.

Tim, as I thought he would be, was excellent and I enjoyed the challenge of the new space, the Royal Exchange. The theatre was a glass construction in the middle of the great old Corn Exchange hall, in the round. I had often seen productions there and found the space a little unsatisfactory. First, the fact that it was in the round and the walls were all made of glass meant that as you looked across the stage you could see, beyond the onstage action, the comings and goings in the café and the bars outside, which I found distracting. I also found that there was a strange acoustic: there was a spot in the middle of the stage where there was some sort of echo. I managed to manipulate Tim to make use of the echo when we needed it and I used the space outside and around the theatre for the battle scenes. I was able to call upon a great number of kids for these scenes and even got the actors from the other production to join in when their play was not being performed. The battle spilled out of and around the theatre: shades of *Julius Caesar* at Alleyn's in 1950!

Work was still a bit thin on the ground when I was asked by Peter Roberts, who had been a student at Rose Bruford, to direct a lunchtime theatre that he had managed to set up. He had found himself a play, a two-hander called *The Manly Bit* about two young men in macho-style competition, and succeeded in getting a booking at the King's Head, Islington, a very good fringe theatre venue. He had the cheek of the devil – he once told me a story of how he had blagged his way in to see Sir Ralph Richardson in his dressing room – but unfortunately he had very little acting talent. The poor kid was exceedingly keen and had a confidence that I felt was not only aggravating, but was standing in the way of his learning about the basic rudiments of acting; I gave him a very hard time. I was particularly harsh on him as I had persuaded Mike Grady, who had been with Paddy in *Once a Catholic* at Wyndham's Theatre, to play the other part, and he was very good, very professional and hard-working. Peter was holding him back, not least because he couldn't learn the lines. He was just not cut out to be an actor and was not working hard enough to make up the shortfall. I would not be surprised to learn that he had gone into production; there were touches of the Bill Kenwright about him.

The play did not do well, and often played to no more than a handful of people. In order to give them some support, I made a habit of being there each lunchtime, at least to see the curtain up. Standing in the bar one day just before the start of the play, I was approached by a tall, slim young man who started the conversation by asking me if I knew Anthony Booth. I said that I didn't exactly know him, but I knew who he was and I had once been at an Equity meeting when he had attracted attention with an aggressively left-wing tirade, and I had formed the opinion that he wasn't my sort of person. The young man then told me that he was in the army, and based at Chelsea Barracks where Tony was in the habit of calling in at the sergeants' mess. Apparently, he had ended up there once after a personal appearance and had taken them at their word when they had said 'call in, any time'! He was beginning to outwear his welcome, as he was in the habit of bumming drinks and getting quite pissed. On a fairly recent occasion, this young man had apparently been in his company and offered to drive him home. On arriving at his house, Tony's wife had bolted the door and refused to let him in; there was apparently an altercation with his wife screaming from an upstairs window and telling him to 'piss off' (according to this young man, that is). Tony then went to the garage, got a can of petrol, and proceeded to douse the front door. Being as pissed as he was, he also drenched himself and when he set light to the door, he went up in flames. This young man, according to the story, took off his coat and rolled Tony on the lawn to put out the fire. He then took him to hospital and continued to visit him regularly there.

There were various aspects of this story that did not exactly ring true: most notably, why did he just stand around and let him do it? I managed to get rid of the young man by getting him in to see the show, and made my escape. A month or so later I received a telephone call from a somewhat camp musical director, who told me the rather sad story of having been in the company of a tall, slim young man who had told him he was in the army and had spoken at length about myself and Anthony Booth (I dread to think of the tale he told about me!). The upshot of his call was that he had taken the young man back with him to his flat and woke up the next morning to find the young soldier had disappeared with a number of valuable items, and he wanted to know if I knew where he could find him. I never bothered to check the story about Anthony Booth; it all sounded too improbable to be true. I did hear that Tony was involved in a burning accident and had spent some time in hospital; but, had there been more to it, I imagine that when his son-in-law became our Prime Minister, the press would have latched on to the story and had a field day!

The work situation was still pretty grim and I was happy to join Jeremy Burnham and Veronica Strong again, this time in a programme of verse, prose and song about marriage, called *Holy Deadlock*. The idea behind this was to put together some sort of show with a group of actors that could be flexible enough in its casting to be taken at any time onto a cruise ship or into foreign hotels, rather like the Derek Nimmo set-up. Apart from Jeremy and Veronica, there was Amanda Grinling, who had been in my year at RADA, and Norman Rossiter, with Jonathan Cohen at the piano, directed by Nicholas Renton. There were shades of my Conservative Club fiasco about this and I can't say that I felt very confident about the singing, but luckily my part in the vocals was not all that great and I managed to scrape through the handful of performances at LAMDA and the Sussex University Theatre in Brighton. When the next stage of the project came up, I was unable to take part as I went into the West End to take over from Bill Marlowe, who had also been a chum at RADA, in *Night and Day* by Tom Stoppard at the Phoenix Theatre in Charing Cross Road.

I loved the West End, and spent quite a bit of time in my dressing room which I regarded rather as a town flat. The play, which had enjoyed great success with Diana Rigg in the main part, had been running for about a year when the cast was changed, or rather some of the cast. Patrick Mower, who had taken over from John Thaw, Edward de Souza, and all the black actors stayed but Susan Hampshire and myself were 'rehearsed in' to take over. Rehearsals were taken by Peter Wood and Tom Stoppard, and I must say I immediately felt I was doing work of a completely different level. This was my first experience of what I would call 'class', and the difference in attitude was very evident. There was a level of discipline and commitment that was never stated, it was just expected, and the direction was exact. When Peter Wood made a comment or suggestion, it was expected to be acted upon, and any comment on performance or delivery came with the understanding that you could and would comply. At the same time you were expected to bring something of yourself to the part; and I opted to make the photographer, George Guthrie, a little more sensitive than Bill had played him, and in the long descriptive speech I made George retch from time to time with the awfulness of the scene. Peter kept his eye on this and made me keep the whole thing very much under control; I really felt I was playing with 'the big boys'.

I had felt dubious about playing a relatively minor part night after night for such a long time, saying the same words over and over again at the same time each night; I had thought that frustration might have got the better of me. Partly because of the quality of the dialogue and the demanding strictures of the direction, and probably most of all because of Patrick Mower, I loved it and was prepared to stay in it for longer than the seven months that I did. Unfortunately, the show was losing its appeal and was taken off. Patrick had the male lead, playing the Australian journalist, and I was the war photographer. The humour of the play was fascinating and not at all easy. The discipline and timing needed to get the comedy was subtle and delicate and Patrick never stopped in his search for improvement and never stopped growing in the part. Every night we would meet up backstage at some time during the show to discuss trying something new. In all probability, nobody would have noticed much difference from one night to the next, but it kept the show alive for me and exciting to play.

Disaster struck towards the end of my run in the West End. Michael Croft was celebrating his sixtieth birthday with a party at his house in Kentish Town and of course I was invited to join them after the show on a Saturday. Unfortunately, because the show came down late, I wouldn't get there until well after eleven o'clock. When I arrived, the party had been going for some time and all the food had gone. I had to make do with champagne, which didn't seem too big an ordeal at the time, but when I came to leave at about two o'clock in the morning I was aware of the fact that I had had far too much to drink, and shouldn't be driving. I reasoned, however, that there would be very little traffic on the roads at that time of the morning and I would take it very easy; I was worried about getting back to the kids as Paddy was away working.

There was indeed very little traffic on the road and I was quite surprised to be pulled up by the police just after passing Euston Station. When they asked if I had been drinking, I admitted that I had and they told me to leave the car, get out and go home. Under the circumstances, they were exceedingly decent and I started off on the walk south, looking for a taxi. The roads were deserted and it started to rain. I was wearing a new velvet jacket that I was very proud of and I was fearful of it getting ruined. Having got to the Embankment without seeing any sign of a taxi, I determined that I must have sobered up by now and decided to return for my car. I had no sooner got behind the wheel and started the engine than the same police knocked on the window and breathalysed me. Of course, I failed and was taken to the police station where I was tested again and found to be well over the limit. Since it was now about four o'clock in the morning I settled down on a chair in the corner of the station reception and slept the few hours left of the night. In the morning, I had to take another test before I was allowed to take the car, but alas I was still positive and had to take the Tube home. Some months later, I was to be up in court to be sentenced, but for the time being I was able to continue to drive.

On leaving the West End, I went almost immediately up to Scotland for a few days to play Daniel Defoe for a Scottish schools TV. It wasn't a great production number, but I always enjoyed playing historical characters as I loved doing the background research. There was the added joy in this instance of meeting up with some old friends. David Andrews had been in the original cast of *The Long and the Short and the Tall* and also in the permanent company of *An Age of Kings*; he was now directing for Scottish TV, as was Julia Smith who was a floor manager on *An Age of Kings* and who was to later be the inspiration behind *EastEnders*.

Back in London once more, things were becoming unbearable at home. Paddy was finding it impossible to accept my infidelity and she was suffering more and more from depressions that I could do nothing about. I felt so helpless; I wasn't any good at handling her moods and everything I did seemed to make matters worse. That summer holiday I took the kids off in a Dormobile for a trip to the south west of France. Partly to give the trip some sort of point, we decided to look at property to buy; we had seen an advertisement in the papers for some dilapidated farm buildings and the price was peanuts. We also took the opportunity of calling on a schoolfriend of Tessa whose family had a converted barn in that area. Whilst visiting we were shown a dilapidated barn, overgrown with brambles, knee-deep internally with the dung of centuries, having no roof to speak of and with only two thirds of the walls still standing. As we were shown around, we were told that the local farmer had said that whoever took that place on would have to have 'courage'. My parents were now retired and spending much of the year on holidays in Spain where they got cheap off-season deals; on returning to England, I spoke with them and we decided to buy it together, contacted the local agent and made an offer of £3,500, which was accepted.

I don't know if, on top of everything else, this upset Paddy, in that she felt out of it, but certainly there was an awful atmosphere at home. Whenever she had moods, there seemed to be no real rationale behind them, other than the fact that my presence seemed to exacerbate them. The final crunch came when, after trying to get to the bottom of her depression, she expressed the thought that we hadn't had any time together away from home and alone together, so I booked a weekend away and arranged for the kids (who were now 18, 16, and 15) to look after themselves. As the time approached, Paddy changed her mind and didn't want to go away for a whole weekend, so the weekend became a day out. She then changed her mind again and the day out was whittled down to a morning drive out to Godstone and a walk down country lanes, a drink in a pub and the drive back with no more than half a dozen words passing between us. The thought of spending the rest of my life in this sort of purgatory was just too much and I now deemed the kids of an age where they could cope with the break-up; on our return home, I packed my bags and moved out.

I went to stay with my old pal Richard Hampton, whose first marriage had also broken up; he now lived in an end-of-terrace house in Selhurst, right beside the railway line, with a spare bedroom that I rented and moved into. I returned a day or so later to put my desk on the roof rack of the car and pick up one or two other belongings. Richard had been living alone in the house for something like three years and the carpet that he had brought with him had still not been fitted, but remained rolled up in the hallway! We were not unlike 'The Odd Couple'. Richard had his foibles and eccentricities, not that he was in any way dirty or unkempt; in fact he was scrupulously clean. I was very amused by the unlaid carpet and the way he would hoover the bare floorboards meticulously, even going to the lengths of putting on the attachment to do the cracks between the boards. I settled into my room, making it very cosy and homely, and I soon got used to the sound of the passing trains.

Shortly after I moved in, I was asked to take over the part of George Oliver in *Getting On*, initially at Bromley Theatre and then due to transfer to Guildford. The part was originally going to be played by someone else but he had broken his arm while out walking his dog and, since I had played the part before, I was asked to take over. My memories of the play, with Dick Tuckey directing and Jane Lowe playing my wife at Liverpool Playhouse, were happy ones and perhaps it was too much to expect this production to measure up to that one. On the other hand, perhaps I was not in the right mental state having just left home. Whatever it was, I found the three weeks at Bromley a bit traumatic.

While playing at Bromley I was able to fit in a Sunday performance of *The Happiest Days of Your Life*, a compilation of verse and prose about school days, devised by Michael Croft, which we performed in the Great Hall at Alleyn's School to raise funds for the National Youth Theatre. I had helped Mike to set it up and with Mike, myself, Julian Glover, Simon Ward, David Weston, Richard Hampton and Paula Wilcox we returned to the school stage for one night.

Back with *Getting On*; when the play moved to Guildford I was a lot happier. After the first week I realised that it was a waste of time and petrol driving up to Selhurst every night after the show and sleeping in Dickey's spare room, even though it was now 'home'. There was a bed in my dressing room, and although I knew it wasn't allowed, I started to work out a way of 'kipping down' in the theatre. After curtain down I would go upstairs to the theatre club and have a few drinks with the rest of the cast, making sure that I was the last to leave, at which point I would take a pint or two with me down the back stairs to my dressing room; if the door was locked I would get the night fireman to let me in and slip him a couple of quid. The set for *Getting On* consisted of a living room and kitchen in the MP's house. Before the week was out, I had managed to get the TV to work and had wired up the refrigerator: I had my own little flat right there on the stage. At one point during the play my son had to come home late at night feeling a little peckish, open the fridge and complain that there was 'nothing in there!' Unfortunately on one occasion after I had been to Marks and Spencer's on a shopping spree, a rather large cooked chicken fell from the top shelf and there was a stunned silence as he sorted out some other dialogue! I had really moved in with a vengeance: I was sleeping in the dressing room, woken most mornings by the cleaning staff with a cup of tea in bed, and then spending the day walking the banks of the canal, returning for lunch on stage and settling down to watch the tennis at Wimbledon on the TV. At the end of the run, I simply went and picked up my car from the multi-storey car park where it had been left for the two and a half weeks and went back to Selhurst.

Despite my newfound freedom, I was not happy; it was a very disturbing time. I hated what I was doing to Paddy and also hated not seeing the kids. I had set myself the objective to not attempt to see Sandra or even let her know that I had left home until I had managed the separation for three months. I must admit that it had always been in my mind that I would wait and hope we could get back together again, but I had first of all to make sure that I could go through with the decision to leave Paddy, and only then face the possibility that Sandra would not want to join me after all. When I returned to Selhurst I was allowed by Paddy to see the kids at weekends; but I found that dreadfully upsetting, taking them to bowling alleys and suchlike, and having to hand them back at the end of the day. That summer I took them off to France with my parents where we had bought the barn and we set about clearing the ground and seeing what was underneath the brambles and the years of cow dung.

When I returned, I determined to let Nicky Glenn know that I had left home, in the hope that she would tell Sandra. In the process of picking up the kids I did occasionally bump into Paddy and realised that there was no way I could go back home again: the damage I had done was irreparable and there was no way that she would ever be able to forgive me. She had understandably lost all respect for me and I needed to have someone who believed in me and who supported me, not someone who despised me. Sandra had made me feel 'special'; and perhaps it was just my age, but I needed that.

Nicky did her bit and it wasn't long before I heard from Sandra. She came over to see me in Selhurst; I was in no position to expect anything from her, I had let her down after the tour and chosen to stay with my family, she had had to return to her forgiving and long-suffering husband and there was no way I could do anything but wait and hope. Consequently I just let her know that I wanted her and made no demands; I would wait. I settled down to my life beside the railway line, took the kids out each weekend, and in the summer holiday I bought a Dormobile and we set off for France to work on our barn.

To cap it all my case came up in Bow Street and I had to face a judge (who looked as if he had a serious drink problem himself) for my drink-driving charge. Being so heavily over the limit, and because it was my second time, I was given a four-year ban.

14

**1980 to 1984 • Ipswich • Greenwich • Indian Tour •
RSC: *Educating Rita* • India • Turkey •
Syria • Kenya**

THERE WASN'T MUCH I could offer Sandra, apart from the position of chauffeuse. The room that I was renting in Dickey's house was not exactly large enough, comfortable enough or in any way attractive enough to offer. Besides, she was not going to find it easy to leave Brian: he had stuck by her, and despite his drinking was still very much in love with her. She also loved her home comforts. Therefore, when Patrick Mower asked if we could housesit for Suzanne Danielle and himself while they went on tour with a play to New Zealand, I jumped at the chance to enjoy a little space and luxury in life. They had a wonderful cottage in Gerrard's Cross, and at last we were able to live together in some sort of comfort; all we had to do was keep the place secure and clean and feed the cat.

It was during our time there that Dick Tuckey offered me the chance to direct *Night and Day* at the Wolsey Theatre, Ipswich. I didn't feel I could turn the job down; so although I didn't like doing it, I left Sandra to feed the cat and, at the end of 1980, went to Ipswich for the three weeks of rehearsal. During those weeks Sandra came to join me for a few days whenever she could. Meanwhile, Paddy had started divorce proceedings and was proposing to sell the house. Whatever the situation, splitting up a relationship after sixteen years is not a pleasant experience; I was riddled with guilt, but I was able to immerse myself totally in my work.

I was lucky to have Barbara Ewing, a very good New Zealand actress, to play the female lead (after she had interviewed me to see if she thought I was up to the job), and Stuart McGugan as the male lead with Tom Mannion playing the young romantic interest. Naturally I was very influenced by the London production that I had played in for seven months, but I was able to take the opportunity to put into practice a theory that I had about the fantasy scenes. Many of my friends had found them difficult to understand, because it was not entirely clear that they were fantasies. I overcame this with a smoke gun that just gave a wisp of smoke on the entrance of Tom Mannion in those scenes. Although I say it myself this did seem to be a worthwhile addition as there were no complaints of lack of comprehension; and I later heard that Barbara Ewing was very taken by my abilities as a director, and wanted to work with me again. However, this was sadly to be my last attempt at directing in what I would call the proper, fully professional theatre. I did later pick up a job directing *Fen* by Caryl Churchill at the Guildford School of Acting, but since it was with students I didn't think it really counted.

In all probability, I had decided too late in my career to want to direct. This is a shame because I think I would have been more suited to directing than acting. It's likely that my dithering between the two had something of a negative effect, and I was thought of too much as a soap actor rather than a serious contender as a director. I have also often thought that my little directing ventures may have led to my not being offered work as an actor, because young directors might have been fearful of my undermining their influence on the rest of the cast. Perhaps I'm just making excuses for myself.

As I have already said, Selhurst was not a wonderful place to offer Sandra; and I was relieved to be cast in *Much Ado About Nothing* for the Horseshoe Theatre Company in Basingstoke, which meant that after the rehearsal period I was able to find wonderful lodgings in the countryside just outside the town. It was the most idyllic Georgian house, set in a beautiful garden, where we were woken in the morning not by passing trains but with the cooing of ring doves. Our landlady, Audrey, was a delightful, elegant, sophisticated widow who happened to be on the board of governors for the theatre, which was soon to prove quite useful.

Two decades on from my first experience of *Much Ado* at the Library Theatre, I felt myself more able to play Benedick, and with Nyree Dawn Porter as Beatrice it should have been better than it was, but unfortunately the director was not really strong enough and there wasn't a great deal of imagination coming from that quarter. Nyree and I had to get together and do most of it ourselves; we often met up at weekends in her house in Barnes and did our own rehearsals. Despite his shortcomings the director was obviously good at spotting talent as he had a young Paul McGann playing one of the Watch. I can remember him pointing to Paul and telling me that one day he would be a great success!

The play wasn't though, and we played to disappointing houses, far less than the show deserved. When we realised that the advance was so bad I set about trying to find out why. I didn't have to look far: the theatre was also the venue for the local amateurs; in fact the professionals only had it for a portion of the year and so hadn't built up a real following. The place was run very much by the amateurs and all of the advertising spots in the foyer were taken up with posters for the Christmas show, which was many months away, the next amateur production and a one-night visit from someone like Ed Stewart, the DJ.

On chatting with Audrey I learnt that she, as a member of the board, was also very frustrated by the state of affairs, and I was encouraged by her to make my usual statement to the press and tell them what was wrong with their theatre! The local press welcomed my outburst, as it gave them something to get their teeth into; but Guy Slater, whom I had known for some years and was now married to Ginny Stride, was not so happy about it. They were living in Basingstoke, and Guy had been the driving force behind the birth of the professional Horseshoe Theatre Company; he called me to say that I had put his work back six months by antagonising the all-powerful local amateur set-up!

On returning to Selhurst, I managed a nice showy BBC TV *Play for Today* directed by Gerald Blake, in which I played an ex-miner dying of cancer, with a lovely long deathbed scene which was touchingly written although the play had the odd title of 'Whistling Wally'. Paul McGann was also in the cast and this was to start him on a very successful career in front of the camera; he certainly looked good on screen.

While I was rehearsing 'Wally' I learnt that Dickey had made the decision to marry again. He had been seeing Jenny Oulton, the former wife of Leslie Lawton, and they were planning to sell the house in Selhurst and move in together. As it happened the timing couldn't have been better. Paddy was well into divorce proceedings and had a buyer for the house in Grafton Square; the residue, after the mortgage had been paid off, would be divided between us and I was to get about £20,000.

I had to start all over again on the housing ladder. I made Dickey an offer which he accepted and, with help from my brother and father, I set about converting the house into two self-contained flats. I had inherited one or two bits of furniture from the Grafton Square house: namely a rather large half-tester bed, which looked very out of place in the tiny bedroom, and a Victorian scroll-end sofa, which I was to take with me everywhere for the next fifteen years! I lived downstairs while the top floor was being converted, and when it was complete I moved up. Once both flats were completed, the upstairs one was sold and I moved back down to the ground floor.

In the middle of this chaos I was asked to do two or three days on a student film at the British Film School at Beaconsfield. The money was little more than expenses, but I accepted; I accepted everything. The script was by Daniel Peacock, son of Trevor Peacock, and directed by Terry Winsor. Entitled *Party Party*, the story was of a wild party held in a suburban house when the parents are out, and their unexpected return at the height of the mayhem; as the mum and dad, Kate Williams and I were the only adults in the picture.

Since I was still banned from driving, I was picked up from Selhurst in a minibus every morning at about five-thirty and dropped off at night. I was the earliest one to be picked up, and also the last to be dropped off at night; and as the filming went on until late into the evening, I wasn't getting home until well after midnight. I wasn't very happy.

On the final day of filming, I was sitting in my dressing room waiting to be called for my last scene; it was already eleven o'clock and, feeling that it was well past the time that I should have been called, I wandered into the studios to find that absolutely nothing was happening: the whole thing had ground to a halt. Apparently the girlfriend of the lad doing the lighting had come into the studios 'throwing a wobbler' because she was feeling neglected, and he had taken her home to calm her down! I was livid and asked to be driven home immediately; I was not going to hang around like that for £20 per day! They managed to placate me and get the lighting guy back, and I agreed to do the scene – just once, no retakes – on condition that they were to drop me home immediately afterwards; first, not last. I really did pull out all the stops and had to be quite unpleasant.

Imagine my surprise when a year or so later *Party Party* was remade for a full cinema release, with an amazing cast and proper money, and I was asked to play the part again. It became something of a cult movie with the younger generation, and it is surprising how many of that young cast went on to play leading parts across the acting spectrum: Gary Olsen, Caroline Quentin, Karl Howman, Nick Berry, Clive Mantle, Perry Fenwick, Phoebe Nicholls, Kim Thomson, to name but a few!

Having sold the two flats in Selhurst, I was back on the property ladder, but not with a great deal of capital. My next venture was again with a chum: this time a member of the Alleyn's Old Boys club who lived in a largish house in Red Post Hill, in the part of London officially called Herne Hill but often referred to as North Dulwich by the residents who were trying to make the area sound a little more upmarket.

It was while I was at Red Post Hill that I was given the opportunity to join the Greenwich Theatre Company for one of the best jobs I had had to date, and one of the worst. I was to play Frank in Willy Russell's *Educating Rita*, and Crabtree in *The School for Scandal*, the Restoration comedy by Sheridan. Both plays were to be taken on a British Council tour of India for ten weeks. *School for Scandal* was to play for two weeks at the Greenwich Theatre, but *Educating Rita* was to open in Bombay!

From the beginning of rehearsals I was very confused by Alan Dossor, the director. To me Crabtree was the conventional Restoration fop, but he wanted it played as an arthritic old man of 80. I have always believed in doing as a director wants, and I relished the challenge, at least at first. I tried and tried but was so uncomfortable that at one point I asked him for some sort of guidance; he hadn't given me any direction at all, nor did he comment during the note sessions. Having approached him, I didn't have much faith in his flattery at the note session after the next run-through when he singled me out for praise!

A company get-together and celebration was planned for after the opening night at Greenwich, and Sandra came to see the first performance; she was still living at home but we were getting together whenever we could. I had one of those sinking feelings, right in the middle of a scene, when I wanted the stage to open up and swallow me! I was concentrating like mad on my arthritic fingers and stooped over my silver-headed cane, leaning on it heavily as an 80-year-old would, when the end broke off the bottom of the cane and I dropped another six inches towards the floor. I felt that the whole audience had seen and registered the embarrassing occurrence, and from that moment I just couldn't convince myself to get into character again – that is, if I ever had been. The comedy wasn't working, not just for me but for everybody.

It was a good cast, led by Philip Voss, David Rintoul, Paul Brooke and David Horovitch. After the show I met Sandra and hustled her straight away to a pub just down the road for a drink away from the rest of the crew and cast; I was so depressed, I didn't want to speak to any of them. The reviews were a disaster and we didn't see Alan Dossor for the next few days. I tried phoning him and left messages everywhere asking if I could talk to him about changing my character-isation; I got no reply or acknowledgment. It wasn't until I was deep into the rehearsals for *Educating Rita* that I received a message from the theatre asking me to go to Greenwich for a rehearsal of the first gossips scene, which Jennie Stoller had asked him to rework because it wasn't working. I pointed out that I had been free to come in for the past two weeks and indeed had asked him for help on a number of occasions; I was now involved with another play and couldn't spare him the time.

Directed by Pippa Broughton, *Educating Rita* was a completely different experience and I was loving it. The play is a two-hander, and Tina Marian was playing Rita to my Frank. We were rehearsing at the British Council at Oxford Circus, and before leaving for India we had a public dress rehearsal for friends and invited guests. Among them was Willy Russell, the play's author, who came to me after the performance in that little room and said, 'Where were you when we cast this in the West End?' I replied, 'Probably out of work.'

Tina and I set off for India ahead of the rest of the company to open in Bombay. I will never forget the first night in the Music Academy Theatre beside the sea. We were warned that there would be a full house, but were not prepared for the multitude that turned up. Tickets were apparently changing hands on the black market; there were ticket touts outside and women were caught trying to smuggle youngsters in under their saris. When the curtain went up there was an air of excitement and expectation that I could almost taste. Absolutely none of the humour was missed; indeed we got reactions that we hadn't even foreseen ourselves. I think the subject of the play – Rita's struggle to educate herself out of the restrictions of her class – and the similarity with the strictures of the Indian caste system made them warm to the subject. When the curtain came down it was like something out of *A Star is Born*; there was a standing ovation that went on for what seemed like an age, and local dignitaries came up onto the stage with sweet, heavy-scented garlands that were placed around our necks.

The rest of the company joined us a few days later and we went through the process of working in *School for Scandal*, which strangely proved to be almost as big a success. We found that the comedy was picked up on in a way that had eluded us in England. We were getting laughs that even we didn't know were there, and played to packed houses with good reviews. Since the cast and the production were the same, the only thing that had changed was the audience, and it is around their neck that we should hang the garlands. They had little in the way of live entertainment, and were accustomed to sitting around talking to each other; as we travelled the country, we would frequently see little groups sitting at the roadside in earnest discussion or listening to a story. Consequently they had acquired the habit of listening, and listening intently: picking up all the little nuances of language that we no longer pick up on as we only half listen. We have become used to switching on the tele or the radio and pottering around the house doing something else. They still have a love and an interest in the English language that we take so much for granted.

We were of course privileged and saw the best of India, staying at the best hotels as guests of the British Council; after the shows we would frequently be royally entertained to lavish hospitality from the resident British and the occasional maharaja. It goes without saying that we saw the poverty too. I will always remember the first arrival at Bombay Airport, getting off the plane to be hit with the humidity and the smell of that massive continent; and as we travelled in the minibus that had been sent for us by the British Council, the excited company was stunned into silence as we passed the mile after mile of cardboard, tin and waste-material constructions that made up the city where millions of people lived in poverty.

A number of us had paid for our partners to join us on the tour and Sandra had come out with the main company. During our separation when I had returned home to my family after the tour of *Dead on Nine*, I had nightly said a little prayer that she should be out front and see me doing work that I was proud of. All through my time at Liverpool Playhouse, I wanted her to see me perform and be proud of me, so when she came to see the first night at Greenwich I had been doubly destroyed when my performance of Crabtree had been such a disaster. However, after the reception *Educating Rita* had received, I was looking forward to the time when she would come to see me in a role that everybody seemed to think I was well suited for and played well.

We chose the moment with care: a night that was in a comfortable theatre with a good audience. I was by now playing with confidence; the performance went well, I seemed to get all of the reactions that I was used to getting and waited in my dressing room for her to come round after the show. As she entered the room there was an embarrassing period of uncertain silence before she said, 'I liked your clothes.' I was devastated and spent the next week or so sulking, and being comforted by Paul Brooke who said he couldn't understand her: she was just wrong. His support helped, but it didn't compensate. When Sandra enlarged upon her reaction, she said that she had seen Julie Walters and Mark Kingston in the original production and she couldn't take the play seriously; she thought I was all right. It didn't help; 'all right' was not good enough!

That aside, we had a wonderful time in India. There were so many highlights: the early-morning breakfast train to Agra and watching the sun go down over the Taj Mahal; a day at the Tollygunge Club in Calcutta; dinner in the Taj Mahal hotel by the gateway to India in Bombay; a visit to the Academy of Music and Dance, just outside Madras, where the course is for seven years and the discipline and exactitude of the training puts our drama schools in the shade; dinner with a maharaja at his palace outside Hyderabad; and many sumptuous after-show receptions thrown by the British Council.

In Madras, Sandra was even offered a part in an Indian film! I had picked up a fan and friend in the shape of Gopi, an Indian character actor who had seen me in *Educating Rita*, and we had struck up a relationship. He followed us from one town to another and often turned up at the hotel, where we would invite him into our company: sometimes with embarrassing effect, as he was a Brahmin, a member of the upper caste, and he would often speak to the waiters who were serving us in a manner that we found difficult to take; but we said nothing as in all other respects he was adorable and friendly.

Sadly, Sandra was not to stay the course in India. We were playing mostly the big cities: Bombay, Delhi, Madras, Hyderabad and Calcutta; and it was Calcutta that finally was the last straw, with its massive poverty and pollution problem. Sandra was not only upset by the poverty, she was also ill with a chest infection and much to my disappointment flew home.

I suppose it was inevitable that the company should split into little groups and factions; it was a large cast and quite a mixture of characters. There was also the heat which occasionally became oppressive and perhaps made some react out of character. Our agents back in England were being paid weekly and we were given a daily *per diem* allowance, which was based on the civil service rate and was therefore more than generous. Given that we were being entertained almost every night and the hotels were all paid for, there was little call on us to spend anything at all, except on ourselves and on presents to take home. We were told that we would not be allowed to take rupees out of India; it being such a poor country, we were expected to spend it all there and not take it home. Nevertheless, and despite the poverty that one encountered everywhere, there were those in the company who went to considerable lengths to change their rupees into sterling and took the money home with them to England! I was also rather dismayed to see the glee that many expressed if they managed to get an extra orange or two when bartering with the young kids who swarmed around our bus whenever we stopped. The haggling that went on in the markets had really got under the skin of some of the company who, I feel, lost a sense of proportion.

Back home in England again, the flats at Red Post Hill having been sold, I found another project just around the corner in Beckwith Road. This was a good buy in that it was riddled with dry rot and had frightened off other buyers so I was able to get it 'at the right price'. As before, I split the house into flats, this time three; once I had moved into the ground floor, I was to stay for some time, with Sandra later joining me. I again got my brother to come up from Hastings and help me with the conversion; I tried a number of times to get him to join me in a partnership, buying up old houses and converting them, but he wouldn't commit himself and indeed this was to be our last venture together.

Beckwith Road was a pleasant tree-lined road close to North Dulwich Station, within walking distance of the Old Boys Club and the Crown and Greyhound pub in Dulwich Village; I was back with my roots. Internally the flat was very pleasant with a split-level lounge/dining room through to the kitchen and bathroom, and the bedroom opening onto a garden in the rear. I had installed the desk and Victorian scroll-end sofa and was very comfortable and well positioned for getting up to town and to the theatre.

For the next few years it was Sandra who bought and sold two houses, having split them into flats with my assistance and advice. Having just got my licence back, I was still without a car; but since I was doing so much in the building and decorating line, I bought an old gas-board van from the auctions in Heathfield, which not only came in handy for the house conversions, it also took Sandra and me on our first trip together to France, loaded to the gunnels with furniture and bits and pieces for the barn.

That trip was a disaster and very nearly marked the end of our relationship. The van was a Transit-sized diesel and, as the engine was in the front, a cloud of black smoke came up in the driver's cabin every time it was started. Dressed more for yachting than for road travel, Sandra had to get out while I started the engine and run up to join me once I had got it going. We got as far as Chartres for our first stop and, finding the hotels all full, we set off with woefully inadequate directions to find a 'Logis' on the outskirts of town and got hopelessly lost. It was dark and a fog came down which made it impossible to drive; visibility was about two yards. It was cold, it was damp and miserable, and we spent the night in a car park trying to sleep in the cabin of the van.

Sandra was in a terrible state, and when she isn't happy, she lets me know. I spent most of the night walking in the fog in the car park and cursing and almost in tears. The next morning we set off again and Sandra was still unhappy, so in a fit of pique I said we would have breakfast and then I would drop her at the nearest railway station and she could go home. I don't know whether it was the threat or the breakfast that changed her attitude, but she decided to continue on the trip south! The sun came out and we had a great time. In a way, that trip is rather symbolic of our relationship.

I hadn't given up acting, and these trips and projects were secondary to my career; I fitted the work in too, whenever it came along. In May of 1982, after the tour of India and whilst doing my conversions, I was surprised to be asked to do the film of *Party Party*, that I had done the student production of the year before. It was about this time that my then agent Richard Eastham decided to retire and I was invited to join Brian Wheeler, who had been Richard's assistant for the last few years. Unfortunately Brian was to give up himself later and become a freelance casting director, but the few years I had with him were quite fruitful. I had a really showy part in the police series *Juliet Bravo*, when I played a stage carpenter for a Bradford amateur drama group, who was a dab hand at make-up and accents and committed a number of burglaries heavily disguised. The director of the 'am dram' society was played by John Savident, who later gave exactly the same performance in *Coronation Street*. Since I have always fancied myself as good at accents and loved disguising myself, I took great delight in appearing as different as I could. On one occasion while filming in Bradford, when I was disguised with a red wig and sporting a Scottish accent, I was moved on by the third assistant who hadn't recognised me and who was clearing the shot for the action.

I was invited back to Manchester Library Theatre for what would prove to be the last time, as David Scase was soon to retire. I was to play Willy Loman in *Death of a Salesman* with Jane Lowe again as my wife. Mac Andrews, who had been one of my students at Rose Bruford, and Sebastian Abineri were my sons; and Alan Rothwell, who had been Ken's brother David Barlow in the early days of *Coronation Street*, played Charlie. We opened at the Library Theatre and transferred to the Forum Theatre, Wythenshawe as in days of old. Although I say it myself, I was feeling very comfortable in the part, enjoyed a good press, and was getting a good reaction from my friends who came to see it. It is sad therefore that everything turned very sour for me and spoilt the aftertaste of what should have been a good experience. I'm not sure how it came to be blown up into such a major storm, but it started with an awareness on my part that young Sebastian Abineri, whose father was an actor that I had come across once and found to be most delightful, was resorting to the most outrageous upstaging tricks that were distracting the attention of the audience and were beginning to aggravate me intensely. He would frequently change his position onstage and was to be found in the strangest of places where he hadn't been at rehearsals. At one point I turned to exit upstage and found that he was blocking my path to the door; to have gone around him would have weakened the exit, so I just shouldered him out of the way and stormed off. The next day David Scase came to my dressing room before the show to tell me that Abineri had registered the complaint that I had struck him on stage! When I explained to David he seemed to sympathise with me and said that he would have done the same thing.

I suppose unpleasant episodes like that tend to undermine the confidence, because my next job too was a disappointment. Brian Wheeler had managed to get me a part in the television mini-series *A Married Man* on the grounds that I had been a pal of Anthony Hopkins, who was playing the lead, and the part of the left-wing reporter was supposed to have been an old chum of the main character. It was a classy production with Charles Jarrott as the director. I had a number of scenes with Tony, the main one being in the saloon bar of a pub where I had a very long and complicated speech. Much to my own surprise I did the first take of the master shot without a break and word perfect.

Charles Jarrott then went for the close-ups and covering shots – and I went to pieces! At the start of the scene I entered through the crowded bar to approach Tony sitting at his table and, on the way into the pub, I happened to pass a make-up girl being chatted up by the chief electrician. They weren't in the shot, but were clearly not interested at all in what was going on, and just continued to chat and giggle throughout the take. Since it was a pub scene with plenty of background action and hubbub, there is no reason why I should have found it so distracting; it just upset me that the attention of the whole crew was not focused upon what was being filmed. I kept drying and had to do retake after retake, getting worse and worse and feeling unable to tell the director what was upsetting me as it would have seemed like telling tales out of school, and it was so childish. I have always had very sensitive feelings in that area; when I was directing, I would insist that anybody who was not in the scene should not sit reading the newspaper but leave the room. I found any concentration not directed towards the production to be destructive and distracting.

I had a very sleepless night after that day's filming as I hate being responsible for a retake and I felt I had let myself down. Tony was delightful though; while he never knew what the matter was, I think he was aware that something was upsetting me, and on my last day of filming he took me out to lunch and insisted that I should have wine with my meal despite the fact that he was unable to join me in a glass.

After playing Frank in *Educating Rita* on the tour of India in 1982, I was invited the following year to take over the role from Tom Baker in the RSC production on its post-London tour. Kate Fitzgerald was playing Rita and would be staying on, so I had to go to Brighton for their last week and be rehearsed in to the play by Michael Ockrent whom I knew vaguely as he had directed Paddy in *Once a Catholic* in the West End.

The tour lasted for ten weeks and since it was under the RSC banner, it played to full houses everywhere. When we arrived at Buxton, though, we were greeted with the news that there were no more than a handful of seats booked on the first night; but we were told that this was not unusual as the likelihood of snow in that area at that time of year meant that people waited until the last moment before buying tickets. I was in my dressing room getting ready when the theatre manager came backstage to say that there was a queue at the box office and we would have to hold the curtain. The queue went right down the road, and we went up forty-five minutes late!

The ten-week tour was a great success, but it ended there and so did my contract with the RSC. I next returned to my role as a teacher-director, this time at a new venue when I was invited to direct *Fen* by Caryl Churchill at the Guildford School of Acting. I hadn't been to Guildford since I had squatted in the dressing room; this time I had no trouble digs-wise as my sister Pauline had moved to Guildford and I was able to spend the odd night with them.

In September/October 1983 I was asked to play Frank in *Educating Rita* again, and again on a tour of India, this time under the auspices of the British Council themselves and without a theatre management involved. Tina Marian was again to play Rita and we were also going to play in tandem with *Duet for One* by Tom Kempinski, my old RADA adversary, with Tina playing the Jacqueline Du Pré part and myself as the psychiatrist. The company was to consist of Tina and myself as the actors, Charles Stephens as the company manager and Teresa Joselyn as the stage manager. We were to have a British Council driver and that was all: the five of us were to take the play to areas where they mostly hadn't had the opportunity to see English touring companies before, and where at times we had to adapt the local village hall to take the two plays, often for no more than two or three performances.

Duet for One was directed by Penny Churns who also joined us for the start of the tour. It seemed that I was surrounded by women; Charles was often busy elsewhere so I spent day after day in female company, and I have to say I enjoyed the experience. Tina had the lion's share of responsibility in that she had virtually all of the dialogue in *Duet for One* and I, as the psychiatrist, just sat and listened with the occasional interjection. At the end of the first act her character breaks down, and in the wonderful and emotional last speech with the constant repetition of the word she cries, 'I will never, never, never, never, never, play the violin again!' As I opened the door for her to pass out for the interval, I whispered softly to her in my Eastern European accent, 'Have you thought of taking up the harmonica?' It became my favourite moment of the play as she tried to get out each night before I could find another little ad lib.

We opened in the Birla Institute of Technology and Science (BITS) in Pilani where we involved many of the students in the lighting and putting up the set in the school hall. Wherever we went we had to involve local labour and found that not only were they surprisingly competent, they were touchingly proud to be involved and there was never a question of extra pay for overtime! We played Jaipur, the pink city, before going up into the hills where the English would retreat, in the heat of Indian summers, playing Roorkee and then Dehra Dun public school, where I had to be treated by the school matron for heat exhaustion, lying down in the sick room for the afternoon before the evening performance; it was like something out of *Tom Brown's Schooldays*! Likewise there were shades of the Raj in Poona (or Pune) where we stayed in the officers' club; when Gopi, my Indian film-actor chum, came to see me he was refused permission to join us in the celebrations in the club afterwards, ostensibly because he hadn't got a tie. Since there were many there who didn't have ties, he was aware of the fact that it was because he was black and said he was going to go home; I persuaded him to stay and join me in my room where we took a bottle of Scotch.

Half way through the Indian leg of the tour, Tina received the news that her mother was dangerously ill and she would have to fly home. There was a panic as we had only the weekend before the next performance, and all the seats had been sold for the rest of the tour. Talks went on all night as they tried to dissuade Tina from going home, but it was only half hearted as they knew it was right that she should go. Trevor Mitchell, the British council official who had set up the tour, happened to be with us at that time and we stayed up all night trying to find a way out of the jam. I gave them what information I had about the whereabouts of Kate Fitzgerald, and they set about arranging the replacements. Tina had to be replaced by two actresses: Kate to play Rita, and Sue Holderness to play Stephanie in *Duet for One*; but they could not be flown out in time for the first performance, so in a flush of 'the show must go on' and patriotic pride, I offered to go on alone and do readings from Shakespeare.

The next problem was to find a copy of the works of Shakespeare and sort out a programme. I naturally only had a few speeches that I could do off the top of my head, but there were many others that I would be capable of sight-reading as I was fairly familiar with them. It took an age to find a library with the complete works which I then spent the night sorting through to compile a programme. The selection was then sent to a secretary at the British Council local office to be typed out in print big enough to sight-read. A copy was to be sent for me to work on, but the next morning it hadn't arrived and I began to panic. After much chasing up, a little Indian arrived on a cycle with a sheaf of papers containing the chosen excerpts, but with all Shakespeare's verse transcribed into prose and the language updated where the typist hadn't been able to understand the original!

By now we were late into the afternoon and it was too late to do anything but just close my eyes and jump in at the deep end. I would like to say that it was a great success but I'm afraid it was one of the more 'cringing' moments of my life. As I was half way through my material, I became aware of the fact that it wasn't going to last for much more than half an hour; I started to think of other bits that I could do, which took my mind off the bits I was doing and made the situation worse as I started to muff them. I eventually extended the introduction to each piece with anecdotes and stories about the productions I had been in and sensed that things were going a little better, but it was too late; and although everybody was very kind at the reception afterwards, I was aware that I hadn't done much more than help pass the time before the after-show drinks. I was greatly relieved when Kate and Sue were settled and rehearsed in to take over.

With the now enlarged company we travelled south to Trivandrum first, and then up to Cochin where we stayed at a hotel on an island and journeyed to the theatre each night in a motor launch which had been put at our command by David McCrirrick, the manager of a local tea plantation who became a very good friend of the company and kept in contact for many years afterwards. We started to collect different ways of travelling to the theatre each evening. Apart from the motor launch we went by elephant, camel, rickshaw, cycle rickshaw, the little adapted Vespas, and many a taxi that was on its last legs. Next was Goa when Kate Fitzgerald, on arriving at the beach and getting out of the British Council Land Rover, just took off every stitch of clothing and strolled off down the beach leaving our poor little Indian driver open-mouthed and speechless.

Before going home for the Christmas break we returned to Bombay where we played the lovely little Prithvi Theatre started, owned, and run by the Kendal family, and where we met up with Felicity Kendal's Indian film-star brother-in-law, Shashi Kapoor. Apparently, the Merchant Ivory film *Shakespeare Wallah* had been based on Felicity's parents.

Bangalore was strange. On checking in to the West End Hotel, I found a note had been left for me at reception by the parents-in-law of my old stagehand companion David Miles. I was wondering at how small the world was that, here in Bangalore, I should come across someone I knew, when the casting director Priscilla John screeched a wild hello from the other side of the reception area. She was staying for a few days to see the locations and cast the locals for *A Passage to India* to be directed by David Lean. Priscilla came to see the show and joined us for a meal afterwards; as she left us that night she said that David Lean would be arriving in the morning and she would be tied up with him, so she said goodbye and good luck. I asked her to give David my love and remember me to him. I had never met him in my life, but it can't be too bad to have your name mentioned occasionally in such illustrious company!

We were leaving the next day and so weren't expecting to see Priscilla at all, but as I was moving out of my bungalow I noticed her talking to two men on the hotel path. Assuming the taller, more distinguished man to be David Lean, I waited until he left before taking her the large bouquet of flowers that had been presented to me on the opening night in Bangalore and which would just go to waste if left in my room. She of course was delighted and, after thanking me, started to introduce her companion to me. 'This is David Lean; David, this is Ken Farrington... oh, but of course you know one another, don't you?'

After the Christmas break, when we all returned home for the month of December, Tina was back in the company and we flew to Istanbul where we alternated with the National Theatre of Turkey; they played one night in Turkish and then we played the next night in English. We became very friendly with the Turkish cast and socialised nightly together. Istanbul became one of my favourite venues; we were royally entertained and I will never forget the restaurant run by two Russian sisters where the duck stew was memorable, and also dining on the Bosphorus, full of jellyfish, on a jetty over the water, fish dish after fish dish and the meal lasting all afternoon.

Next we set off to Damascus where, on arrival, we discovered that our set and costumes had been lost somewhere in transit; we had to tour the houses of the English residents and borrow books, desk, chairs and improvise a set, and also dress in hand-me-down clothing borrowed from the local ex-pats! Things were seeming to fall apart a little and in Damascus I found myself in a hotel where the nocturnal comings and goings made it impossible to sleep, so I got up the next day and moved myself into another hotel, much to the dismay of the British Council, as it was a little more expensive, but I was desperate for a good night's sleep. Although the street markets in Damascus and the oldest street called 'Straight' (as it is referred to in the Bible) enthralled me I was relieved to get away to play Ankara, motoring across the Syrian Desert. We had been spoilt in general with our accommodation and I think we were getting a little tired, so when Trevor Mitchell sent a message to ask if we would be prepared to extend the tour to go to Sweden, we weren't really all that keen and he was a little hurt. The tour wasn't finished, however; we returned home for a week out before setting off for the final leg to Kenya.

When I had embarked upon the tour, I had been under the impression, and the hope, that Sandra would be coming with me. In the event, she said that she wasn't too keen on becoming a camp follower and I was left to go alone. She did, however, agree to come with me on the last leg of the tour when we were to play in the National Theatre in Nairobi. Things started badly even before we set off from England on a Sunday evening. As we were packing on the Sunday morning, Sandra discovered that her passport was out of date; after making various urgent phone calls we learnt that there was nothing we could do about it in the time available! We also learnt that there was no problem in getting out of England: the problems lay in getting into Kenya and also in trying to get back into England. We decided to take the risk. Sure enough, passport control at Heathrow noticed the date on the passport but allowed us through. On landing in Nairobi, at an ungodly hour in the morning, I presented my passport and, as Sandra handed hers over, I distracted the attention of the official; he automatically stamped Sandra's without looking, and we were in.

At the reception after the first performance, I made a point of introducing myself to the British Consul. The next day we were invited to the consular office and Sandra was issued with a temporary passport. I also took the opportunity to arrange to rent one of their little cottages on the beach at Mombasa for the week after the play finished, as we were planning to stay on for a week's holiday.

One day during the first week of playing, we received a message at the hotel that David Mayers, who had been with me in the film *Submarine X-1*, was in reception to see me. Sandra was looking forward to us having some quality time together and her nose was initially a little put out of joint. It didn't take long, however, for David's charm to effect a complete U-turn and win her over.

The last time I had seen David was when he had bought the house next door to us in Grafton Square with his wife Charlie, but much had happened since, including the disastrously tragic road accident that had left David paralysed from the waist down and confined to a wheelchair. David's family had been farmers in Kenya and we were invited to spend a few days at their farm in the hills outside Nairobi with David's mother. David himself had been a farmer for some time after giving up acting, but had been driven off his farm and out of the house when the blacks had 'walked on' to his land and claimed it and the house. He took us to see the rather wonderful farmhouse, which had been ruined; the natives had put their animals into the house and built themselves little huts outside! His mother had been allowed to stay, or rather had managed to reclaim her house, and kept a Masai village on the farm where she helped them and took visitors, who bought their artefacts and paid to be entertained with the Masai warriors' dance before taking tea with her on the farm. Although it may sound as if it was a little condescending, she was greatly respected by the Masai and she had a great respect for them in return.

The atmosphere on the farm was delightful, which is more than could be said for the centre of Nairobi. During our week in Mombasa, I had bought a pair of wicker chairs made by a little craftsman in the bush. We had taken a coach from Mombasa and they wouldn't take the chairs, so I had to go to the bus company and put them in the luggage compartment of another bus to Nairobi, which seemed to be one that was more for the natives than for tourists; I had to pay, of course. I then had to meet that bus at the terminal in Nairobi and collect the chairs later that day. I went alone to the bus station which was in a decidedly dodgy part of the city; there seemed to be a lot of aggression and drunkenness around, and I was the only white face. When the bus arrived, they refused to let me take the chairs until the bus had completed its journey, so I got on board and stubbornly sat upstairs while it travelled around the outlying villages and then went to the depot to be washed!

As the bus emptied progressively from stop to stop, until there was just me and a couple of black guys upstairs, I began to fear for my life and sat with my feet up and my fists ready with my imagination running riot. I realised that I had been set up; at first I thought it was just bloody-mindedness because I was white, but it was beginning to get a bit more serious, and it was now quite well into the evening and was dark. As soon as the empty bus arrived back at the city centre I got off, let myself into the luggage compartment and took the chairs without reference to the driver, before legging it back to the hotel where they were about to call the police as I had been missing for something like five hours!

Those two chairs became something of another personal challenge because when we got back to London Heathrow, I had to make a special return trip to the airport with a car large enough to take them. They only cost about £10 for the pair originally, but they loom very large in my legend and remind me of the idyllic week we had on the deserted beach in Mombasa where we lived in a little cottage on the beach and spent the hot nights eating succulent pineapples the like of which I have never tasted since.

15

1984 to 1990 • *Coronation Street* •
Bill Waddington • Barry Foster •
Nottingham Playhouse • *It's a Madhouse* • *Run for
Your Wife* • Farnham: *The Complaisant Lover* •
Leicester: *The Crucible* • Eastbourne • Leeds: *Ghosts*

ONE OF THE PROBLEMS with returning every once in a while to *Coronation Street* was that they usually required about three months' advance notice in order to get the storylines sorted and scripts written, and I was reluctant to commit myself that far ahead; I was always hoping that that elusive career-changing offer might come through in the meantime. So when I was approached in February of 1984 and asked if I could come up immediately, I didn't hesitate, but I did use the urgency of the situation to negotiate an extension of the three-week offer; I was getting fed up with enduring the negative side of playing Billy Walker without reaping the financial rewards.

The need for my return at such swift notice had been occasioned by Fred Feast (who played Fred Gee, the Rovers potman) having some sort of breakdown. I was to take over his role; still as Billy, of course, but with the lines changed appropriately where needed. Unfortunately, they also took the opportunity to alter Billy's character, making him a much nastier piece of work than he had been hitherto. I'm not sure what the reasoning behind this change was. Doris had left the previous year, so perhaps they felt that Billy needed to change direction, as he was no longer required to be a feed for Annie. Meanwhile Johnny Briggs had been built up as Mike Baldwin, and his character was not dissimilar to the lovable rogue I felt I had been playing, although not so lovable! Mervyn Watson was now producer (with Bill Podmore as executive producer) and maybe he wanted to mix things up a little to establish his authority. At the same time, *Dallas* was extremely popular and the cruel and scheming J. R. Ewing had become a national icon; perhaps they were thinking to echo that and cash in.

Whatever the reasoning, I found myself week after week trying to play against the unpleasantness of the scripts in order to try and retain some sort of continuity with the character I had been playing on and off for the past twenty-odd years. After a long discussion with Doris who, although no longer in the Street, watched it avidly and took a great deal of interest, I went to see Mervyn Watson to talk over the way the character was going. The meeting was not only fruitless, it was destructive; he more or less accused me of wanting to play a lovable character because I didn't like being disliked by the audience, an assertion I found insulting.

Doris was now living in a home in Bury and I would make a point of going to visit her regularly. It wasn't done as a chore or a duty; she was genuinely good company and a joy to be with. She was, though, always complaining about what they were doing with my character; it upset her greatly. On her demise from the Street, I had taken over as landlord of the Rovers Return; and because I felt this would give me a more prominent role in the storylines and thus more rewarding work to get my teeth into, and despite the fact that I was unhappy with the way the characterisation was going, I had more or less decided to remain in the Street for the foreseeable future – long enough, at least, for me to not want to live in digs or a hotel.

By now I had sold my terraced house in Whalley Range, and I also wanted another project to stimulate me in my 'easy weeks' which were bound to crop up, so I bought a two-bedroomed farmhouse in the little village of Combs in the Peak District, just outside Buxton. The views across the rolling Peaks were wonderful, with the drystone walls stretching away towards Kinder Scout, clearly visible in the distance. It was a beautiful solid stone building with flagstone floors downstairs and roof slates the size of paving slabs, and had a spring in the back garden supplying its own water, filtered through the Buxton moors.

The place was above the snow line and hadn't been lived in for some years, and was consequently in dire need of renovation and modernisation. Since I was fairly taken up with rehearsals in central Manchester, I employed a builder to oversee the conversion and was surprised to discover that he was the father of one of my former students in the MYT, David Threlfall. He was quite an eccentric character – he once turned up in his working clothes in the rehearsal room at Granada, having 'blagged' his way past reception, and I sometimes came home to find that he had taken it upon himself to make some rather strange decisions – but in general the result was stunning and retained all of the original features. I now had my dream cottage within an hour's drive of the studios, and within walking distance of the Beehive Inn where I stayed for the initial stages of the conversion, and where I soon became one of the favoured few who would be allowed to drink into the early hours.

When I first arrived back in the Street I was still without a car (and indeed a licence), and had started my house-hunting catching trains and buses, until Bill Waddington very kindly took me under his wing and opted to join me after work and drive me everywhere. Bill had been brought into the Street to play Percy Sugden, the somewhat boring war veteran. Bill had been a stand-up comic and it showed – not only in his performance, but off screen too. He was constantly cracking old jokes that eventually became funny merely because of his insistence rather than their quality. I got on very well with him though, and he was very flattering in the way he constantly asked my opinion and advice about his acting. Once when we were rehearsing a scene in the Rovers, in which I was behind the bar talking to him, he was fiddling with the loose change in his pocket, a nervous habit of his, and I had quite a long speech which was accompanied by this jingling of coins. Without breaking the speech, I came around the bar, took his hand out of his pocket, put the change on the bar, and went back to the other side by the end of my dialogue. Whenever I met him in later years, he would recount this moment with some joy. He was devoted to the Street. He had lost his wife and was a very lonely man; he had also, as far as I can gather, been quite wealthy, owning racehorses that he was very heavily into.

Another newcomer (to me) was Bill Tarmey, playing Jack Duckworth; and once again I was flattered to find him asking for advice and assistance when he hit a problem. Bill had also been a club singer, and was keen to do the job properly and make the transition to acting. There seemed to be a regular influx of club entertainers; Lynne Perrie had been the first, and I guess the casting department were encouraged by her success to try others: Bill Tarmey, Bill Waddington, Jill Summers, Liz Dawn; there may have been others that I wasn't aware of. Whilst they may have been lacking in the techniques of television acting, they certainly brought with them the confidence of being solo performers and created some good, strong and unusual characters.

It must be said though that there was a considerable amount of fluffing and drying going on; perhaps because of the lack of theatre discipline and experience, and also, since the show was now coming up to its quarter century and some of the cast had been with it for most, if not all, of that time, there was a touch of complacency too. Nevertheless, in the main, the approach was very professional and most of the cast were extremely conscientious.

Whatever the reason, Mervyn Watson sent a memo to all the cast, reminding them that they were being well paid to learn their lines, be punctual and not let their personal appearances get in the way of performance! It was quite a strongly worded letter with the implied threat of the sack. It was true that Pat Phoenix, who had left the cast at this point, would often read her lines from a script in her handbag, and Doris Speed would have pages of the script set at various strategic places around the set. It was true too that one or two of the cast had difficulty with punctuality, and with line learning, but they were very much in the minority; and I was livid at receiving the letter, as indeed were many of the others. It was a cowardly way of dodging the awkward situation of singling out the guilty and facing them with the admonition. It was last thing on a Friday that I received my letter and took it home to Dulwich to fume over the weekend. By now, I was well ensconced in the ground-floor flat in Beckwith Road, having sold the two flats upstairs, one of them to Kit Miller, a fellow member of the Old Boys' club who happened to be a journalist for the *News of the World* at that time.

Kit was one of three sons to Gary Miller, and was exasperatingly unreliable, but possessing immense charm. When he had bought the flat from me, I learnt at the last moment from our mutual solicitor Bob Joyce (who was also an Alleyn's Old Boy) that Kit had got a mortgage, but he hadn't got a deposit. I therefore had to lend him the £5,000 deposit to buy my flat! He was due to pay me back at the rate of £1,000 per month, but I was fearful of his ability to do this and when I went back into the Street, I agreed to give him an exclusive interview, for which the paper paid me £1,000, which was to be deducted from the debt. I was trying to create a situation that would help him to pay back my money; and when I showed him Mervyn Watson's letter that Friday evening in the pub, he begged me to let him have it. Still smarting from my indignation at having received it, I rather stupidly gave it to him on condition that it was never divulged whom he had got it from.

The next I heard was when it was nationally announced on the Sunday early-morning news that the cast of *Coronation Street* had received a rocket from the show's producer and threatened with the sack unless they 'pulled their socks up'. I then found it on the front page of the *News of the World*, including a photocopy of the original letter (without my name), and it was to be followed up with articles in the daily papers, including a cartoon in the *Daily Mail*. My blood ran cold; what had I done?

There was already an enquiry under way at Granada because somebody was leaking storylines to the press and the company were very 'mole aware'. When I arrived back at the studios after the weekend, the place was buzzing with the publication of the letter and I felt that everybody was looking at me! One of the first people I met was Thelma Barlow, who played Mavis Riley, and she asked, 'How much did you get for it?' I think she was only joking, and I bluffed it out and pretended not to know what she was talking about, but I could feel myself blushing scarlet. Mervyn Watson muttered something like, 'We'll find out where it came from; we're working on it.' Apart from that, although I was expecting at any moment to be unmasked and denounced as 'the Granada Mole', nobody said a word; I was later relieved to hear that Adele Rose, who had been a scriptwriter for the Street, had been caught selling stories to the papers and I hoped that they might think she had also given them the letter.

Things quietened down and I continued in my struggling way to try and take the edge off the unpleasant scenes that I was being given to play. One day, when I was having a little time off in my remote farmhouse in the Peak District, I was amazed to see Kit Miller coming across the fields with somebody else who, it turned out, was a photographer. The *Coronation Street* contracts were coming up for renewal and Kit said he had come to see if I was leaving. I must admit I was puzzled, and rather naively didn't cotton on to what he was really saying. I simply said that I had no intention to leave, just yet; they took some pictures and left. It can't have been more than a few days later that Julie Goodyear came back from her usual sycophantic lunchtime drink with Bill Podmore, the executive producer, and I learnt from her that I would not be invited to stay on; and sure enough later that day I received a letter to that effect from the office.

It took me some time to take it on board and get an interview with Bill. I wanted to let him know that I was prepared to stay on; perhaps they hadn't been aware? When I did eventually get to see him, he said they had thought that I would, as usual, want to move on; but he didn't offer to retract the decision, so that was obviously not the truth.

Of course, I was tortured by the thought that they had discovered it was me that had given the letter to the papers, and I felt I had really let myself down, but it was never stated. Despite my spending a drunken night with Bill Podmore in Belfast some years later, when a lot of home truths were explored, he never said that he had known. I have twice met Mervyn Watson since, once at the TV awards and once at the Street fortieth birthday thrash, and he has been nothing but friendly and warm towards me. I have too met up from time to time with my old mates from the cast and there has never been any mention, yet I am convinced they must have known and I live with a feeling of guilt. The exit storyline was that I lost the licence because of late-night drinking in the Rovers; I was last seen driving along the motorway on my return to Jersey, and have not been seen since.

I had been in the Street for the best part of 1984; Sandra and I then went off for a fortnight to the island of Nevis in the Caribbean, and the *News of the World* sent a photographer to take pictures of 'Billy away from it all'. At first we weren't too keen, even though they were paying half of the holiday cost for the privilege; but we were lucky enough to get Arthur Edwards, who has since made a name for himself as a royal photographer, and he turned out to be an absolutely charming man and was very unobtrusive. Also on the island at the time was Diana Hardcastle and her then partner Martin Campbell who had recently had a great success with his wonderful production of the TV series *Edge of Darkness*, and the designer Tom Rand who used to sit beside the pool, in the most outlandish gear, doing his needlework with his partner Ian.

We all got on extremely well together and were somewhat thrown out of kilter when Barry Foster turned up out of the blue. We knew he was on the island as we had met him at the airport. I had noticed him at Heathrow, although he seemed to be disguising himself with dark glasses that made him stand out in a crowd; and when I found myself sitting one seat away from him, I felt I had to say something. We had been in the film *Robbery* together, both as train robbers, and had become 'partners in crime' of a different sort when we slipped away from the night filming standby and found the local pub. He had also just finished playing in the West End with Paddy, my now ex-wife, in *Passion Play* by Peter Nichols, so I felt the connection strong enough to at least say hello. His reaction was to say the least completely uninterested and I wish I hadn't spoken.

After we had been on the island a week we were told that an actor would be joining us at the hotel that night, and when I heard it was Barry I must have registered some disappointment because the receptionist said, 'It's funny you should be like that. When we told him we had an actor here he said, "Oh no, keep him away from me!"'

When he arrived that evening for the pre-dinner drinks I was taken aback by his friendly advance, but it all made sense when he tried to bum a cigar off me, and when I didn't respond he bummed cigarettes off Martin Campbell instead. We managed to keep out of his way, as he rather liked to dine on the top table with the hotel owners where we could hear him telling tales of *Van Der Valk*, and we preferred to be on our own on a little side table. He didn't stay long but we did bump into him while we were waiting for our return flight from Antigua; he had joined up with some of the crew from a big yacht who were rather arrogant, loud and boisterous, possibly drunk, so once again we escaped. Some years later we discovered that he was a close friend of the neighbours to our barn in France; he was a frequent visitor and we saw him often, but he never seemed to acknowledge that we had ever met before.

We reluctantly returned to England for Christmas 1984 and I found I had been offered *A Man For All Seasons* at Nottingham Playhouse, this time playing Thomas More. It wasn't a role that I thought myself ideally suited for, but I liked the idea of playing such a heroic part, and was prepared to work hard to face the challenge. Kenneth Alan Taylor directed it and Jane Lowe was again to play my wife. The rehearsal period was hard, but I enjoyed working with Ken, and as usual Jane was a joy to play with. Although I had had reservations about being able to play the part, I did well, not only getting decent 'crits' but also a good reception from my fellow actors. Paul McGann visited and was particularly flattering about my performance as we chatted late into the night in the bar backstage. There was, at Nottingham Playhouse, an innovative idea of the actors having their own little mess-room bar backstage, which was very civilised.

With the end of my *Coronation Street* back-up, I was to spend the next six years mostly on tour, intermingled with the odd television, radio, and corporate video; starting with a touring production of *The Last of the Red Hot Lovers* by

Neil Simon, directed for the Channel Theatre Company by Kevin Wood, who ran the company with his wife. I loved Neil Simon, and also loved the idea of carrying a play. *The Last of the Red Hot Lovers* consists of three acts, each with a different woman and the same man, so as far as I was concerned it was virtually a two-hander. The play was not a financial or artistic success; I found that Kevin was not too happy about it either and he ceased to visit us on tour, so I imagined he had either given us up or had other things to do.

I did also learn that the fact that I had been in the Street was not sufficient to attract people to the theatre. We played some terrible dates that would obviously struggle with rustling up an audience at the best of times. The worst were those that were run by local authorities; the publicity was virtually non-existent and was usually handled by someone who had been promoted from 'Parks and Gardens'. The best publicists are working for commercial firms; and the theatre, because it pays so badly, is left with either the inexperienced who, if they are any good, move off as soon as they have learnt the trade, or the inept, who can't get work elsewhere. The theatres too were badly run. Gone were the days when the theatre manager would come round just before curtain up on the first night, welcome you to the theatre, give you a copy of the programme and invite you for a drink after the show. More often than not, you would never see the theatre manager, and you got your own drink after the show in the empty theatre bar – that is, if it was still open! There was rarely any pride or interest in the local theatre, and it is no wonder that they were always struggling to get together a half-way decent audience. Darlington, alone of the theatres we visited, could not be accused in some aspect of any of these criticisms.

I think one of the worst must have been Milton Keynes, where the theatre is situated in the middle of a shopping precinct that dies when the shops close, and is unbelievably unenticing to visit in the evenings. I could hear, during the first act, the continual hum of a conversation from the back of the auditorium, and at the interval I asked our company manager to do something about it. I learnt after the show that it was the man operating the lighting board, who was almost deaf and was communicating with his operators. The next night as I went before the show to the front-of-house bar, I noticed a man coming along the corridor who seemed very much the worse for drink; I warned the staff that there was a drunk backstage, only to be informed that he was the deaf man who was operating the lighting board! When I asked why he was allowed to continue in his post I was told that he had been with the council for so long that they would have difficulty in getting rid of him. There really were some terrible and depressing dates and I was glad to get back home after the tour, although I was out of work for the next two months and was soon ready to accept anything again.

As it happens, the next job was a peach: a week's filming in Switzerland, staying at the Gstaad Palace hotel and playing the part of a French waiter in an episode of *Lime Street*, made by Columbia Pictures Television for the American ABC network. The series starred Robert Wagner and was directed by Ray Austin, who had been the stunt co-ordinator on *The Splendid Spur* and now lived in Hollywood. I was called to a London hotel for the casting where I was interviewed by Ray in his private suite wearing a red monogrammed smoking jacket, mono-grammed bedroom slippers and smoking what looked like a monogrammed cigar! It wasn't a large part, possibly one or two days' filming; but I was to stay in that wonderful hotel in Gstaad for at least a week, in case I was needed.

John Standing was among the show's regular cast, and since he didn't seem to remember me from the pilot for *Scandal* that we had done together in about 1965 I didn't mention it; he seemed a little aloof. On the other hand, John Woodvine, who had come out to India to join his then girlfriend Jennie Stoller, was extremely warm and friendly despite the fact that I had had a running feud with his ex-girlfriend. He, Gayle Hunnicutt and I spent most of our hanging-around time together, walking in the Swiss mountains and waiting to be used. In the evenings, we would join the rest of the company for a meal in the delightful village of Gstaad; it was all very upmarket and glamorous.

While the trip to Switzerland was a great experience, my part in *Lime Street* wasn't much to write home about; and although I didn't know it at the time, the series was cancelled after only a handful of episodes when Samantha Smith, the 13-year-old actress who played Robert Wagner's young daughter in the show, was tragically killed in a plane crash.

Just before I returned to England, Sandra telephoned to say that we had been burgled and my lovely Bang and Olufsen TV and VCR had been stolen. I was brought back to earth with a thump and arrived home in Dulwich to find that the thieves had entered though the front-room window while Sandra had been asleep in the back! This was the first of four burglaries that were to make us move from London. Dulwich was an area much targeted by the druggies from Brixton and the surrounding district because of the apparent wealth. They just made an error in choosing my 'pad'; after the Bang and Olufsen had gone there was no apparent wealth!

After this depressing incident I was relieved to be invited to Derby Playhouse to play the lead, a bombastic and domineering football-club chairman, in a new play by Stephen Bill called *Over the Bar*. The director was Chris Honer and while I got on well with him, I had the feeling that he was a little bit wary of me. I went out of my way to make him feel comfortable because I would have liked to work with him again, but this was the one and only time, although I did meet up with him again when he took over Manchester Library Theatre. I was still very heavily involved with football, arranging charity soccer games as well as playing in them, which made this play a bit special to me. I could also commute to Derby from my farmhouse in Combs, and so I was disappointed not to be invited back – especially since I had another two months with nothing but a radio play for Tony Cliff, who was now based in the studios in Manchester. Although they were great fun to do, they didn't do more than give the morale a boost as the money was not enough to live on.

I was consequently delighted when, at the beginning of 1986, I was asked to play Father Keegan in a tour of *John Bull's Other Island* by Shaw, directed for the Cambridge Theatre Company by Bill Pryde. Apart from Jeremy Sinden as the one English character, Broadbent, the rest of the cast were all genuine Irish, including Des McAleer, Brendan Conroy, Declan Mulholland and Shay Gorman. I have always prided myself on being good at dialects and I had already played a number of Irish roles and been generally accepted as convincing. This time it was different though; I was playing the best Irish part in the play, and the casting of an Englishman caused a certain amount of resentment.

That wasn't my biggest problem, although it contributed to my feeling a little undermined and consequently lacking in confidence. Matters came to a head when Bill Pryde was missing for a day and the assistant director took rehearsals. He did not have Bill's sensitivity and, after a tentative run-through, made some comment about me lacking the necessary charisma; that put the final nail into my coffin. I enjoyed the tour (it was classier than the general run of tours) and liked the company; but I felt aware that I was the weak link and that ruined it for me. I never recovered, and I was glad when the tour came to a close.

The next tour followed hard upon *John Bull's Other Island* and was nowhere near as good a play or as good a company, but I was much more comfortable in the part of Hardy, a manservant who turns out to be a Russian spy! The play was called *The Edge of Darkness*, written by Brian Clemens and directed by Peter Clapham. It was the usual touring-type thriller where the twists and turns of plot were more important than the characters. Perhaps it was a better play than I gave it credit for, because we didn't do it at all well.

The fault lay with the fact that the leading part was played by Anthony Steel, a heart-throb film star of the sixties who had never been more than a good-looking and photogenic young man. He was not merely inadequate as an actor; because of a dependence on drink, he had also lost his ability to learn lines. The whole of the rehearsal period was just a line-learning process as we all stood around watching him try to muddle through and never had much of a chance to get to work on our own parts. Virginia Stride had the most difficult task as she had to play most of her scenes opposite him; without her patience and help he would never have made it. By 'made it', I mean just learnt the lines because that in reality was the limit of his achievement, and indeed ours too. The only bright spot in the production was the maid, played by Helen Pearson who managed to bring a welcome touch of comedy to the evening.

I wasn't beyond reproach myself though, as I forgot one night to take on with me a key that I had to take an imprint of, which was a very important development in the plot. Finding myself on stage without this vital prop, I mimed it; unconvincingly I'm sure, but nobody seemed to notice – although probably by that point nobody in the audience cared any more as they had ceased to follow the plot anyway!

The last I saw of Anthony Steel was after the last night at Dartmouth when we all said goodbye in the pub next to the theatre, where he was staying. When I returned with a play a year later, I was told that he had stayed in the pub for some weeks after that, running up a bill he couldn't afford to pay; it was very sad.

It was in the middle of November 1986 that I received the news of Michael Croft's death. I had last seen him in the summer of that year when he had called me to come and help him with his production of *Henry V* in Regent's Park. I had worked for a week, mainly on the French court scenes with a very impressive Tom Hollander playing the Dauphin, and had given private tuition to the lad playing Fluellen. At the end of my week I had to go to Manchester for the opening night of the Manchester Youth Theatre; although no longer a director, I was a vice president and liked to give my support. I called in to Mike's rehearsals at Camden Town Hall where they had just broken for lunch, and found Mike sitting on the terrace outside a very upmarket restaurant with a bottle of Chardonnay and a Dover sole. He was alone while the surrounding benches, the bus shelter, even the steps of the Town Hall were swarming with young would-be actors eating fish and chips or sandwiches. I had a glass of wine with him before continuing on my way; and although I saw him some days later at the first night of his *Henry V*, he was far too busy to give me any time. He was looking decidedly thin and had aged a good deal; he was grey, and had lost a lot of his youthful fire and enthusiasm. Some of the young actors were hungry for the sort of advice I was giving them, and complained that Croft hardly gave them any direction at all. It was sad to hear them talk of him in this way, but perhaps he had said all he had to say.

He was cremated in north London not far from where he lived in Kentish Town, attended by the chosen few chums that he had designated in his last wishes. Afterwards we were invited to a typically northern funeral tea where there was a lot of laughter and much sadness. It was at this tea that I was approached by Esta Charkham and asked if I would submit my name to be considered to succeed Mike. At first I was somewhat doubtful of being able to do the job justice and suggested I might get together with Geoff Sykes and put in a bid for joint leadership; but Esta dissuaded me from this idea as Hazel and Geoff had somewhat blotted their copybook with their drinking escapades. I decided to think about it for a while.

A few days later I was telephoned to say that I had inherited a set of hand-painted plates depicting scenes from Paris. Mike had prepared a long list of his belongings and every one of his old chums had been left some little memento.

Some three weeks after the funeral, a memorial service was held in the church opposite Euston Station which, although large, was only just about able to hold the multitude that turned up. I have never seen so many grown men in tears, and I have never seen such a collection of theatrical luminaries; not just past members of the National Youth Theatre but everybody who was anybody in the theatre was there. I found myself sitting next to Fulton Mackay, who had played the doctor in *Coronation Street* before making his mark in the wonderful comedy series *Porridge*; Vanessa Redgrave was a few seats away, and there were many old friends including Froggie French and John Stride. What a send-off!

I was again invited to put my name forward to take over the running of the NYT and by now I had a real taste for the job. I felt that my seven years directing the Manchester Youth Theatre would stand me in good stead, and I was very much in tune with Mike's original concept. The council of the NYT met to sort out the various applicants and I was informed that I had been shortlisted. Geoff Sykes telephoned to say that he had been asked to give me some sort of reference; I got the impression that his testimonial had been a little short of glowing!

For the final selection process I was interviewed by the then NYT president Bryan Forbes along with Simon Ward, Esta Charkham, Stanley Vereker, Illtyd Harrington, and I can't remember who else. I felt the interview was going quite well until Simon asked if I believed I had the necessary diplomatic discretion for the job, and I replied by asking if he thought Mike had been what you might call diplomatic and discreet. I got the impression that he was referring to something Geoff had said in his letter and that my goose had been cooked.

I didn't get the job; Ed Wilson, who had been working with Mike as an assistant director for some time, was appointed artistic director of the National Youth Theatre, a position he held for the next sixteen years. During that time he did a very good job and although I didn't agree with everything he did, I think he took the Youth Theatre forward and made a number of improvements. I am only disappointed that I was never invited back to direct a show, despite offering on numerous occasions.

My frustrating experience with *The Edge of Darkness* had put me off touring for a while, and I was glad to get a part in the TV mini-series *A Killing on the Exchange*. Although not a large part (again), it was spread over several episodes and kept me going until the end of the year. That and another radio play for Tony Cliff were all I had during a very lean period, so I was relieved when Kenneth Alan Taylor came up with an offer to do the play *It's a Madhouse* even though I wasn't too happy about the touring aspect.

How I got the part was a series of accidents. I had been watching on television a repeat of *Boys from the Black Stuff*, and had been overwhelmed by the writing and the acting; I particularly recall the scene where 'Yosser' is in dire straits and visits the priest in the confessional, who encourages him not to call him Father, but to be less formal and use his Christian name, Dan. Whereupon Yosser says, 'I'm desperate Dan!' The bravery of putting such a gag in such a pitiable situation struck me as brilliant; and, although I was not in the habit of writing fan letters and didn't have more than a nodding acquaintance with Alan Bleasdale, the writer, I wrote to say how wonderful I thought the series. He told me later that he had received the letter the day he had agreed with Bill Kenwright to let him do a tour of his play *It's a Madhouse* and had suggested me for the cast.

Perhaps Bill had forgotten that he had said he would never employ me, or perhaps Alan was too persuasive; maybe even Kenneth Alan Taylor, who was by then employed to direct, had reinforced Alan's suggestion. In any event I was asked to play the part of Eddie which Ken himself had played in a production I had seen at the University Theatre in Manchester some years earlier when Paddy had played Christine, the part now played by Ken's wife, Judith Barker.

The coincidences were unhappily not to end there. In rehearsals, Ken told me that during the Manchester production Paddy had been in a bad emotional state because of the situation in our marriage and had made his life a misery; he said she had ruined the play for him and he would never work with her again. I'm sure it wasn't intentional, but the tables were turned when his wife Judith Barker ruined the play for me and made the tour a very unhappy one that I would not wish to repeat.

I think the essence of the problem was that I was the only one in the company who had not played their part before, and they were all well ensconced in their characters. There was also the fact that Ken, the director, had played the part that I was playing, and as I remember was very good. The sexuality of the character, who was an orderly in a mental home, was a bit questionable; and Ken himself being something of a puzzle in that area, despite the fact that he was married to Judith, gave him a head start. The result was that I felt decidedly uncomfortable during rehearsals; I felt I was holding everybody up and was terribly conscious of Judith's exasperation at the time I was taking to find my own way into the character. In consequence I never felt at all settled in the part.

As the tour progressed, I found that I was being ostracised by the majority of the cast, and I put this down to Judith's antipathy towards me. Off stage she played very much the Thora Hird of the company, 'Mrs Warm Straight Northerner' with the heart of gold and the ready ear for the troubled, and if you were prepared to worship this and join her clique you were accepted with an overpoweringly warm embrace, but I was not of this mind and was the subject of much backbiting.

The end to any pretence came in Belfast when we happened to be staying in the same hotel and at breakfast one morning she informed me that we would be having the matinee afternoon off, as the understudies would be going on in our stead. Since she was enjoying the attentions of the young man who was understudying me, I could see where this was coming from and said that I did not agree with that. The public were paying to see the advertised cast and, unless they were informed and given the choice, I did not think it was right.

From that moment forth, the antagonism was more open and I had an even unhappier tour. It must be said that the play was superb, which only served to double my frustration at the fact that I couldn't enjoy and grow in the part. The most outstanding performance was from David Ross, who was quite brilliant and I am glad to say was to develop in more of Alan Bleasdale's work.

Money was a bit short at that time and I had great hopes of things improving when I was offered a role in a new situation comedy called *Valentine Park* for Central TV. The cast included Ken Jones, whom I had known and admired from RADA, and Daniel Peacock who had written and starred in the film *Party Party*. It was also introducing a new and talented young actor, David Thewlis, and the old hand Liz Smith. I was playing the husband of Penny Morrell who was married in real life to George Cole. We played to a studio audience and it wasn't long before we realised that the scripts weren't working. At least, they weren't as far as Penny and I were concerned; we didn't get much reaction from the audience and a lot of the fault has to be laid at Penny's feet because on getting no reaction she tried harder and eventually was so over the top that it became embarrassing rather than funny. Once again I didn't enjoy a studio audience, but they were not wrong!

Apart from the depressing lack of work, we had been burgled another three times. Once, Sandra had got up in the night to go to the loo and on coming back to bed told me I had left the light on in the lounge. I got up and went through to turn it off, and when we discovered the next morning that we had been visited, we realised they were probably still there when I came to turn out the light; which can't have been too pleasant for them as I don't wear anything in bed!

By now it was 1988 and work was pretty thin on the ground again. I did a small character part in *Hannay* starring Robert Powell in which I met up with Ted de Souza again; I also met for the first time Gary Bond who impressed me immensely, not just with his performance, but by being completely unspoilt and probably one of the nicest guys I had ever come across. I played the eccentric inventor of the Gatling gun, which was a nice part but, as I said, small. Two other embarrassingly brief visits, in *Boon* and *Minder*, made up the sum total of my TV appearances that year. Esta Charkham was the producer on *Boon* and offered me the part. I have always had a great admiration for Michael Elphick's work; he was a character actor of great depth and it was tragic that he fell into the same pattern of drink dependency that seem to afflict all of the actors that I most admire, like Wilfrid Lawson, Freddie Jones and my old mate Graham Haberfield.

Even though I had nothing else to do, I rather wish I hadn't done these small roles. Not only was it embarrassing to be so little involved when soccer mates like Dennis Waterman and Mark Kingston were playing leads, but it also put me into an employment bracket that I didn't really wish to be considered for; once there, it is difficult to claw your way out. I am fairly convinced that John Thaw created his reputation as a leading man by turning down work that was not 'big enough' for him; not that he wasn't good: he was, but he was somewhat overrated, in my opinion, and clever.

While television that year was negligible, so was theatre! *Not Later Than Six* was the English translation of a French play that had originally been a success in Paris; we were to try our luck with a fringe production in Guildford – not the main theatre unfortunately, but in the little studio theatre. Directed by Chris Masters for the Millstream Theatre Company, this was to be one of my favourite roles, when I recreated the character I had played with Graham Haberfield in the Stables Theatre, Manchester. When I say recreated, I used the same voice which was a mixture of Alastair Sim and Wilfrid Lawson. The play was about a recluse whose life is shattered one night when a car crashes though the wall of his cottage. The driver, an inept young crook who has just robbed the casino, ties him up and, somewhat reminiscent of *Sleuth*, they play mind games, the old man eventually coming out on top.

Although the play itself was little more than an hour long, I contrived to extend the evening by being on stage as the audience arrived and took their seats, going through the lengthy and eccentric process of putting the cat out and getting washed and ready for bed, which lulled the audience into a state of tranquillity before the car came crashing through the wall. It was one of the best openings to a play that I had ever been in, and I absolutely loved the freedom of being on stage for all that time with no words but just improvising the nightly ritual. The play too I found very funny, but it depended a great deal on interplay and I'm afraid I had little faith in my partner; he seemed to me more of a male model than an actor, and definitely brought nothing to the party in the way of comic invention. I have since tried to get the play put on elsewhere with another fellow actor, but so far with little success. Who knows; one day...

The dreadful lack of employment that year, plus the fact that Sandra had set herself up in Surrey, prompted me to put Beckwith Road up for sale and look for something else. I turned my attention to Brixton; not exactly a desirable area at that time, mainly due to the riots, but one which I felt would surely be a good investment as it could only go up. The fact that the Northern Line of the Tube started there was a definite bonus, as the traffic situation was making driving in London more and more impossible. I bought a dreadfully run-down terraced house in Nursery Road, behind Marks and Spencer's and a two-minute walk from the Tube.

The house had to be gutted and I set about doing most of the clearing up myself, only employing Kit Miller's younger brother Jonty to come in and do the specialist conversion later. Jonty was also an actor and had been very successful in commercials having a nice humorous quality, and charm, as all of the Miller boys had. I must say that for an out-of-work actor he was charging top specialist rates – almost commercial money! But he did seem to know what he was doing and I didn't resent it until I found that the roofers, whom I had employed under a separate agreement and a fixed price, were paying him to do something that was within their remit and in my time, so he was getting paid twice!

As the work on Nursery Road was coming to completion, I did a three-month stint in Ray Cooney's *Run For Your Wife* at the home of farce, the Whitehall Theatre. I'm not a great lover of farce, but I must say I had to admire the technical expertise and know-how of the writer, cast, and director. It was directed by my old boss from the Liverpool Playhouse, Leslie Lawton, who I think had been instrumental in getting me the part, and Ray Cooney himself came into rehearsals towards the end. Paul Shane and myself were being rehearsed into our parts; he was playing the lead, and I was playing Sergeant Troughton. The production by this point had been running in the West End for some six years and the rehearsals were frighteningly exacting; all of the comic business, reactions and dialogue stresses had been handed down and any alteration was frowned upon. While I enjoyed the challenge, I missed the freedom of being able to discover a perform-ance for myself and I can't say that I did it very well, or that I ever felt really comfortable in the role.

It was with some relief therefore that, immediately after my West End run, I accepted the leading role in Graham Greene's *The Complaisant Lover* at the

Redgrave Theatre, Farnham. Graham Watkins, whose father had been a boyhood friend of my father, and whom I had a vague recollection of as a child growing up in Peckham, directed the play. Although I don't think he was a great director, we got on very well together, perhaps because of our family history, and I had a wonderful time in the part because I felt that he had confidence in me and that gave me the self-assurance to be quite bold.

Sir Ralph Richardson had originally played the part I played; I had seen him in the role when I was a student. One of the joys of the character was that he was a rather lovable joker, which gave me almost *carte blanche* on stage. It took quite a bit of persuading but I managed to get Graham to let me have a pair of Noddy slippers made, consisting of carpet slippers with little cloth replicas of Noddy on the top, with a little bell in his little red bonnet that tinkled as I walked. He admitted later that the scene where I read the farewell letter from my wife and walked off with the slippers tinkling became for him a *coup de théâtre*.

I did a brief visit to *The Bill* and a training film for Shell. Three episodes of *The Chief*, starring Tim Pigott-Smith, saved me at the end of the year, although once again the part was not one that I remember with any sense of achievement as I only had a few scenes spread over the three months so the part seemed to disappear into nothing with dilution, and so did the money. It proved quite useful though as I was able to spend much of my time on the renovation of Nursery Road, which was to be my new home.

1990 started a little more promisingly with a production of Arthur Miller's *The Crucible* at the relatively new theatre in Leicester: the Haymarket. I did take a trip down memory lane one free day when I went back to the Phoenix, by the bus shelter. When I had played there in 1964, it was a new theatre, but was only meant to be temporary; it was still there, and so was the Bowling Green, the pub where Tony Hopkins, Alex Henry and myself had spent so much of our post-performance winding down.

In the more magnificent Haymarket, I was playing Danforth who doesn't appear in the first act but when he does appear more or less dominates the action. Because I was not involved in the rehearsals for the first half of the play I was able to fit in an episode of *All Creatures Great and Small* for BBC TV, in which I played a carpenter whose dog swallows a bit of wood or something. It was quite a sweet little part, but all I can remember is that the collie that I was supposed to be so in love with stank to high heaven. We filmed in the Yorkshire Dales; the dog they gave me was kept on a farm, where it was never bathed or brushed, and I had to cuddle it and show it a lot of affection.

I was relieved to get back to Leicester where Peter Lichtenfels, the director, did a magnificent job on me. He got me to play the part so laid back that I didn't appear or feel as if I was doing a thing. As it happens I found this difficult, but in the end it was very rewarding. When Struan Rodger came into the dressing room and said he had just been sick at the review that was pinned to the company notice board, I knew I had got a good mention. In fact it turned out to be a rave; and although Struan got some good reviews later in the week, he really resented the fact that I had been selected for praise. I found he was almost obsessive in his competitive attitude towards acting, which took on an aggravating aspect on stage. He was constantly engineering himself into the most prominent or advantageous positions, and I found that, instead of concentrating on the scene and what was going on in the action, I was constantly looking to see what Struan was up to and where he was! I was joined in my objection to this destructive approach by David Gwillim, the son of Jack Gwillim who had been a leading actor at the Old Vic in the days of my youth. He has a strong belief in the truth and a dedicated attitude that was a pleasure to work with.

Kevin Whateley was playing the lead role, and after the show one night he had to make a curtain speech to appeal for donations to help keep the theatre going. In his speech, he happened to mention that the cause of the theatre's position was the meanness of the Thatcher government which had cut the theatre's grant. At this point Edwina Currie who was in the audience shouted out 'Rubbish!' and left the theatre.

After Leicester, everything went quiet once more; and I started to think again about stimulating my dwindling financial prospects with a venture into property development. This was coupled with a concern for my parents: my mother was finding the hill where they were, in the old town of Eastbourne, somewhat hard on her faulty breathing, and my father was becoming a little erratic behind the wheel of his car! I managed to find a large five-storey house in the centre of Eastbourne, with fine views over Devonshire Park and the tennis club, and within level walking distance of the shops, theatres and station. After lengthy discussion with my parents it was agreed that I should buy the property with a large commercial mortgage and convert it into five flats, after which they would sell their property and have first choice of the five flats at a knockdown price. This would not only give them a new home that was much more manageable and convenient but would also free up money to help them in their later years.

The project was a large one, more ambitious and risky than anything I had tackled hitherto. I bought a van, again from the auctions at Heathfield, and set about the clearance and planning. I was to employ my father and also, whenever he was available, my brother. It was a depressing time. Although I thought I had bought at the bottom of the market, it continued to go down; meanwhile the unemployment figures were rising, not only as far as I was concerned but throughout the country. I was beginning to feel that I had bitten off more than I could chew, and employed a labourer at rock-bottom rates; I felt bad about it, but I had to try and get myself out of this dreadful situation where the money was running out.

A glimmer of light appeared at the end of the tunnel, however, when my worried bank manager (in the days when Nat West had bank managers who gave a damn) came to Eastbourne to view the situation, and purely by chance we happened to meet Brian Murphy in the street outside the house. He was appearing at the Devonshire Park Theatre and said he was thinking of buying a flat in Eastbourne! He expressed the desire to have a look at my conversions, promptly fell in love with the flat that I had taken up semi-residence in and committed himself to buying it on the spot, thus wiping out my overdraft and saving my life!

The year was coming to a better end when I was also offered the part of Pastor Manders in Ibsen's *Ghosts* at the Leeds Playhouse. Rosemary Leach played Mrs Alving, and a young girl called Tal Rubens directed it. I'm not sure why, but I have the feeling that I wasn't very good in the role. Unfortunately I had strong memories of Michael Hordern playing it at the Old Vic when I had ruined the first night with my late 'tabs', and I think I set off on the wrong foot by trying to play him as an older man. They all quite sweetly set about trying to get me to stop acting older and just be myself; I'm not sure if I succeeded or not because nobody said anything and the reviews were lukewarm. Rosemary was of course excellent and it is surprising that it wasn't a more joyful production. It may have been the gloom of Ibsen, the fact that Rosemary was suffering with arthritis or simply that I wasn't as good as I wanted to be!

It was while I was at Leeds that David Clapham asked me to direct and act in a training film about self-defence that was to see the end of our friendship when he later reneged on payment.

16

1991 to 1994 • *Trainer* • Farnham • Ipswich • New Victoria, Staffordshire • Sir Stanley Matthews • Doris Speed

THINGS HAD GOT marginally better with the clearance of the overdraft when Brian Murphy bought the flat. But I still had to find £2,000 per month to cover the heavy mortgage, so I was much relieved when I was put under contract by the BBC to play Jack Ross, an injured jump-jockey working to get back on a horse again in a new and exciting TV drama series about horse racing, called *Trainer*. I was at first a bit miffed at being considered small enough to be a jump jockey, but was consoled with the assertion that jump jockeys are not that small.

I was also put under strict orders to lose weight and sent off to go on a diet. This proved easy enough before the series started as I was living at home, but once we got out filming, I found it difficult to resist the location caterers who were phenomenal! Gerard Glaister, who had been the producer when I did *Moonstrike* for the BBC in 1963, was one of the old school and liked his creature comforts, and consequently he had really gone to town and booked the best caterers he could find. We had real *cordon bleu* cuisine with duck, lobster, and many mouth-watering dishes; plus a daily selection of curries and salads. I have always had a love of eating and a healthy appetite and I hated the thought of missing out on any of it. I had made heavy weather of the fact that I was on a diet, and everybody seemed to take an interest in my weight loss; so I had to exercise extreme caution when it came to the lunch breaks, making sure that I was constantly changing seats so nobody could check on how much I was eating. I usually managed to break early and grab a seafood salad as a starter and then join the crowd for the main meal, followed by a little sample from the curry selection (usually eaten behind the wagon) before returning to the main area for a small dessert. Needless to say, I did not lose any weight, but then I hadn't lost any weight when I had been on a strict diet at home, before the series started!

The series was directed in turns by Jeremy Summers and Frank Smith, and featured quite a starry cast with Susannah York, David McCallum and Nigel Davenport in supporting roles and a relative newcomer, Mark Greenstreet, playing the leading part of the trainer. I was also to come across Dudley Sutton again after having only occasionally met up since RADA days. The contract was for the best part of a year and although I wasn't used a great deal, I was on regular money and quite good money at that. The only problem was that I never saw any of it; it was all swallowed up by the greedy mortgage.

Consequently, I was unable to do more than just keep my head above water for most of the time while I tried to sell the rest of the flats. The bottom had fallen out of the property market and since it was such a bad time for selling, I decided to rent. This was to prove a decision that I would live to rue and later count a blessing; but for the moment I had no choice.

In the spring of 1991, I went into hospital for an operation on my cruciate ligaments. I had had an accident on the soccer pitch, playing for the Alleyn's Old Boys, when the goalkeeper fell onto my leg and bent my knee the wrong way; now the knee kept 'coming out', and the ligaments were so weakened that they had to be replaced. This, at the age of 54, brought a painful and abrupt halt to my soccer career. I had hoped to play into my sixties and emulate the achievement of Billy Wilson, who played for the Old Boys up until he was 60 and would turn out on a Saturday afternoon with his fags and matches in the pocket of his long shorts, and light up at half time! I consoled myself with the thought that it was the same operation that attracted so much attention when 'Gazza' hit the head-lines, although in my case the surgeon said I was not to play any contact sport again; if I did and it went wrong, he would refuse to operate. I had taken up squash and I had to give that up too. I was quite lost without my sport, although later when my knee settled down I was able to play a gentle game of tennis.

Luckily, although the operation was a big one and I would be on crutches for several weeks afterwards, I was able to fit it in during a period when I was not required for filming on *Trainer*. I didn't tell any of the production team, I just took the chance and went ahead. I only just got away with it because in the story-line, as the injured jump jockey, I was supposed to try my hand at some jumps again, against medical advice, and come a cropper. They had got a stunt rider to do the difficult jump when I was supposed to fall from my horse and put a final end to my career. Apart from the fact that I would have liked to do my own stunt, the stuntman insisted on riding with a long stirrup, whereas as a jump jockey I should have been much higher and out of the saddle. I managed to get them to let me have a go as well and although I say it myself, I made a much better job of falling from the horse than the stuntman and my new knee held out.

Since I was still strapped for cash, I was unable to upgrade my transport from the Talbot Express van that I had been using for my building work. To avoid embarrassment, while filming in the Newbury area when we were booked in to the motel beside the motorway, I would park my unimpressive and conspicuous old gas-board van at the motorway service station and negotiate my way across the dual carriageway to enter the motel from the car park looking as if I had just arrived and parked my limousine. When I later, to save money, took up lodgings with Peter Cudlip, the racehorse trainer who was adviser to the series and owned the stables that we were using for filming, I tried to camouflage my unimpressive chariot by parking it among his stable vehicles outside his house, but was caught out one morning when I was found sleeping in the van; I had arrived so late the previous night that they had all gone to bed and I was reluctant to beat on the door and wake them up.

It may have been compassion and a desire to cheer me up when, towards the end of the first series, Peter told me that he had been at a conference the night before to discuss the guidelines for the next year's series. They were aware that *Trainer* had not been the success they were hoping for, but they were to make some changes and push ahead. He then told me that they were disappointed with Mark Greenstreet; he was not a good enough actor to carry a series, and they were going to set me up as a rival trainer. The Susannah York character was to finance me and we were to have some sort of relationship! I was sworn to secrecy but obviously elated and said nothing to anybody, even at the end-of-series party at Newbury Racecourse.

It came as a complete surprise therefore and a dreadful blow to be told later that year, while I was waiting to be officially informed of my promotion, that both Nigel Davenport and myself were to be axed from the new series! The reason I was given was that they had been unhappy with the girl who was playing my daughter and was providing the other half of the love interest, and as my part was so closely allied to hers, I had to go. I was aware that she and Mark hadn't hit it off, but I had been led to believe that I was to be saved from the chop.

I was not only devastated because of the loss of income and the humiliation of feeling that the blame for the failure of the first series was being laid at my door; I was also devastated because I loved the job. I have always had a love of horses, and revelled in the privilege of being able to saddle up a horse on my time off and just set off on my own. I had also enjoyed the special relationship I had developed with Joe Mercer, the jockey, whose house was being used as my home for filming, and I would often spend the off-set hours chatting with him in his country-cottage kitchen. I also had a bicycle on which I would set off to Newbury when I was not wanted for an hour or so.

When I received the news I tried to phone Nigel Davenport, whom I heard was equally devastated, and left a message on his answerphone; I think he must have been too cut up to talk because he never phoned back. The only bright spot was when Lynda Lee-Potter, in her column in the *Daily Mail*, said that the BBC had made the fatal error of axing the two best actors in the series!

The second series proved to be even less of a success than the first and it ended there, which was tragic as it had great possibilities. The horses and the country-side were beautiful and there was plenty of drama to be found on the racecourses and in the stables, but unfortunately the fault lay with Gerard Glaister's rather old-fashioned idea of a leading man. Instead of going for somebody like Mike Elphick to play the trainer, with passion and an inner life, he opted for Mark, who was really a very nice lad and extremely good-looking but more of a male model than an actor; and gone were the days when the viewing audience thought that was enough. He was still thinking along the lines of Roger Moore and *The Saint*!

Rejection is part of the job and learning to handle it is all part of an actor's necessary development. The moment you step on stage in a performance, you are opening yourself up to being rejected and asking the audience to judge your work in terms of 'am I believable enough to have been worth the price of your ticket?' It starts at the very beginning, of course, with entry into a drama school or the process of casting, when you present yourself to a director or a panel of strangers who ask you to perform or read from a script and then, when you have left the room, sit and discuss your quality, or lack of it; again, you are submitting yourself to being rejected. Sometimes that can be a rewarding process, even if you don't get the job; you get the chance to meet and perhaps impress a director who might in the future remember you for something else. Sometimes a director may get you to redo a piece and try it a different way and you might find out something new about yourself. In the early days I remember Michael Benthall at the Old Vic getting me to redo my Hotspur speech: 'My liege, I did deny no prisoners...' as if I was talking to the king sitting next to me at the dinner table and not as if in front of the whole court, and I was struck by the different meanings that were possible on that level. Television directors too might ask you to reread a part with a different emphasis and I have found that this can also be rewarding, even if you don't get the part.

Far and away the worst, in my experience, are the castings for commercials. When you first arrive, they take a Polaroid photo of you against a blank wall, and get you to fill in a questionnaire about yourself, mainly about your agent and most recent work. As you hand it back you often get a glimpse of the Polaroid and feel like going home straight away and doing something about your hair and the dead look in your eyes. There's no point in asking them to take another one as, no matter what you try and think about, the smile still comes over as an uncomfortable leer. You join the waiting horde of lookalikes, some of whom you know from dreadful performances in the past and some who, despite forty years in the profession, you have never seen either in the flesh or on the screen, and you wonder where the hell they've been to get this selection of 'suspects' from. Even worse, you know that the casting is taking place over several days so they are just the tip of the iceberg.

When it's your turn you are led into the room with your questionnaire and worse-than-passport photo and interviewed by a child who has just left school, who invariably asks you what you have done and doesn't make any pretence at listening to the answer, let alone know what the hell you are talking about when you reel off the list of productions. He or she is sometimes accompanied by the clients who, enjoying their day out from the office and playing at being in the theatre, are anxious to impress their importance on you and ask the most asinine of questions, which are designed to make you think they have some knowledge of the entertainment business. You are then frequently told that the script has not been written yet, so would you please improvise around something like: you have just stepped outside into the rain and are sheltering in a shop doorway when a beautiful girl walks past and offers you shelter under her umbrella but you are particularly unimpressed until she offers you also a bite from her Mars bar when your face lights up and you step out into the rain, happy again!

I think one of the worst cases of this sort of torturous exercise in humiliation was when, after arriving at the casting and going through the reception process, I had to sit in the waiting room with the words of a popular song written on a blackboard and the tune being relayed to the waiting queue of actors who had all been told to be prepared to sing the jaunty little number when their turn came. At first I was mystified by the actions of several employees of the casting company who were exiting at regular intervals to a little side room and returning in fits of laughter and trying to make token attempts to control their mirth; they were obviously ensconced in some sort of viewing chamber beside the main interview room. When it came to my turn for the ritual degradation I discovered that when you were in front of the casting panel, there was no blackboard with the words, and if you didn't know them you were encouraged to just go ahead and have a go. The results were disastrous and I was so enraged that I phoned my then agent, Scott Marshall, and asked his wife Denise (who at that time ran the commercial side) to register a complaint on my behalf. I was given a little lecture and told to behave myself; if I didn't want the work I wouldn't be sent for the castings.

Commercials can be good money; indeed they can be fantastic money if they are what are known as 'buy outs', when they pay for the right to run the ad as many times as they like without paying a fee each time. They are easy to do, but hard to get; in my case, impossible. I have done two commercials, both for Brian de Salvo, one in Spain and the other in Ireland, but in this country – nothing! I must have done at least a couple of hundred castings and got nowhere. Lesley Grayburn, with whom I'd worked at the Liverpool Playhouse and who later became a casting director dealing with many commercials, once told me that it was because my eyes were hooded! Sandra too, who had made a career from commercials, said that my eyes were the main problem; so I took myself to the doctor, explained that the excess of flesh above my eyes was hampering my career and could I have an operation on the National Health?

I was rather expecting him to send me off with a flea in my ear and tell me there was nothing wrong with my eyes. In the event, he sent me to see a specialist who booked me in for cosmetic surgery. I was in overnight and came out of the Queen Elizabeth Hospital at Roehampton, where they have the brilliant burns unit, with a couple of black eyes which lasted for a few weeks and made no difference to my work whatsoever; I still haven't done any commercials. I think the worst part of not getting a commercial is not the great desire to be in one; it is being rejected, time after time, for something I had no great admiration for.

The rejection from *Trainer* was even worse because it was so public. To make matters worse, there then followed another year of depressingly minor parts in *Boon*, *The Bill* and a couple of training films. These of course were not big money as they were not big parts; in fact, they were no more than a day's filming here and there.

I was also invited over to Belfast for the *Kelly* show which was a late-night chat show, live from the Ulster TV studios with a live audience. The theme of the evening was the fact that *Coronation Street* had reached its thirtieth year and I was appearing with Shirin Taylor, who had played the wife of Mike Baldwin, and the show's former producer, Bill Podmore. We were flown over to Belfast and put up in a rather grand hotel in idyllic surroundings just outside the city; we had been invited to come early and make a day of it, availing ourselves of the gymnasium and swimming pool at the hotel.

The show didn't start until about eleven o'clock and so we were treated to dinner at the hotel, where I remember Bill Podmore ordering a very handsomely expensive bottle of wine, before being picked up and transported to the studios. Once there we were entertained in the hospitality suite while we waited for our entrance. Nobody seemed too worried about the amount of booze that was being consumed and, fearful of making a fool of myself, I didn't drink as much as I was invited to. The actor's instinct is, if it's free, to take it while the going is good and while it's still on offer. However, I needn't have worried because the hospitality room remained open after the show and then, when we were taken back to the hotel, there was another spread there and a well-stocked bar to boot.

Bill had a reputation for being somewhat of a boozer and he certainly didn't disappoint. The drink loosened his tongue and I learnt quite a bit about his feelings for Julie Goodyear, and many others. I discovered that he was not at all blind to the weaknesses of some of the cast, both in performance and in their private lives. When I came down to breakfast the next morning I was told that

Bill had just left, having stayed up at the bar all night! They certainly know how to entertain in Ireland!

Back in Eastbourne, the flat rental situation was proving more problematic than I had ever considered. I had enlisted a lettings agency to find me tenants, and at first it went quite well. Unfortunately the Iranian who ran the agency did a moonlight flit with his clients' deposits; luckily, I had just changed to another agency run by another Iranian, which happened to be a case of out of the frying pan into the fire. I was twice called to the ground-floor flat because they were having trouble with the central heating system. There was nothing wrong; they were just unaccustomed to the way it worked. The first time, I made a special trip to explain how to operate the system; the guy who had rented the flat was in bed so I spoke to his girlfriend, demonstrated to her how to set up the system and returned home.

Two days later I had to make the one-and-a-half-hour drive again to go through the whole routine once more, because the tenant had parted company with his girlfriend! When I arrived this time, his mate came to the door, said he was busy and could I come back in twenty minutes. I was a bit put out, but returned half an hour later to find that he was still 'in conference'. This time I got quite shirty, and said I would show his mate and he could pass the instruction on. I was not best pleased and let them know in no uncertain terms.

A few days after that I was telephoned by the police who informed me that they had had to break into the flat above, which happened to be the one I had sold to Brian Murphy, because they were trying to arrest the occupants in the ground-floor flat and had thought they heard sounds from the flat above. The tenants were eventually charged with armed robbery! How close had I been to getting my kneecaps shot off!

Since I was still feeding the hungry mortgage, I had to take housing-benefit tenants just to make sure that the flats were never empty, but this proved to be a false economy. My Iranian agent next put two Scousers in the third-floor flat. Now, because of my associations with the Liverpool Playhouse, I was very fond of the people of Liverpool; but these two were the scum of the earth. They paid no rent, they would sit in the windows, drunk, and were aggressive and offensive to me and to local residents. There were constant nocturnal comings and goings; they chased the two girls out of the flat above and took not only the furniture but also the cooker and sold them. They played soccer in the lounge and broke most of the windows, and when I came to try and evict them I found that the Iranian agent had, first of all, no deposit from them, and second that he had not made them sign a contract. I then found that the law was strongly weighted in their favour; it took me six months to get them evicted, and it cost me £4,500 in legal fees to go to court to try and get some sort of recompense from the agent. In the end I had to take over the case myself as the solicitors were not only expensive, but also inept. I eventually won the case, but got no money as the Iranian disappeared and I have had to content myself with a charge on his house where his deserted wife now lives. I have also, consequentially, fairly strong views about the legal profession, Iranian letting agents, and Scousers outside of Liverpool!

The only bright spot in this period was three episodes of *Grange Hill*, which were not in themselves of any great note, as they seemed extremely badly written, but constituted a pleasurable experience for me because I was cast and directed by Nigel Douglas. There was just something about him that made me feel that he would be successful. I liked his approach, and the way that he handled his actors and crew filled me with a sense of confidence. I have worked with him a couple of times since then; not in any great venture, but I have often referred to him in later years with regard to my attempts at writing and found him very willing to help.

It was financially a bad year again, and the rents I was getting from Eastbourne were not enough to subsidise my acting career, so I had to take drastic measures. I took a job as a labourer, working on a neighbour's house for the daily rate of £40. I still had my gas-board van and it came in quite handy. When socialising in the rather upmarket commuter regions of Surrey, where Sandra had her house, I found the conversation would frequently turn to 'What car do you drive?' I have never really been taken with this macho-male infatuation with the car; for me, it has always been just a mode of transport and not an outward sign of inner masculinity. So I took a certain delight in watching them try and cover their confusion when I replied, 'I drive a Talbot Express, actually.' It was usually obvious that they hadn't a clue what sort of vehicle that was, but were reluctant to show their ignorance. I did, however, find that I was very popular when someone wanted a wardrobe picked up or a removal done.

At the beginning of 1993 came the invitation to play Lopachin in Graham Watkins' production of Chekhov's *The Cherry Orchard* at the Redgrave Theatre in Farnham, with Rula Lenska playing the lead role. I have always had a great love of Chekhov and found him absolutely fascinating to play, especially when approached with a sense of fun. There were certain clashes of temperament with a variety of opposing views about how Chekhov should be approached, but Rula was a strong personality and was ideal casting with her Slavic heritage. At that time she was still married to Dennis Waterman, whom I knew fairly well from charity football, so it was pleasant to sometimes meet up in the bar after the show when he arrived with his driver to pick up Rula. Dennis was on tour himself at that time, so I don't believe he ever got to see the production, but I think Rula was having trouble keeping Dennis's drinking under control and so the driver was under strict instructions to keep him in check, and to report in to Rula after the show with Dennis in tow whenever their tour brought them within driving distance of Farnham. Sadly, the battle was not a victorious one, and shortly after the tour I heard that they had split up again. This was to be my last appearance at the Redgrave, as Graham Watkins moved away and the incoming director was unable to keep the theatre open due to financial problems. They weren't the only ones! I was still under considerable stress with troubles on the rental front and the mortgage.

It was quite a relief to get offered a nice reasonable character part in *Heartbeat* by Yorkshire Television almost immediately after the end of *Cherry Orchard*, and I had a few days' filming in the wonderful picturesque village of Goathland on the Yorkshire moors. It was in the days of Nick Berry, who it has always seemed to me was an extremely likeable lad, but how he managed to be the highest paid actor on British television, as he was rumoured to be at that time, I find a mystery. I also didn't really understand why *Heartbeat* was so popular. Nevertheless it was a very pleasant job; I met up with Derek Fowlds, another RADA contemporary, and with William Simons who had been with me and Paddy in the days of the Phoenix Theatre, Leicester. I played the part of a rustic eccentric who was swindled out of an antique motorbike by the devious Greengrass, played by Bill Maynard.

While I was staying in Goathland I took a walk one afternoon when I was not needed to see the waterfall or spring behind the hotel. I had to go down a steep path through the wood, and halfway down I was forced to stop and hold on to the fence because of the pain in my knees. It wasn't the operation; it was in both knees and it was excruciating. I continued the descent like an old man, clinging to the fence and creeping gingerly with the pain. It was very frightening and, as soon as I returned home, I went to see my doctor, who diagnosed arthritis.

I was also at that time experiencing trouble with my voice. It felt as if I was always talking through a muslin screen; it had a permanent husky quality and I felt impelled to cough at frequent intervals to clear my vocal cords. I went to King's College Hospital for tests, including a barium scan and various other ear, nose and throat tests, but they could find nothing wrong. At the same time I was losing weight at an alarming rate despite having a tremendous appetite. I once went with Sandra and her parents to the local Harvester restaurant, whose boast was that you would be unable to finish their gargantuan mixed grill. I not only succeeded in finishing mine, I also ate a good third of Sandra's as well as a quarter of the chicken that her stepfather had left plus her mother's chips!

I happened to be visiting a local ex-gamekeeper, whose wife had some years previously suffered from an overactive thyroid; if the doctor hadn't called at the house to attend to her son, and noticed how thin she was, she could have died. On being told this story, something rang bells in my head and I immediately contacted my doctor and asked to have my thyroid count tested. Sure enough, I was diagnosed as being chronically overactive!

It had taken eighteen months to diagnose and I was not looking at all at my best. The initial treatment was to take pills and get the whole thing under control, but this couldn't be done for too long because of the side effects. I was then tried out with a system called 'block and replace', whereby pills are taken to knock out the thyroid gland altogether and the necessary thyroid count is supplied with other pills. At the end of a course of this treatment I had to cease and see if the thyroid had been kick-started back into performing properly. I have been, touch wood, one of the lucky ones in that it seems to have settled. Strangely enough, the arthritis that had been diagnosed was not arthritis, but another symptom of the overactive thyroid. Normally the main symptom is bulging eyes but I escaped that one. In the past those displaying the symptoms were probably dismissed as village idiots! I did learn that it is indeed life-threatening; the causes are often apparently hereditary, but in my case I have always felt that it was because of the stress during that disastrous period of the Eastbourne flats, when I think I really was near to behaving like the village idiot!

Just after we had found out what was wrong, I was invited back to the Wolsey Theatre, Ipswich to play Hirst, the Ralph Richardson part in Pinter's *No Man's Land*. The John Gielgud part was admirably played by Donald Pelmear, who many years ago was at the Phoenix, Leicester in *Othello* with me. The play was directed by Dick Tuckey and was to be among his last at the Wolsey as he was on the point of retiring.

I can't say that I had a great understanding of the play; in fact I saw it again a few years ago at the National Theatre and still didn't really know what it was all about. The nearest to an explanation that in any way seems satisfactory is that the two main characters are two sides of Pinter's personality: one the serious and respected writer of integrity, and the other the commercial success with less integrity but a greater position. Whilst I loved Pinter's *The Caretaker* and *The Birthday Party* and much of his early work, I find that a lot of his later stuff is just too obscure for me; although I can appreciate the rhythms of the dialogue and the interesting characters, I find him too much hard work to follow and I feel a lot of the reaction to him is a case of 'the Emperor's new clothes'.

It was while I was rehearsing for *No Man's Land* that Sandra had her fiftieth birthday, and it looked as if she would have to spend the occasion alone. I organised a surprise party in a neighbour's house, employing caterers to do the food and getting my friends, whose house we were using, to invite her to dinner to make up a foursome. I managed to obtain special permission to get away early from rehearsals, and drove down to the neighbours' where I met up with a host of Sandra's old friends just before she was due to arrive. They all hid in the lounge and I hid upstairs; I had earlier phoned her to say that we had been rehearsing late and that I had to go to the hospital in Ipswich as my back was playing up. Once the first surprise was over and she had squealed her greetings to all of the friends I had dug up from the past, a tune was played, one very redolent of our first weeks together: 'We Do It' by R&J Stone. At this point she screamed, 'He's here, I know it!' and I came down the stairs. Unfortunately, I had to return to Ipswich the next day as I had only managed to persuade them to let me have the morning off.

Television had more or less dried up for me again. A lot was to do with my age, of course; most plays have a preponderance of young men, and there is usually only the odd father figure, and a wealth of actors my age to play the parts. I managed to fit in a brief visit to *The Bill* again and a corporate video for Nigel Douglas before I was invited to the New Victoria Theatre in Newcastle-under-Lyme, Staffordshire, to play the part of Sir Stanley Matthews in a new stage play about his life. The play was written by Rony Robinson and directed by Rob Swain. Once again, it wasn't a job that was going to sort out my financial situation, but it was to prove a great boost to my flagging spirits.

I got the job after an interview in which my footballing activities came very much to the fore and I was even asked to kick a ball or two. Having been offered the part and accepted, I arranged to stay with my old mate Danny Farley in the village of Combs where I had once lived. They had a chalet in their garden overlooking the lake and I was able to feel almost as if I was in a self-contained flat. Danny and Pat had become very close friends of both myself and Sandra and we were very fond not only of them but also of Pat's mother Joan, who lived with them, and their two children William and Emma. I had managed to persuade Emma to join the MYT, through which she found a new purpose for her life and developed as a designer.

In the first days of rehearsal we were introduced to Sir Stanley Matthews, an adored figure in the Staffordshire Potteries who is universally recognised and loved. He apparently had strong reservations about letting them do his life story, so they were pretty apprehensive about him meeting and getting on with us. I was to play him in his later years and Karl Woolley was to play him as a young man. I was quite nervous and overawed at the chance of meeting him; more so than the others, possibly because he was more of my era and had been a schoolboy hero of mine. In the event I think he was as nervous as I was, because he turned out to be quite a shy and unassuming man. In some strange way he made ordinariness a star quality.

The first meeting was just a chat and then a photo-call with the local papers, but we got on so well that he offered to take me the next morning and show me the area where he had been brought up. He took me to the school he had attended as an infant and then to the little terraced cottage (which looked just like the early *Coronation Street*) where he had learnt to play, kicking a tennis ball in the minute back yard. He knocked on the door of the cottage and the completely unfazed pensioner who was living there invited us in and let Stan show me around. Our relationship, and the play, nearly ended that morning as he drove his little car very badly and we nearly had an accident on a roundabout. Stan was oblivious to the fact that he had nearly caused a nasty collision, and just carried on chatting as hooters blared and I flinched and ducked the almost certain moment of impact.

Our friendship developed as he came once or twice to rehearsals, and we recorded some of the chats that he had with us about his life and times. He also invited me to join him on some evenings when he had to go to various functions. On one occasion we went to a boxing tournament where Prince Naseem, who was then just starting his career, was fighting an exhibition bout. I have never seen such a fantastic display of boxing skills. At one point he stood with his feet as if glued to the floor and just weaved his upper body, like a reed in the wind, and was impossible for his opponent to hit. In interviews since, I have seen him come across as extremely arrogant, but that night he joined us on the top table after the fight and was an extremely pleasant and modest young man in front of Sir Stan, who was idolised everywhere he went but seemed completely unaware of the fact.

In fact, in company, he tried to deflect the attention he received onto others. In my case he was much amused by the fact that I was trying to master the way he walked, slightly bow-legged and with his toes turned in, and he would get me to demonstrate my imitation of his walk to the assembled company, and giggle with delight. He was equally moved to laughter when later I had trouble with my knees again because of the awkward gait.

Stan became a constant visitor to rehearsals, not to watch us work but to chat to us and enjoy the company which was a young, vibrant and friendly mixture; he didn't see the show until the first night when he came with Lady Mila, his wife. It was a packed night and we received a standing ovation. I wanted to pull Sir Stan from the audience and bring him down onto the stage, but I had been specifically told not to. He had told the theatre that he wanted 'no fuss', which was one of his favourite expressions; but when I asked him afterwards if he would have come on stage if I'd gone for him, he said he would. He was so pleased with the production and the audience's reaction that I got the impression he regretted being so adamant about not wanting to be involved.

Just like a game of football, it was a show of two halves. The first half dealt with his growing up and his early career and as the elder Stan, I acted as a sort of chorus, wandering and commenting on the action. Karl, playing young Stan, was luckily very adept at the necessary ball control and showed many skills beyond those expected of an actor. The second half dealt with the rest of his amazingly long career and his romantic meeting and eventual marriage to Mila, including the invasion of Hungary when he was trapped and was helped to escape by Mila's first husband; it was a fascinating story. Stan came to see the play a couple of times during the run, creeping in at odd times during the three weeks. He was also at the last night with Mila, and this time I didn't take any notice of the directive not to get Stan on stage. The audience was clapping, stamping and cheering as I brought him down on stage, and Liz Brailsford who played Mila brought Mila onto the stage; it was a very emotional moment and one that I will cherish for the rest of my life.

The wonderful experience of that production was shattered when my mother died in the last week of the run. As the curtain came down on the Friday-night performance I was taken aside by Peter Cheeseman, the artistic director of the theatre, and told that they had received a message from my sister during the show and I was to telephone immediately the curtain was down. Guessing what was wrong, I phoned my father to discover that my mother had been taken into Eastbourne Hospital, having had a stroke during the night. I made arrangements to drive down after the show on the Saturday night; but in the meantime, the next evening after the show, I received the news that she had died. There was nothing I could do, but I spoke to my father and set off at curtain down to drive south.

I had no idea how long it would take, so I asked him to leave a key under the doormat. I arrived at about 4.30 a.m. after a nightmare drive, only to discover that he had left the wrong key and I couldn't get in. I didn't want to wake my father so I went into the back yard and tried to wake my brother whom I knew would be sleeping in the back bedroom. Unfortunately, my brother is more than a little deaf and I could get no joy with whispered shouts or the odd thrown stone, but I did manage to unearth a ladder and climbed to his bedroom window. I was concentrating on trying to open the window when the parting of the curtains and the appearance of my brother startled me and I nearly fell off the ladder. He let me in and we started a bottle of whiskey, soon to be joined by my father when he heard us downstairs.

The funeral was arranged for the following week. I went down the night before and spent the day with my father; my youngest sister Michelle joined us that afternoon. After the service and a brief moment back at the house, I set off back to

Newcastle-under-Lyme; I was glad to get away from the depressing atmosphere and return to the sanity of my imaginary life as Sir Stan.

1994 was fast becoming a year of death. Sandra's mother had died on March 19th after battling for eighteen months against lung cancer. It was not an easy death and I was amazed at her courage and dignity in the face of the dreadful deterioration. Her end, when it came, was a blessed release, not only for her but also for her husband and Sandra who were suffering greatly in watching her battling with her pain. We were all very much involved and at her side when she ended her days in the hospice. Then came the sudden death of my mother on June 3rd (my brother's birthday), followed by the death of Doris Speed at the age of 95 on November 17th.

I had made a habit of visiting Doris in the home in Bury as often as I could and made a point of trying to take her out for a lunch at least once a month. To celebrate the thirty years of *Coronation Street*, Granada transmitted a special show when Judy Finnigan was to interview Doris and myself together; I suspect Doris hadn't wanted to do it alone. It wasn't a pleasant experience. She was nervous and tetchy, and Judy Finnigan didn't help by being so nervous herself that she put Doris on edge. Doris was not at all happy and I don't think she took to Judy; as I walked her to her waiting car she was grumbling away about 'the dreadful girl'. I handed her over to her driver who took her the last few yards to her car, and I watched her totter away in her shoes which were much too big, her feet having shrunk with age. She looked so tiny and vulnerable and I choked as I thought this could be the last time I saw her.

In reality she lasted another four years, although she was of course very frail towards the end, which wasn't just to do with age. After leaving the Street she had lived quite happily in her house in Chorlton-cum-Hardy, alone now that her mother was no longer alive, until she was burgled which caused her to become a bit of a recluse. This was exacerbated by the almost criminal activities of a photographer who installed himself in the house opposite and got a photo of her opening the door first thing in the morning, with her dreadfully thinning hair and looking as if she were mental. The picture was published disgracefully by the *News of the World*, together with the revelation of her real age, which she had kept secret for years. She was a proud lady and didn't deserve this vile treatment. The press often excuse their intrusive behaviour by saying that, if you are in the public eye and court publicity, you must be prepared to face it when you don't want it. While I have sympathy with this argument, it is completely hypocritical since, in Doris's case, she was always a private person who shunned publicity, and this intrusion had a disastrous effect on her.

I was told that she looked forward to my visits and when I arrived would be sitting in her room, all made up and ready with her handbag on her lap, waiting for her rare trip into the outside world. I would drive her to a nearby pub where she had booked a table and we would spend an hour or two on lunch, which she usually insisted on paying for. As we walked from the car to the pub, she would announce that she was not wearing her hearing aid and would do all the talking; and as we arrived at the door she would take off her shoes, which were dangerous to walk in as they were too big for her tiny feet, and go barefoot to the table. After lunch, we would go back to her little room on the first floor overlooking the fields and we would have tea and gossip for another few hours, watching the antics of the white horse in the field, which gave her so much pleasure. These visits were never a chore and we would spend much of the time laughing.

A few months before her death she had phoned me at Sandra's house; I was out at the time but she spent a long time chatting to Sandra, telling her how much she loved me, and asked for me to call her back. When I returned her call she asked for my official address because she said she wanted to leave me something in her will. 'It will probably only be about fourpence by the time I go,' she said, 'but I want you to have what there is.' I was very touched and since I was also still in financial trouble, which I hadn't told her, it was a nice bit of news to receive. I wrote to her to say that I was very proud that she would think enough of me to want to do something like that but that I hoped she would live long enough to enjoy her money herself. When I next went to see her, she was glowing with the news that she had just changed her accountant who had discovered that her previous accountant had been at best incompetent, and she now had more money than she had ever had before! When I said that I was very happy for her she said, 'Oh no dear. It's for you.'

I was on tour with *Deathtrap* when I was telephoned by the home and told of her death. Apparently she had left word that myself and Tony Warren, the creator of *Coronation Street*, were to be informed before the press or Granada, and we were the only two who were to be allowed to speak at her funeral. It was arranged for the funeral to be on a Monday as I wouldn't be performing and I duly, together with Tony, gave the oration. It was not much of a service; her distant family, a cousin, belonged to the Kearsley New Jerusalem Church, some strange religious sect, and they themselves were not particularly impressed with Doris's chosen career. The family vicar in particular was a nasty little man; I met him in the toilet after the service and he made some insensitive and trite comment about emotional speeches, obviously referring to my oration, when I had a lump in my throat as I came to the end of my speech. I wish now that I had challenged him, but I was too taken aback with the viciousness of the comment.

Before the service, there was some consternation at Granada when Julie

Goodyear was playing games again. Doris had particularly asked that she should not be at the funeral, but of course it put Granada in a difficult situation; how could they tell her? The problem seemed to have been resolved for them when Julie announced a few days before the funeral that she wouldn't be going as she thought it was Doris's day and she didn't want to be a distraction from that (a pretty arrogant statement to my mind!). Nevertheless, unable to miss out on a photo opportunity, she turned up on the day, on the arm of Tony Warren; like so many gay men, he was one of her admirers and she played up to him. At the end of the service Tony, who made a wonderful speech, asked me if I would look after Julie while he went to the loo, which shows how aware he was of what was going on around him! I said that I would rather go to the loo with him, which is where I chanced upon the despicable vicar.

Because I was on tour, I had asked the home to arrange for a wreath on my behalf; two weeks after the service, I telephoned to see about paying, although admittedly I was wanting to know also about the will, but didn't like to ask. I was told that they had been aware of the fact that Doris had planned to make me a beneficiary in her will, but in the event she hadn't got around to it! The main beneficiary had been a cousin of hers whom she hadn't seen for five years as they had fallen out, and whom she didn't like. They also told me that she had left nearly half a million. There was much about it that didn't seem right; it had been well over a year since she informed me that she had changed her will, but I did not feel it would be dignified or right to start haggling over the money. I just hope they didn't enjoy it!

17

1994 to 2000 • *Deathtrap* • The RSC • *Hard Times* •
Philip Madoc • Aled Jones • Janet Brown •
Family Affairs • Brian Park

IN THE MIDST of all this death and destruction, apart from funeral orations, I was still working from time to time and had a brief but pleasant trip to Bristol for an episode of *Casualty*, where I met up with Ian Redford whom I had known as a young man in the National Youth Theatre. We made a pleasant job even more pleasant by staying outside Bristol in a village that I can no longer recall the name of, and cannot find on the map, but it was like being in a Mediterranean hamlet as we sat in the square in the balmy July evenings reminiscing about the days of Michael Croft. I also met up with one of the daughters of Ann Beach, who was in the permanent company of *Casualty* and seemed intrigued by the fact that I had strongly fancied her mother in my student days.

The year 1994 had ended with the tour of *Deathtrap*, an excellent thriller by Ira Levin. The play was directed by Philip Dart under the auspices of the Channel Theatre Company which he had taken over from Kevin Wood. My co-star in this production was John Wheatley. We had worked before in *A Man For All Seasons* at Nottingham, and at first I thought we were going to be at loggerheads as he had just recently starred in quite a prominent role in *Coronation Street* and I think he felt he had to make some sort of stand against me. Whatever the reason, the rehearsal period was a series of confrontations, but once we had settled down we really got on very well together and I became quite fond of him. We spent most of our days off together playing tennis, which was to take the place of my love for football.

The play is based upon the homosexual relationship of two writers: the well-known and successful thriller writer that I played, and his young protégé played by John. A week or so into the run, in a mischievous mood, I took John by surprise when I caught hold of him in a passionate embrace and kissed him on the mouth just before the first-act curtain. He then had to run offstage, up the stairs, and I heard him exclaim 'Yuck!' as soon as he was out of sight of the audience. Originally, I had only done it as a gag, but it had such a startling effect on the audience that we decided to keep it in!

1994 was the year of death for me in that I lost three mothers: first my virtual mother-in-law of whom I was very fond, followed by my natural birth mother, and finally my stage mother Doris. I wasn't alone in losing people who were dear to me: Sandra also lost her husband, and although she had left him for me, she still kept in touch and saw him fairly regularly, as she was worried about his alcohol dependence and naturally felt guilty and responsible. It is no doubt that drink had hastened his end, that and smoking; he was a very unfit man and died at a tragically early age which has weighed on both of our consciences since. I met him only briefly once but I am sure that under different circumstances we could have been quite friendly; he seemed to me to have been the sort of guy I would have got on with.

Sandra's experience with his heavy drinking, plus the fact that her maternal grandmother was something of a lush and met her end because of drink, means that she has a deep aversion to the influence of alcohol and has kept strict control of the amount that I drink! This has of course had its social implications as my life was pretty much centred on the amber nectar. Although I never regarded myself as more than a heavy drinker, I have since learnt that my mother was rather worried about the amount that I drank; and while I still enjoy beer very occasionally and wine daily, I have been encouraged to cut back drastically.

This has had an effect not only on my health but also my pocket and my weight, and also on my smoking. I gave up smoking cigarettes when my first son was born in 1962. I had watched my uncle Bill's last days in hospital with lung cancer and determined that my son was not going to end his days in that way. I then reasoned that I could not forbid him to smoke with a cigarette hanging from my mouth, so I gave up myself, without too much of a struggle. I am of the belief that one only has to have a strong enough reason. After a few years of not smoking at all, I started to smoke cigars, but only when I was drinking; I was under the impression that they were not as damaging. Since I drank a lot, I smoked a lot, and it wasn't until the financial crisis of 1990, when I realised that I could save myself about thirty-five quid a week if I gave up cigars, that I stopped altogether; so together with a cutback on cigars came a cutback on booze. This of course had the effect of increasing my appetite which counteracted the effect of the weight loss from not drinking so much. You can't win them all!

I was glad to see the back of that dreadful year of 1994, but '95 seemed to be starting in much the same way with an appearance in *Space Precinct*, a futuristic series made by Gerry Anderson, who had hitherto made his name in puppet films. I don't think it ever really took off as a series, but it was fun to do, if not very comfortable as I had to wear contact lenses that gave my eyes a kaleidoscope effect at the moments when I was possessed by the aliens. Ironically, I was playing a somewhat despotic futuristic landlord, and my main source of income at that time was from my Eastbourne property!

I have never regarded myself as particularly superstitious, but when, on the way for an interview for the Royal Shakespeare Company, I saw one magpie, I made a point of driving the more rural route to London in order to increase the probability of seeing another! I remember Alan Bleasdale telling me that if Willy Russell saw one magpie on his way to dinner with him, he would not turn up until he had seen another. I wanted so much to be part of the RSC that I was prepared to take whatever precautions necessary to increase my chances. I was to read for the part of Gonzalo in a touring production of *The Tempest* that was destined to go on a world tour, including Japan, South America, Europe, and also a tour of England, playing in sports centres in towns that rarely got theatre because they had no proper venue in which to receive productions. We were to travel with our own collapsible seating and play in the round.

I read first of all for the casting department and then was recalled, after seeing another double magpie, to read for David Thacker, the director. I had of course played for the RSC twice before in my career, once with *Nil Carborundum* at the Arts Theatre in 1962 and later in the post-London tour of *Educating Rita* in 1982, but I had never really felt that I had been part of the RSC proper. I was therefore absolutely thrilled when I was offered the part of Gonzalo, and also 'The Old Man' in Edward Bond's *Bingo* which was to play in tandem. I immediately phoned my old mate David Weston, who had originally told me about the upcoming tour, and discovered that he was to be in it as well, playing Alonso.

Rehearsals were in Clapham, just around the corner from Grafton Square, where I parked my car every morning outside my old house and walked to the rehearsal rooms. I was in seventh heaven; the rehearsals were everything that I had hoped for. I was playing not only with dedicated proper actors, but with an erudite and accomplished director and with the best scriptwriter in the world. We had early-morning warm-up sessions, and also private voice tuition with Cicely Berry who had been with the RSC for decades. It was a long six-week rehearsal period, and I loved every moment of it. I also loved the direction of David Thacker, who was open to ideas and suggestions from any quarter. Since the production was in the round, and the play a fantasy, it was decided that we would all be on stage from the start, waking up to play our scenes and then melting into the side of the stage and lying asleep until our next involvement.

Unfortunately, when we opened at the Young Vic, it was in the middle of a heatwave with the highest temperatures recorded for many years. To make things worse, our specially designed costumes were heavy, voluminous, thick, and hot. We were uncomfortable, the audience were uncomfortable and the critics were irascible with the heat and cruel with their assessment. After the first night, the play was reworked and re-rehearsed with exits and entrances, and by the time we went to play for three weeks at the Swan Theatre in Stratford it was a different production. In fact, it was very well received there and played to full houses and a wonderful reception. We were shattered therefore when we were all called to the theatre one morning to receive the distressing news that our world tour had been reduced to a week in the Polish capital, Warsaw, and a week in Halle in Germany! St Petersburg, Venezuela, Japan, and many other rumoured exotic venues were out. There was a stunned silence followed by outrage: this wasn't the job that we had all signed up for. The reason given was that the six weeks in Japan had been cancelled because of technical difficulties and that the British Council, which was financing some of the tour, had withdrawn because of the bad press reviews.

I had previously been elected Equity representative of the company and, after a discussion with the rest of the cast, I requested a meeting with Adrian Noble, the artistic director of the RSC who was responsible for these decisions. I also asked for him to come up to Stratford to see the reworked production at the Swan. On the day of the meeting I travelled down early to London to discuss the situation with David Thacker prior to my appointment with Adrian Noble. I learnt that the background to all this was a little more complicated, as David had been shortlisted with Adrian for the RSC job of artistic director and there was considerable history of a competitive attitude between the two.

My loyalties were obviously with David, and during the meeting I managed to expose Adrian Noble as being devious to the point of lying. By sheer chance, Paul Jesson, who was playing Prospero, had a girlfriend who was working at the Japanese end of the organisation and who had sent Paul a copy of a message from Adrian Noble to the Japanese theatre, to the effect that the production was not good enough to send abroad, and effectively pulling the plug on the tour. When I challenged him with the discrepancy between this memo and his previously stated excuse of 'technical difficulties', he was somewhat taken aback and hid behind his company manager who was also at the meeting.

I further destroyed any future relationship I might have had with Adrian Noble when I asked if he had seen the reworked production that was enjoying such success at the Swan; in fact it was generally held to be the best production at Stratford that season, *Julius Caesar* and *Romeo and Juliet* not having been wildly acclaimed. He replied that he had not, because he had just returned from holiday. At this point, I asked if he had considered the possibility that he had taken his holiday at the wrong time? He wasn't best pleased, but it seems to me ludicrous that the leader of the most renowned theatrical company in the world should be allowed to absent himself in the middle of a full season; he should take his holiday in the closed season.

I did manage to get them to agree to invite the British Council to come and see the play again and reassess their decision, which they did; but although when I had tea with their representative after the show she admitted that it had much changed and that she had enjoyed it, it was all too late. Meanwhile Adrian Noble continued to run down the prestige of that wonderful company while taking time out to earn himself a small fortune in commercial productions. In due course he quit the RSC to pursue his new money-making opportunities, leaving behind many a disaster for the new management to sort out.

Far from being dispirited, the setback seemed to draw the company closer together, and having enjoyed reasonable success at Stratford we set off on our tour of England. Before we left, however, I was to receive another personal shock, but this time of a more pleasant nature.

My agent Scott Marshall had forwarded a letter to me from Australia, from a young lady called Sally Anne, who said she was under the impression that I was her father! To be absolutely honest I had been expecting something like this, but it had been so long in coming that I had thought perhaps it never would. She said she was coming to England for a short visit and, after communicating with her, we arranged to meet between shows.

As it happened, that day it was *Bingo* in which I played a mentally retarded dirty old man in an exceedingly unattractive woolly hat, with a demented look on my face and blacked-out teeth; hardly the best way to meet a long-lost father. After all these years I was amazed that she was late, and I stood outside the stage door looking expectantly at every young lady of about the age of 35! When she did turn up, having had difficulty parking her car, I could see that she was indeed my daughter; and as we chatted over a drink in the actors' pub, the Black Swan (more commonly known as the Dirty Duck), I found that the poor girl had also inherited my bloody-mindedness. Our first meeting was a great success and I fixed for her to see *Bingo* that evening; afterwards I took her out to dinner where we got to know each other a bit more, and then she came and stayed with David and me, in our digs that we shared.

Despite the disappointment of not going to the luxurious countries, I enjoyed the tour. As the eldest member of the company, I also enjoyed the status of senior statesman and was often called upon to make the thank-you speech to our sponsors, NatWest Bank, at the reception that invariably followed the first night in each of the venues. I frequently took the opportunity to express my personal dismay at the latest trend of centralised telephone banking; I used to enjoy the relationship that I had with my bank manager in Clapham and had missed that personal touch. I found that in general they themselves didn't like the new system and were very sympathetic. Eventually, after one of the receptions, I was offered a bank manager of my very own who would look after me personally; the only trouble was that he was based in Middlesbrough and we only met when I was in that area on tour!

When we took the production to Warsaw, Sandra came with me and David Weston took his wife Dora. Since she has always for some reason blamed me for a break in their relationship some years past, she refuses to acknowledge my existence; for that week, David and I only met on stage. Both Warsaw and Halle were depressing places, although much of that may have been because we were there when the weather was grim.

Whenever we arrived somewhere new, I would spend the first day wandering around on foot getting my bearings and finding out the best places to drink and to eat; it was a habit I had acquired while touring India, when I had been left on my own without Sandra. On the last night in Halle, while the stage crew did the 'get out', Paul Jesson and I set off in a snowstorm to find a bierkeller that I had discovered earlier in the week. Not only would we get a good drink there, but I had noticed 'goose breast' on the menu at an unbelievable price. After walking for half an hour in the blizzard, we sat in the steamy warmth of the buzzing bar where we were presented with a goose breast each: the whole breast, both sides, each. I never finished mine; I took half of it back to England for Sandra.

It was a happy and united company despite the disappointment of the curtailed tour. Apart from David Weston and Paul Jesson, who became a good friend, as did Ian Driver who became my main tennis adversary throughout the tour, there was Ian Holm's daughter Sarah-Jane Holm, newcomer Bonnie Engstrom who was given the opportunity to play Ariel because of recasting at the rehearsal stage, and Dominic Letts, who gave probably the best performance in the show as Caliban, but who was apparently on his best behaviour as he has a drink problem.

Dominic is a very talented redhead with an eccentric and aggressive attitude. Something of a rebel, he saved money on accommodation by sleeping in a tent that he travelled with from place to place, despite the fact that the tour encompassed some of the worst weather months of the year. It was the common belief that he was also substituting 'pot' for the 'pint' in an attempt to honour his pledge to stay away from alcohol. He did slip once, and was castigated by his fellow actors for letting them down on stage. Why is it that so very often the best actors have this dreadful weakness? He was a super little actor and should be getting a lot more work than he does.

There was no demarcation between stage staff and actors; we all socialised together. The stage manager, Martyn Sargent, was a source of great strength and amusement. I remember him singing and playing the piano, just slightly off key and hilariously funny, in a bar in Halle. There was also little Jo Mo, who became a lasting friend after the tour and invited Sandra and me to stay with her in Stratford whenever we came up to see a show.

I was sad when the tour came to an end, but touched by the presentation of a collection they had taken for me to buy a tennis racquet to replace one that had been stolen when we were in Newbury. I was aware that my confrontation with Adrian Noble meant I was unlikely to be returning to the RSC, but I was not alone in my amazement that the only person to be recalled for the next season was a black actor who not only turned in what was universally acclaimed as the worst performance of the tour, he was also the most unreliable member of the company, being frequently late. It was a definite case of positive discrimination, which does more harm than good and is more likely to encourage racialism than discourage it, when it is so obviously unjustified and misplaced.

When it comes to minorities the theatre has always been more sympathetic than any other profession. Homosexuality was accepted in the theatre long before it was legalised; political extremists like Vanessa Redgrave and her brother Corin were tolerated with their left-wing Workers Revolutionary Party. In general the performance is what matters and takes priority of judgement. The perverse practice of casting according to colour rather than ability can only foster resentment and nurture prejudice, not eradicate it. There are many extremely talented black actors around and it is imperative that they should be cast within the range of their capabilities. To do otherwise does them no more favours than if we were to insist on a white runner being included in the Olympic hundred-metre squad, where black athletes seem to hold supremacy.

The RSC tour ran from April 1995 until February of the following year, and it was five months before I was to work again. On this occasion, it was not to be a happy experience; another tour, but this time on a shoestring for the so-called Good Company, which was something of a misnomer! The company was based in Brighton and was rumoured to be financed by Christian Science. The play was a stage version of Charles Dickens' *Hard Times*, adapted by Dennis Saunders and directed by his wife, Sue Pomeroy. I played Thomas Gradgrind and my adversary was Philip Madoc, playing Bounderby. The large cast also included Janet Brown, who was famous as a variety artist and for her impression of Maggie Thatcher, Aled Jones who had been a celebrated child choral and solo singer, Tom Cotcher who had been a regular in *The Bill* for a number of years, and Dermot Walsh, the now ageing film star with whom I had worked years ago in *The Little Hut*.

On paper it was quite an impressive company and should have done well, in that there was a lot of experience on stage and enough in the way of known faces to attract a decent audience. In reality it was a disaster, which started with the rehearsals in south London. The adaptation of the book was disappointingly fragmented and a little immature in its conception, and Sue Pomeroy's direction turned out to be exceedingly amateur. She failed in the basic requirement to ensure that she did not expose her actors to humiliation and embarrassment. The opening circus scene with poor Dermot Walsh, as the ringmaster, attempting to juggle and dropping every other ball, set the show off on its downward journey. The worst moment was probably the suicide scene when Tom Cotcher had to throw himself to his death from a well-lit bridge and was forced to just drop to his knees and give forth a strangulated squawk, hoping for a blackout that never came.

We should have seen the danger signs at the outset when Sue started every morning with warm-up exercises that seemed designed for the day nursery. Every corner that could be cut was cut. When the tour started, the props and musical instruments were all shared out amongst those of us who had transport, which is not in itself wrong, but one would have liked to have been asked. Once again, I was the Equity Deputy and more or less ended up as the social secretary as well, running the lottery syndicate and organising a number of dinners and nights out.

As before, the company were united in their antagonism towards the management and, rather like the Blitz, we were all drawn together in a tight and loyal band. All that is except Philip Madoc, who kept himself strangely aloof; and not only did he not join in, I found him extremely competitive on stage. My scenes with him became something of a battle as I found him a very selfish actor to play with, or in this case against. His performance was in fact very good and probably saved the play from being worse than it was. He had a magnificent resonant voice with a beautiful and impressive Welsh timbre, reminiscent of Hugh Griffith, and indeed his onstage selfishness fitted in well with his characterisation. I just found it a battle trying to deal with his technique of upstaging and his constant need to walk away in the middle of a conversation, taking the audience's attention with him.

Since he didn't join in with many of the evenings out, we didn't strike up more than a token relationship; and indeed the only time he did condescend to join Janet Brown and myself for dinner in Leeds, I had cause to vow 'never again'. The restaurant was a little drive away, and so he asked if he could come in the car with Janet and myself, and of course I said yes and waited for him after curtain down. As we drove away from the theatre he asked if I could do a slight detour to drop him at his flat to pick up his wallet. After sitting outside his flat waiting for him for what seemed like an age, but must have been about twenty minutes, he came down to say that he had been getting his washing in. At the best of times I am always wanting to 'get a move on' – my father nicknamed me 'Mr Hurry-Up' – but after a show, when my adrenalin has been racing and I am dying for a drink, I am doubly impatient. To add insult to injury I discovered that he had his own car, parked outside his flat all the time, but was reluctant to use it; he was also reluctant to give anybody else a lift as we discovered throughout the tour!

My main pal became Aled Jones who I discovered had been a very fine tennis player, and represented Wales as a junior. We played regularly and continued to meet up for about two years after the tour finished, playing together at the David Lloyd Club. He then disappeared from my life as if he had been whisked away. I heard nothing from him and despite many letters, cards, phone messages and invitations there was complete silence until Sandra and I were invited to his wedding to Claire at St Paul's, Covent Garden (affectionately known as the Actors' Church) and the reception afterwards at the Connaught Rooms. We were indeed honoured because there were no other theatricals there apart from a couple of his student pals from the Bristol Old Vic School and our mutual agents Scott and Denise Marshall. After the wedding he disappeared from my life once more and it wasn't until Thames TV did *This Is Your Life* on him that we met up again and got together for another tennis session. Nothing had changed: he was still the unspoiled Aled and I was still unable to win a single set. Even when I did win a point I got the feeling that it was more a case of him giving it to me than me winning.

It would appear that the *Hard Times* experience had been equally traumatic for Aled, as he went back to singing and didn't try his hand at acting again for many years! Sandra and I also remained very pally with Janet Brown who sometimes joined us at our place in France and whom we saw fairly regularly until she passed away in 2011 at the age of 87.

When the tour came to a close, most of the company except myself were asked if they would go out again with another tour of the same play! Philip accepted, but all of the other main cast players declined the offer to extend their purgatory, including young Joanne Thirsk who had turned in a lovely performance and was a favourite of the management. Little Rebecca Rainsford, who had played the clarinet, helped the stage management and played a variety of small parts, was more or less promised that she would take over from Joanna, and was asked to attend the recasting read-throughs in London. Apparently she stayed with them all day, reading with a whole succession of would-be victims, and in the end was not offered a part and not paid for her time; she was also treated as a menial in that she was asked to leave the room whenever they discussed someone. That was fairly indicative of what sort of management Good Company was. When Brian Murphy phoned me a year later to say that he had been offered a part for them I advised him not to touch it with a bargepole.

A little over a month after the tour ended, I was asked to read for a new soap series for Channel Five. Barbara Ewing, whom I had directed in *Night and Day* in Ipswich, telephoned me to say that she too was with Scott Marshall and had been invited to read; she suggested that we meet up before the read-through. Not knowing the studios in Hayes, where the reading was to take place, I had driven up the previous day to do a recce and arranged to meet her for breakfast in the nearby Tesco.

There was quite a collection of old mates when we got to the studios. There was Delena Kidd and Bruce Montague, whom I knew from RADA days, and some other recognisable faces. I read first of all with Barbara Ewing and was then asked to stay behind and possibly read with someone else. Barbara left telling me that she wasn't interested as she had just married a Maori and was returning to New Zealand for the Maori marriage ritual. I next read with Delena Kidd; I can remember being very distracted and amused when I saw the window cleaner in a cradle outside, cleaning the office window behind the selection committee and showing bewildered interest in the proceedings. Two days later Delena and I were offered the parts of Jack and Elsa Gates, the grandparents of the family upon which the series *Family Affairs* was to be based.

Barbara missed out; this was to be one of the pleasantest and most enjoyable jobs that I had ever done, although it was not without the occasional battle. Our daughter was played by Liz Crowther, the real-life daughter of Leslie Crowther; she was married in the series to Ian Ashpitel, known as Ash. Their four children, our grandchildren, were played by Rocky Marshall, Sandra Huggett (the real-life daughter of Brian Huggett, the golfer), Cordelia Bugeja (known as Codge), and Michael Cole playing Jamie, the baby of the family. There was also the paternal grandfather played by Ian Cullen, who had been in *Z Cars* in the year dot.

This was the family around which the stories were to be written; and it was to prove a pretty heavy schedule, as it was to be the first attempt at a five-day-a-week serial. There were other regulars of course: the very glamorous duo of Tina Landini and Tina Hall, the narcissistic David Easter, the more mature *femme fatale* Annie Miles, and the scallywag Scouser Barry McCormick. There was also Idris Elba, a remarkably good-looking and very talented black actor who was destined to do great things.

It was one of the happiest and closest-knit companies I have ever worked with, and I think the reasons for this were manifold. First, the schedule threw us all very closely together for concentrated periods in the middle of the industrial wasteland of Hayes. Second, as a ground-breaking soap for the new channel, Channel Five, it wasn't received in a great number of households so they weren't made stars overnight and everybody, with one or two exceptions, kept their feet on the ground. Lastly, Morag Bain the originating producer had selected not only a talented little bunch of youngsters, but also a decidedly pleasant collection.

It was not only the cast which had been selected with such care; the make-up, wardrobe, props, grips and even the vision mixer and the script editors were all unbelievably pleasant, and we all joined in together as a very close-knit community. Once again I took over the role of daddy of the company, organising the lottery syndicate, tennis tournaments and greyhound racing. The youngsters also did their bit with organising trips to the musical *Rent* and a soccer and cricket team. It wasn't all just fun and games though; the work schedule was very, very demanding, and Morag had to keep a tight rein on the team discipline. There were too the occasional differences of opinion and flare-ups, and I seemed to be at the centre of most of the disputes with regard to the scripts.

My biggest conflict with Morag came when the script called for some jiggery-pokery with the closing of a joint bank account and the withdrawal of funds which, when I read the script two weeks before we were to film it, I realised was inaccurate and not at all following bank procedure, so I went to the script editor and asked for it to be checked out. I called again just before we were due to film and was told that it was being checked, but by the time we came to recording the scene in the studio, I had heard nothing more and the script had still not been changed. Just before we did the scene I told the director that it was inaccurate; he contacted Morag and was told that it had been checked and was in order, and that I had been informed of this. I was obliged to do the scene as written, but I didn't do it with good grace. As the scene was coming to an end I noticed that Morag had come down to the studio floor and was waiting for me. She was livid that I had dared to question her in public and had decried the script, and we left the studio together shouting at each other; everything around went very quiet.

Later that day I got a summons to go and see Morag in her office. She said she had been looking into the dispute and had to apologise on both counts: first, that I hadn't been informed that the script had been checked, and second, that I was right about the facts being inaccurate. We hugged and kissed and made up. I was in fact very fond indeed of Morag, and could see that she was beginning to feel the strain of the pressure she had been under and was taking too much on board; she even bothered herself with the car-parking arrangements!

We also came head to head, but in a much more friendly and jokey manner, over my accommodation arrangements. The studios were owned by a Sikh family with whom I had struck up a good relationship, often nipping into their offices for a cup of coffee and a chat between scenes. I found that when I was called for filming first thing in the morning, I had to leave home at 5.30 a.m. in order to miss the motorway traffic, and if I had been filming at the end of the previous day I didn't get home until about nine or ten; it was almost a case of turning around and coming straight back! We each had a dressing room in portacabins just outside the studios and, after obtaining permission from my Indian friends, I decided to make a little nest out of my portacabin and stay overnight. It started with just a bed, or rather a futon, but within a few weeks I had erected a TV aerial and bought a little fridge, a coffee maker, a music centre and an electric hob. I would sometimes nip out for a takeaway, get back before they locked the gates and settle down for the night with my meal and a bottle of wine. Sometimes I was joined for a drink or two by a late-working director, like Kenny Glenaan, or another of the cast who would occasionally follow my example.

Morag first found out about it when she caught me up on the roof, putting up my TV aerial, and worried about my safety; then she worried about the legality of what I was doing. It became a cat-and-mouse game as she tried to dissuade me from staying overnight. At first she argued that I was not covered by insurance, and I assured her that I was perfectly adequately covered; then she argued that if anything happened to me, my wife would be in touch and create problems, and I pointed out that I wasn't married. Eventually I explained that the journey was killing me, and that I spent most of the night working on my lines anyway, so in fact my staying overnight meant that I was fitter and more ready to do my job properly. We agreed that she should turn a blind eye and I was to keep an eye out for any of the others who did it; I think she was worried about drugs.

Our first year was a great success. We were even nominated for the most popular soap at the National Television Awards. Although we knew there was no hope of winning anything, we were delighted to be invited to the awards evening in the Royal Albert Hall and we set off from Hayes in taxis all togged up and excited. I must say it was an eye-opener to see the cavorting of the girls as they walked down the red carpet responding to the crowd and the photographers. David Easter had asked Rocky Marshall to share a stretch limo with him and arrive in style, but Rocky was not that sort of exhibitionist; when he told me, I suggested that he decline the offer and make plans to arrive at the same time as David, on his pushbike!

We had had a good first year and I must say I was in general impressed with the performances, particularly the youngsters'. I wasn't too keen on my opposite grandfather, but a lot of that might have been jealousy as he did seem to get some good storylines and some better comedy situations than my character. Taking into consideration the fact that we had taken on five shows a week and with a new and very much untried cast, I think we had achieved a remarkable standard as far as soaps were concerned; but it appeared that Channel Five were not happy with the viewing figures and there was talk of another producer coming in to take over from Morag. There were many rumours, and Corinne Hollingsworth, who was our boss at Pearson Television, invited me to lunch. We were all upset at the fact that Morag was going, but she told me that Morag was not well and that they had to do something about the viewing figures. To that end they were bringing in a new executive producer to revamp the series; she wouldn't tell me who they had got but she did say it was a high-profile figure.

When I later heard the rumour that it was to be Brian Park, who was currently producing *Coronation Street*, I telephoned my mates in the Street cast, who warned me that he was poison. He had been called in to axe some of the old characters and to bring in some young blood; he had performed the first part of his task with a certain amount of glee, and performed the second part with a predatory delight in making sure he was around when the handsome young men were on set.

I remember being appalled at the press release issued when Peter Baldwin, who played Derek Wilton, was axed because he was so boring! For Granada to issue such a destructive comment about an actor who had been playing the part for ten years was to me unforgivable. If he was boring, surely one should look to the scripts or the storylines; but it turned out to be typical of Brian Park's approach. I can only hope that, eventually, Granada became aware of the damage that he did to the Street. Before Brian Park, *EastEnders* was definitely in second place; after Brian Park, they took the lead. He may have had the effect of raising viewing figures for the brief period of curiosity as viewers followed the changes, but the result was to lower the standard. As soon as I received my report from 'up north', I contacted Corinne and told her what I had been told. She replied that he couldn't wield the axe as he had done at Granada as they couldn't afford the cost; he wouldn't have the money.

Our first experience of Brian was when we were all called to the studio to meet him and some of his team. He made a speech that upset many of us when he said he was going to 'put the show on the map', and introduced us to a new producer and company manager that he was leaving behind with us, to get a feel of the problems for the next three months before his takeover. We then had a glass of warm wine and a few nibbles and he disappeared for three months.

The team he had left behind started to make their presence felt as one by one the various departments were cut down and we saw some of our best friends disappear, along with the Monday rehearsal day that we had fought for. The morale of the company, which had been high and exciting, dropped day by day and the wonderful atmosphere was changing.

At the end of the three months, Brian Park appeared back on the scene and a list was put up on the board of times that he wanted to see us, one by one. I was the first on the list: in at 10.15 a.m. I had a very heavy day with sixteen scenes to do starting at 7.30 a.m. and with just the one break at 10.15. We had caught a whiff of the rumour that he was going to axe the family, so I was a little prepared, and had decided not to go. I was in my dressing room when the runner came to say that Brian Park was waiting for me; when I said I wasn't going, he didn't know what to do and left bewildered. A few moments later a more senior member of the staff came to say that Brian Park was still waiting, and I took great delight in telling him to tell Brian Park to 'f--k off' and begging him to use those words.

Within ten minutes I received a call from my agent; Brian Park had phoned to say that they were killing off my character, Jack Gates, and I would be the first to be written out in November, committing suicide in my car after murdering my wife Delena! Shortly after that the rest of the family were to be blown up in a gas explosion on board a boat. We learnt from the office staff that on the fateful day when he axed the whole family, he was running back and forth to the press office making sure that they put out the press release at the right time in order to catch the weekend papers; but when he did release, they weren't interested. There then followed a series of advertisements, some on the radio and others in the newspapers, announcing Brian Park as the 'great axe man'; these had been taken out by Brian to advertise himself, as his great press release had not really caught the imagination of the daily papers.

Once I had ascertained that they were obliged to pay me until the end of my contract in February, I was not at all dismayed and I wrote the following letter.

21.09.98

Dear Brian Park,

I am fully aware that what I have to say may sound like the rantings of an embittered rejected actor. However, I would like to assure you that nothing could be further from the truth. I was in fact planning to not renew my contract in February (had I been offered it), not a decision that I was looking forward to as I have really enjoyed my time with *Family Affairs*.

I have never stayed anywhere for longer than 2 years, even in my 25 years with *Coronation Street* I was constantly leaving and returning. One of the reasons why I have stayed so long with *Family Affairs* is the wonderful atmosphere and team spirit that existed before your arrival. There have been no stars, no tantrums and the whole team, cameras, sound, art, costume, make up etc., all have been the nicest I have ever worked with and despite the pressures and financial restrictions, they have all pulled together making many sacrifices to make this show the 'flop' that you obviously think it is!

Since your arrival however, when it would appear that four people are now covering the work previously done by Morag Bain alone, all of the other departments have been ordered to cut back on staff. The daily hours and shooting schedule have been altered, without so much as a courtesy chat with the people involved. We have seen nothing of the new trio who have kept themselves aloof and made no effort to join in with the rest of us, and to cap it all, after a pathetic welcoming speech and a warm glass of wine you disappeared on holiday leaving enough information behind to set off a series of alarming and disturbing rumours which have destroyed the morale of the company and created dishonouring between departments and unease amongst the cast. You then returned from holiday and summoned us one by one to your office. As I hope you are aware I was told to report to you at 10.15 and I refused.

I had a heavy schedule that day, both in the studio and on location, and I find it quite unbelievable that someone in your position should be so lacking in sensitivity and common sense, to ask an actor to come and be told that he was no longer wanted, and then expect him to return to work and retain his concentration. Even though I had no intention of staying with the show, it is never pleasant to be told that you are not wanted and I was not prepared to jeopardise (?) my performance in order to give you your little moment of sadistic pleasure. After 40 odd years in the profession I am completely unimpressed with your little power parade and I am extremely angry and bitter that your callous, insensitive and unprofessional behaviour has been allowed to destroy the wonderful humour, dedication and team spirit that existed before – something that money cannot buy.

We are all aware that you childishly enjoy your reputation as the 'Axe-Man' but from my many friends at Granada it would appear that you are more commonly known as the 'Poisonous Ginger Dwarf'? and I cannot understand how Pearson's, who have been bombarding us with newsletters and information to make us feel that we are part of the Big Brother company and that we all matter so dreadfully, could have left us in the hands of someone who has left such a trail of misery and hatred in his wake.

I have not mentioned your choice to axe the whole Hart family, because it may well be the right decision, although arrived at for the wrong reasons and done in the wrong manner. It is apparent that you were looking for the most sensational act that would attract attention to yourself and grab the headlines. What a miserable failure that was! I can only pray that the rest of your reign has similar success.

I feel sorry for my friends that I leave behind, they don't deserve you. The 18 months or so that I have spent with them will remain as one of the pleasantest and happiest work experiences of my career. It was not going to be easy for me to refuse an extension of contract – you have made it easy and thanks for the 3 months pay without having to come in to work.

Happy Christmas.

I was prevailed upon by Sandra and Delena to take out the references to 'the poisonous ginger dwarf', and a few days later received his brief reply.

23rd September 1998
Ken Farrington
C/o *Family Affairs*

Dear Ken,

The words 'Bitter' – 'Rejected' and 'Actor' must remain yours. I do not share your taste for personal abuse.

Last Thursday's meeting was intended as an opportunity for Liz and myself to explain face to face the reasons why we felt it necessary to write out the Hart family. It was a professional courtesy though you obviously choose to characterise it otherwise. As you pointedly declined this invitation, I certainly feel under no compulsion to address your remarks now in correspondence.

If this vituperative outburst has provided you with a catharsis – so much the better. If not, *Family Affairs* will rely on your professionalism to fulfil your contractual obligations.

For my part I see no useful purpose in further communication with you on this subject. Doubtless you would agree.

Yours sincerely,
Brian Park
Executive Producer

A few weeks after the demise of the whole family, Pearson Television threw a party for the leaving members of the cast. Greg Dyke was still with Pearson's at that time; he had been present at the launch of *Family Affairs* two years before and I had seemed to get on quite well with him, so I took advantage of the fact that he was very approachable and told him the story of Brian Park's disgraceful behaviour. He expressed surprise and alarm at the way the whole thing had been handled and promised to look into it. I would like to think that I had been in some way responsible for Brian Park's departure from Pearson's within the year of his start; and I was delighted to note that the show's viewing figures did not increase following the tampering by that objectionable little man!

Although not what I would call a proper acting job, I was asked to go up to Granada for a celebration of *Coronation Street*'s fortieth year. The dinner dance in the Town Hall with the Lord Mayor of Manchester was a most magnificent affair; with one or two exceptions it was great to meet up with some really old chums, and the guest list looked like 'Who's Who in the Theatre'.

Unfortunately the celebrations had started with *The Richard and Judy Show* doing a *Coronation Street* special and I had the misfortune of accepting an invitation to appear on their morning show. They had asked me to be at the studios at nine o'clock, and since there was a great deal of trouble with British Rail at that time they agreed to my driving up and staying in a hotel the night before, for which they would pay expenses on top of a nominal fee. When I turned up at the studio at nine in the morning, nobody seemed to know who I was; I hung around the green room for two hours before anybody took any notice and I was given a dressing room in which to change.

Others began arriving at eleven and I took some comfort in meeting Daphne Oxenford who had been in episode one, way back in 1960. There were four of us from the distant past who were to appear in a special nostalgia spot, interviewed by Richard and Judy. There was to be no rehearsal and we did not meet Richard and Judy until we had made our entrance and were sitting on the set. The floor manager gave us instruction that on cue for action we were to make our entrance one by one through the doors of the Rovers Return, to smile and wave at the camera, and to take our seats opposite Richard and Judy. I have never felt such a prat; it was like something from the lottery show where you get the partners of the contestants outside the studio waving and giving the thumbs-up sign like demented idiots on happy pills. The interview itself was not much better, though much to my delight Ken Morley, who had played Reg Holdsworth for many years, sent the whole thing up nicely, getting one or two good laughs. At the end of the interview Richard and Judy scooted off to their next set and we were just left to find our own way out of the studio and home; nobody came to say thank you or to show us the way out. To cap it all, my agent had to chase them for months to pay the expenses that they had promised, and eventually gave up when they reneged on the overnight hotel!

I think these latest experiences took their toll. I had been exceedingly happy with the experience of *Family Affairs*; apart from the spirit of the company, I enjoyed working at that sort of pressure and, since the directors were under such pressure too, I found that they welcomed, in the main, any sort of constructive input. At one time I was even invited by one of the directors to direct a scene. They weren't all of them pliable, of course, and towards the end when the Park team took over they often weren't pleasant. I found that I had lost my appetite for work, and felt sad at the changes that were coming over the business. I found that we were being administered by business people, who were manipulated by the accounts and the accountants, not by people who had a love of acting or entertainment. Corinne Hollingsworth had sacrificed a loyal and talented team at the altar of her own progress in the corridors of power at Pearson's.

I decided that I no longer wanted to tour or to go for any length of time to the provinces for peanuts and live out of a suitcase, and I started to wind down my career.

AFTER LEAVING *FAMILY AFFAIRS* in 1999, I did a couple of corporate videos, a play reading for the RSC and guest roles in *Holby City* and *Doctors*, both for the BBC. I had decided that I was going to try my hand at writing and would only accept an acting job if they asked me very nicely! This arrogant attitude persisted for a couple of years as I was not offered anything of any worth and consequently didn't work.

Meanwhile I busied myself making alterations to the barn in France and travelling. It was during one of our expeditions to the south of France that we came across the seaside resort of Sanary-sur-Mer, a very pretty fishing port between Marseille and Toulon which was completely unspoilt, being more of a holiday resort for the French and not swamped by the British influx as the coast tends to become further east around Nice and Cannes.

We fell in love with the place; and, rather half-heartedly, because we didn't have the finance, started to look around for a new home. Sandra had taken herself off for a wander while I chilled out on the beach, and after a few minutes she returned bubbling with excitement and claiming to have found her dream home. At the end of a promontory, which overlooked a sandy beach on one side and the port with all of the shops and restaurants on the other, was a cluster of ten or so villas. On enquiring at one of the villas we learnt that it was extremely unlikely that any of them would be for sale; and if ever one of the owners did want to sell, the property was so sought after that it would most likely be snapped up by a friend or relative without being offered on the open market.

We visited a recommended local estate agent and asked her to investigate the possibility of any of the properties coming onto the market. She didn't hold out much hope and, after unfruitful preliminary enquiries, we left her with instructions to contact us if ever there was a chance of purchasing any one of the ten properties. To be honest since we were in no position to buy anything I was a little relieved, and the dream could continue with no threat of realisation. The barn had become too big for just the two of us and I was becoming more and more disenchanted with renting it out, so it was put on the market at a slightly inflated price (much to the chagrin of my son Mark who spent every summer there with his extended family); but there seemed little hope either of getting a buyer or of one of the villas in Sanary coming onto the market.

Robin Hawdon, a fellow student at RADA who was now well established as a playwright, had come back into my life after meeting up at the barn when he was also house hunting in France. My new freedom was still not being challenged with any offers of work that I could deem acceptable, and when Robin offered to rent me his flat in Tenerife for a six-month period, I jumped at the chance to settle down to try writing, although I was not sure what. I had previously tried writing a situation comedy based on my experiences working on my allotment; I had written some three episodes and résumés for another ten, but I hadn't had any success in getting it accepted anywhere and had lost heart.

From time to time I would visit my mother's grave in the picturesque village churchyard at Stonegate in Sussex, and since David Mayers lived with his wife Charlie just outside Wadhurst I frequently took the opportunity to call in and see them. During these visits I would talk to them about the accident that had left David paralysed from the waist down and the effect it had on them both. They were both very open about all the aspects of coming to terms with the disaster and how they had to adjust both mentally and physically. Although the subject matter was not a joyful one, they talked about it frequently in humorous terms and many of the incidents that they related had their funny side. With their permission, I had taped these conversations, and talked to them about turning their story into a drama; and this is what I set about doing during our six-month tenure of Robin's flat in Tenerife.

Luckily Robin was in residence at his flat for the first week or two of our rental and he was able to show us that Tenerife is not all like the horrendous resorts of Las Americas or Los Cristianos. We found some wonderful eating places which were not frequented by the lager-swilling, tattooed, shaved-head brigade. Robin was to become a 'new best friend'; Sandra took to him immediately and I found it strange that I had not been all that friendly with him when we had been at drama school together, as we had quite a lot in common. Perhaps it was an indication of how much I had changed from those early student days. Whilst I enjoyed life in the sun, with swimming daily and very good eating out, I found that I really did have to write, not because I felt the need to be creative but because I had to have some project on the go.

Towards the end of our time in Tenerife, as 2001 was coming to a close, I received news from Mme Malaret, our estate agent in Sanary, that there was the possibility of one of Sandra's dream cottages coming up for sale. Apparently one of the owners was in dispute with her neighbours and was so fed up that she wanted to sell. There was some degree of urgency, not solely because this was a rare opportunity to buy but also because she was quite liable to change her mind. Sandra and I talked it over at great length and finally came to the conclusion that

I could rustle up enough for a deposit and, if I sold one of the remaining flats in Eastbourne, I could soon pay off the rest. I also hoped to sell the barn at some point which would completely repay the mortgage. I immediately emailed Mme Malaret and told her to go ahead with the agreed price of £200,000. She asked when I could come and view the property and was amazed when I said I would be unable to come until the New Year, but that I would send her a deposit to secure the sale. Thus I became the potential owner of a property that I had not seen; I didn't even know which of the ten properties it was!

Early in the New Year I flew to Marseille and took the train to Sanary to meet the seller and view the property. Arriving the night before the appointment, I took an evening stroll around the area to identify which of the properties it was; I was delighted to find that it was one that was in the best condition and one of the few that was semi-detached. It had a wonderful little courtyard garden on one side and superb views of the Mediterranean on the other. I was able to sleep soundly in the knowledge that I had not been conned.

The next day I met Mme Corti, the owner, who was a fairly typical French-woman in her early sixties: heftily built, average height and pretty middle class. She had quite a dominant personality and declared herself to be a medium. She laid great weight on the information that I was an Aries, and claimed she had been aware of my presence the previous evening when I had approached the house to take stock of its position, despite the fact that the shutters were all closed and there was no sign of anybody in residence.

Before visiting the solicitor to agree the contract I was made aware of a number of problems with the property. There was an ongoing dispute over some alterations that Mme Corti had effected without planning permission or the agreement of her neighbours. However, her neighbours had also made alter-ations to their properties, likewise without permission, and there was a court hearing pending to sort the matter out. In any event the agent assured me that it was mainly a question of personalities and that she was sure we would be able to charm them into some sort of agreement. The next problem was that the vendor also wanted some £80,000 to be paid in euros, in cash, before the exchange of contracts. It appeared that this was not uncommon in France despite the fact that it was not legal. I didn't care; I wanted that house and I was prepared to accept any conditions. The sale was agreed; I flew back to the UK to get the cash and returned with Sandra for the official exchange of contracts in February of 2002.

The problems of that hasty purchase and the ensuing court cases with the variety of lawyers and alterations to the property were to preoccupy my waking hours for the next ten years and indeed are still ongoing. However, these sorts of shenanigans appear to be so commonplace in that area of France that it is like having a bad back: when you mention it to someone, they immediately regale you with the story of their own spinal problem. Property disputes are a French national sport and this tale is a story on its own that I will write of in detail elsewhere. Suffice to say that the whole of 2002 and 2003 were taken up with moving from the barn and redecorating the house in Sanary which, although it was in good condition and had obviously been cared for, was a disaster taste-wise. The interior was almost entirely clad in lacquered tongue and groove, even the ceilings, giving the effect of living in a wooden coffin.

In a way I suppose I was lucky that I was not being distracted by seeking work, or tempted by being offered work. I was left free to upgrade the barn and the flats in Eastbourne for selling; and when I was invited to travel to Leeds on January 16th 2004 for an interview for a part in the Yorkshire soap *Emmerdale*, it was so long since I had worked that I looked upon it as more of a day out up north rather than a serious offer of employment.

I had been sent a page or two of dialogue that was to be used as a test reading and, since I had a day or two to think about it, I decided to learn the lines, more by way of getting the feel of being an actor again than a ploy for landing the job. As usual I set off for my interview much earlier than I needed to have done and arrived at Leeds station with time enough to spare, so I decided to walk to the studios; even then I arrived very early and found myself sitting in the reception with several others who had been called for the part. There was Mark Eden, who had been very heavily featured in *Coronation Street* as the murderous partner of Rita and had been run down by a tram in Blackpool. John Forgeham, who was currently starring in *Footballer's Wives*, arrived complete with a minder and a fistful of rings and bangles still dressed for his part. After a quick sly look at the list of candidates I decided that I was somewhat out of my league; these were far higher-profiled actors than me and I did not hold out much hope of getting the part. I also noticed Tony Valentine's name on the list but I don't know if he turned up.

I caught the train back to London, and by the time I reached Victoria I had received the news that, much to my surprise, I had got the part of Tom King and would be starting a three-month contract the next week. This seemed remarkably soon, but it was in line with the now common practice of casting at the last moment, probably to minimise the time during which negotiations could take place over the fee. If an actor was available it was unlikely that he would use the argument that he had something else in the air as a lever to up his fee, or to claim that he would rather wait for a better offer.

Emmerdale was introducing a new family: the Kings. I was to play Tom King, the widowed head of the family of three boys, Jimmy, Matt and Carl, played by

Nick Miles, Matt Healy and Tom Lister in that order. The hope was that they would catch on as a unit and continue in the series for some time, although I learnt in the first few weeks that the plan was to kill off my character and leave the three boys fighting to take over the family business, a very profitable road haulage and property development firm. I discovered that I was to be killed off purely by chance when one of the directors casually let slip the chance remark that it was a pity my character wasn't planned to live long. I must confess that when I heard this news I was very upset as I was settling in nicely and was enjoying immensely being back in harness. On the other hand I was glad that I received the news at the beginning of my term and not at the end, as I would then have come to the conclusion that it was because I was not good enough in the part. I made sure to let everyone know that I was aware of my intended demise so that they would not think the same.

Shortly after accidentally hearing of this disturbing storyline I was summoned to the office of the then producer, Steve Frost, and asked if I would be prepared to sign a six-month extension to my contract as they liked what I was doing and had changed their mind about killing me off. I was of course over the moon and started looking for a flat to rent. I initially rented a flat in the city centre opposite the Army & Navy store, but after a few nights of being woken by the clubs turning out at three and four in the morning, followed by the rubbish collectors and then the early-morning deliveries to the A&N, I had to look for something quieter and ended up buying a flat, still in the city centre but on a quiet backwater of the canal. I spent much of my spare time and cash renovating it and turning it into a wonderful place to come home to after a hard day at work.

While the studios in Leeds were used for interior scenes, most exteriors were recorded on location in the village that had been specially built for the series on the Harewood estate, some ten miles from the city. The village location was idyllic and I was amazed to see that the houses, the pub, village hall and church were all very solidly built of genuine stone, but with no interiors. With my property acquirer's hat on I was very interested in them, but I was astonished to learn that if and when the series finished they were to be pulled down. They had been built on agricultural land and permission had been granted just for the run of the series; they were not to be used for habitation despite their desirability and the beauty of the setting. I was to enjoy many hours of walking in the surrounding woods between scenes over the next three years.

At first sight my fellow actors were a very happy and warm bunch. Patrick Mower, with whom I had played in Tom Stoppard's *Night and Day*, made a point of taking me out to TGI Friday's in my first week and filling me in on all the little dos and don'ts of the set-up as well as filling me up with his favourite chicken dish. The main gist of his advice was to keep my head down and not make any waves; not something I'm very good at, but at the beginning it all made sense and I was very happy. The show was on the box for five nights of the week and the schedule was therefore arduous, but that was something that I loved. I responded to working under pressure and found that I had not lost my ability to learn lines very quickly, or rather that I could learn the thoughts and the lines seemed to come – although sometimes not exactly as the writer had written, which was to prove to be something of a problem in the future.

For the moment, though, I was very happy; although my relationship with my eldest son was gradually turning sour. At first Nick seemed OK. He was a mindless ardent supporter of Arsenal, and since the city pubs all had vast screens for soccer games, I joined him in the first few weeks when football was on. It wasn't long though before I opted out of further socialising, not wishing to drink at his pace. Since I had not been exactly teetotal when I was his age I was in no position to be judgemental, except that I cannot recall it ever having affected my work whereas he was frequently late and the worse for wear. I also observed that he enjoyed being recognised and tended to attract attention to himself to increase the likelihood of getting noticed; this too did not appeal to me, although it is a common failing of many young actors when they first achieve success. Here again I couldn't swear to the fact that I didn't do likewise when I was starting out.

However, since we frequently had to share transport to work, I was forced to become a little more acquainted with his attitude towards his profession. The form was that if you were filming in the studios you had to get yourself to work, but if you were on location then you were picked up by the company car or, if that was in great demand, then by taxi. After our first few weeks of travelling together, Nick approached me and suggested we insist on having the company car because the taxis were not as comfortable, besides which the driver obviously changed from one journey to the next. Needless to say I advised him against making any such request and reminded him that some few weeks prior to getting this job he had been driving a delivery van with little prospect of employment.

Not long after this there was an occasion when the car was to pick me up first and then Nick about five minutes later; unfortunately the time of the pickup was changed at short notice and Nick was left sheltering in the rain outside his block of flats for some fifteen minutes. When he got in the car he was furious and started to berate the poor driver for being late, which was rich coming from him. I explained that we had received a message late the previous evening informing us that the car would be fifteen minutes late; and Nick then, as soon as we arrived, turned his ire on the third assistant who had failed to contact him. The poor girl was nearly in tears and once again I pointed out to Nick that, if he wanted to make an issue of it, he should remember his days as a delivery driver, and be prepared to return to them or put up with the odd few minutes in the rain.

This bullying and high-handed manner was becoming common with him and he was getting a very bad reputation with the taxi drivers, who more than once told me he was prone to keeping them waiting and inclined to be very rude to them depending on how he was feeling that morning. It seemed that he was living it up around the Leeds nightspots, and was also rumoured to be taking dubious substances; he was certainly subject to vast mood swings and had fallen in with the 'lunatic fringe' on the series which I was to learn later was pretty rampant.

As far as I was concerned Nick was in no way talented enough to behave in this manner; his acting was to my mind crude, unsubtle and uncontrolled. It was obvious that he had not been properly trained, and I was not surprised to learn that he was the product not of a drama school but of some media course at a polytechnic or university. I was not at all dismayed to learn shortly before our first six months was up that they were not planning to renew his contract.

Nick was distraught when he learnt this news, and indignant that the King family had been such a success which he felt was in no small measure due to him. I don't know how he did it, but shortly after receiving the news of his dismissal we learnt that his departure had been rescinded and he was to stay. Rumour had it that he had been grooming on the internet a fan club known as 'Jimmy's Angels' and that he had somehow used this to engineer a new lease of life.

Nick had become my *bête noir*, my whipping boy; I always seem to find one. It wasn't his behaviour that earned him this distinction – that certainly didn't help, but he was by no means the worst of the bunch. It was his acting that affected me so badly because, as my eldest son, I had to work closely with him. I found him a nightmare to act with and took steps to avoid having too much to do with him. Unfortunately the scriptwriters found it necessary for our paths to cross quite frequently, which only exacerbated the problem.

With regard to his behaviour socially, I was to learn that he was by no means alone, not only in his attitude to drink but in his uncouth ways. There were some three or four of the younger members of the cast (together with one of the more middle-aged) who had something of a reputation on the social scene; strangely, I first came across it at work. I had been filming on the village set and went to the green room between scenes to find that the place had been trashed. The furniture, although not broken, was piled up in the middle of the room, the prints on the wall were all defiled with foul language and there was a strong smell of vinegar. On investigation I found that this had been the work of two of the cast members who, finding themselves a little bored and no doubt still pissed from the night before, had decided to have a little fun.

When I bearded one of the guilty party he was quite unrepentant and more or less accused me of having no sense of humour. This incident released a whole host of stories from the more sober members of the cast who expressed their disgust at this sort of behaviour but were not prepared to do anything about it for fear of causing unpleasantness.

Shortly after this I was due to catch an afternoon flight to Nice to spend some time off with Sandra in Sanary. The day before, I learnt that the filming schedule had been changed and instead of working the next morning I had been shifted to the afternoon, which meant that I would miss my flight. At first I took this to be one of the hazards of the job, but on enquiring why the schedule had been altered I discovered that three of the younger but very well established members of the cast, on their way back from playing in a charity soccer match in Ireland, had cut off the seatbelts on the plane, causing the airline to have to cancel some poor holidaymakers' flights until the damaged equipment could be replaced. The three young blades were to appear in court in Manchester the next morning, and thus the filming schedule had to be rearranged. I'm afraid I did not share my fellow actors' reluctance to cause unpleasantness and I promptly refused to cancel my flight to Nice in order to accommodate the behaviour of these three louts.

At first my refusal was not taken too seriously and the first assistant continued to address me as if he assumed I was going to cave in and accept the change. When he realised I was in earnest he conveyed my decision to the top office and Tim Fee, the 'Mr Fixit' of *Emmerdale* without whom they would undoubtedly flounder, came to see me and offered to fix me another flight and get me a taxi to the airport; he was prepared to do more or less anything to get me to change my flight. I was adamant that I was not going to change my plans and he retired, defeated, to send down Steve Frost the producer.

Steve listened much more sympathetically, and when I recounted the various stories I had heard with regard to the trio's behaviour on many other occasions, he said that he had been made aware of some of their goings-on but that nobody would make a specific complaint; they were all too loyal. I, on the other hand, was under no such constraint and repeated a number of horror stories to him. One of the trio had clouted a girl in a fish-and-chip shop when he was the worse for drink; another had thrown a microwave out through the window of some girl's flat. Worst of all was the story of one of them peeing on the toothbrush of a young nurse who was repelling his advances. I told Steve that I was not going to let the antics of such people have any influence on my life whatsoever, and invited him to sack me if he wanted. I was at the end of my career anyway and it didn't matter to me, unlike the others who were desperate to hang on to their jobs and would not risk making waves.

Steve was very understanding, rearranged the schedule so that I could catch my flight and after an investigation suspended the main culprit for three months and admonished the other two. There was not much more he could do; if the characters they were playing were successful it was very difficult to get rid of them, and they knew it. I can understand that, in a way. Storylines are planned and written months in advance and it creates a massive problem to have to write a main character out at short notice. On another later occasion one of the popular Dingle family simply didn't turn up for work and disappeared for three weeks, apparently on a bender, refusing to answer calls or acknowledge knocks at his door. When he did come back they simply rapped his knuckles and he returned, rather sheepishly I must admit; he obviously had a massive drink problem.

After that initial skirmish with Steve and standing up against the loutish behaviour, I was of course not popular with a certain section of the cast, but it didn't stop me from continuing to enjoy the work. There were enough of the saner members of the cast who were on my side even though they didn't voice their support too volubly, and I was getting good storylines.

My main storyline though was more than a little disturbing. I was to woo and eventually wed Charity Dingle, a very popular and feisty character who was decidedly too young for a man of my age. She was 28 and I found the gap in our ages somewhat distasteful; when it came to my character, Tom, celebrating his 65th birthday I tentatively asked if they could perhaps make it his 60th birthday just to narrow the gap just a little. It wasn't an ardent request, and when it was turned down I was not really upset and got on with it.

However, since I received the scripts some two weeks in advance I did ask to talk to them with regard to a scene that I had with my middle son Matt, wherein I discussed my relationship with this young girl. The scene as it was written was more like two young girls discussing their conquests in the ladies' toilet; I wanted to make a stronger case for his attraction and make it more realistic. There was a process for this sort of discussion, and if you got in early enough it was often possible to secure minor rewrites. Following the procedure I applied to see the producer, who at this point was Kathy Beedles as Steve was on holiday. I tried three times and even left messages which were not replied to.

Come the day of the filming, when we got to that scene I asked the director if we could show him a proposed revision of the scene that Matt and I had prepared. He was very impressed with our suggested rewrite, and at this point the continuity girl piped up and said Kathy Beedles had warned her that I was unhappy with the scene but that I was to play it as written.

The director was marvellous and completely supportive of our suggestion, so he opted to hold up the filming schedule and telephone Kathy himself. He was on the phone for well over half an hour, which is an age in filming terms when the pressure is on. He won the day and in the main our suggested rewrite was accepted, with one minor concession; but once the scene was shot the continuity girl said that Kathy had sent the message that if I wanted any changes made I must speak to her sooner. I sent a reply back to say that I had tried three times and left various messages, which Kathy evidently received as she had said she was aware that I was not happy with the scene. I added that I would appreciate her talking to me direct, not through the continuity girl. Thus began my relationship with the woman who in due course was to take over from Steve and become the full-time producer of the show; from then on, it was downhill all the way.

Up until that point I had always had a reasonable response when I asked for a script alteration. I wasn't 'anti' the writers; I thought most of them did a very difficult job very well, but given the number of different writers that were on the team, and the fact that between them they were churning out scripts at the rate of five half-hours a week, it was only to be expected that occasionally the standard would fluctuate. Also, they were writing for some thirty-plus characters and there is no way that all the writers would write well for all of the characters. Certain writers wrote well for some characters and not for others. I only had to look after one character, Tom King, and it was quite natural that I should occasionally feel the need to protect that character from inconsistencies in the writing. As I said, a procedure was in place for questions on the script and I always followed it to the letter, being aware that I was inclined to be more picky when it came to scripts than most, and had got something of a reputation for rewriting.

At one particular point when the writers appeared to be obsessed with the confrontational relationship between Tom King and his eldest son Jimmy the storyline reached the tense point where Jimmy, together with his wife Sadie, had torpedoed the wedding by spreading false rumours about Tom's fiancée, Charity Dingle. Sadie, played by Patsy Kensit, also made a video of Jimmy *in flagrante delicto* with Charity and deliberately played the tape to the King family by way of getting revenge, at which point Tom disowned his son Jimmy and kicked him out of the firm. Possibly a storyline that pushed the bounds of credibility to its extremes, but then all the soaps are guilty of this constant desperation to come up with something new and explosive. However, when I was required in the very next episode to walk into the Woolpack, shake Jimmy by the hand and welcome him back into the firm, I felt that I had to fight hard to get this reconciliation watered down or at least postponed for a plausible amount of time to elapse to accommodate the change of heart. The writer, who happened to be the girlfriend of the then head of series at Yorkshire, had possibly not seen the episodes immediately prior to this one because it created an impossible situation.

I went immediately to Kathy Beedles with some suggested rewrites which she agreed would be acceptable and which I felt would make the scene in the pub at least playable. When it came to shoot the scene in the studio, however, Nick claimed that he had not received the rewrites and knew nothing of the changes. He was prevailed upon to go along with them, but must have complained afterwards to Kathy because she then summoned me to her office and started to remonstrate about changing the scripts. When I pointed out that she had okayed the changes she was somewhat flustered and changed her tack.

I did not have a happy time during her tenure as producer and it was obvious she had no great love for me. I found I had no respect for her decisions. When she took over from Steve Frost she made the questionable choice to get rid of two of the best young actors in the show, Amy Nuttall and Dale Meeks, and bring in a doll-like young actress with no experience who had falsified her CV and was continually late, or didn't turn up at all if she felt she hadn't enough to do in a scene. Kathy also appeared to champion Nick Miles to such an extent that when it was leaked that he was to be axed for a second time, she reversed the decision and once again he wheedled his way back onto the payroll.

I was coming to the end of my third year in the show and the time was arriving when the new contracts were to be offered. I had never before stayed anywhere for longer than two years; and although I was very comfortable and enjoying the regular income, I was too often getting frustrated with some of the weird storylines. No matter how good an actor is, over-exposure playing the same part year after year will inevitably diminish the excitement and the unexpectedness of his performances, and the best actors know when to give up and change tack. I had had some very good (or at least prominent) storylines and there wasn't a great deal that could be more exciting without delving into the realms of the absurd.

I have always maintained that working in soaps is about making bad scripts work, and by bad I don't necessarily mean badly written; it is often a case of trying to make an unrealistic situation believable when, in the competition to come up with something more stunning than the other soaps, they create a ridiculously outlandish series of events that stretch the imagination beyond the bounds of believability. This is not by way of a complaint. I very much enjoyed the challenge and the process of working with fellow actors, the director and the crew to make these situations work. It was my belief that right up until the last moment when the scene has been shot and is 'in the can' the process should be open for input from any quarter; and in most cases I found the directors very sympathetic to this attitude, and often the writers too. It was only occasionally that Kathy Beedles would show her lack of understanding of how an actor works by trying to demonstrate the power of her position and put me in my place. She was so opposed to me that I was surprised to be nominated twice, or was it three times, as best actor in a soap opera; I am sure she must have had some say in who was nominated. Needless to say I never won, but I did pick up the award for best scene and the next year the award for best storyline. These are quite meaningless awards as they should have been presented to the director in the first instance and the writer in the second, not to the actors.

If I have given the impression that I was unhappy then I have been misleading. I was happy enough to recommend it to Freddie Jones, an actor I have always admired. Some years before, Freddie had been a resident in a village in Surrey near where Sandra lived and, on one of his return visits to the local pub that he used to frequent, he expressed the desire to do a soap; in fact, he went so far as to say he would pay me a thousand pounds if I could get him in. This was not all that unusual; Sir Laurence Olivier had told Doris Speed that he would love to be in *Coronation Street*, even as just a customer in the Rovers Return, and Sir Ian McKellen had just finished a spell in the Street himself.

When I got back up to Leeds I telephoned the executive producer of most of the Granada continuing dramas, told him that Freddie had expressed the desire to join the cast and asked if was he interested. I didn't go to Kathy Beedles, not for the obvious reason but because I was fairly sure she wouldn't know who Freddie was. I called Freddie and said he should insist on a six-month contract as he would only make money from a decent run. I told him to forget the thousand pounds, but to propose me as a member of the Garrick Club.

I loved working under the pressure of turning out five shows a week. I loved the battles and the struggle to make the scenes work, and with a few exceptions I got on very well with the cast. I spent my spare time, such as it was, between France and Surrey, and in my time off when I couldn't get home I played tennis at the Roundhay Tennis Club. In spite of my gut feeling that I should not do another year, I must admit that I was going to have trouble turning it down.

In the event I needn't have worried as Kathy Beedles made the decision for me. She called me into her office and unless I am mistaken took a certain pleasure in telling me they were not going to renew my contract. I hope I didn't betray my surprise at this; I just shrugged and said that was fine by me as I was not planning to accept another extension to my contract anyway. I had come for three months, stayed for three years and it was time for me to go; I had never stayed even in *Coronation Street* for longer than two years at a stretch. Kathy went on to explain that my exit storyline was going to one of the biggest in the history of the series and although it was a secret at the moment I would be very pleased with it. I went back to work in the studios a little deflated as I would have rather made the choice myself and not been effectively given the push.

I didn't tell anybody of the decision and when it did eventually come out that I was to leave, it caused quite a stir. Many of the directors said they were appalled and even a number of the writers and storyliners came to me and said they had been very much against the decision. Linda Thorson, who had been brought in to marry Tom King, reportedly stormed into Kathy's office and blew her top; she even wrote me a charming letter expressing her disgust at what had happened. I of course kept my cool and protested that I was planning to leave anyway, which was ninety-per-cent true. The view generally expressed was that Kathy could not have made the decision without the acquiescence of the powers above as my character had been very popular; she had obviously used the angle of the mammoth exit story to persuade them and get permission to axe my character. An Australian company was being imported to mastermind the internet coverage, and the nation was to be invited to vote on who murdered Tom King.

In my last few weeks with the show, we were alarmed to find that ITV were planning to do away with the cast list at the end of each episode. Two Equity negotiators came up from London for a meeting with the cast and a representative from management who was obviously an accountant. I'm not too sure of the reason behind the proposed scrapping of the credits, unless it was to make a little more time available for adverts; the accountant didn't put a very good case except to say that ITV was in dire financial straits and had to find ways of cutting costs. Arguing that actors needed the credits in order to generate further employment (although admittedly they were usually run at such a speed that they were impossible to read), we won the day and the accountant was sent off with his tail between his legs.

Only a week or so later we were told that travel and overnight expenses were to be cut for any actor who was in the show for over six months. A withdrawal of labour was threatened and once again Equity was called in. The same accountant came to defend his plan, which revolved around the assumption that anyone who was in the series that long would relocate permanently to Yorkshire. There was a heated discussion in which it became clear that the accountant did not know anything about the show or about show business, and the Equity duo were left to meet with him and thrash out some sort of deal.

In a week or so they came back offering to increase the episode fee for those who were on a contract that paid overnight and travel, which was the majority of the regular cast; in exchange for this increase they were to relinquish their right to expenses, and all future contracts would incorporate this change. I was strongly against the agreement and saw it as a bribe to the old guard to sell off their birthright. However, it was put to the vote, and greed and selfishness won. They got their increase, so they lost nothing, while new contracts would contain the expenses restriction, meaning that anyone who joined the cast in future would be worse off. I wrote to Equity and resigned my membership on the grounds that they were tasked with protecting the whole of the acting profession, not just those who were already in comfortable employment in a long-running soap. From a position of strength, where we could have taught the accountants that they couldn't get away with running the show merely as a financial exercise, they had won their point and bought us off.

My last few weeks story-wise were manic. Tom King's recent controversial building development in the village blew up during the opening ceremony because of a gas leak, killing a number of the villagers. I was kidnapped along with Sadie by Cain Dingle and tied up in the boot of a car. I was married to Linda Thorson and then pushed from an upper-floor window and fell to my death. All fairly everyday for a soap opera, but this story was doomed to be dragged out for the next six months after my demise. The final scene of my exit through the bedroom window was to be filmed twelve times, each time with a different suspect as the murderer. There were my three sons, who all bore grudges; there was my new wife who was obviously after the money, et cetera.

On Friday November 17th 2006 I shot my last scene, and Kathy Beedles came out to the location to make a brief insincere speech and present me with an expensive bottle of brandy, the traditional way of saying goodbye after one's last scene is shot. I noticed that there was a bigger crowd than normal at the other side of the camera; they had all come in the expectation of me making a speech and laying into Kathy, but in the event I remained as dignified as I could. In fact I became quite emotional in saying goodbye and had to fight the lump in my throat; I had made a good many friends and the northerners are by tradition a very warm lot.

The cast had clubbed together to buy me a top-of-the-range harpoon gun and various other bits of diving equipment, and that evening I invited whoever was around to dine in a nearby restaurant. Being a Friday night most of the cast were homeward bound but my sons turned up, even Nick Miles with his new girl-friend; and as we were finishing our meal Freddie Jones, who just happened to be passing on his way home from the pub, dropped in and got the management of the restaurant to mix me a very potent cocktail that saw me off for the rest of the night.

WHAT A CHANGE IN lifestyle. Everything seemed to stop and I was in serious retirement, but I still had plenty to do: so much in fact that I don't know how I had found time to go to work.

Things were not so bright on the Sanary front. The dispute over the alterations made by the previous owner without permission had rumbled on; we had tried various ways to resolve the matter peaceably with the neighbours, but they were adamant in having their day in court. As a result they shot themselves in the foot, for as well as getting a judgement requiring me to reduce the size of our terrace, three of the other house owners were ordered to demolish certain alterations that they had likewise effected without permission.

The confrontation had existed since 1996 when the objections had first been raised; and despite the judgement of the tribunal in early 2006, an appeal was made to the court in Aix-en-Provence. This extended the uncertainty until April 2007 when the court of appeal came up with a far more draconian decision requiring all the properties to be returned to their original condition within six months, after which a charge of up to €1,000 per day could be paid in penalty!

Luckily I was in the process of selling the fourth of my five flats in Eastbourne and had the money to finance the demolition of the terrace, the lowering of the roof and the bricking up of four windows at the cost of some £35,000, thinking this would see the matter closed. I was not prepared for the French psyche which seems to flourish on these property disputes, and I was amazed and distraught when the neighbours claimed that I had not carried out the alterations as designated in the judgement and then set about another court action, in spite of the fact that they had not complied with the judgement themselves! It is obviously a long and complicated story and certainly tarnished my view of the French in that area. The situation is still the same a further ten years on and we appear to have arrived at a position of stalemate.

On leaving *Emmerdale* I was looking forward to enjoying my new home in our pad on the Côte D'Azur. I wasn't really bothered about working. I was not at all unhappy with the Scott Marshall Agency; although no longer run by Scott and Denise Marshall, it was still one of the bigger and more respectable agencies and I was loath to leave them, but the lure of someone young, keen and hungry proved to be strong and I left Scott Marshall to join Grantham and Hazeldine.

Caroline Hazeldine was the sister of Anthony Horowitz, the writer of many TV shows but most notably at that time the superb *Foyle's War* starring Michael Kitchen, which I found compulsive viewing; and, tempted with the thought that they might be able to pull strings and get me in it, I jumped ship, much to the consternation of the Scott Marshall office who were not best pleased even though I wrote them a very apologetic letter to explain and ask their forgiveness. I didn't think it would have been of much consequence to them as they had a very full list of well-established actors on their books and I was, I felt, small fry.

This sea change did not kick-start my career as it was intended to do. Six months after my exit from *Emmerdale*, the 'who killed Tom King' campaign was still motoring; my new agents said they had difficulty in getting me work because I was too closely identified with Tom. Since other actors were leaving soaps and going from one thing to another I was not entirely convinced with this argument, but I had set a limit on the work that I wanted to do and did not push too hard. Anyway, at the age of 71 I considered myself semi-retired, and with the various investments and pensions that I had subscribed to I was not rich but comfortable enough not to be desperate to work.

The year went by with only one acting role: a guest appearance in *Doctors*, the 'continuing drama' (as the soaps were now called) filmed in the BBC studios in Birmingham. The director, Piotr Szkopiak, had been a director on *Emmerdale*; the job impressed my new agents but did nothing for my career as it was a further eighteen months before I was to work again. This was not entirely the fault of my agents as, while I was available for interviews or auditions if I was in Surrey, I was spending half my time in France and was not prepared to come all the way back for an interview unless the job was more or less guaranteed.

I was in fact enjoying life immensely. In France, in spite of the uncertainty of the legal conflict with the neighbours, I spent most of the sunshine days sleeping on the beach, reading and swimming and in the evening enjoying the profusion of nearby restaurants. In Surrey, I took to playing tennis two or three times a week. There was, however, the nagging thought that I was still an actor, and this I satisfied in a number of ways.

First, I was writing from time to time and had a number of projects on the go, principally my memoirs which I hoped might one day be of interest since they covered the birth of the National Youth Theatre and the start of *Coronation Street*. Also, thanks to Freddie Jones who had honoured his promise to propose me and Tim West who seconded me, I was now a member of the Garrick Club which I deemed a great honour as it seemed to me to confirm that I had achieved some sort of credibility in the acting profession. I make the effort to attend the actors' lunch on the first Thursday of every month, where I usually join up with

Gary Raymond who is married to Delena Kidd, who played my wife in *Family Affairs*. I keep in contact with them both and see them fairly regularly since they have a country cottage near Sandra, and we are asked to their New Year party every year in their house on the banks of the river Thames in Chiswick. This is one of the highlights of my year and I always attempt to be around for it as it is a great chance to meet up with old friends who have managed to cling by their fingernails to a career in the theatre. I was also a member of BAFTA, the main perk of which is to receive DVDs of most of the nominated films each year. Since they all arrive around Christmastime, they are great for viewing in the wintry weeks and well make up for the membership fee as I am not near enough to London to be able to avail myself of the many invitations to view the films in their little cinema in Piccadilly.

Then there were the Soap Awards that are held every year in London and to which I had been invited up until the year following my exit from *Emmerdale*. I had been nominated three times for best actor and had attended in hope and left deflated. The awards are dominated by *Coronation Street* and *EastEnders*, though we did pick up the odd award for best scene and best storyline. In the years that I was nominated for best actor, I was provided with a suite in a top-class hotel, picked up from home by a chauffeur-driven car and delivered back the next morning. One year the hotel was the Soho which had just won the award for the best designed hotel, and on two other occasions it was the Royal Garden where Sandra and I had a wonderful suite with a grand view over Kensington Park and which we learnt was normally £525 per night. At that price I imagined the breakfast to be included, but I was amazed to be asked for £7.50 when I went to sign out because I had a full English breakfast and the £525 which the sponsors had paid only included the continental self-service.

I had heard stories of the vast sums that soap stars could command at Christmastime when the panto season provides work for hundreds of actors, keeping some of them going for the next year. Just when I was beginning to believe that I was never going to be able to cash in on my time as Tom King in this way, I was offered the chance to play Captain Hook in a production of *Peter Pan* at Lowestoft for Christmas 2008. Unfortunately it was not one of the really big-paying productions as Lowestoft had not had a professional panto before and it was more or less a try-out for the company UK Productions Ltd.

For my first ever panto I was lucky to be playing Captain Hook which I saw as more of a 'proper actor's part'. This in no way though made me complacent and when I met with Jamie Rickers who was playing Smee, Hook's sidekick, and Sarah Jane Buckley who was playing Mrs Darling and the Mermaid, I threw myself on their mercy by explaining that this was very different territory from what I had been used to and I would be looking very much to them for help and guidance. As seasoned campaigners despite their junior years, they were clearly well on top of the job and knew what they were doing. They were also very charming and looked as if they were going to be fun to work with.

I first met these two members of the cast at a press launch in mid September when, after a fitting in London, I had to go to Lowestoft for the day and prance about on board a yacht in Lowestoft harbour. I also took the opportunity to look for digs; when I saw how depressing and deprived an area Lowestoft was, I came to the conclusion that I would have to find somewhere very comfortable because it was not going to be a jolly place to pass the winter. After chatting with the box-office staff I managed to get a terraced cottage just out of the town centre which, although it was in a depressing back street, was decorated and furnished with loving care if not with marvellous taste, and was clean, warm and comfortable, with two bedrooms, a kitchen, bathroom and a lounge that opened straight out onto the street.

This was to prove a wise move as the rehearsals were only for ten days and I was flying in unknown territory. It wasn't the characterisation that worried me; I had learnt when doing my research, very early on before rehearsals began, that Captain Hook was an Old Harrovian and I therefore played him as a 'toff'. My main problem was the song. On his first entrance in this particular version he sings a song about hating children. My insecurity as a singer dated back to my early years when I was evacuated to Wales and had been asked in school to mime during choral singing and not to vocalise. During my first year at RADA, when we made a return visit to the British Legion and I managed to torpedo the whole evening by starting in the wrong key, I felt that perhaps the Welsh had been right all the time. However, I decided that with a little help from the musical director I would be able to overcome this insecurity and that there was a masterful voice in there somewhere which was dying to come out. The song wasn't really a very difficult one musically, but it required the verbal dexterity of a Danny Kaye as it was a real tongue twister.

Either the musical director was not very good, or he was too busy to bother much with me, or I was a lost case from the off and there was nothing he felt he could do. In any event I didn't get much help and, though I mastered the words when singing alone, I seemed to go to pot when I had to sing in front of anybody. In the three-week run of two performances daily I don't think I got it together more than a handful of times and I was glad when that part of the show was over.

The rehearsals were somewhat frenetic and were held in a dance school just outside the centre of town. There were three rooms: the dance room where the dance captain and choreographer worked tirelessly; the music room where the musical director sat at his keyboard with a strange dog at his feet which made a weird sound, somewhere between chuckling and retching, in the middle of any singing (not only mine, I hasten to add) and had to be banned from the rehearsal room and left in the car; and then there was the main room where the director was putting all of the different sections of the show together. It was chaos, and as the days passed and I couldn't see where the final show was coming from I was told not to worry; it was always like this.

The ten days of chaos over, we moved into the theatre and what little organisation there was seemed to disintegrate altogether; I could sense a feeling of panic all around. The backstage was not very spacious, and when the crowd of local kids joined the cast with all of their chaperones and minders I felt that this was going to be a rather ignominious end to a career. The DSM (deputy stage manager) in the prompt corner became more and more desperate as the director became more and more angry and she eventually burst into tears and looked as if she was going to leave the sinking ship. Eventually the company manager joined her in the prompt corner and between them a sort of order was restored, although it became painfully obvious that we had big problems on the stage-management front. We later learnt that this was her first job as a DSM and the company had tried to save money on the technical side; their excuse was that they had been let down when the company manager that had agreed to take the job had dropped out, necessitating a desperate last-minute engagement. As the 'new boy' I stayed well out of any objections and kept my head down.

In any case I had my own problems to contend with. My first entrance was described roughly thus: a large ship with a huge sail comes into view and, as the ship approaches, the sail drops down to reveal Captain Hook, who then breaks into his song 'I Hate Children'. My insecurity about the song was compounded during rehearsals when I couldn't find any sign of a large ship, although there was a tub resembling a small dinghy parked in the restricted area backstage, with a sail having the dimensions of a large towel which would not be able to conceal a medium-sized dog. This seemed hardly the ideal way to start my variety career, launching into a song that I had little confidence in. At the technical rehearsal we tried various ways of making this undignified entrance, but there seemed no way that it was going to look anything but ridiculously inadequate. In the end I came up with the suggestion that I should make no attempt to hide but merely sit in the tub with an oar and row myself onstage, thus saving a great deal of technical time wasted trying to make the ship work. I received no acknowledgement or gratitude from the director for this imaginative solving of the problem, but I understood that I was the least of his worries. Not only did he have the main cast who were all quite young to whip into shape, he also had a crowd of amateurs, gymnasts and dancers to meld together into a show. In the end, miraculous as it might seem, the whole thing did come together and we made the first night without any major mishap.

There were certain aspects of the show that I thought were more than adequate and really quite good. The girl playing Peter, Jessica Punch, was a good singer, dancer and actor and handled herself with professional poise and dignity, turning in a superb performance and never letting the situation disturb her in any way. Jamie Rickers was extremely good at communicating with the audience and was greatly loved by the kids, and also managed to charm the adults as well. He was imaginative and creative, as indeed was Sarah Jane Buckley who played Mrs Darling, my wife, and the Mermaid, although I did find that I had difficulty in coming to terms with some of her deviations from the script. I was astonished that after the show opened we never saw the director again and there were quite a few little niggles that needed to be sorted out. I was off on my hobby horse again but uncharacteristically managed to keep my mouth shut.

I'm not sure just how bad our panto was; there were certainly areas that were decidedly tacky and amateurish, but then I suspect that many pantos are the same because of the ground they cover and the mixture of talent levels. I do know that some of the performances had charm and some had considerable talent. On one occasion, on leaving the theatre between shows to grab a bite to eat, I was stopped by a young mother who asked if she could take a photo of me with her little boy who was about four years old. As I crouched to get down to the mite's level, his mother said to the child, 'Don't you recognise Captain Hook?' – at which point the little kid legged it up the road without even turning to look. I found that very encouraging.

Needless to say we played mostly to full houses and, with two shows a day, by the end of the run I was exhausted. I can't really say that my role was particularly arduous, but I seemed to be continually fighting a cold; and I was also tired, as when we did get our one day a week off I drove back to Surrey which took three hours each way. It also cost me a speeding charge, picked up at eight o'clock on Christmas Eve after failing to slow down on a stretch of deserted rural road in Suffolk where the speed limit dropped from sixty to fifty miles per hour.

It is apparently panto tradition that the cast should on the last performance play little tricks on each other and generally misbehave. Of course, a lot of these stunts are rather childish and not really very funny; if they were, they would have been incorporated into the show a lot sooner. It needed them. I didn't join in the pranks and it must have looked as if I was aloof and disapproving, but on the curtain call I made my solo entrance carrying my bags and my coat ready to leave the theatre and go home, which reduced most of the cast to hysterics.

The panto had been a good learning experience and, although I don't think I lit any fireworks, I had survived and had been well paid, although I hasten to add not as well paid as Paul O'Grady. It wasn't until a few weeks later that I realised that my theatre talisman had been stolen. It was a leather wallet signed by Sir Laurence Olivier and Vivien Leigh on the occasion of their opening night of *The Skin of Our Teeth* and presented to Richard Eastham, my former and now late agent, when he was company manager for that production. He had given it to me just before he died and I was quite proud of it. I kept it in my make-up box and it was quite some time before I realised that it was missing. It put a rather sour taste to the panto experience, because it must have been one of the cast or crew and there were so many of them that I wouldn't know where to start.

The panto finished in January 2009 and in May of that year I had a guest appearance in *New Tricks* for the BBC. Not much of a part, in fact just two scenes that were polished off in the morning, but I don't think I have laughed so much in ages. I had last met my old charity football teammate Dennis Waterman when I did *The Cherry Orchard* with Rula Lenska, but I was warned not to remind him of that as the divorce had been acrimonious and he never talked about her. James Bolam I had worked with in Manchester many moons ago but I had run into him once since then at a Youth Theatre first night when I think his daughter was in the production. Alun Armstrong I had met on a number of occasions but I can't recall exactly where or when, which is strange because I found him the most hilarious of them all; he kept us in fits of laughter throughout the morning and all through lunch. Amanda Redman stayed strongly focused on her role during the morning's shoot but when we broke for lunch she changed immediately and became very warm and friendly. It was a very enjoyable experience and one that was going to have to keep me going for quite some time because it wasn't until the November of 2011 that I was to be offered another job.

I love musicals and although I had little confidence in my vocal abilities I had always harboured the secret desire to be in one; and when I was offered the part of the General in *White Christmas* by Irving Berlin, I couldn't believe my luck. The fact that he doesn't have to sing made no difference. I was in a musical! I got the part because Aled Jones had asked for me. He was starring in the show with Adam Cooper, the dance star. I must say it was a great eye-opener when I saw how hard they worked and how talented they all were; from Adam and Aled down through the whole cast of singers and dancers, they were all so multi-talented and dedicated. A very humbling experience, and when my car was broken into in Liverpool and all of my Christmas presents for my grandchildren were stolen, they showed just what a nice bunch they were by having a whipround. The only bugbear was that the run covered the Christmas period in Southampton, Dublin and Liverpool and it's not the right time of year to be away from home; although it wasn't as long away as the panto, it proved to be another possibility crossed off the list.

When, in 2016, Trio Entertainments offered me the part of the Wizard in *The Wizard of Oz* my first instinct was to say no, but as I thought longer about it I felt I couldn't resist the challenge and I really did miss the stage. The deciding factor was that it was only for two and a half weeks in total: four days' rehearsal, a week in Melton Mowbray and another in Exmouth. I must admit that there were fears of looking rather pitiful at my age of life but what the hell!

Any thoughts of being too good for the job were dispelled at the first rehearsal. The rest of the cast had all played their parts before, and were all so well cast and excellent in their roles; I was suitably humbled and was constantly seeking their help and advice. Dorothy was played by the producer's partner, Bessie McMillan, and seemed to have been born to play the part; she could sing and dance and also did the choreography and the wardrobe! Stuart Earp played the Scarecrow and more or less carried the show with his unbounded energy. Stephen Hall played the Lion with beautifully underplayed humour, and young Gary Amos was delightful as the Tin Man. Lucinda Rhodes was an extremely adept good fairy and Grace Adams-Short a delightfully wicked witch. There was of course the input from the local dancing schools; and although it was obviously not a lavish or expensive production, I was amazed at the standard they managed to achieve and I grew to be very fond of them all.

However, rehearsals started badly when I learnt that my new agent, who had got me the job, had a reputation for not paying up. Kevin Brown, the producer, was very supportive, and with his help the situation was resolved; and after a couple of sleepless nights when it looked like I was going to withdraw from the production, I settled down to face the new challenge of what was to be probably my last job. In fact I was so convinced that I would probably never need it again, I gave away my make-up box to young Gary Amos as he had been so helpful with my musical attempts.

I am frequently asked if I have retired and I can't bring myself to say outright that I have. Old actors don't retire, they just don't get asked any more; and, with this in mind, I do still have an agent. Not the one at the centre of the *Wizard of Oz* fiasco, but the daughter of my old school chum and co-founding member of the NYT, the late Paul Hill. You see, that big break may still be just around the corner!

20 Conclusions

IN THE LAST SIXTY years the profession has changed, and while there have been technical developments that have opened many doors, much of the feeling of belonging to one large family has disappeared. In the early days of my involvement in television, when there was just one BBC channel and one ITV, we all seemed to know one another, not only in television but also in the theatre, as we were generally expected to do both. Television drama was much the same as theatre drama, in that there was a rehearsal period, a technical rehearsal followed by a dress rehearsal and then a recorded or live performance. Nowadays, the technical advancements mean that television has adopted the techniques of the film industry. At the same time it has developed not only its own unique drama form, in the shape of soaps, but it has also thrown up its own type of actor.

The requirements are simply that they should appear real and relaxed in front of the camera, and little more is demanded of them. Sometimes, when they have to give more, and perhaps act out a dramatic moment, they lose their appearance of reality and become laboured and unreal. They are not required to repeat the performance time and again with any degree of accuracy. Nor are they required to project their voice. One of the first rules of the old theatre was that everybody should be able to hear, even the little deaf old lady in the back row, but there are times in so many dramas these days when I cannot understand a word they are saying. Sometimes it can be put down to one's hearing faculty deteriorating as one gets older, but so often it is a matter of bad diction and mumbling acting which is meant to be realistic, and no matter how high I turn up the volume I still cannot make out what is being said.

With the spiralling number of television channels, the ever-growing competition for the same audience has led to the situation where the public dominate; and the accountants, who now run the profession, respond to that, measuring the actors' popularity and more or less controlling not only the casting but also the choice of programmes. It is for this reason that our viewing is dominated by cheap and mindless shows like *Big Brother*, *The Jeremy Kyle Show*, *You've Been Framed*, *The Only Way is Essex*, *Through the Keyhole*; the list goes on. We are getting less and less proper drama and have to put up with an endless procession of soaps: *Coronation Street*, *EastEnders*, *Hollyoaks*, *Emmerdale*, *Home and Away*, *Neighbours*, *Doctors*; and regular series with a similar appeal to the soaps, like

Casualty and *Holby City*, are likewise falling into the slough of mediocrity in their constant frantic search for something new or more shocking to grab the attention of 'Joe Public'. The talent shows too, such as *The X Factor* and *Britain's Got Talent*, appeal to the lowest common denominator as they stretch out the decisions with lengthy and contrived pauses, and cruelly dwell on the loser to see how they are going to take defeat. They also border on the verge of fraud as they manufacture situations and misleadingly edit footage to create fake jeopardy and phoney drama.

The culture of cruelty seems to have seeped over into every genre of TV. On *The Weakest Link* Anne Robinson broke the mould of quiz show hosts by being gratuitously nasty to everybody in a very amateurish and unconvincing performance. Meanwhile in the highly competitive and backstabbing world of *The Apprentice*, Alan Sugar takes delight in bullying his rejects and pointing the finger with his mantra 'You're fired'.

This dumbing down not only lowers the standards of excellence that have been set over the past years; it also creeps into everyday life, promoting aggressive rudery and a lack of manners and respect for your fellow man. I am aware that this may appear a snobbish view. I am not saying that these shows shouldn't exist, or that there should be no soaps; I am just crying out for fewer of them and more serious quality drama to set the standards higher. There are too many dramas of questionable quality and, coupled with the cheap game shows and fly-on-the-wall television, our choice of viewing is becoming increasingly poor.

There has been a knock-on effect too in the theatre, where the provincial towns, those not lucky enough to boast their own repertory theatre, are subjected to tours of often mediocre plays that demand little of their audience, and with dubious stars that have seen better days on television. I have myself been guilty of appearing in some of the worst examples and can speak with experience when I say that the damage they do to the live theatre is inestimable, but once again it is the managements that must shoulder the blame. They have even managed to get their greedy little fingers into the wonderful traditional Christmas pantomimes, with the ridiculous casting of everyone from sportsmen to Australian soap stars in productions that will be the first magical theatrical experience of thousands if not millions of youngsters up and down the country.

This may sound like the rantings of a bitter failed actor, which indeed they might well be except that they were echoed some years ago by Sir Peter Hall when he complained about the dumbing down of television. I think too I can safely say that I haven't completely failed. It is true that I have not tasted the success that I had wanted to; I was sidetracked at the start of my career into the first of the soaps and never managed to get back into the classical stream to any lasting extent. However, I have managed to earn a living from acting; and eventually, while not ending up as rich as I would like to have been, I have secured a certain amount of comfort for my retirement years – mainly through wise investment of my earnings in property, sometimes more by accident than design.

I have too managed to keep going after leaving the Street and occasionally done work of which I am reasonably proud. Not unnaturally, I have made many wrong decisions. I think my first major mistake was not to follow up on the possibility of a place at Oxford. Of course, even with hindsight one can never be absolutely certain, but it may well have transpired that I could have made the move into directing, and been more in charge of what was happening to me. Looking back there have also been times when I behaved in a manner of which I am not proud. Mostly it was a desire to improve and make things better; I found it frustrating to be in the position of seeing what I thought was wrong and being thwarted in my attempts to improve either myself or the situation.

Having said that, I can't have been too impossible as many of my jobs were long-lasting or were repeat engagements. My association with *Coronation Street* spanned twenty-five years; my relationships with Manchester Library Theatre, Liverpool Playhouse and the Leicester Phoenix also encompassed many visits over many years, and there are many directors with whom I worked more than just the once, so I think I am justified in coming to the conclusion that I did not upset all of the people all of the time. I do not say all this in any way boastfully, but merely to analyse why I haven't accomplished what I set out to achieve.

In reality, therefore, I do not consider myself to be bitter; in fact, I appreciate that I have, in many ways, been very lucky. However, I am very strong in my love of the theatre and of what it should be about. The theatre is not simply a way of passing a few pleasurable moments being entertained by gifted and talented people; it has a very important role to play in our society. Of course Shakespeare put it superbly when he said 'it is to hold as 'twere the mirror up to nature', and in fulfilling this role it teaches us compassion and understanding of others. In sitting through a play we view other people in situations that we recognise, or people that we recognise in situations we have not experienced, and in watching the action unfold we share to some extent their emotions and their dilemmas and are led into a greater understanding of our fellow human travellers in this journey through life. There is too the potential for exposure of wrongs or evil that can be powerfully illustrated, ridiculed and possibly changed.

We have, in this country, the best actors, the best technicians, the best theatre and the best television in the world and if we are not careful, if we allow it to be controlled by the accountants and dictated to by the mass appeal, we will destroy that rich and wonderful heritage.

In recent times I have found myself drawn more and more to living in France where I enjoy the better weather, and where I feel myself more in tune with their priorities in life, where they put food and drink before the flashy car and the decoration of the outside of their houses to impress the neighbours – though I must admit the standard of their television leaves much to be desired. Hopefully I will find more time for writing and will not turn into a pitiful old man who has little else to do, and nothing to talk about except the fascinating and incredible grandchildren, boring others with tales of their groundbreaking achievements to such an extent that I make the listener dislike them intensely without ever having met them.

All the soaps, and in particular the main ones – *Coronation Street, EastEnders* and *Emmerdale* – now seem to have a strong leaning towards the younger viewer. With talent shows like *The X Factor* and *Britain's Got Talent* and other such inducements to reach for celebrity, the carrot is dangled in front of the young to make them feel there is the possibility of a career in showbiz just around the corner and that you don't really need much to be successful if you happen to look good. I recall the comment once made by a neighbour of ours who was lamenting that her son was in his teens and not doing very well at school and, worried that he was not fitted to anything in particular, asked if I couldn't get him a job as an actor!